mediterranean:
food of the sun

mediterranean:
food of the sun

a culinary tour of sun-drenched shores
with evocative dishes from southern Europe

Jacqueline Clark and Joanna Farrow

HH
HERMES
HOUSE

This edition is published by Hermes House

Hermes House is an imprint of Anness Publishing Ltd
Hermes House, 88–89 Blackfriars Road, London SE1 8HA
tel. 020 7401 2077; fax 020 7633 9499; info@anness.com

A CIP catalogue record for this book is available from the British Library.

Publisher: Joanna Lorenz
Senior Cookery Editor: Linda Fraser
Editor: Emma Gray
Designer: Nigel Partridge
Proofreader: Richard McGinlay
Illustrator: Anna Koska
Main jacket images: Nicki Dowey

The majority of the recipes for this book were provided by Jacqueline Clark and Joanna Farrow; other recipes were contributed by Angela Boggiano, Jacqueline Clark, Carole Clements, Roz Denny, Christine France, Silvano Franco, Rebekah Hassan, Christine Ingram, Judy Jackson, Soheila Kimberley, Lesley Mackley, Maggie Mayhew, Anne Sheasby, Steven Wheeler, Elizabeth Wolf-Cohen, Jeni Wright.

The majority of the photographs in this book were taken by Michelle Garrett, assisted by Dulce Ribiero; other photographs were taken by William Adams-Lingwood, Karl Adamson, Edward Allwright, John Heseltine, Amanda Heywood, Janine Hosegood, Patrick McLeavey.

1 3 5 7 9 10 8 6 4 2

NOTES

For all recipes, quantities are given in both metric and imperial measures and, where appropriate, measures are also given in standard cups and spoons. Follow one set, but not a mixture, because they are not interchangeable.

Standard spoon and cup measures are level. 1 tsp = 5ml, 1 tbsp = 15ml, 1 cup = 250ml/8 fl oz

Australian standard tablespoons are 20ml. Australian readers should use 3 tsp in place of 1 tbsp for measuring small quantities of gelatine, cornflour, salt etc.

Medium eggs should be used unless otherwise stated.

CONTENTS

INTRODUCTION

The countries bordered by the Mediterranean sea

produce some of the finest food the world has to

offer—set sail with us on a culinary tour.

ABOVE: A grove of old olive trees lit by the afternoon sun in Provence.

Azure skies, even bluer seas, white-gold sands, bright, whitewashed walls, the vibrant reds, greens, yellows, purples and oranges of the flowers, fruits and vegetables on display in the market—these are the paint palette colors of the Mediterranean. These evocative images are familiar to many of us, although, of course, we will not all be thinking of the same country—after all, there are fifteen to consider. A quick tour will take us from the shores of Spain, to France, Italy, Greece, Turkey, Syria, Lebanon, Israel, and into Africa to Egypt, Libya, Tunisia, Algeria and Morocco. The islands of Malta and Cyprus are truly Mediterranean, encircled by the sea. In many ways these fifteen countries are completely different from each other, but one thread links them all—the love of good food.

Centuries before Christ, the area surrounding the Mediterranean sea was colonized by the Phoenicians, Greeks and Romans, who shared a basic cultivation of wheat, olives and grapes. These, in turn, became bread, oil and wine, three components that are still very important in today's Mediterranean diet. With the building of ships came import and export, and the various countries began a sort of cross-pollination of crops, ingredients and recipes. Spices and flavorings were introduced through North Africa and Arabia, and saffron, cloves, chiles, ginger and allspice continue to be popular all over the Mediterranean, appearing in sweet and savory dishes. Nuts, too, are an ingredient common to many of the countries. Almonds, pistachios and pine nuts are perhaps the most popular, as they are native to the region.

When thinking of Mediterranean food, however, it is the fresh fruit, vegetables and herbs that immediately spring to mind. Open-air markets from Marseilles to Morocco are a feast for the senses. Fabulous arrays of

tomatoes, eggplant, zucchini, peaches, figs, garlic and pungent herbs such as basil and thyme are tantalizingly displayed; the experience is completed by the hot sun drawing out the flavors and aromas. Mediterranean cooking depends on the freshest of ingredients; it is honest, simple and prepared with respect.

Recent research has proved the Mediterranean diet to be a very healthy one, thus increasing its popularity. Olive oil is at the heart of this theory; it contains a high proportion of monounsaturated fats. Olive oils vary in color, from the golden Spanish varieties to the deep greens of some Greek, Provençal and Italian oils. Color is not really an indication of quality; the oils have to be tasted, and flavor, like color, varies immensely.

BELOW: Glossy green leaves shade juicy oranges in a grove near Seville.

ABOVE. Melons, including the familiar tiger watermelons in the background, lie piled in the sun in a Greek market.

The people of the Mediterranean have known great hardship and poverty. Although we may have images of endless sunny days, the weather can be wild and unjust. Lack of rain, terrible winds and a capricious sea ruin crops and the fishermen's haul; in the past, foreign domination and disease caused poverty and death. Because of this, the most basic foods are, even today, a celebration of life to the Mediterranean people. Bread is an important staple and always accompanies a meal, be it a bowl of soup or a platter of grilled fish.

Perhaps Mediterranean food could be described as "peasant food," not in a derogatory sense, but as an homage to the people who have provided and inspired us with such a vast and wonderful repertoire of recipes, ancient and new. In this book, we give you just a few of the countless dishes from around the Mediterranean. Some are traditional—for example, Gazpacho, Ratatouille, Greek Salad and Provençal Beef Daube, while others are more contemporary, using Mediterranean ingredients but creating something new. Among these recipes are Grilled Vegetable Terrine, Pan-fried Red Mullet with Basil, Mushroom and Pesto Pizza, and Turkish Delight Ice Cream.

As in the Mediterranean, ingredients should be fresh and of the highest quality, even if this means waiting for some of them, such as tomatoes or figs, to be in season. We hope to bring you a true taste of the Mediterranean.

INGREDIENTS

Mediterranean markets are sheer delight. Colorful displays of seasonal fruits and vegetables vie for your attention alongside stalls selling hams, cheeses, oils and herbs. Fresh fish is displayed on crushed ice, and culinary advice is freely offered.

VEGETABLES

Vegetables have always played an important role in Mediterranean cooking. They are sometimes served as dishes in their own right, and sometimes as accompaniments. Either way, the range of imaginative vegetable recipes from all over the Mediterranean is infinite.

ARTICHOKES There are two different types of artichoke, the globe and the Jerusalem, neither of which is in any way related to the other. The globe artichoke belongs to the thistle family and is common throughout the Mediterranean. It appears as different varieties, depending on the country, and ranges from tiny purple plants with tapered leaves, which are so tender that they can be eaten raw, to large bright or pale green globes, whose cooked leaves are pulled off one by one by the diner, who strips off the succulent flesh at the base with his or her teeth. The base is also edible. Baby varieties are completely edible and are sometimes eaten raw.

Globe artichokes were once thought to be aphrodisiacs, and women were forbidden to eat them.

They may not win any beauty contests, but Jerusalem artichokes taste delicious.

Globe artichokes are at their best in summer. Whichever variety you are buying, look for tightly packed leaves, as open leaves indicate that they are too mature. Look, too, for a very fresh color. When an artichoke is old, the tips of the leaves will turn brown. If possible, buy artichokes that are still attached to their stems, as these will stay fresh for longer. Artichokes will stay fresh for several days if you place the stalks in water. If they have no stalks, wrap them in plastic wrap and keep in the vegetable drawer of the refrigerator for a day or two.

The Jerusalem Artichoke is an entirely different vegetable. It is, in fact, a tuber, belonging to the sunflower family, and has nothing to do with Jerusalem. One explanation is that its name is a corruption of *girasole,* "sunflower," because its yellow flower turns toward the sun. Jerusalem artichokes look a lot like bumpy potatoes, and can be treated as such. They have an appealing, distinctive flavor and are good in soups. They are also delicious baked, braised, sautéed or puréed.

Buy asparagus spears of uniform thickness, so that they cook evenly.

ASPARAGUS Asparagus has been cultivated in the Mediterranean for hundreds of years and is still highly prized there as a luxury vegetable. It has a short growing season, from spring to early summer, and is really only worth eating during this period. Both green and white asparagus are cultivated. The green variety is grown above ground, so that the entire spear is bright green, and is harvested when it is about 6 inches high. The fat white spears with their pale yellow tips are grown under mounds of soil to protect them from the light, and harvested almost as soon as the tips appear above the soil, to retain their pale color.

Asparagus spears can be boiled, steamed or roasted in olive oil, and served as a first course with butter and freshly grated Parmesan, or with a vinaigrette. When served as an accompaniment, they can be dipped in egg and bread crumbs and fried. Asparagus tips also make a luxurious addition to risotto. Allow about eight medium spears per serving as a first course and always buy spears of uniform thickness.

EGGPLANT Although eggplant originated in Asia, it is featured in dishes from every Mediterranean country. The plump purple variety is the most common. Look for firm, taut, shiny-skinned specimens with green stalks.

Some people believe sliced eggplant should be salted for about 30 minutes and drained before cooking, which helps to extract bitter juices. Others maintain that this is unnecessary. Salting does stop the eggplant from absorbing large quantities of oil during cooking, so overall it seems worth doing.

When buying eggplant, look for specimens that feel quite heavy for their size, as a light eggplant may indicate a dry, spongy inside that may contain a lot of seeds. Do not buy eggplants with wrinkled or damaged skins. Eggplant will keep in the refrigerator for up to a week, and it is a very versatile vegetable. It can be grilled, baked, stuffed, stewed and sautéed, either on its own or with other vegetables, and since it absorbs flavors well, it can be used with most seasonings.

Glossy and good to eat, eggplants are among the most popular Mediterranean vegetables.

Fava beans are at their best when they are small and tender. Young ones can be eaten pods and all.

FAVA BEANS In the spring these beans are often exported from various Mediterranean countries to countries whose growing seasons are later.

The beans are at their best when they are small and tender, with a bittersweet flavor. When young, they can be cooked and eaten, pods and all, or shelled and eaten raw with cheese, as in Italy. When the beans are older, they are shelled, cooked, and sometimes peeled. Cooked fava beans have a milder flavor than raw.

Dried fava beans are popular in the Middle East, where they are cooked with spices or added to stews.

ZUCCHINI These squash have shiny green skin, a sweet delicate flavor and a crisp texture. They are at their best when they are small. They can be sliced or grated and eaten raw, or they can be cooked, as they combine well with other Mediterranean vegetables.

Zucchini can also be battered and deep-fried, made into fritters or served with a white sauce flavored with Parmesan or nutmeg. Served cold with a mint-flavored vinaigrette or tomato sauce, they can be served as part of a first course. They can also be halved and stuffed with a meat or vegetable filling.

The larger a zucchini becomes, the less flavor it has. When buying, choose firm, shiny specimens. Do not buy limp zucchini, or those with blemished skins. Yellow varieties, sometimes called "summer squash" are also available and, although there is little difference in flavor, they make a pretty alternative to the usual green variety.

In Italy and France, the golden zucchini flowers are highly prized; they are frequently stuffed and cooked, or deep-fried in batter. Zucchini is available almost all year round, but is at its best in spring and summer. Allow 9 ounces zucchini per serving. Zucchini will keep in the vegetable drawer of the refrigerator for up to one week.

FENNEL Originally a medicinal remedy for flatulence, fennel has become one of the most important Mediterranean vegetables, especially in Italy.

Bulb or Florence fennel—so called to distinguish it from the feathery green herb, resembles a fat white celery root with overlapping leaves and green, wispy fronds. It has a delicate but distinctive flavor of aniseed and a crisp, refreshing texture. It can be eaten raw, dressed with a vinaigrette or served in a mixed salad. It can also be cooked—either sautéed, baked or braised. When it is

For the finest flavor and texture, choose young zucchini that are firm, not limp.

cooked, the aniseed flavor becomes more subtle, and the texture resembles cooked celery. Braised fennel is particularly good with white fish or chicken, but it is also delicious served as a separate vegetable course, either roasted or baked with a cheese sauce.

Fennel is available all year round. Choose firm, rounded bulbs, in which the outer layers are crisp and white, not wizened and yellow. Some people claim that the plumper "female" bulbs have the better flavor. If possible, buy fennel bulbs with their topknots of feathery green fronds intact, which you can chop and use for garnishing or as an herb in any dish in which you would use dill.

Whole fennel bulbs will keep in the refrigerator for up to a week. Once cut, however, they must be used immediately, or the cut surfaces will discolor and the texture will soften. Allow a whole bulb per serving. If using raw, toss the slices in lemon juice to prevent them from discoloring.

Delicious raw or cooked, fennel is a versatile vegetable. It is particularly good braised.

Wild mushrooms are still collected in many parts of the Mediterranean. These are oyster mushrooms.

GARLIC Sold in "strings" or as separate bulbs, the main consideration when buying garlic is that the cloves are plump and firm. Garlic is one of the most vital ingredients in Mediterranean cooking and there are few recipes in which its addition would be out of place. Used crushed, sliced or even whole, garlic develops a smooth, gentle flavor with long, slow cooking. Used raw in salads, sauces and mayonnaise, garlic packs a punch.

MUSHROOMS Man has collected and eaten mushrooms for centuries, and people still collect wild mushrooms in many parts of the Mediterranean region. The varieties used in Mediterranean cooking are button, open cup and flat, but regional wild species, such as cepes, chanterelles and oyster mushrooms are to be found in the markets during autumn.

Mushrooms can be finely sliced and eaten raw, dressed with extra virgin olive oil, or they can be brushed with olive oil and grilled.

Mushrooms should never be washed, or they will become waterlogged and mushy. To clean them, cut off the earthy base of the stalk and lightly brush the caps with a soft brush, or wipe them clean with a damp cloth.

Never store mushrooms in a plastic bag, as they will sweat and turn slimy and moldy. Put them in a paper bag and keep in the vegetable drawer of the refrigerator for one or two days.

OKRA This unusual vegetable, is a five-sided green pod with a tapering end. It has a subtle flavor and a gelatinous texture that helps to thicken and enrich certain dishes. Used in Middle Eastern and Greek cooking, its most successful partners are garlic, onion and tomatoes. Choose small, firm pods and use sliced or whole in cooking.

ONIONS The starting point of so many dishes, the onion is invaluable to Mediterranean cooking. There are many varieties, differing in color, size and strength of flavor, from mild yellow onions to stronger-flavored white onions. For salads, or when onion is to be used raw, choose red or mild white globes, which have a sweet, mellow flavor. Large Spanish onions have a mild flavor, too, and are a good choice when a large amount of onion is called for in a recipe. Baby onions are perfect for adding whole to stews, or for serving as a vegetable dish on their own. Large onions can be stuffed with ground meat and herbs or cheese, and baked.

There are many different types of onions, be sure to choose the appropriate variety for each recipe.

You may be lucky enough to find young fresh onions in markets. These are sold in bunches like large, bulbous scallions, complete with their leaves. They have a mild flavor and can be used for pickling or in salads. They will keep in the refrigerator for three or four days, but should be wrapped tightly to prevent their smell from pervading everything else.

Older onions have thin, almost papery skins that should be unblemished. The onions should feel firm and should not be sprouting. They quickly deteriorate once cut, so buy assorted sizes, then you can use a small onion when the recipe calls for only a small amount. Stored in a dry, airy place, onions will keep for several weeks.

Some onions are easier to peel than others. The skins of red and yellow onions can be removed without much difficulty, but white onions may need to be plunged into boiling water for 30 seconds to make peeling easier.

For most cooked dishes, onions should be sliced or chopped, but for salads they are sliced into very thin rings.

In Mediterranean cooking, onions are seldom browned, which can give them a slightly bitter taste, but are generally sweated gently in olive oil to add a mellow flavor to a multitude of dishes.

Okra has an unusual texture and is an acquired taste, but is popular in Greek and Middle Eastern cooking.

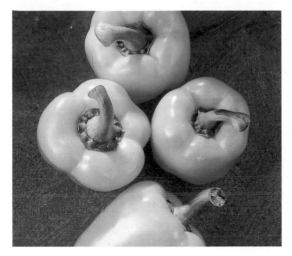

Bell peppers are a delicious addition to salad, they add a lovely crunch and a wonderful color, ranging from green to red.

BELL PEPPERS Generically known as capsicums, the shape of those peppers gives them the name "bell peppers." They come in a range of colors, including green, red, yellow, orange and even a purplish-black—and add color to markets throughout the Mediterranean region—though they all have very much the same sweet flavor and crunchy texture. They are a very healthy food, being rich in vitamin C and a good source of fiber. Peppers can be used raw or lightly roasted in salads or for antipasto, and can be cooked in a variety of ways roasted and dressed with olive oil or a vinaigrette and capers, stewed, marinated in olive oil, or stuffed and baked. To make the most of their flavor, broil peppers until charred, then rub off and discard the skins. Peppers have a great affinity with other Mediterranean ingredients, such as olives, capers, eggplant, zucchini, tomatoes and anchovies.

RADICCHIO This red chicory is one of the most popular salad leaves in Mediterranean countries, especially in Italy. There are several varieties, but the most common is the round type that looks like a head of lettuce. The leaves are crisp and pleasantly bitter and can be eaten raw or cooked.

SPINACH This dark green leafy vegetable is popular in Mediterranean countries. Originally cultivated in Persia in the 6th century, it was brought to Europe by Arab traders some thousand years later. Cooked or raw, it is a particularly good source of vitamins A and C, and is also rich in minerals, especially iron.

Young spinach leaves can be eaten raw and need little preparation, but older leaves should be washed in several changes of water and then picked over and the tough stalks removed.

Spinach is used in Middle Eastern pastries, Spanish tapas, French tarts and many more dishes—eggs and fish, for instance, make good partners. All types of spinach should look very fresh and green, with no signs of wilting. The leaves should be unblemished and the stalks crisp. Spinach leaves wilt down to about half their weight during cooking, so you always need to buy far more than you think you will need—if the spinach is to be cooked, allow 9 ounces raw weight per person. Using a heavy pan will aid even cooking.

Mediterranean cooks love versatile spinach, often using it in pastries.

Buy tomatoes on the vine if possible, as they will have ripened naturally.

TOMATOES Some of the best tomatoes in the world are to be found in Mediterranean markets, so it is hardly surprising that it is impossible to imagine Mediterranean food without them. But these "golden apples" were unknown in the Mediterranean until the 16th century, when they were brought from Mexico. In some countries, they were known as "love-apples" because they resembled the heart. Their popularity soon spread and they were cultivated all over the Mediterranean region and incorporated into the cooking of almost every country.

Sun-ripened and full of flavor, tomatoes come in many varieties—beefsteak tomatoes, plum tomatoes, cherry tomatoes and baby pear-shaped ones. Bright red fruits literally bursting with aroma and flavor, tomatoes are essential ingredients in so many Mediterranean dishes. They are used in so many different ways that it is hard to know where to start. They can be eaten raw, sliced and served with a trickle of extra virgin olive oil and some torn basil leaves. They are the red component in insalata tricolore, partnering with white mozzarella and green basil

to make up the colors of the Italian flag. Raw ripe tomatoes can be chopped with herbs and garlic to make a fresh-tasting pasta sauce. Tomatoes are at their best in summer, when they have ripened naturally in the sun.

Choose your tomatoes according to how you wish to prepare them. Salad tomatoes should be firm and easy to slice. The best tomatoes for cooking are plum tomatoes, which have a superb flavor and hold their shape well. Beefsteak tomatoes are the best for stuffing. Tomatoes will only ripen properly if they are left for long enough on the vine, so try to buy "vine-ripened" varieties. As well as fresh tomatoes, canned and sun-dried tomatoes are invaluable pantry items.

GRAPE LEAVES These pretty leaves have been used in cooking for hundreds of years. They can be stuffed with a variety of fillings and also make perfect, and very decorative, wrappers for meat, fish and poultry. Fresh leaves must be young and soft. If using brined grape leaves, soak them in hot water for 20–30 minutes before stuffing or wrapping.

Grape leaves make ideal wrappers for rice, and are famously used to make the Greek dolmades.

FRUIT

Dates Plump and slightly wrinkled fresh dates have a rich honey-like flavor and dense texture. They are delicious pitted and served with plain yogurt. The dried dates can be used in the same way, but fewer will be needed, as the flavor is very concentrated.

Figs Fresh figs are delicious served on their own, but they have an affinity with nuts such as walnuts, pistachios and almonds. They can be served raw as a first course with prosciutto or salami, or with plain yogurt and honey or stuffed with raspberry coulis or mascarpone and served as a dessert. Poached in a little water or wine flavored with cinnamon or nutmeg, they make an excellent accompaniment to duck, game or lamb. Ripe figs are extremely delicate and do not travel well, so it is hard to find imported fruit at a perfect stage of maturity, but they can be ripened at home, by storing them on a high shelf. In season throughout the Mediterranean, you will find delectable local figs that are just ripe for eating. They should be soft and yielding, but not mushy.

There are few fruits more delicious than ripe figs, but treat them with care, as they bruise very easily.

Grapes grow all over the Mediterranean region, and make the perfect finale to a simple meal.

Grapes Grapes grow all over the Mediterranean. As well as being delicious, fresh grapes are extremely good for you, rich in potassium, iron, enzymes and vitamins. Grapes are best eaten on their own or as an accompaniment to cheese, but they can also be used in pastries or as a fruit garnish for cooked quail, guinea fowl or other poultry. The seeds are pressed into grapeseed oil, which has a fairly neutral taste and is high in polyunsaturated fatty acids. Choosing white, black or red grapes is simply a matter of preference. Beneath the skin, the flesh is always pale green and juicy. Buy bunches of grapes with fruit that is of equal size and not too densely packed on the stalk. Check that none is withered or bad. The skins should have a delicate bloom, that you should not be able to taste, and be firm to the touch. Try to eat one grape from a bunch to see how they taste. Grapes should be washed immediately after being purchased, drained, then placed in a bowl and kept in the refrigerator for up to three days. Keeping them in a plastic bag causes them to become over-ripe very quickly.

Melons that ripen naturally in the sun have a wonderful perfume and flavor.

LEMONS These bright yellow citrus fruits originated in India and Malaysia and were brought by the Assyrians to Greece, which in turn took them to Italy. The Greeks and Romans greatly appreciated their culinary and medicinal qualities. Later, seafarers ate them in large amounts to protect against scurvy, and society ladies used them as a beauty treatment to whiten their skin, bleach their hair and redden their lips. They are rich in vitamin C and have a tangy flavor that enhances almost any dish. Lemons are an extraordinarily versatile fruit. The juice can be squeezed to make a refreshing drink, or it can be added to tea, dressings and sauces. It is an antioxidant, and prevents discoloration when brushed on fruits and vegetables that have a tendency to turn brown when cut. A squeeze of lemon juice makes a difference to bland foods, such as fish, poultry, veal or certain vegetables. Its acidity also helps to bring out the flavor of other fruits.

A bowl of fresh lemons is a common sight in the Mediterranean kitchen.

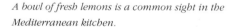

The zest makes a wonderfully aromatic flavoring for cakes and pastries, and is an essential ingredient in many desserts. Quartered lemons are served with fried fish and other foods fried in batter. Depending on the variety, lemons may have thick indented skins, or be perfectly smooth. Their appearance does not affect the flavor, but they should feel heavy for their size, which indicates plenty of juice. If you intend to use the zest, buy unwaxed lemons. Lemons will keep in the refrigerator for up to two weeks.

MELONS This fruit comes in many different sizes, shapes and colors—cantaloupe, charentais, galia, honeydew, ogen, orange- and green-fleshed varieties, and the wonderful pink watermelon. Melons can be eaten as an appetizer, sometimes accompanied by wafer-thin prosciutto or cured meats. In the Mediterranean, melons and watermelons are often served as dessert fruit on their own, but sometimes appear as part of a fruit salad. Ripe melons should yield to gentle pressure from your thumbs at the stalk end and have a fragrant, slightly sweet scent. If they smell highly perfumed and musky, they will probably be over-ripe. A melon should feel heavy for its size, and the skin should not be bruised or damaged. Melons will ripen quickly at room temperature and should be eaten within two or three days.

Oranges—and orange zest—are favorite flavorings, used in savory as well as sweet dishes.

ORANGES Many varieties of the orange are grown all over the Mediterranean, particularly in Spain. Seville oranges, the bitter marmalade variety, have a very short season, just after Christmas. The best of the orange flavor comes from the zest—the outer layer of the skin—that is often included in recipes using oranges. Sweet oranges are used for both sweet and savory recipes and are a favorite addition to salads. Oranges are available all year round, but are at their best in winter. They should have unblemished shiny skins and feel heavy for their size, which indicates that they contain plenty of juice and that the flesh is not dry. If you intend to candy the zest or to incorporate it into a recipe, choose unwaxed oranges. Oranges will keep at room temperature for a week and for at least two weeks in the refrigerator. Bring them back to room temperature before eating.

PEACHES AND NECTARINES These are among the most delicious summer fruits. Peaches need plenty of sun to ripen them and grow in France, Spain and Italy. There are yellow-, pink- and white-fleshed varieties, with velvety skin. Look for bruise-free specimens that just give when squeezed gently. Nectarines are smooth-skinned, with all the luscious flavor of peaches. They also come in yellow and white varieties and, like peaches, the white nectarines have a finer flavor. Some people prefer nectarines to peaches as a dessert fruit because they do not require peeling. Peaches and nectarines are interchangeable in cooked dishes. They can both be macerated in fortified wine or spirits or poached in white wine and syrup. They also have a special affinity with almonds. Peaches are also delicious served with raspberries, or made into fruit drinks and ice creams and sorbets. Peaches are in season during the Mediterranean summer. Make sure they are ripe, but not too soft, with unwrinkled and unblemished skins. They should have a sweet, intense scent. Peaches and nectarines bruise very easily, so try to buy those that have been kept in compartmented trays rather than piled into crates. Do not keep peaches and nectarines for more than a day or two. If they are very ripe, store them in the refrigerator.

A nectarine or peach makes the perfect dessert, either fresh or baked.

The best Parmesan has the words "Parmigiano Reggiano" stamped on the rind.

DAIRY PRODUCE

CHEESE The variety of cheeses from Mediterranean countries is huge and diverse, ranging from fresh mild cheeses such as mozzarella, to soft, blue-veined ones such as Gorgonzola and aged hard types with a strong, mature flavor such as Parmesan and Pecorino. Cheeses are made from cow's, goat's, sheep's and, in the case of Italian mozzarella, buffalo's milk. Cream cheese is also common to many countries, varying a little according to the milk and the method used for preparing it.

Perhaps the best known Mediterranean cheese is Parmesan. There are two types, Parmigiano Reggiano and Grana Padano, but the former is infinitely superior. A really fine Parmesan may be aged for up to seven years, during which time it matures, becoming pale golden with a slightly granular, flaky texture and a nutty, mildly salty flavor. Always buy Parmesan in a block and grate it yourself.

YOGURT This live product (pasteurized milk combined with two beneficial bacteria) is perhaps most associated with the Middle Eastern countries, where it is used extensively in cooking. Yogurt is thick and creamy, and French yogurt is traditionally of the set variety. Yogurt is used as a marinade, a dip and to enrich soups and stews. It can be made from goat's, sheep's or cow's milk.

FISH AND SHELLFISH

RED MULLET Very popular along the coasts of the Mediterranean, the red mullet is a pretty fish. It is rarely available in the United States, however, so use red snapper instead.

SALT COD Most salt cod is prepared in Norway, Iceland and Newfoundland and then exported to Mediterranean countries. It looks very unappetizing, and has a pungent smell, but after being soaked for 48 hours and cooked in the Mediterranean style, it is delicious.

SEA BASS This is quite an expensive fish and is usually sold and cooked whole. The flesh is soft and delicate and needs careful attention when cooking. Methods include poaching, steaming, grilling and baking.

SQUID Popular in the Mediterranean region, particularly in Spain, Italy and Portugal, squid vary in size from the tiny specimens that can be eaten whole, to larger varieties, which are good for stuffing, grilling or stewing. The flesh is sweet and, when carefully cooked, tender.

When buying fresh fish, bright eyes, fresh red gills and firmly attached scales are signs to look for.

SWORDFISH This delicious fish is widely available through-out the Mediterranean. Swordfish steaks can be very large, so do not automatically order one per person. Brush them with oil when grilling.

TUNA An oily fish belonging to the same family as the mackerel. The flesh, which is sold in steaks or large pieces, is dark red and very dense, and has a tendency to dry out when cooked. Marinating before cooking helps to keep the flesh moist, as does basting while cooking. Tuna can be baked, fried, grilled or stewed.

CRAB There are thousands of species of crab around the world. In the Mediterranean countries, brown and spider crabs are the most common. The meat of the crab is divided into two kinds—brown and white. Crabs are often sold cooked and dressed, which means that the crab is ready to eat. Choose cooked crabs that are heavy for their size and therefore meaty.

MUSSELS Available in the Mediterranean through the win-ter, mussels usually need to be scrubbed and have the beard—the hairy tuft attached to the shell—removed. Any open mussels should be discarded if they do not close after a sharp tap, as this indicates that they are old and therefore should not be eaten. Mussels vary in size from very small to quite large, and the shell can be blue-black to dappled brown. They are easy to cook—just steam for a few minutes in a covered pan. Discard any that fail to open after cooking.

SHRIMP These vary enormously in size. The classic Mediterranean shrimp is very large, about 8 inches long and reddish brown in color when raw. When shrimp are cooked over intense heat, such as on a barbecue, the shell is often left on to protect the flesh from charring. Shrimp can be bought ready-cooked and frozen.

Mediterranean shrimp are a treat. Cooked fresh from the sea, with garlic and olive oil, they are delicious.

GRAINS

BULGHUR WHEAT Also known as bulghur, this cereal has been partially processed, so it cooks quickly.

COUSCOUS This semolina product simply needs moisten-ing, then steaming to swell the grains. It is usually served with a spicy meat or vegetable stew.

RICE There are many varieties of this world-wide staple food. In Italy, which produces more and a greater vari-ety of rice than anywhere else in Europe, there are at least four short-grained types used for risotto, and in Spain, Valencia rice is the preferred variety for paella. In the Middle East, rice is served with every meal, either boiled or cooked with saffron and other spices to create fragrant pilafs.

POLENTA This grainy yellow flour is a type of cornmeal. It is cooked into a kind of porridge with a wide variety of uses. Polenta is available ground to various degrees of coarseness to suit different dishes.

Pasta comes in a remarkable range of shapes and sizes, from tiny soup shells to long strands.

PULSES

CHICKPEAS This pulse looks like a golden hazelnut and has a nutty flavor. In the Middle East they are made into flour, and in Greece they are puréed to produce a dip. Soak them for 5 hours before cooking, and cook for up to 4 hours until tender. Timing will vary, depending on the age of the chickpeas.

HARICOT BEANS These white beans are quite soft when cooked, and are used in casseroles in Spain, Portugal and France. They need to be soaked for 4 hours before being cooked, and are also good in soups and salads. They taste great with a rich tomato sauce.

LENTILS These come in different sizes and can be yellow, red, brown or green. The tiny green Puy lentils are favored in France, and the brown and red ones favored in the Middle East, where they are cooked with spices to make dhals. They do not need soaking. Red lentils cook quite quickly—in about 20 minutes, but Puy lentils take considerably longer.

One of the most colorful stalls on the market is the one selling pulses.

PASTA

Pasta is simply the Latin word for "paste," the flour-and-egg-based dough from which it is made. Although a staple of Italian cooking, pasta is also widely used throughout the Mediterranean and has much in common with Chinese noodles, which filtered from China via the Middle-Eastern trade routes. In Italy today there are countless varieties of pasta, from flat sheets of lasagne and ribbon noodles to pressed and molded shapes specifically designed to pocket substantial amounts of the sauce with which they are served. Dried pasta, made from hard durum wheat, is a good standby and keeps for weeks in an airtight container. Fresh pasta has a better flavor and texture, but will only keep for a couple of days, although it can be successfully frozen. Fresh pasta is usually made by hand, using all-purpose flour enriched with eggs. Commercially-made fresh pasta is made with durum wheat flour, water and eggs. The flavor and texture of all fresh pasta is very delicate, so it is best suited to creamier sauces. Pasta is a wonderfully simple and nutritious staple food. Both fresh and dried pasta can be bought flavored with tomato, olive, spinach or mushroom paste. Black pasta, made with the addition of squid ink, is increasingly popular. Pasta is easy to make at home, if time is allowed for chilling the fresh dough. Rolling it can be done effortlessly using a pasta machine.

Browning pine nuts, either under the broiler or in a dry frying pan, really brings out their wonderful flavor.

NUTS

ALMONDS Cultivated commercially in Spain, Italy and Portugal, the almond is widely used in the Arab-influenced countries. It is an important ingredient in sweet pastries and is often added to savory dishes, too. Almonds are sold fresh in their velvety green shells in Mediterranean markets.

HAZELNUTS Used in desserts and candy, hazelnuts are particularly good in halva.

PINE NUTS These little nuts are used in both sweet and savory dishes, and are one of the principal ingredients in pesto, the basil sauce from Italy.

PISTACHIOS These colorful nuts originated in the Middle East. They have flesh that ranges from pale to dark green, and a papery, purple-tinged skin. Pistachios have a subtle flavor and are used in a wide range of dishes, from pastries to ice creams and nougat.

WALNUTS These versatile nuts are used in both sweet and savory dishes. Walnut oil is a popular addition to salad dressings in France. Elsewhere, walnuts are chopped and added to pastries, ground to make sauces, or eaten fresh.

HERBS

BASIL One of the herbs most crucial to Mediterranean cooking, particularly in Italian dishes, basil has a wonderful aroma and flavor. The sweet, tender leaves, sometimes as large as cabbage leaves, have a great affinity with tomatoes, eggplant, bell peppers, zucchini and cheese. A handful of torn leaves enlivens a green salad and is a great addition to a tomato sandwich. Basil is perhaps best known as the basis of pesto, that glorious green sauce that is so widely used in Italy and beyond. Pesto also includes pine nuts and olive oil, but it is basil that gives it its incomparable flavor. The herb is easy to grow in pots and should be picked just before use, though it will not survive the colder winter months outdoors if the temperature drops. Tear the leaves, rather than chopping them, if possible. Chopping the leaves can reduce them to an unappealing pulp and sometimes leave an unpleasant flavor from the metal on the leaves, a taste that may transfer to the dish you are preparing and spoil it.

Under the Mediterranean sun, basil leaves grow better and bigger than they do in colder climates.

Tied in bunches, chives look as good as they taste.

BAY LEAVES Taken from the bay shrub or tree, these are widely used to flavor slow-cooked recipes like stocks, soups and stews. They are also added to marinades, threaded onto kebab skewers, thrown on the barbecue to invigorate the smoky flavor, or used for decoration. One or two young bay leaves, infused with milk or cream in custard, add a warm, pungent flavor. They do not soften with cooking, so it is advisable to remove them before serving.

CHERVIL This delicate gentle herb with its lacy leaves, tastes rather like a mild parsley and needs to be used generously to impart sufficient flavor. Widely used in French cooking, it works well in herb butters and with eggs and cheese.

CHIVES Thin stems with a mild onion flavor, chives are one of the easiest herbs to grow. They are cut in short lengths and used in salads and egg dishes.

BOUQUET GARNI A collection of herbs that classically includes parsley, thyme and bay, although other herbs like rosemary and marjoram can be added; different regions vary the combination of herbs. Bouquet garni is available dried, tied in muslin bundles or in teabag-like sachets. Fresh bouquet garni can be tied together with string for easy removal from the dish before serving.

CILANTRO Huge bundles of fresh cilantro are a familiar sight in eastern Mediterranean markets, their warm, pungent aroma rising at the merest touch. The leaves impart a distinctive flavor to soups, stews, sauces and spicy dishes when added toward the end of cooking. They are also used sparingly in salads and yogurt dips.

Oregano grows wild all over the Mediterranean. Its pungent scent seems to linger in the air.

DILL Feathery dill leaves have a mild aniseed taste, popular in the eastern Mediterranean, particularly in Greece and Turkey. Dill is chopped into fish and chicken dishes, as well as stuffings and rice. Pickled gherkins and cucumbers are often flavored with dill.

MARJORAM A versatile herb of which there are several varieties. It grows wild and is also cultivated and goes very well with red meats, game and tomato dishes.

MINT One of the oldest and most widely used herbs. In Greece, chopped mint accompanies other herbs to enhance stuffed vegetables and fish dishes, and in Turkey and the Middle East finely chopped mint adds a cooling tang to yogurt dips as well as teas and iced drinks.

24

OREGANO is a wild form of marjoram, with a far more pungent flavor. The name means "joy of the mountains" in Greek, which is appropriate, as the scent makes walking in the mountains pure pleasure. Oregano is a very popular herb, widely used throughout the Mediterranean region.

PARSLEY Flat-leaf parsley is far more widely used in Mediterranean cooking than the tightly curled variety. Mixed with garlic and lemon zest, it makes a wonderfully aromatic gremolata, a colorful, refreshing garnish for sprinkling on tomato and rice dishes.

ROSEMARY Cut from the pretty flowering shrub, rosemary grows well throughout the Mediterranean and is most widely used when cooking meat. Several sprigs, tucked under a roast chicken or lamb with plenty of garlic, impart an inviting warm, sweet flavor.

SAGE Native to the northern Mediterranean, soft, velvety sage leaves vary in color from yellow to green to purple and have a strong, distinctive flavor that is used sparingly in meat and game dishes. Sage can be added to stuffings and nut dishes or pan-fried with squab and liver.

TARRAGON Long, lank tarragon leaves have a very individual aroma and flavor, most widely appreciated in French cooking. The herb is used generously in chicken and egg dishes, and with salmon and trout. Tarragon-flavored vinegar makes a delicious ingredient in a good mayonnaise or Hollandaise sauce.

THYME There are many types of thyme, from lemon thyme to plain garden thyme, ranging in color from yellow to gray-green. A few sprigs will add a warm, earthy flavor to slow-cooked meat and poultry dishes, pâtés, marinades, soups and vegetable dishes.

A rosemary bush is a gift to any gardener who likes cooking Mediterranean food.

SPICES

CARDAMOM Usually a spice associated with Indian cooking, the use of cardamom extends as far as the eastern Mediterranean. The pods should be pounded to release the black seeds, which are bruised to release the flavor.

CHILES These are the small fiery relatives of the sweet pepper family. Mediterranean chiles are generally milder in flavor than the unbearably fiery South American ones but should still be used with caution.

CINNAMON Cinnamon sticks, the thin curled bark of the cinnamon tree, have an aromatic, sweet flavor that is used extensively in the eastern Mediterranean for savory dishes, and in many desserts. Ground cinnamon is convenient but lacks the intensity of stick cinnamon.

CORIANDER SEEDS The seeds of the cilantro herb have a warm, slightly orangey flavor that is essential to many dishes of the eastern Mediterranean. Their flavor can be accentuated if they are crushed before use and used in either sweet or savory dishes.

Nutmeg has a wonderful warm flavor. Buy whole nutmegs and grate them as needed.

CUMIN SEEDS These dark, spindly seeds are frequently married with coriander when making spicy dishes that are typical of north Africa and the eastern Mediterranean.

MACE This is the thin, lacy covering of nutmeg, available ground to a powder or as thin "blades." It has a gentler flavor than nutmeg.

NUTMEG Nutmeg's beautiful, sweet warm aroma makes a good addition to sweet and savory dishes, particularly with spinach, cheese and eggs or in terrines and pâtés.

PEPPER There are several different types of peppercorns, all of which are picked from the pepper vine, a plant unrelated to the capsicum family. Black peppercorns have the strongest flavor. Green peppercorns are fresh unripe berries.

SAFFRON The color and flavor of this exotic spice are indispensable in many Mediterranean dishes, such as French fish stews, Spanish rice dishes and Italian risottos. Crush the strands and soak them in boiling water before use.

PRESERVES, PICKLES AND FLAVORINGS

CAPERS These are the pickled buds of a shrub native to the Mediterranean region. The best are those preserved in salt rather than brine or vinegar. When capers are roughly chopped, their sharp piquant tang is used to cut the richness of lamb, enliven fish sauces and flavor salads and pastes such as tapenade.

HARISSA A fiery, hot paste used mostly in north African cooking. It is made from a blend of chiles, garlic, cumin, coriander and cayenne and can be bought in small jars.

HONEY An ancient sweetener that depends on the flowers on which the bees have fed for its individual fragrance and flavor. The Turks and Greeks use it in their syrupy pastries and desserts and small amounts are added to some savory dishes.

PRESERVED LEMONS AND LIMES Lemons or limes preserved in salt develop a rich, mellow flavor. To make preserved

lemons, scrub and quarter the fruits almost through to the base and rub the cut sides with salt. Pack tightly into a large sterilized jar. Half fill the jar with more salt, adding some bay leaves, peppercorns and cinnamon, and any other spices, if desired. Cover completely with lemon juice. Top with a lid and store for two weeks, shaking the jar daily. Add a little olive oil to seal and use within one to six months, washing off the salt before use.

Preserved lemons give a mellow flavor to Mediterranean dishes.

One of the Mediterranean's most important ingredients, olive oil has been called liquid gold.

ROSE WATER This distilled essence of rose petals is used mainly in eastern Mediterranean desserts, giving a mild rose fragrance and flavor.

TAHINI A smooth, oily paste ground from sesame seeds, tahini gives a nutty flavor to Middle Eastern dishes.

TOMATO PASTE A concentrated paste made from fresh tomatoes, perfect for boosting the flavor of bland tomatoes in soups, stews and sauces.

OLIVES The fruit of one of the earliest known trees native to the Mediterranean. There are hundreds of varieties, differing widely in size, quality and taste. Color depends purely on ripeness—the fruit changes from yellow to green, violet, purple, brown and finally black when fully ripened. Fresh olives are picked at the desired stage of ripeness, then soaked in water, bruised and immersed in brine. They can be bought whole or pitted, sometimes stuffed with peppers, anchovies or nuts, or bottled with flavorings.

Perfect for antipasto, tapas, salads or savory dishes of all types, olives have a wonderful flavor.

OLIVE OIL

Unlike other oils, which are extracted from the seeds or dried fruits of plants, olive oil is pressed from the pulp of ripe olives, which give it an inimitable richness and flavor. Besides being polyunsaturated and a natural fat, making it a healthy alternative to many other fats, olive oil is valued for its fine, nutty flavor. Italy, France and Spain produce some of the best, and different regions produce distinctively different olive oils. The production of olive oil is strictly controlled and regulated, rather like wine. The richest and best oil comes from the first cold pressing of the olives, with no further processing, producing a rich green "extra virgin" oil. It must have an acidity level of less than 1 percent. The distinctive fruity flavor of this oil makes it ideal for dressings and using raw. Virgin oil is pressed in the same way, but usually from a second pressing, and has a higher acidity level and not such a fruity flavor. It, too, can be used as a condiment, but is also suitable for cooking. Unclassified olive oil is refined, often using heat and chemicals to aid extraction, then blended with virgin oil to add flavor. It has an undistinguished taste but is ideal for cooking. The best olive oil is expensive. It is made with slightly under-ripe olives, which give it a luminous green color. Once opened, keep olive oil in a cool, dark place. Use it within six months of opening.

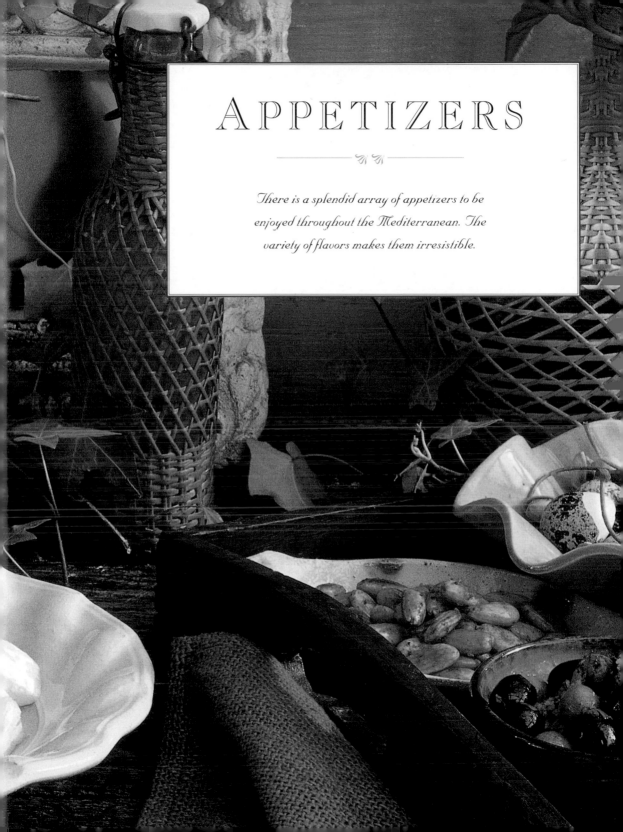

APPETIZERS

❧ ❧

There is a splendid array of appetizers to be
enjoyed throughout the Mediterranean. The
variety of flavors makes them irresistible.

Tapas, apéritifs, mezze, mezedes—all these terms describe the inexhaustible and highly flavored range of appetizers that are served with drinks before a meal or as a light snack at almost any time of day. This is one of the most enticing aspects of Mediterranean cooking—the irresistible nibbles enjoyed in a casual, unhurried atmosphere, offering a culinary glimpse of the good things to follow. For the cook, the preparation of these savories can be as simple or as demanding as time and circumstances allow. Whether it is a selection of marinated olives, regional cheeses or fresh seafood or, on a more elaborate scale, delicious baked vegetables, pickles and spicy pastries, this informal style of enjoying food is quintessentially Mediterranean.

In Spanish, "tapa" means a lid, and it was the custom

RIGHT: Bent double, Moroccan farmworkers bring in the olive harvest.

LEFT: On the mountainous Greek island of Naxos, arable land is precious, and hillsides are extensively terraced.

of bartenders to serve glasses of sherry covered with a slice of bread topped with sausage or ham that evolved into the fascinating and imaginative selection of "little dishes" served today. Tapas bars, particularly abundant in southern Spain, serve a variety of such dishes. In these bars you can enjoy predinner bites or thoroughly indulge yourself with a selection of dishes as a main meal. Fried new potatoes, chorizo sausage in olive oil, garlic shrimp and empanadillas are tapas classics. The tortilla, an omelet in which fried potatoes are layered in a pan, covered with beaten eggs and baked to a set "cake," is another well- established dish. It is served warm or cold, cut into wedges, and washed down with local chilled wines or, like other tapas, with sherry, port or beer.

In the eastern Mediterranean, in places like Turkey, Greece, Lebanon and North Africa, local and specialized variations of mezze are popular with both locals and visitors. Arak, raki and ouzo, as well as wine, are drunk with a wonderful selection of foods to whet the appetite. These are usually highly spiced and aromatic. In Greece, sheep's and goat's milk yogurt are strained to produce thickened cheeses that are preserved in spiced olive oil. Spread on warm toast, this delicious snack is good

ABOVE: With his scales at the ready, a Turkish fisherman sets out his catch on his stall.

enough to enjoy as a complete meal. Stuffed tomatoes, fried halloumi or kefalotyri cheese drizzled with lemon juice and pepper and a bowl of garlic-flavored Greek yogurt complete a mouthwatering spread.

Vegetables, salads and beans feature prominently in North African or Lebanese mezze. Simple vegetable crudités such as carrots, turnips and cucumber are scattered with coarse salt and left to marinate lightly before being moistened with lemon juice or wine vinegar. Miniature versions of national dishes such as kibbeh and little phyllo pastries are also ideal for whetting the appetite.

Sampling a selection of nibbles before a Turkish meal is almost compulsory, and the range of dishes is very extensive. A rich, thick sauce of tomato and chile and a refreshing cacik, or cucumber and yogurt salad, provide a stimulating contrast alongside specialties such as garlic mussels, broiled vegetables and stuffed bell peppers.

The classic Italian appetizer is the antipasto, usually an assortment of salami, prosciutto and other cured meats, served alongside roasted bell pepper salads, artichokes in olive oil, green bean vinaigrette, anchovy fillets and breads such as crostini and focaccia.

Tasty dips like tapenade, herb aïoli and a very garlicky vinaigrette are essential appetizers in France, often accompanied by a selection of raw or roasted crudités, herb salads and radishes with salt and butter.

Part of the pleasure of serving appetizers is that they can be as simple or as complicated as desired. Serve several as a light summer meal, two or three as a simple appetizer or a varied selection for a larger party. Added interest can be provided, with little extra effort, by serving a variety of olives, interesting Mediterranean breads and salted or spiced nuts.

Essentially, plenty of time must be allowed so that the nibbles can be enjoyed in the unhurried and relaxed atmosphere that is an integral part of the Mediterranean way of life.

TAPENADE AND HERB AIOLI WITH SUMMER VEGETABLES

A beautiful platter of salad vegetables served with one or two interesting sauces makes a thoroughly delicious and informal appetizer. This colorful French dish is perfect for entertaining, as it can be prepared in advance.

FOR THE TAPENADE
1½ cups pitted black olives
2-ounce can anchovy fillets, drained
2 tablespoons capers
½ cup olive oil
finely grated zest of 1 lemon
1 tablespoon brandy (optional)
ground black pepper

FOR THE HERB AIOLI
2 egg yolks
1 teaspoon Dijon mustard
2 teaspoons white wine vinegar
1 cup light olive oil
3 tablespoons chopped mixed fresh
herbs, such as chervil, parsley
or tarragon
2 tablespoons chopped watercress
5 garlic cloves, crushed
salt and ground black pepper

TO SERVE
2 red bell peppers, seeded and cut into
wide strips
2 tablespoons olive oil
8 ounces new potatoes
4 ounces green beans
8 ounces baby carrots
8 ounces young asparagus
12 quail's eggs (optional)
fresh herbs, to garnish
coarse salt for sprinkling

SERVES 6

1 To make the tapenade, finely chop the olives, anchovies and capers and beat together with the oil, lemon zest and brandy if using. (Alternatively, lightly process the ingredients in a blender or food processor, scraping down the mixture from the sides of the bowl if necessary.)

2 Season with pepper and blend in a little more oil if the mixture is very dry. Transfer to a serving dish.

3 To make the aïoli, beat together the egg yolks, mustard and vinegar. Gradually blend in the oil, a trickle at a time, whisking well after each addition until thick and smooth. Season with salt and pepper to taste, adding a little more vinegar if the aïoli tastes bland.

4 Stir in the mixed herbs, watercress and garlic, then transfer to a serving dish. Cover and put in the refrigerator.

5 Put the peppers on a foil-lined broiler rack and brush with the oil. Broil under high heat until just beginning to char.

6 Cook the potatoes in a large pan of boiling salted water until just tender. Add the beans and carrots and cook for 1 minute. Add the asparagus and cook for another 30 seconds. Drain the vegetables.

7 Cook the quail's eggs (if using) in boiling water for 2 minutes. Drain and remove half of each shell.

8 Arrange all the vegetables, eggs and sauces on a serving platter. Garnish with fresh herbs and serve with coarse salt for sprinkling.

COOK'S TIP
Keep any leftover sauces for serving with salads. The tapenade is also delicious tossed with pasta or spread on warm toast.

EGGPLANT DIP

This is an appetizer to serve with drinks and crisp sticks of raw vegetables. Eggplant is particularly popular in Israel, where it is almost a staple food.

2 eggplant, about 10 ounces each
⅔ cup olive oil
2 onions, chopped
3 garlic cloves, crushed
freshly squeezed juice of 1 lemon
salt and ground black pepper
cilantro sprigs, to garnish
black and green olives, to serve

SERVES 4 AS AN APPETIZER, OR MORE
AS A DIP WITH PITA BREAD

1 Preheat the broiler. Cut both the eggplant in half lengthwise and put them on a sheet of aluminum foil, skin side up. Broil at least 2 inches away from the heat for 20 minutes. The skin will start to wrinkle and the flesh will become slightly smoky and soft.

2 Meanwhile, heat about 4 tablespoons of the oil and sauté the onions in a frying pan over medium heat. Then add the garlic and cook both the onions and garlic until they are soft but not brown. Season with plenty of salt and pepper.

3 Scoop the flesh out of all the eggplant halves and put it into a food processor or blender with the onion and garlic. Pour in the freshly squeezed lemon juice.

4 With the blades running, slowly pour in the remaining olive oil to make a smooth mixture. Taste to check the seasoning and add more salt or pepper if needed.

5 Spoon the dip into bowls. Garnish with sprigs of fresh cilantro and serve with black and green olives.

CHARRED ARTICHOKES WITH LEMON OIL DIP

This citrus dressing marries particularly well with roasted artichokes. They are usually boiled, but dry-heat cooking also works well.

🌿 🌿

1 tablespoon lemon juice or
white wine vinegar
2 globe artichokes, trimmed
12 garlic cloves, unpeeled
6 tablespoons olive oil
1 lemon
sea salt
sprigs of flat-leaf parsley, to garnish

SERVES 4

🌿 🌿

1 Preheat the oven to 400°F. Add the lemon juice or vinegar to a bowl of cold water. Cut each artichoke into wedges. Pull the hairy choke out from the center, then drop them into the acidulated water until needed.

2 Drain the artichoke wedges and place in a roasting pan with the garlic. Add half the oil and toss well to coat. Sprinkle with salt and roast for 40 minutes, stirring once or twice, until the artichoke wedges are tender and a little charred.

3 Next, begin to make the dip. Using a small, sharp knife, thinly pare away two strips of zest from the lemon. Lay the strips on a board and carefully scrape off any remaining pith. Place the zest in a small pan with water to cover. Bring to a boil, then simmer for 5 minutes. Drain the zest, refresh it in cold water, then chop it roughly. Set aside.

4 Arrange the cooked artichokes on a serving plate and set aside to cool for 5 minutes. Using the back of a fork, gently flatten the garlic cloves so that the flesh squeezes out of the skins. Transfer the garlic flesh to a bowl, mash to a paste, then add the lemon zest. Squeeze the juice from the lemon and, using the fork, whisk it into the garlic mixture, together with the remaining oil. Serve the artichokes warm with the lemon dip. Garnish with a few sprigs of flat-leaf parsley.

BABA GANOUSH WITH LEBANESE FLATBREAD

Baba Ganoush is a delectable puréed eggplant dip from the Middle East. Tahini—a sesame seed paste with cumin—is the main flavoring, giving a subtle yet significant hint of spice.

2 small eggplant
1 garlic clove, crushed
¼ cup tahini paste
¼ cup ground almonds
juice of ½ lemon
½ teaspoon ground cumin
2 tablespoons fresh mint leaves
2 tablespoons olive oil
salt and ground black pepper
fresh thyme sprigs, to garnish

FOR THE LEBANESE FLATBREAD
6 pita breads
3 tablespoons toasted sesame seeds
3 tablespoons chopped fresh thyme leaves
3 tablespoons poppy seeds
⅔ cup olive oil

SERVES 6

3 Broil the eggplant, turning them frequently, until the skin is blackened and blistered. Remove the peel, chop the flesh roughly and let drain in a colander.

1 Start by making the Lebanese flatbread. Split the pita breads through the middle and carefully open them. Mix the sesame seeds, chopped thyme and poppy seeds in a mortar. Crush them lightly with a pestle to release the flavor.

2 Stir in the olive oil. Spread the mixture lightly over the insides of the pita bread. Broil until golden brown and crisp. When cool, break the pita breads into rough pieces and set aside.

4 Squeeze out as much liquid from the eggplant as possible. Place the flesh in a blender or food processor. Add the garlic, tahini, ground almonds, lemon juice and cumin, season to taste and process to a smooth paste. Roughly chop half the mint and stir into the dip.

5 Spoon the dip into a bowl, sprinkle the remaining leaves on top and drizzle with olive oil. Place the bowl on a platter, surround with the Lebanese flatbread and garnish with the fresh thyme sprigs.

HUMMUS BI TAHINA

Blending chickpeas with garlic and oil makes a surprisingly creamy purée that is delicious as part of a Turkish-style mezze, or as a dip with vegetables. Leftovers make good sandwiches.

¾ *cup dried chickpeas*
juice of 2 lemons
2 garlic cloves, sliced
2 tablespoons olive oil
pinch of cayenne pepper
⅔ *cup tahini paste*
salt and ground black pepper
extra olive oil and cayenne pepper
for sprinkling
flat-leaf parsley, to garnish

SERVES 4–6

1. Put the chickpeas in a bowl with plenty of cold water and let soak overnight.

2. Drain the chickpeas and cover with fresh water in a saucepan. Bring to a boil and boil rapidly for 10 minutes. Reduce the heat and simmer gently for about 1 hour, until soft. Drain.

3. Process the chickpeas in a food processor to a smooth purée. Add the lemon juice, garlic, olive oil, cayenne pepper and tahini and blend until creamy, scraping the mixture down from the sides of the bowl.

4. Season the purée with salt and pepper and transfer to a serving dish. Sprinkle with oil and cayenne pepper and serve garnished with a few parsley sprigs.

COOK'S TIP
For convenience, canned chickpeas can be used instead of dried. Use two 14-ounce cans and drain them thoroughly. Tahini paste can now be purchased at most supermarkets or health-food stores.

FONDUTA

Fontina is a medium-fat Italian cheese with a rich salty flavor, a little like that of Gruyère, which makes a good substitute. This delicious cheese dip needs only some warm ciabatta or focaccia, an herb salad and some robust red wine to make a thoroughly enjoyable meal.

9 ounces fontina cheese, diced
1 cup milk
1 tablespoon butter
2 eggs, lightly beaten
ground black pepper

SERVES 4

1 Place the cheese in a bowl, add the milk and let soak for 2 3 hours. Transfer to a double boiler or a heatproof bowl set over a pan of simmering water.

2 Add the butter and eggs and cook gently, stirring, until the cheese has melted to a smooth sauce with the consistency of custard.

3 Remove from heat and transfer to a serving dish. Grind on some pepper and serve immediately.

COOK'S TIP
Don't overheat the sauce, or the eggs might curdle. Very gentle heat will produce a lovely, smooth sauce.

SPICY MOROCCAN OLIVES

*Green olives, marinated in these two spicy herbal concoctions,
are simple to prepare and absolutely delicious.*

2⅔ cups green or tan olives (unpitted)
for each marinade

FOR THE SPICY HERBAL MARINADE
3 tablespoons chopped cilantro
3 tablespoons chopped fresh
flat-leaf parsley
1 garlic clove, finely chopped
good pinch of cayenne pepper
good pinch of ground cumin
2–3 tablespoons olive oil,
plus extra if necessary
2–3 tablespoons lemon juice,
plus extra if necessary

FOR THE HOT CHILI MARINADE
¼ cup chopped cilantro
¼ cup chopped fresh
flat-leaf parsley
1 garlic clove, finely chopped
1 teaspoon grated fresh ginger root
1 red chile, seeded and finely sliced
¼ preserved lemon, cut into thin strips

SERVES 6–8

1. Crack the olives, hard enough to break the flesh but taking care not to crack the pits. Place in a bowl of cold water and let sit overnight to remove the excess brine. Drain thoroughly and divide the olives between two jars.

2. Mix all the ingredients for the spicy herbal marinade in a pitcher. Pour over the olives in one of the jars, adding more olive oil and lemon juice to cover, if necessary.

COOK'S TIP
A jar of marinated olives makes the perfect present for anyone who appreciates their delectable flavor. Experiment with different herbs and spices in the marinade—try oregano and basil, and substitute lime juice for the lemon juice, or even use flavored vinegars.

3. To make the hot chili marinade, combine all the ingredients. Pour over the olives in the second jar. Store both jars in the refrigerator for at least 1 week, shaking them occasionally.

TAPAS OF ALMONDS, OLIVES AND CHEESE

These three simple ingredients are lightly flavored to create a delicious Spanish tapas medley that's perfect for a casual appetizer or nibbles to serve with cocktails.

FOR THE MARINATED OLIVES
½ teaspoon coriander seeds
½ teaspoon fennel seeds
1 teaspoon chopped fresh rosemary
2 teaspoons chopped fresh parsley
2 garlic cloves, crushed
1 tablespoon sherry vinegar
2 tablespoons olive oil
⅔ cup black olives
⅔ cup green olives

FOR THE MARINATED CHEESE
5 ounces goat cheese, or Spanish sheep's milk cheese
6 tablespoons olive oil
1 tablespoon white wine vinegar
1 teaspoon black peppercorns
1 garlic clove, sliced
3 fresh tarragon or thyme sprigs
tarragon sprigs, to garnish

FOR THE SALTED ALMONDS
¼ teaspoon cayenne pepper
2 tablespoons sea salt
2 tablespoons butter
4 tablespoons olive oil
1¾ cups blanched almonds
extra salt for sprinkling (optional)

SERVES 6–8

1 To make the marinated olives, crush the coriander and fennel seeds with a mortar and pestle. Combine with the rosemary, parsley, garlic, vinegar and oil and pour over the olives in a small bowl. Cover and chill for up to 1 week.

2 To make the marinated cheese, cut the cheese into bite-size pieces, leaving the rind on. Combine the oil, vinegar, peppercorns, garlic and herb sprigs and pour over the cheese in a small bowl. Cover and chill for up to 3 days.

COOK'S TIP
If serving with cocktails, provide toothpicks for spearing the olives and cheese.

3 To make the salted almonds, combine the cayenne pepper and salt in a bowl. Melt the butter with the olive oil in a frying pan. Add the almonds to the pan and fry, stirring, for about 5 minutes, until the almonds are golden.

4 Pour the almonds out of the frying pan into the salt mixture and toss together until the almonds are coated. Let cool, then store them in a jar or airtight container for up to 1 week.

5 To serve the tapas, arrange in small, shallow serving dishes. Use fresh sprigs of tarragon to garnish the cheese and sprinkle a little more salt on the almonds, if desired.

YOGURT CHEESE IN OLIVE OIL

Sheep's milk is widely used in cheese making in the eastern Mediterranean, particularly in Greece, where sheep's milk yogurt is hung in cheesecloth to drain off the whey before being patted into balls of soft cheese. Here it's preserved in olive oil with chiles and herbs—an appropriate gift for a "foodie" friend.

1¾ pounds sheep's milk yogurt
½ teaspoon salt
2 teaspoons crushed dried chiles or chili powder
1 tablespoon chopped fresh rosemary
1 tablespoon chopped fresh thyme or oregano
1¼ cups olive oil, preferably garlic-flavored

FILLS TWO 1-POUND JARS

1 Sterilize a 12-inch square of cheesecloth by steeping it in boiling water. Drain and lay over a large plate. Mix the yogurt with the salt and pour onto the center of the cheesecloth. Bring up the sides of the cheesecloth and tie firmly with string.

2 Hang the bag on a kitchen cupboard handle or in a suitable position where the bag can be suspended with a bowl underneath to catch the whey. Leave for 2–3 days, until the yogurt stops

3 Sterilize two 1-pound glass preserving or jam jars by heating them in the oven at 300°F for 15 minutes.

4 Combine the chiles and herbs. Take teaspoonfuls of the cheese and roll into balls with your hands. Lower into the jars, sprinkling each layer with the herb mixture.

5 Pour the oil over the cheese until completely covered. Store in the refrigerator for up to 3 weeks.

6 To serve the cheese, spoon out of the jars with a little of the flavored olive oil and spread on lightly toasted bread.

COOK'S TIP
If your kitchen is particularly warm, find a cooler place to suspend the cheese. Alternatively, drain the cheese in the refrigerator, suspending the bag from one of the shelves.

STUFFED GRAPE LEAVES WITH GARLIC YOGURT

An old Greek recipe that comes in many guises. This meatless version is highly flavored with fresh herbs, lemon and a little chile.

8 ounces preserved grape leaves
1 onion, finely chopped
½ bunch of scallions, trimmed and finely chopped
¼ cup chopped fresh parsley
10 large mint sprigs, chopped
finely grated zest of 1 lemon
½ teaspoon crushed dried chiles
1½ teaspoons fennel seeds, crushed
scant 1 cup long-grain rice
½ cup olive oil
⅔ cup thick plain yogurt
2 garlic cloves, crushed
salt
lemon wedges and mint leaves, to garnish (optional)

SERVES 6

1   Rinse the grape leaves in plenty of cold water. Put in a bowl, cover with boiling water and let sit for 10 minutes. Drain thoroughly.

2   Combine the onion, scallions, parsley, mint, lemon, chiles, fennel, rice and 1½ tablespoons of the olive oil. Mix thoroughly and season with salt.

3   Place a grape leaf, veined side facing upward, on a work surface and cut off any stem. Place a heaping teaspoonful of the rice mixture near the stem end of the leaf.

4   Fold the stem end of the leaf over the rice filling, then fold over the sides and carefully roll up into a neat cigar shape.

5   Repeat with the remaining filling to make about 28 stuffed leaves. If some of the grape leaves are quite small, use two and patch them together to make parcels of the same size as the others.

6   Place any remaining leaves in the bottom of a large, heavy saucepan. Pack the stuffed leaves in a single layer in the pan. Spoon on the remaining oil, then add about 1¼ cups boiling water.

COOK'S TIP
To check that the rice is cooked, lift out one stuffed leaf and cut in half. The rice should have expanded and softened to make a firm parcel. If necessary, cook the stuffed leaves a little longer, adding boiling water if the pan is becoming dry.

7   Place a small plate over the leaves to keep them submerged in the water. Cover the pan and cook over very low heat for 45 minutes.

8   Combine the yogurt and garlic and place in a small serving dish. Transfer the stuffed leaves to a serving plate and garnish with lemon wedges and mint, if desired. Serve with the garlic yogurt.

BROILED VEGETABLE TERRINE

A colorful layered terrine, using vegetables associated with the Mediterranean.

2 large red bell peppers, quartered,
cored and seeded
2 large yellow bell peppers, quartered,
cored and seeded
1 large eggplant, sliced lengthwise
2 large zucchini, sliced lengthwise
6 tablespoons olive oil
1 large red onion, thinly sliced
½ cup raisins
1 tablespoon tomato paste
1 tablespoon red wine vinegar
1⅔ cups tomato juice
2 tablespoons powdered gelatin
fresh basil leaves, to garnish

FOR THE DRESSING
6 tablespoons extra virgin olive oil
2 tablespoons red wine vinegar
salt and ground black pepper

SERVES 6

2 Arrange the eggplant and zucchini slices on separate baking sheets. Brush them with a little oil and cook under the broiler, turning occasionally, until tender and golden.

3 Heat the remaining olive oil in a frying pan and add the sliced onion, raisins, tomato paste and red wine vinegar. Cook gently until soft and syrupy. Let the mixture cool in the frying pan.

4 Line a 7½-cup terrine with plastic wrap (it helps to oil the terrine lightly first), leaving a little hanging over the sides.

5 Pour half the tomato juice into a saucepan and sprinkle with the gelatin. Dissolve gently over low heat, stirring.

6 Place a layer of red peppers in the bottom of the terrine and pour in enough of the tomato juice with gelatin to cover. Continue layering the eggplant, zucchini, yellow peppers and onion mixture, finishing with another layer of red peppers. Pour tomato juice over each layer of vegetables.

7 Add the remaining tomato juice to any left in the pan, and pour into the terrine. Give it a sharp tap, to disperse the juice. Cover the terrine and chill until set.

8 To make the dressing, whisk together the oil and vinegar and season with salt and pepper. Turn out the terrine and remove the plastic wrap. Serve in thick slices, drizzled with dressing. Garnish with basil leaves.

1 Place the prepared red and yellow peppers skin side up under a hot broiler and cook until the skins are blackened. Transfer to a bowl and cover with a plate. Let cool.

48

MARINATED BABY EGGPLANT WITH RAISINS AND PINE NUTS

Eggplant is popular in all the Mediterranean countries. This is a recipe with an Italian influence, using ingredients that have been included in recipes since Renaissance times. Make a day in advance, to let the sweet and sour flavors develop.

❦ ❦

12 baby eggplant, halved lengthwise
1 cup extra virgin olive oil
juice of 1 lemon
2 tablespoons balsamic vinegar
3 cloves
⅓ cup pine nuts
2 tablespoons raisins
1 tablespoon sugar
1 bay leaf
large pinch of dried red pepper flakes
salt and ground black pepper

SERVES 4

❦ ❦

1 Preheat the broiler to high. Place the eggplant, cut side up, in the broiler pan and brush with a little of the olive oil. Broil for about 10 minutes, until slightly blackened, turning them over halfway through cooking.

2 To make the marinade, put the remaining olive oil, the lemon juice, vinegar, cloves, pine nuts, raisins, sugar and bay leaf in a bowl. Add the red pepper flakes and salt and pepper and mix well.

3 Place the hot eggplant in an earthenware or glass bowl, and pour the marinade over. Let cool, turning the eggplant once or twice. Serve cold.

ROASTED BELL PEPPER ANTIPASTO

Jars of Italian mixed peppers in olive oil are now a common sight in many supermarkets. None, however, can compete with this colorful, freshly made version, perfect as an appetizer on its own, or with some Italian salamis and cold meats.

3 red bell peppers
2 yellow or orange bell peppers
2 green bell peppers
½ cup sun-dried tomatoes in oil, drained
2 tablespoons balsamic vinegar
5 tablespoons olive oil
few drops of hot pepper sauce
4 canned artichoke hearts, drained and sliced
1 garlic clove, sliced
salt and ground black pepper
basil leaves, to garnish

SERVES 6

1 Preheat the oven to 400°F. Lightly oil a foil-lined baking sheet and place the whole peppers on the foil. Bake for about 45 minutes, until beginning to char. Remove from the oven, cover with a dish towel and let cool for 5 minutes.

2 Slice the sun-dried tomatoes. Remove the core and seeds from the peppers and peel away the skins. Slice each pepper into thick strips.

3 Beat together the vinegar, oil and hot pepper sauce, then season with a little salt and pepper.

4 Toss the peppers with the sliced artichokes, tomatoes and garlic. Pour the dressing over and sprinkle the basil leaves on top.

SHERRIED PIMIENTOS

Pimientos are simply cooked, skinned peppers. You can buy them in cans or jars, but they are much tastier when made at home.

3 red bell peppers
2 small garlic cloves, crushed
3 tablespoons chopped fresh parsley
1 tablespoon sherry vinegar
2 tablespoons olive oil
salt

SERVES 2–4

3 Using a sharp knife, cut each halved pepper lengthwise into ½-inch wide strips and place them in a small bowl.

4 Whisk the garlic, parsley, vinegar and oil into the pepper juices. Add salt to taste. Toss with the strips. Serve at room temperature.

1 Preheat the broiler to high. Place the peppers on a baking sheet and broil for 8–12 minutes, turning occasionally, until the skins have blistered and blackened. Remove the peppers from heat, cover with a clean dish towel and let stand for 5 minutes so that the steam softens the skins and makes them easy to peel.

2 Make a small cut in the bottom of each pepper and squeeze out the juice into a pitcher and reserve for later use. Peel off the skin and cut each pepper in half. Remove and discard the cores and scrape out the seeds. Place the peppers on a cutting board.

LEMON-SOAKED ANCHOVIES

Make these at least 1 hour and up to 24 hours in advance. Fresh anchovies are tiny, so be prepared to spend time filleting them—the results will be well worth the effort.

8 ounces fresh anchovies
juice of 3 lemons
2 tablespoons extra virgin olive oil
2 garlic cloves, finely chopped
1 tablespoon chopped fresh parsley
flaked sea salt

SERVES 4

1 Cut off the heads and tails from the anchovies, then split them open down one side, using a small knife with a short, sharp blade.

2 Open each anchovy out flat and carefully lift out the bone.

3 Arrange the anchovies, skin-side down, in a single layer on a plate. Pour on two-thirds of the lemon juice and sprinkle with sea salt. Cover and let sit for 1–24 hours, basting occasionally with the juices, until the flesh is white and opaque.

4 Put the fish on a platter. Drizzle on the oil and the remaining lemon juice. Sprinkle on the garlic and parsley, cover and chill.

DEEP-FRIED NEW POTATOES WITH SAFFRON AIOLI

Aïoli is a well-known garlic mayonnaise from Southern France; this Spanish version is very similar. In this recipe, saffron adds color and flavor.

1 egg yolk
½ teaspoon Dijon mustard
1¼ cups extra virgin olive oil
1–2 tablespoons lemon juice
1 garlic clove, crushed
½ teaspoon saffron strands
20 very small new potatoes
vegetable oil for frying
salt and ground black pepper

SERVES 4

 To make the aïoli, put the egg yolk in a bowl with the mustard and a pinch of salt. Beat together with a wooden spoon. Still beating, add the olive oil very slowly, drop by drop to begin with, then, as the aïoli gradually thickens, in a thin stream. Add the lemon juice and salt and pepper to taste, then beat in the crushed garlic.

 Place the saffron in a small bowl, and add 2 teaspoons hot water. Press the saffron with the back of a teaspoon to extract the color and flavor, and let infuse for about 5 minutes. Beat the saffron and the liquid into the mayonnaise.

3 Cook the potatoes in boiling salted water for 5 minutes, then turn off the heat. Cover the pan and let sit for 15 minutes. Drain the potatoes, then dry them thoroughly.

4 Heat ½ inch oil in a deep pan. When the oil is very hot, add the potatoes and fry quickly, turning, until crisp and golden. Drain on paper towels and serve with the saffron aïoli.

DATES STUFFED WITH CHORIZO

A delicious combination from Spain, using fresh dates and spicy chorizo sausage.

2 ounces chorizo sausage
12 fresh dates, pitted
6 bacon slices
oil for frying
all-purpose flour for dusting
1 egg, beaten
1 cup fresh bread crumbs
toothpicks for serving

SERVES 4–6

 Trim the ends of the chorizo sausage and peel away the skin. Cut into three ¾-inch slices. Cut these in half lengthwise, then into quarters, giving 12 pieces.

2 Stuff each date with a piece of chorizo, closing the date around it. Stretch the bacon by running the back of a knife along each slice. Cut each slice in half crosswise. Wrap a piece of bacon around each date and secure with a toothpick.

3 In a deep pan, heat ½ inch of oil. Dust the dates with flour, dip them in the beaten egg, then coat in bread crumbs. Fry the dates in the hot oil, turning them, until golden. Remove the dates with a slotted spoon and drain on paper towels. Serve immediately.

GARLIC SHRIMP

For this simple Spanish tapas dish, you really need fresh raw shrimp, which absorb the flavors of the garlic and chiles as they cook. Have everything ready for last-minute cooking so you can take the dish to the table still sizzling.

*12 ounces—1 pound large
raw shrimp
2 fresh red chiles
5 tablespoons olive oil
3 garlic cloves, crushed
salt and ground black pepper*

SERVES 4

1   Remove the heads and shells from the shrimp, leaving the tails intact.

2   Halve each chile lengthwise and discard the seeds. Heat the oil in a flameproof pan, suitable for serving. (Alternatively, use a frying pan and have a warmed serving dish ready in the oven.)

3   Add all the shrimp, chiles and garlic to the pan and cook over high heat for about 3 minutes, stirring, until the shrimp turn pink. Season lightly with salt and pepper and serve immediately.

CHORIZO IN OLIVE OIL

Spanish chorizo sausage has a deliciously pungent taste; its robust seasoning of garlic, chile and paprika flavors the ingredients it is cooked with. Frying chorizo with onions and olive oil is one of its simplest and most delicious uses.

*5 tablespoons extra virgin olive oil
12 ounces chorizo sausage, sliced
1 large onion, thinly sliced
coarsely chopped flat-leaf parsley,
to garnish*

SERVES 4

1   Heat the oil in a frying pan and fry the chorizo sausage over high heat until beginning to color. Remove from pan with slotted spoon.

2   Add the onion to the pan and fry until colored. Return the sausage slices to the pan and heat through for 1 minute.

3   Pour the mixture into a shallow serving dish and sprinkle with the parsley. Serve with warm bread.

VARIATION
Chorizo is usually available in large supermarkets or delicatessens. Other similarly rich, spicy sausages can be used as a substitute.

JUMBO SHRIMP IN SHERRY

These shrimp couldn't be simpler, or quicker, to prepare—yet they're deceptively impressive in terms of flavor and appearance. A great appetizer for any special meal.

12 raw jumbo shrimp, peeled
2 tablespoons olive oil
2 tablespoons sherry
a few drops of Tabasco sauce
salt and ground black pepper

SERVES 4

1   Make a shallow cut down the back of each shrimp, then pull out and discard the dark intestinal tract. Leave the tails on the shrimp; when they are cooked they will curl and look more decorative.

2   Heat the oil in a frying pan and fry the shrimp for 2–3 minutes, until pink. Pour on the sherry and season with Tabasco sauce, salt and pepper. Transfer the shrimp to a dish and serve immediately.

SIZZLING SHRIMP

This dish works particularly well with tiny shrimp, which can be eaten whole, but any type of shrimp in the shell will be fine. Choose a small flameproof dish or frying pan that can be taken to the table for serving while the shrimp are still sizzling.

2 garlic cloves, peeled
and halved
2 tablespoons butter
1 small red chile, seeded and
finely sliced
4 ounces cooked shrimp, in the shell
sea salt and coarsely ground
black pepper
lime wedges, to serve

SERVES 4

1   Rub the cut surfaces of the garlic cloves on the surface of a frying pan. This will delicately flavor the shrimp and make them a little sweet. After use, discard the garlic cloves. Add the butter to the pan and melt over fairly high heat until it just begins to turn golden brown.

2   Toss in the chile and shrimp. Stir-fry for 1–2 minutes, until heated through, then season to taste and serve with lime wedges to squeeze over.

SCALLOPS WITH BROWN BUTTER

This is a very striking dish, as the scallops are served on the half-shell, still sizzling from the broiler.
Reserve this dish for a special occasion, when you want to impress your guests.

¼ cup unsalted butter, diced
8 scallops, prepared on the half-shell
1 tablespoon chopped fresh parsley
salt and ground black pepper
4 lemon wedges, to serve

SERVES 4

1 Preheat the broiler to high. Melt the butter in a small saucepan over medium heat until it is pale golden brown. Remove the pan from heat immediately; the butter must not be allowed to burn.

2 Arrange the scallop shells in a single layer in a flameproof serving dish or a shallow roasting pan. Brush a little of the brown butter on the scallops and broil for 4 minutes— it will not be necessary to turn the scallops in the shells.

3 Brush on the remaining brown butter, then sprinkle with a little salt and pepper, together with the parsley. Serve the scallops immediately, with lemon wedges.

FRIED SQUID

The squid is simply dusted in flour and dipped in egg before being fried, so that the coating is light,
and does not mask the flavor.

4 ounces squid rings
2 tablespoons seasoned flour
1 egg
2 tablespoons milk
olive oil, for frying
sea salt
lemon wedges, to serve

SERVES 4

1 Toss the squid rings in the seasoned flour in a bowl or strong plastic bag. Beat together the egg and milk in a shallow bowl. Heat the oil in a heavy frying pan.

COOK'S TIP
For a crispier coating, dust the rings in flour, then dip them in batter.

2 Dip the floured squid rings one at a time into the egg mixture, shaking off any excess liquid. Add to the hot oil, in batches if necessary, and fry for 2–3 minutes on each side until golden.

3 Drain the fried squid on paper towels, then sprinkle with salt. Transfer to a small, warm bowl and serve with the lemon wedges. Offer finger bowls and napkins.

FRIED WHITEBAIT WITH TOMATO SALSA

Fresh, crispy whitebait is served with a slightly spicy tomato salsa for a sensational combination of flavors and textures.

8 ounces whitebait,
thawed if frozen
2 tablespoons seasoned flour
¼ cup olive oil
¼ cup vegetable oil

FOR THE SALSA
1 shallot, finely chopped
2 garlic cloves, finely chopped
4 ripe tomatoes, roughly chopped
1 small red chile, seeded and
finely chopped
2 tablespoons olive oil
¼ cup sweet sherry
2–3 tablespoons chopped fresh herbs
½ cup fresh white bread crumbs
salt and ground black pepper

SERVES 4

1 To make the salsa, place the shallot, garlic, tomatoes, chile and oil in a pan. Cover with a lid and cook gently for 10 minutes.

2 Pour in the sherry and add salt and pepper to taste. Stir in the herbs—basil, parsley or cilantro could be used—then add the bread crumbs. Stir to mix, then cover and keep hot while the whitebait is being prepared.

3 Wash the whitebait, drain, then dust in the seasoned flour. Heat both oils together in a frying pan and cook the fish in batches until crisp and golden. Drain on paper towels and keep warm in a low oven.

4 Spoon the whitebait into a bowl. Stir the tomato salsa, spoon it into a separate bowl and serve immediately, with the whitebait.

CRISPY FISH BALLS

You can use any white fish to make these crispy balls. Cod, haddock and monkfish fillets all work well.

1 egg
a pinch of saffron threads
2 garlic cloves, roughly chopped
3 tablespoons fresh parsley leaves
8 ounces white fish, skinned,
boned and cubed
3 ounces white bread, crusts removed
¼ cup seasoned flour
vegetable oil, for frying
salt and ground black pepper
lemon wedges, to serve

SERVES 4

1 Beat together the egg and saffron threads in a cup, then set aside for 5 minutes.

2 In a food processor, combine the garlic and parsley until finely chopped. Add the fish and bread and process until well blended. Scrape the fish mixture into a bowl and stir in the egg and saffron. Season with plenty of salt and pepper.

3 Shape the mixture into 24 small balls. Spread out the seasoned flour in a shallow dish and add the balls. Shake the bowl to coat the fish balls on all sides.

4 Heat the oil in a deep frying pan. Fry the fish balls, in batches if necessary, until crisp and golden, shaking the pan to keep them moving. Drain on paper towels and serve immediately with lemon wedges. Offer a small bowl of plain or garlic-flavored mayonnaise for dipping, if desired, and toothpicks for spearing.

SARDINES IN ESCABECHE

*This spicy marinade is widely used in Spain and Portugal as a traditional means of preserving fish,
poultry or game. It is particularly good with fried fish.*

16 sardines
1 pound seasoned flour
2 tablespoons olive oil
roasted red onion, green bell pepper
and tomatoes, to garnish

FOR THE MARINADE
6 tablespoons olive oil
1 onion, sliced
1 garlic clove, crushed
3–4 bay leaves
2 cloves
1 dried red chile
1 teaspoon paprika
½ cup wine or sherry vinegar
½ cup white wine
salt and ground black pepper

SERVES 8

1   Cut the heads off the sardines and split each of them along the belly. Clean them, if necessary, then turn them over so that the backbone is on top. Press down along the backbone to loosen it, then carefully lift out the backbone and as many other bones as possible.

2   Close the sardines up again and dust them with seasoned flour. Heat the olive oil in a deep pan and fry the sardines for 2–3 minutes on each side. Remove the fish from the pan and let cool, then place in a single layer in a large shallow dish.

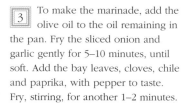

3   To make the marinade, add the olive oil to the oil remaining in the pan. Fry the sliced onion and garlic gently for 5–10 minutes, until soft. Add the bay leaves, cloves, chile and paprika, with pepper to taste. Fry, stirring, for another 1–2 minutes.

4   Stir in the vinegar, wine and a little salt. Let it bubble up, then pour over the sardines. When cool, cover and chill overnight or for up to 3 days. Serve on individual plates, garnished with roasted red onion, pepper and tomatoes. Offer bread for mopping up the marinade.

SAUTEED MUSSELS WITH GARLIC AND HERBS

These mussels are served without their shells, in a delicious paprika-flavored sauce.
Eat them with toothpicks.

2 pounds fresh mussels
1 lemon slice
6 tablespoons olive oil
2 shallots, finely chopped
1 garlic clove, finely chopped
1 tablespoon chopped fresh parsley
½ teaspoon sweet paprika
¼ teaspoon dried red pepper flakes
parsley sprigs, to garnish

SERVES 4

1 Scrub the mussels, discarding any damaged ones that do not close when tapped with a knife. Put the mussels in a large pan with 1 cup water and the slice of lemon. Bring to a boil and let boil for 3–4 minutes, removing the mussels as they open. Discard any that remain closed. Take the mussels out of the shells and drain them on paper towels.

2 Heat the oil in a sauté pan, add the mussels *(left)* and cook, stirring, for a minute. Remove from the pan. Add the shallots and garlic and cook, covered, over low heat for about 5 minutes, until soft. Stir in the parsley, paprika and red pepper flakes, then add the mussels with any juices. Cook briefly. Remove the pan from the heat, cover and let sit for 1–2 minutes to let the flavors mingle. Serve, garnished with parsley.

SUPPLI AL TELEFONO

These are risotto fritters with nuggets of mozzarella inside. When they are bitten into, the cheese is drawn out in thin strings, like telephone wires—hence the name.

3 tablespoons finely chopped
fresh parsley
6 cups risotto
7 ounces mozzarella cheese,
cut into 20 cubes
2 eggs, beaten
1¼ cups natural-colored
dried bread crumbs
corn or vegetable oil, for deep-frying
fresh herbs, to garnish

MAKES 20

1 Stir the parsley into the risotto, cool, then chill until firm. Divide into 20 portions and shape each into a ball. Press a cube of cheese into each ball and reshape neatly. Coat the rice balls in the beaten egg, then the bread crumbs, and chill again for 30 minutes to set the coating.

2 Heat the oil for deep-frying to 350°F. Cook about five fritters at a time for 3–5 minutes, until golden brown and crisp. Drain the fritters on paper towels and keep warm on an uncovered plate so that the coating remains crisp. Serve, garnished with fresh herbs.

MOZZARELLA IN CARROZA WITH FRESH TOMATO SALSA

The name of this delectable Italian snack translates as cheese "in a carriage." It contains mozzarella and is dipped in beaten egg and fried like French toast.

7 ounces mozzarella cheese,
finely sliced
8 thin slices of bread, crusts removed
a little dried oregano
2 tablespoons freshly grated
Parmesan cheese
3 eggs, beaten
olive oil, for frying
salt and freshly ground black pepper
fresh herbs, to garnish

FOR THE SALSA
4 ripe plum tomatoes, peeled, seeded
and finely chopped
1 tablespoon chopped fresh parsley
1 teaspoon balsamic vinegar
1 tablespoon extra virgin olive oil
salt and freshly ground black pepper

SERVES 4

1 Arrange the mozzarella on 4 slices of the bread. Season with salt and pepper and sprinkle with a little dried oregano and the Parmesan. Top with the other bread slices and press them firmly together.

2 Pour the beaten eggs into a large shallow dish and season with salt and pepper.

3 Add the cheese sandwiches, two at a time, pressing them into the egg with a spatula until they are well coated. Repeat with the remaining sandwiches, then let them stand for 10 minutes.

4 To make the salsa, put the chopped tomatoes in a bowl and add the parsley. Stir in the vinegar and the extra virgin olive oil. Season well with salt and pepper and set aside.

5 Heat oil for frying to a depth of ¼ inch in a large frying pan. Carefully add the sandwiches in batches and cook for about 2 minutes on each side, until golden and crisp. Drain well. Cut in half, garnish with herbs and serve with the salsa.

ARTICHOKE RICE CAKES WITH MELTING MANCHEGO

For really impressive tapas, serve these rice cakes with a tangy garlic mayonnaise.

1 globe artichoke
¼ cup butter
1 small onion, finely chopped
1 garlic clove, finely chopped
⅔ cup arborio rice
scant 2 cups hot chicken stock
⅔ cup freshly grated Parmesan cheese
5 ounces Manchego cheese,
finely diced
3–4 tablespoons fine cornmeal
olive oil, for frying
salt and ground black pepper
flat-leaf parsley, to garnish

SERVES 6

1 Remove the stalk, leaves and choke from the artichoke, leaving the heart; finely chop this. Melt the butter in a saucepan and gently fry the chopped artichoke heart, onion and garlic for 5 minutes, until softened. Stir in the rice and cook for about 1 minute.

2 Keeping the heat fairly high, gradually add the stock, stirring constantly for about 20 minutes, until all the liquid has been absorbed and the rice is cooked. Season well, then stir in the Parmesan. Transfer to a bowl. Let cool, then cover and chill for at least 2 hours.

3 Spoon about 1 tablespoon of the mixture into the palm of one hand, flatten slightly, and place a few pieces of diced Manchego cheese in the center. Shape the rice around the cheese to make a small ball. Flatten slightly, then roll it in the cornmeal. Repeat with the remaining mixture to make about 12 cakes in all.

4 Heat the oil and shallow-fry the rice cakes, in batches of three or four if necessary, for 4–5 minutes, until they are crisp and golden brown. Drain on paper towels and serve hot, garnished with flat-leaf parsley.

CHEESE CHOUX

Deliciously light, these cheese puffs are perfect for parties.

¼ cup butter, cubed
¼ teaspoon salt
1 cup water
1 cup all-purpose flour
2 whole eggs, plus 1 yolk
½ teaspoon dry mustard
½ teaspoon cayenne pepper
½ cup finely grated well-flavored
cheese, such as
Manchego or Gruyère

SERVES 4

1 Preheat the oven to 425°F. Bring the butter, salt and water to a boil in a pan. Sift the flour onto a sheet of waxed paper, then pour the flour into the boiling liquid and stir it in very quickly.

2 Beat the mixture with a wooden spoon into a thick paste that leaves the sides of the pan clean. Remove the pan from heat.

3 Beat in the eggs and yolk, one at a time, then add the mustard, cayenne pepper and grated cheese.

4 Place teaspoonfuls of the mixture on a nonstick baking sheet and bake for 10 minutes. Lower the oven temperature to 350°F and cook for another 15 minutes, until well browned. Serve hot or cold.

SPICY MEATBALLS WITH CHILI SAUCE

These meatballs are delicious served piping hot, with chili sauce on the side so guests can add as much heat as they like.

4 ounces fresh spicy sausages
4 ounces ground beef
2 shallots, finely chopped
2 garlic cloves, finely chopped
1½ cups fresh white bread crumbs
1 egg, beaten
2 tablespoons chopped fresh parsley,
plus extra to garnish
1 tablespoon olive oil
salt and ground black pepper
Tabasco sauce or other hot chili sauce,
to serve

SERVES 6

[3] Heat the olive oil in a large frying pan and cook the meatballs, in batches if necessary, for 15–20 minutes, stirring regularly, until browned and cooked through.

[4] Transfer the meatballs to a warmed plate and sprinkle with the extra chopped parsley. Serve with chili sauce on the side, and offer toothpicks for spearing.

[1] With a sharp knife, nick the skin of each sausage to create a small split and carefully peel off the skin. Repeat until all the sausages have been skinned. Place the sausage meat in a small mixing bowl.

[2] Add the ground beef, shallots, garlic, bread crumbs, beaten egg, parsley and plenty of salt and pepper to the sausage meat. Mix the ingredients well, then shape into 18 small balls.

SWEET-CRUSTED LAMB

These little noisettes are just big enough for two mouthfuls and so are ideal for tapas. If you would prefer something a little more substantial, small lamb cutlets or chops can be prepared in the same way.

2   Remove the broiler pan from the oven. Turn over the lamb rounds and spread with the mustard.

3   Sprinkle the sugar evenly on the lamb rounds, then return the broiler pan to the oven.

4   Cook the lamb for 2–3 more minutes until the sugar has melted, but the lamb is still pink in the center. Serve with toothpicks for spearing.

6 ounces tender lamb fillet, sliced into
½-inch rounds
1 teaspoon mild mustard
2 tablespoons light brown sugar
salt and ground black pepper

SERVES 8

1   Preheat the broiler to high. Sprinkle the lamb with salt and pepper, and broil on one side for 2 minutes, until well browned.

SHRIMP BRIOUATES

In Morocco, briouates are made using a special pastry called ouarka. Like phyllo, it is very thin but even more tricky to make and requires a great deal of practice. Phyllo makes a good substitute.

6 ounces phyllo pastry
3 tablespoons butter, melted
sunflower oil, for frying
scallions and cilantro leaves,
to garnish
ground cinnamon and confectioners'
sugar, to serve (optional)

FOR THE SHRIMP FILLING
1 tablespoon olive oil
1 tablespoon butter
2–3 scallions, finely chopped
2 tablespoons all-purpose flour
1¼ cups milk
½ teaspoon paprika
12 ounces cooked peeled
shrimp, chopped
salt and ground black pepper

MAKES ABOUT 24

1 First, make the filling. Heat the olive oil and butter in a saucepan and fry the scallions over low heat for 2–3 minutes, until soft. Stir in the flour, and then slowly add the milk to make a thick, smooth sauce. Season the filling with paprika, salt and pepper, and stir in the shrimp.

2 Take a sheet of phyllo pastry and cut it in half horizontally, to make a rectangle measuring about 7 × 5½ inches. Cover all the remaining pastry with a damp dish towel to prevent it from drying out while you make the first briouate.

3 Brush the pastry with melted butter and then place a heaping teaspoon of filling along one edge. Roll up the pastry like a cigar, tucking in the sides as you go. Continue in this way until you have used all the filling.

4 Heat about ½ inch of oil in a heavy pan and fry the briouates, in batches if necessary, for 2–3 minutes, until golden, turning occasionally. Drain on paper towels, then serve garnished with a scallions and cilantro leaves, and sprinkled with cinnamon and confectioners' sugar, if desired.

MEAT BRIOUATES

The Moroccans, who enjoy mixing sweet and savory tastes, traditionally sprinkle these little pastry snacks with ground cinnamon and confectioners' sugar. It is an unusual but delicious combination.

6 ounces phyllo pastry
3 tablespoons butter, melted
sunflower oil, for frying
fresh flat-leaf parsley, to garnish
ground cinnamon and confectioners'
sugar, to serve (optional)

FOR THE MEAT FILLING
2 tablespoons sunflower oil
1 onion, finely chopped
1 small bunch cilantro, chopped
1 small bunch parsley, chopped
12 ounces lean ground beef or lamb
½ teaspoon paprika
1 teaspoon ground coriander
good pinch of ground ginger
2 eggs, beaten

MAKES ABOUT 24

1 First, make the filling. Heat the oil in a frying pan and fry the onion and herbs over low heat for about 4 minutes, until the onion is softened. Add the meat and cook for about 5 minutes, stirring frequently, until the meat is evenly browned and most of the moisture has evaporated.

2 Drain off any excess fat and stir in the spices. Cook for 1 minute, remove the pan from heat and stir in the beaten eggs. Stir until they begin to set and resemble lightly scrambled eggs. Set aside.

3 Take a sheet of phyllo pastry and cut into 3½-inch strips. Cover the remaining pastry with damp dish towels to prevent it from drying out. Brush the strip with melted butter, then place a heaping teaspoon of the meat filling at one end of the strip, about ½ inch from the end. Fold one corner over the filling to make a triangular shape.

4 Fold the "triangle" over itself and then continue to fold, keeping the triangle shape, until you reach the end of the strip. Continue in this way until all the mixture has been used up. Make about 23 more in the same way.

5 Heat about ½ inch of oil in a heavy pan and fry the *briouates* in batches for 2–3 minutes, until golden, turning once. Drain on paper towels and arrange on a serving plate. Serve garnished with fresh parsley and sprinkled with ground cinnamon and confectioners' sugar, if you like the combination.

PASTRY-WRAPPED CHORIZO PUFFS

These flaky pastry puffs, filled with spicy chorizo sausage and grated cheese, make a perfect accompaniment to a glass of cold sherry or beer. You can use any type of hard cheese for the puffs, but for the best results choose a mild variety, as the chorizo has plenty of flavor.

8 ounces puff pastry
4 ounces chorizo sausage, chopped
½ cup grated cheese
1 small egg, beaten
1 teaspoon paprika, to dust

MAKES 16

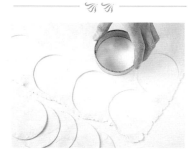

1 Roll out the pastry thinly on a floured surface. Using a 3-inch cutter, stamp out as many rounds as possible, then re-roll the trimmings, if necessary, and stamp out more rounds to make 16 in all.

COOK'S TIP
You can prepare the chorizo puffs a day or two ahead. Chill them without the glaze, wrapped in a plastic bag, until ready to bake, then let them come back to room temperature while you preheat the oven. Glaze before baking.

2 Preheat the oven to 450°F. Put the chopped chorizo sausage and grated cheese in a bowl and toss together lightly until well mixed.

3 Lay one of the pastry rounds on the palm of your hand and place a little of the chorizo mixture across the center.

4 Using your other hand, pinch the edges of the pastry together along the top to seal, as when making a two-crust pie. Repeat the process with the remaining rounds.

5 Place the pastries on a nonstick baking sheet and brush lightly with the beaten egg. Using a small sieve or tea strainer, dust the tops lightly with a little of the paprika.

6 Bake the pastries for 10–12 minutes, until puffed and golden brown. Transfer the pastries to a wire rack and let cool for 5 minutes. Transfer to a plate and serve warm, dusted with the rest of the paprika.

VARIATION
Try cutting the pastry in different shapes, such as stars and hearts. They are ideal snacks for children's parties.

SPINACH EMPANADILLAS

These are little pastry turnovers, filled with ingredients that show a strong Moorish influence—pine nuts and raisins.

2 tablespoons raisins
1½ tablespoons olive oil
1 pound fresh spinach, washed
and chopped
6 drained canned anchovies, chopped
2 garlic cloves, finely chopped
⅓ cup pine nuts, chopped
1 egg, beaten
12 ounces puff pastry
salt and ground black pepper

MAKES 20

1 To make the filling, soak the raisins in a little warm water for 10 minutes. Drain, then chop them coarsely. Heat the oil in a large sauté pan or wok, add the spinach, stir, then cover and cook over low heat for about 2 minutes. Uncover, turn up the heat and let any liquid evaporate. Add the anchovies, garlic and seasoning. Cook, stirring, for another minute. Remove from the heat, add the raisins and pine nuts, and cool.

2 Preheat the oven to 350°F. On a floured surface, roll out the pastry to a ⅛-inch thickness.

3 Using a 3-inch pastry cutter, cut out 20 circles, re-rolling the dough if necessary. Place about 2 teaspoons of the filling in the middle of each circle, then brush the edges with a little water. Bring up the sides of the pastry and seal well (*left*). Press the edges together with the back of a fork. Brush with egg. Place the turnovers on a lightly greased baking sheet and bake for about 15 minutes, until golden. Serve warm.

FALAFEL

In North Africa, these spicy fritters are made using dried fava beans, but chickpeas are much easier to find. Falafel are great served as a snack with garlicky yogurt or stuffed into warmed pita bread.

¾ cup dried chickpeas
1 large onion, coarsely chopped
2 garlic cloves, coarsely chopped
4 tablespoons coarsely chopped parsley
1 teaspoon cumin seeds, crushed
1 teaspoon coriander seeds, crushed
½ teaspoon baking powder
salt and ground black pepper
oil for deep-frying
pita bread, salad and yogurt,
to serve

SERVES 4

1 Put the chickpeas in a bowl with plenty of cold water. Let soak overnight.

2 Drain the chickpeas and cover with water in a pan. Bring to a boil. Boil rapidly for 10 minutes Reduce the heat and simmer for about 1 hour, until soft. Drain.

3 Place in a food processor with the onion, garlic, parsley, cumin, coriander and baking powder. Add salt and pepper to taste. Process until the mixture forms a firm paste.

4 Shape the mixture into walnut-size balls and flatten them slightly. In a deep pan, heat 2 inches oil until a little of the mixture sizzles on the surface when added. Fry the falafel in batches until golden. Drain on paper towels and keep hot while frying the remainder. Serve warm, in pita bread, with salad and yogurt.

CROSTINI

These are Italian canapés, consisting of toasted slices of bread spread with various toppings. The following recipes are for a chicken liver pâté and a shrimp butter.

FOR THE CHICKEN LIVER PATE
10 tablespoons butter
1 small onion, finely chopped
1 garlic clove, crushed
8 ounces chicken livers
4 sage leaves, chopped
salt and ground black pepper

FOR THE SHRIMP BUTTER
8 ounces cooked, peeled shrimp
2 drained canned anchovies
4 tablespoons butter, softened
1 tablespoon lemon juice
1 tablespoon chopped fresh parsley
salt and ground black pepper

FOR THE CROSTINI
12 slices crusty Italian or
French bread, cut ½-inch thick
6 tablespoons butter, melted

FOR THE GARNISH
sage leaves
flat-leaf parsley

SERVES 6

 Bake for 8–10 minutes, until pale golden. Spread half the hot crostini with the pâté and the rest with the shrimp butter, garnishing with sage and parsley, respectively. Serve the crostini immediately.

 To make the chicken liver pâté, melt half the butter in a frying pan, add the onion and garlic, and fry gently until soft. Add the chicken livers and sage and sauté for about 8 minutes, until the livers are brown and firm. Season with salt and pepper and process in a blender or food processor with the remaining butter.

To make the shrimp butter, chop the shrimp and anchovies finely. Place in a bowl with the butter and beat together until well blended. Add the lemon juice and parsley and season with salt and pepper. Preheat the oven to 400°F. Place the bread slices on one or two baking sheets and brush with the butter.

COOK'S TIP
Both the chicken liver pâté and the shrimp butter can be made ahead, but should be used within two days. Cover both toppings tightly and store them in the refrigerator.

GOAT CHEESE AND CROSTINI WITH FRUIT

*A sherry marinade accentuates the flavor of the goat cheese and contrasts beautifully
with the fruity tomato, orange and basil salsa.*

8 slices of goat cheese
1 tablespoon sherry
2 tablespoons walnut oil
2 tablespoons olive oil
4 slices of Italian or French bread
1 garlic clove, halved
2 scallions, sliced
6 shelled walnut halves,
roughly broken
1 tablespoon chopped fresh parsley
salt and ground black pepper
tomatoes and mixed salad greens,
to serve

FOR THE SALSA
5 tomatoes, peeled, seeded
and chopped
2 oranges, peeled and segmented
1 tablespoon chopped fresh basil
2 tablespoons olive oil
pinch of light brown sugar
fresh basil sprig, to garnish

SERVES 4

2 In a bowl, combine all the
ingredients for the salsa. Season
to taste. Garnish with the basil.

3 Toast the slices of bread on one
side, then turn them over and
rub the untoasted surfaces with the
cut sides of the garlic. Brush with the
marinade, then sprinkle the sliced
scallions on top. Arrange two of the
marinated slices of cheese on each
slice of bread.

4 Pour on any remaining
marinade, sprinkle with pepper
and cook the crostini under a hot
broiler until the cheese has browned.
Sprinkle the walnuts and parsley on
top. Serve with the tomatoes, salad
and the bowl of salsa.

COOK'S TIP
French goat cheese, or chèvre,
is often cylindrical in shape, which
makes it perfect for this dish.

1 Put the goat cheese slices into a
shallow bowl, pour in the
sherry, walnut oil and olive oil, then
marinate in a cool place for 1 hour.

TOMATO AND GARLIC BREAD

A basket of warm, crusty, garlic-flavored bread is always welcome when appetizers are being served.

4 large ripe tomatoes,
roughly chopped
2 garlic cloves, roughly chopped
¼ teaspoon sea salt
grated zest and juice of ½ lemon
1 teaspoon light brown sugar
1 flat loaf of bread, such as ciabatta
2 tablespoons olive oil
ground black pepper

SERVES 4–6

1 Preheat the oven to 400°F. Place the tomatoes, garlic, salt, lemon zest and brown sugar in a small pan. Cover and cook gently for 5 minutes, until the tomatoes have released their juices.

2 Split the loaf in half horizontally, then cut each half widthwise into 2–3 pieces. Bake on a baking sheet for 5–8 minutes, until hot, crisp and golden brown.

3 While the bread is baking, stir the lemon juice and olive oil into the tomato mixture. Cook uncovered for 8 more minutes, until the mixture is thick and pulpy.

4 Spread the tomato mixture on the hot bread, sprinkle with pepper and serve immediately, in a basket or on a platter.

OLIVE AND ANCHOVY BITES

*These melt-in-your-mouth morsels store very well; freeze them for up to 3 months or
keep in an airtight container for 2–3 days before serving.*

*1 cup all-purpose flour
½ cup chilled butter
1 cup finely grated cheese,
such as Manchego or Gruyère
2-ounce can anchovy fillets in oil,
drained and roughly chopped
½ cup pitted black olives,
roughly chopped
½ teaspoon cayenne pepper
sea salt*

MAKES 40–45

1 Place the flour, butter, cheese, anchovies, olives and cayenne in a food processor and pulse until the mixture forms a firm dough.

2 Wrap the dough loosely in plastic wrap. Chill for 20 minutes.

3 Preheat the oven to 400°F. Roll out the dough thinly on a lightly floured surface.

4 Cut the dough into 2-inch-wide strips, then cut across each strip diagonally, in alternate directions, to make triangles. Place on baking sheets. Bake for 8–10 minutes, until golden. Cool on a wire rack. Sprinkle with sea salt and serve.

BLACK PUDDING CANAPES

Black pudding (morcilla) is a very popular tapas dish. In Spain, the sausage is often homemade.

1 tablespoon olive oil
1 onion, thinly sliced
2 garlic cloves, thinly sliced
1 teaspoon dried oregano or marjoram
1 teaspoon paprika
8 ounces black pudding,
  cut in 12 thick slices
1 small loaf French bread,
  sliced into 12 rounds
2 tablespoons dry sherry
sugar, to taste
salt and ground black pepper
chopped fresh oregano, to garnish

SERVES 4

1   Heat the oil in a large frying pan and fry the onion, garlic, oregano and paprika for 7–8 minutes, until the onion is soft and golden.

COOK'S TIP
If you find real *morcilla*, fry slices in olive oil and then top the bread rounds.

2   Add the slices of black pudding, raise the heat and cook for 3 minutes on each side, until crisp.

3   Arrange the rounds of bread on a large serving plate and top each with a slice of black pudding. Stir the sherry into the mixture remaining in the frying pan, with sugar to taste. Heat, stirring, until the mixture bubbles, then season.

4   Spoon a little of the onion mixture on top of each slice of black pudding. Sprinkle on the oregano and serve immediately.

ROASTED BELL PEPPER TARTLETS

*These individual little tarts, topped with red and yellow bell peppers,
are as colorful as they are scrumptious.*

1½ cups all-purpose flour,
plus extra for rolling
a pinch of salt
6 tablespoons chilled butter, diced
2–3 tablespoons water
1 red bell pepper, seeded and quartered
1 yellow bell pepper, seeded and
quartered
¼ cup heavy cream
1 egg
1 tablespoon freshly grated Parmesan
salt and ground black pepper
MAKES 12

1 Sift the flour and salt into a bowl. Add the butter and rub it in with your fingertips until the mixture resembles fine bread crumbs. Stir in enough of the water to make a firm, but not sticky, dough.

2 Preheat the oven to 400°F. Roll out the dough thinly on a lightly floured surface and line 12 individual molds or a 12-hole tartlet pan. Prick the pastry shells with a fork and cover them with crumpled aluminum foil. Bake blind for 10 minutes.

3 Meanwhile, place the peppers, skin side up, on a baking sheet and broil for 10 minutes, until the skin is blistered and blackened. Cover with a dish towel and let sit for 5 minutes, then peel off the skin.

4 Cut each piece of pepper lengthwise into very thin strips. Remove the aluminum foil from the pastry shells and divide the pepper strips among them.

5 Whisk the cream and egg in a bowl. Add plenty of salt and pepper and pour over the peppers in the pastry shells. Sprinkle the Parmesan over each filled tartlet and bake for 15–20 minutes, until firm and golden brown. Cool for 2 minutes before removing from the molds and transferring to wire racks. Serve the tartlets warm or cold.

SOUPS

❧ ❧

*Soups are a vital part of the culinary heritage of
the Mediterranean. From winter warmers to
summer coolers, there's a soup for every season.*

LEFT: In Morocco the nights can be bitterly cold, and a bowl of hot, spicy soup is very welcome.

BELOW: In autumn, when Majorca's almond trees are heavy with the delicious nuts, farmworkers spread nets on the ground and use long poles to knock them down. The reward for their labors is a delicately flavored soup.

Soups have long been an important part of the Mediterranean diet. In the past, when a lot of the countries were poverty-stricken, soup constituted a meal for many. These broths were made with dried beans, peas and lentils, particularly during the cold winter months. Eaten with plenty of bread, they were filling and provided nourishment. Fresh vegetables were added in season, and sometimes eggs. Many of these soups, therefore, were extremely simple. Some of the recipes that exist today have been passed down through the generations, only to be given new life, and new status, with the rising popularity of "peasant food" in restaurants and cookbooks. These are unfussy recipes, which rely for their success on the quality of the ingredients. Take garlic soup, for example, which is made in various ways throughout Spain and France; in its simplest form, it is nothing but garlic, water and seasoning, but with the best garlic, these basic ingredients are transformed into a delicious and fragrant liquor. This basic method is applied to many vegetables, with the water sometimes replaced with a meat stock, and the mixture sometimes put through a strainer, to produce a smooth soup.

Pumpkins, Jerusalem artichokes, tomatoes, bell peppers,

asparagus and spinach are just a few of the many varieties of vegetables used to make soup.

Soups containing meat are usually hearty, combined as they are with pulses such as lentils or chickpeas, or potatoes, rice or pasta. In the Middle East, beef and lamb are used, and soups are seasoned with spices and herbs. There are special feast day soups, and soups to eat after sunset during the fast of Ramadan. However, the more typical Mediterranean soup is based on vegetables, beans,

ABOVE: Dawn in Corfu, and a fisherman prepares to head out to sea.

and of course, fish and shellfish. Wonderful fish soups come in numerous different guises; the now famous, and often poorly imitated, bouillabaisse is a "stew" of various varieties of fish and seafood native to the coast of the south of France. The dish originated in the port of Marseilles. Again, these soups serve as complete meals, sometimes with the fish and broth offered separately, accompanied by bread or toasted croutons.

Every country and coastal region has its own specialty, and the soup will never be quite the same, the ingredients depending on the fishermen's catch that day. Many of the recipes were originated by the fishermen themselves, who cooked them on their boats, using fish that they couldn't sell in the market, because it had no commercial value. Today, with a wide choice of fish available in fish stores and supermarkets, it is possible to re-cre-

ate many of these wonderful dishes at home.

Chilled soups come from the south of Spain, where gazpacho is extremely popular—this is a delicious and refreshing mixture of raw tomatoes, bell peppers and cucumbers, which makes the perfect lunch for a hot summer day. Again, there are variations on this classic recipe, with such diverse ingredients as almonds and grapes. Cold soups are also featured in the Middle East—these are yogurt-based, usually mixed with cucumber and garlic, spiked with mint.

Tourists who travel to the Mediterranean seldom sample more than a few of the many different soups available, but it is worth investigating that delicious smell wafting from a restaurant kitchen, or asking the name of the delectable-looking soup that is being enjoyed at the next table.

Changing at the whim of the cook, or to take best advantage of the finest market produce, Mediterranean soups are certainly a cause for celebration.

BOUILLABAISSE

Perhaps the most famous of all Mediterranean fish soups, this dish, originating in Marseilles in the south of France, is a rich and colorful mixture of fish and shellfish, flavored with tomatoes, saffron and orange.

3–3½ pounds mixed fish and raw
shellfish, such as red mullet, porgy,
monkfish, red snapper,
whiting, large shrimp and clams
8 ounces ripe tomatoes
pinch of saffron strands
6 tablespoons olive oil
1 onion, sliced
1 leek, sliced
1 celery stalk, sliced
2 garlic cloves, crushed
1 bouquet garni
1 strip pared orange zest
½ teaspoon fennel seeds
1 tablespoon tomato paste
2 teaspoons Pernod
4–6 thick slices French bread
3 tablespoons chopped fresh parsley
salt and ground black pepper

SERVES 4–6

2   Cut the fish into large chunks.
Leave the shellfish in their
shells. Scald the tomatoes, then drain
and refresh in cold water. Peel and
coarsely chop them. Soak the saffron
in 1–2 tablespoons hot water.

3   Heat the oil in a large pan,
add the onion, leek and celery
and cook until softened. Add the
garlic, bouquet garni, orange zest,
fennel seeds and tomatoes, then stir
in the saffron and liquid and the fish
stock. Season with salt and pepper,
then bring to a boil and simmer for
30–40 minutes.

4   Add the shellfish and boil for
about 6 minutes. Add the fish
and cook for another 6–8 minutes,
until it flakes easily.

5   Using a slotted spoon, transfer
the fish to a warmed serving
platter. Keep the liquid boiling, to
allow the oil to emulsify with the
broth. Add the tomato paste and
Pernod, then check the seasoning. To
serve, place a slice of French bread in
each soup bowl, pour the broth on
top and serve the fish and shellfish
separately, sprinkled with the parsley.

1   Remove the heads, tails and
fins from the fish and put them
in a large pan with about 5 cups
water. Bring to a boil and simmer for
15 minutes. Strain, reserving
the liquid.

SAFFRON MUSSEL SOUP

This is one of France's most delicious seafood soups. Serve it with plenty of French bread to mop up all the delectable juices.

3 tablespoons unsalted butter
8 shallots, finely chopped
1 bouquet garni
1 teaspoon black peppercorns
1½ cups dry white wine
2¼ pounds fresh mussels,
scrubbed and bearded
2 medium leeks, trimmed and
finely chopped
1 fennel bulb, finely chopped
1 carrot, finely chopped
several saffron strands
4 cups fish or chicken stock
2–3 tablespoons cornstarch, blended
with 3 tablespoons cold water
½ cup whipping cream
1 medium tomato, peeled, seeded and
finely chopped
2 tablespoons Pernod (optional)
salt and ground black pepper

SERVES 4–6

1 In a large heavy pan, melt half the butter over medium-high heat. Add half the shallots and cook for 1–2 minutes, until softened but not colored. Add the bouquet garni, peppercorns and white wine and bring to a boil. Add the mussels, cover tightly and cook over high heat for 3–5 minutes, shaking the pan occasionally, until the mussels have opened.

2 With a slotted spoon, transfer the mussels to a bowl. Strain the cooking liquid through a muslin-lined sieve and reserve.

3 When the mussels are cool enough to handle, discard any that are closed. Pull open and remove the flesh from the rest Add any juices to the reserved liquid.

4 Rinse the saucepan and melt the remaining butter over medium heat. Add the remaining shallots and cook for 1–2 minutes. Add the leeks, fennel, carrot and saffron and cook for 3–5 minutes.

5 Stir in the reserved cooking liquid, bring to a boil and cook for 5 minutes, until the vegetables are tender and the liquid is slightly reduced. Add the stock and bring to a boil, skimming any foam that rises to the surface. Season with salt, if needed, and black pepper. Cook for another 5 minutes.

6 Stir the blended cornstarch into the soup. Simmer for 2–3 minutes, until the soup is slightly thickened, then add the cream, mussels and chopped tomato. Stir in the Pernod, if using, and cook for 1–2 minutes, until hot, then serve.

SHRIMP BISQUE

The classic French way to make a bisque requires you to push the shellfish through a tamis, or drum sieve. This is a much simpler method, and the results are just as smooth.

1½ pounds small or medium cooked
shrimp in their shells
1½ tablespoons vegetable oil
2 onions, halved and sliced
1 large carrot, sliced
2 celery stalks, sliced
8 cups water
a few drops of lemon juice
2 tablespoons tomato paste
bouquet garni
¼ cup butter
½ cup all-purpose flour
3–4 tablespoons brandy
⅔ cup whipping cream
salt and white pepper

SERVES 6–8

1 Remove the heads from the shrimp and peel off the shells, reserving the heads and shells for the stock. Chill the peeled shrimp.

2 Heat the oil in a large pan, add the shrimp heads and shells and cook over high heat, stirring, until they start to brown. Reduce the heat, add the onions, carrot and celery, and fry gently for about 5 minutes.

3 Add the water, some lemon juice, tomato paste and the bouquet garni. Bring the stock to a boil, then reduce the heat, cover and simmer gently for 25 minutes. Strain the stock through a sieve.

4 Melt the butter in a heavy saucepan over medium heat. Stir in the flour and cook until just golden, stirring occasionally. Add the brandy and gradually pour in about half of the shrimp stock, whisking vigorously until smooth, then whisk in the remaining liquid. Season with salt, if necessary, and white pepper. Reduce the heat, cover and simmer for 5 minutes, stirring frequently.

5 Strain the soup into a clean saucepan. Add the cream and a little extra lemon juice to taste, then stir in most of the reserved shrimp and cook over medium heat, stirring frequently, until hot. Serve immediately, garnished with the remaining reserved shrimps. Add a sprig of flat-leaf parsley to each portion, if desired.

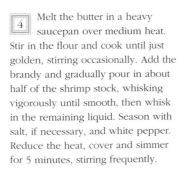

SEAFOOD SOUP WITH ROUILLE

This is a chunky, aromatic mixed fish soup from France, flavored with plenty of saffron and herbs.
Rouille, a fiery hot paste, is served separately for diners to swirl into their soup to flavor.

3 snapper or red mullet, scaled
and gutted
12 large shrimp
1½ pounds white fish, such as cod,
haddock, halibut or monkfish
½ pound fresh mussels
1 onion, quartered
1 teaspoon saffron strands
5 tablespoons olive oil
1 fennel bulb, coarsely chopped
4 garlic cloves, crushed
3 strips pared orange zest
4 thyme sprigs
1½ pounds tomatoes or 14-ounce can
chopped tomatoes
2 tablespoons sun-dried tomato paste
3 bay leaves
salt and ground black pepper

FOR THE ROUILLE
1 red bell pepper, seeded and
coarsely chopped
1 red chile, seeded and sliced
2 garlic cloves, chopped
5 tablespoons olive oil
¼ cup fresh bread crumbs

SERVES 6

2. Fillet the snapper or mullet by cutting the flesh from either side of the backbone, reserving the heads and bones. Cut the fillets into small chunks. Shell half the shrimp and reserve the trimmings for the stock. Skin the white fish, discarding any bones, and cut into chunks. Thoroughly scrub the mussels, discarding any that are damaged or any open ones that do not close when tapped with a knife.

3. Put the fish heads and bones and shrimp trimmings in a large saucepan with the onion and about 5 cups water. Bring to a boil, then simmer gently for 30 minutes. Cool slightly and strain.

4. Soak the saffron in 1 tablespoon boiling water. Heat about 2 tablespoons of the oil in a large sauté pan or saucepan. Add the snapper or mullet and white fish and sauté over high heat for 1 minute. Drain.

1. To make the rouille, process the pepper, chile, garlic, oil and bread crumbs in a blender or food processor until smooth. Transfer to a serving dish and chill.

5. Heat the remaining oil and sauté the fennel, garlic, orange zest and thyme until beginning to color. Make up the strained stock to about 5 cups with water.

COOK'S TIP
To save time, order the fish and ask the fish seller to fillet the snapper or mullet for you.

6. If using fresh tomatoes, plunge them into boiling water for 30 seconds, then refresh in cold water. Peel and chop. Add the stock to the pan with the saffron, tomatoes, tomato paste and bay leaves. Season, bring almost to a boil, then simmer gently, covered, for 20 minutes.

7. Stir in the snapper or mullet, white fish and shrimp and add the mussels. Cover the pan and cook for 3–4 minutes. Discard any mussels that do not open. Serve the soup hot with the rouille.

FISH AND OKRA SOUP

The inspiration for this soup originally came from north Africa. Chop the okra for a more authentic consistency, if desired.

 Melt the butter in a large pan and sauté the onion for about 5 minutes, until soft. Stir in the chopped tomatoes and okra, and fry gently for another 10 minutes.

Add the fish, fish stock, chile and seasoning. Bring to a boil, then reduce the heat and simmer for about 20 minutes or until the fish is cooked through and flakes easily.

2 green bananas
¼ cup butter
1 onion, finely chopped
2 tomatoes, peeled and finely chopped
4 ounces okra, trimmed
8 ounces smoked haddock or cod fillet, cut into bite-size pieces
3¾ cups fish stock
1 chile, seeded and chopped
salt and ground black pepper
chopped fresh parsley, to garnish

SERVES 4

1 Slit the skins of the green bananas and place in a large saucepan. Cover with water, bring to a boil and cook over medium heat for about 25 minutes or until the bananas are tender. Transfer to a plate and let cool.

4 Peel and slice the bananas. Stir into the soup and heat through. Serve sprinkled with parsley.

FISH AND VEGETABLE SOUP

---

*Liguria, in Italy, is famous for its fish soups. In this one, the fish are cooked in a broth with vegetables
and then puréed. This mixture can also be used to dress pasta.*

2¼ pounds mixed fish or fish pieces
(such as sole, whiting, red mullet,
salmon, haddock, etc)
6 tablespoons olive oil, plus extra
to serve
1 medium onion, finely chopped
1 celery stalk, chopped
1 carrot, chopped
¼ cup chopped fresh parsley
¾ cup dry white wine
3 medium tomatoes, peeled
and chopped
2 garlic cloves, finely chopped
6 cups boiling water
salt and ground black pepper
rounds of French bread, to serve

SERVES 6

3 Pour in the wine, raise the heat, and cook until it reduces by about half. Stir in the tomatoes and garlic. Cook for 3–4 minutes, stirring occasionally. Add the boiling water, and bring back to a boil. Cook for another 15 minutes.

4 Stir in the fish, and simmer for 10–15 minutes or until it is tender. Season well.

5 Remove the fish from the soup. Discard any skin and bones. Purée the flesh in a food processor and return it to the soup. Season to taste. If the soup is too thick, add more water.

6 Heat the soup to simmering. Toast the bread, and sprinkle with olive oil. Place 2 or 3 rounds in each soup bowl before pouring over the soup.

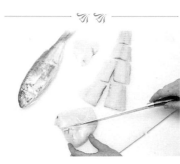

1 Scale and clean the fish, discarding all innards, but leaving the heads on. Cut into large pieces. Rinse well in cool water.

2 Heat the oil in a large saucepan and add the onion. Cook over low heat until it softens. Stir in the celery and carrot, and cook for 5 more minutes. Add the parsley.

SPICED MUSSEL SOUP

Chunky and colorful, this Turkish fish soup is like a chowder in its consistency. It's flavored with harissa, a spicy paste more familiar in North African cooking.

3–3½ pounds fresh mussels
⅔ cup white wine
3 tomatoes
2 tablespoons olive oil
1 onion, finely chopped
2 garlic cloves, crushed
2 celery stalks, thinly sliced
bunch of scallions, thinly sliced
1 potato, diced
1½ teaspoons harissa
3 tablespoons chopped fresh parsley
ground black pepper
thick yogurt, to serve (optional)

SERVES 6

1 Scrub the mussels, discarding any damaged ones or any open ones that do not close when tapped with a knife.

2 Bring the wine to a boil in a large saucepan. Add the mussels and cover with a lid. Cook for 4–5 minutes, until the mussels have opened wide. Discard any mussels that remain closed. Drain the mussels, reserving the cooking liquid. Reserve a few mussels in their shells for garnish and shell the rest.

3 Peel the tomatoes and dice them. Heat the oil in a pan and sauté the onion, garlic, celery and scallions for 5 minutes.

4 Add the shelled mussels, reserved liquid, potato, harissa and tomatoes. Bring just to a boil, reduce the heat and cover. Simmer gently for 25 minutes or until the potatoes are breaking up.

5 Stir in the parsley and pepper and add the reserved mussels. Heat through for 1 minute. Serve hot, with a spoonful of yogurt, if desired.

GREEN LENTIL SOUP

Lentil soup is an eastern Mediterranean classic, varying in its spiciness according to region. Red or puy lentils make equally good substitutes for the green lentils used here.

1 cup green lentils
5 tablespoons olive oil
3 onions, finely chopped
2 garlic cloves, thinly sliced
2 teaspoons cumin seeds, crushed
¼ teaspoon ground turmeric
2½ cups chicken or vegetable stock
salt and ground black pepper
2 tablespoons coarsely chopped
chopped cilantro

SERVES 4–6

1 Put the lentils in a saucepan and cover with cold water. Bring to a boil and boil rapidly for 10 minutes. Drain.

2 Heat 2 tablespoons of the oil in a pan and sauté two-thirds of the chopped onions with the garlic, cumin and turmeric for 3 minutes, stirring. Add the lentils, stock and 2½ cups water. Bring to a boil, reduce the heat, cover and simmer gently for 30 minutes, until the lentils are soft.

3 Sauté the remaining onion in the remaining oil until golden.

4 Use a potato masher to lightly mash the lentils and make the soup pulpy. Reheat gently and season with salt and pepper to taste. Pour the soup into bowls. Stir the chopped cilantro into the sautéed onion and sprinkle on the soup. Serve with warm bread.

CHICKPEA AND PARSLEY SOUP

Thick, tasty and comforting, this is perfect for winter evenings.

🌿 🌿

*1⅓ cups chickpeas,
soaked overnight
1 small onion
1 bunch fresh parsley, about
1½ ounces
2 tablespoons olive oil and
sunflower oil, mixed
5 cups chicken stock
juice of ½ lemon
salt and ground black pepper
lemon wedges and finely pared strips
of zest, to garnish
crusty bread, to serve*

SERVES 6

🌿 🌿

 1   Drain the chickpeas and rinse them under cold water. Cook them in rapidly boiling water for 10 minutes, then simmer for 1–1½ hours, until just tender. Drain.

2   Place the onion and parsley in a food processor or blender and process until finely chopped.

3   Heat the olive and sunflower oils in a saucepan or flameproof casserole and fry the onion mixture for about 5 minutes over low heat, until the onion is slightly softened.

4   Add the chickpeas, cook gently for 1–2 minutes and add the stock. Season well with salt and pepper. Bring the soup to a boil, then cover and simmer for 20 minutes, until the chickpeas are soft.

5   Let the soup cool a little. Part-purée the soup in a food processor or blender, or by mashing the chickpeas fairly roughly with a fork, so that the soup is thick but still has plenty of texture.

6   Return the soup to a clean pan, add the lemon juice and adjust the seasoning if necessary. Heat gently and then serve, garnished with lemon wedges and finely pared lemon zest, and accompanied by crusty bread.

🌿 🌿

COOK'S TIP
Chickpeas are easier to purée if the outer skin is rubbed off. If you don't have time to cook the chickpeas yourself use canned chickpeas.

MEDITERRANEAN BEAN SOUP

There are many versions of this wonderful soup. This one uses cannellini beans, leeks, cabbage and good olive oil—and tastes even better reheated.

3 tablespoons extra virgin olive oil
1 onion, roughly chopped
2 leeks, roughly chopped
1 large potato, peeled and diced
2 garlic cloves, finely chopped
5 cups vegetable stock
14 ounces canned cannellini beans,
    drained, liquid reserved
6 ounces Savoy cabbage, shredded
3 tablespoons chopped fresh
    flat-leaf parsley
2 tablespoons chopped fresh oregano
3 ounces Parmesan cheese, shaved
salt and ground black pepper

FOR THE GARLIC TOASTS
2–3 tablespoons extra virgin
    olive oil
6 thick slices country bread
1 garlic clove, peeled and bruised

SERVES 4

2 Stir in the cabbage and beans, with half of the herbs, season and cook for 10 minutes more. Spoon about one-third of the soup into a food processor or blender and process until fairly smooth. Return to the soup in the pan, taste for seasoning and then heat through for 5 minutes.

3 Meanwhile, make the garlic toasts. Drizzle a little oil on the slices of bread, then rub both sides of each slice with the garlic. Toast until browned on both sides. Ladle the soup into bowls. Sprinkle with the remaining herbs and the Parmesan shavings. Add a drizzle of olive oil and serve with the toasts.

1 Heat the oil and gently cook the onion, leeks, potato and garlic for 4–5 minutes. Pour on the stock and add the liquid from the beans. Cover and simmer for 15 minutes.

RIBOLLITA

Ribollita is a lot like minestrone. In Italy it is traditionally served ladled over bread and a rich green vegetable, although you could omit this for a lighter version.

3 tablespoons olive oil
2 onions, chopped
2 carrots, sliced
4 garlic cloves, crushed
2 celery stalks, thinly sliced
1 fennel bulb, trimmed and chopped
2 large zucchini, thinly sliced
14-ounce can chopped tomatoes
2 tablespoons homemade or
store-bought pesto
3¾ cups vegetable stock
14-ounce can navy or pinto
beans, drained
salt and ground black pepper

TO FINISH
1 pound young spinach
1 tablespoon extra virgin olive oil, plus
extra for drizzling
6–8 slices crusty white bread
Parmesan cheese shavings

SERVES 6–8

VARIATION
Use other dark greens, such as chard
or cabbage, instead of the spinach;
shred and cook until tender.

 1 Heat the oil in a large saucepan. Add the onions, carrots, garlic, celery and fennel and sauté gently for 10 minutes. Add the zucchini and sauté for another 2 minutes.

2 Add the chopped tomatoes, pesto, stock and beans and bring to a boil. Reduce the heat, cover and simmer gently for 25–30 minutes, until the vegetables are completely tender. Season with salt and pepper to taste.

 **3** To serve, sauté the spinach in the oil for 2 minutes or until wilted. Spoon over the bread in soup bowls, then ladle the soup over the spinach. Serve with extra olive oil for drizzling onto the soup and Parmesan cheese to sprinkle on top.

MOROCCAN HARIRA

This is a hearty meat and vegetable soup, eaten during the month of Ramadan, when the Muslim population fasts between sunrise and sunset.

1 pound ripe tomatoes
½ pound lamb, cut into ½-inch pieces
½ teaspoon ground turmeric
½ teaspoon ground cinnamon
2 tablespoons butter
4 tablespoons chopped cilantro
2 tablespoons chopped fresh parsley
1 onion, chopped
¼ cup split red lentils
½ cup dried chickpeas, soaked overnight
4 baby onions or small shallots, peeled
¼ cup soup noodles
salt and ground black pepper
chopped fresh cilantro, lemon slices
and ground cinnamon, to garnish

SERVES 4

1 Plunge the tomatoes into boiling water for 30 seconds, then refresh in cold water. Peel away the skins. Cut into quarters and remove the seeds. Chop coarsely.

2 Put the lamb, turmeric, cinnamon, butter, cilantro, parsley and onion into a large pan, and cook over medium heat, stirring, for 5 minutes. Add the chopped tomatoes and continue to cook for 10 minutes.

3 Rinse the lentils under running water and add to the pan with the drained chickpeas and 2½ cups water. Season with salt and pepper. Bring to a boil, cover, and simmer gently for 1½ hours.

4 Add the onions and cook for another 30 minutes. Add the noodles 5 minutes before the end of the cooking time. Garnish with the cilantro, lemon slices and cinnamon.

CHICKEN SOUP WITH VERMICELLI

In Morocco, the cook—who is almost always the most senior female of the household—uses a whole chicken for this nourishing soup, to serve her large extended family. This is a slightly simplified version of the classic recipe, using individual pieces of chicken.

2 tablespoons sunflower oil
1 tablespoon butter
1 onion, chopped
2 chicken legs or breast pieces,
    halved or quartered
seasoned flour, for dusting
2 carrots, cut into 1½-inch pieces
1 parsnip, cut into 1½-inch pieces
6 cups chicken stock
1 cinnamon stick
a good pinch of paprika
a pinch of saffron strands
2 egg yolks
juice of ½ lemon
2 tablespoons chopped cilantro
2 tablespoons chopped fresh parsley
5 ounces vermicelli
salt and ground black pepper
rustic bread, to serve

SERVES 4–6

1 Heat the oil and butter in a saucepan or flameproof casserole and fry the onion for 3–4 minutes, until softened. Dust the chicken pieces in seasoned flour and fry gently until evenly browned.

2 Transfer the chicken to a plate and add the carrots and parsnip to the pan. Cook over low heat for 3–4 minutes, stirring frequently, then return the chicken to the pan. Add the stock, cinnamon stick and paprika and season well with salt and black pepper.

3 Bring the soup to a boil, cover and simmer for 1 hour, until the vegetables are very tender. While the soup is cooking, mix the saffron with 2 tablespoons of boiling water.

4 Beat the egg yolks with the lemon juice in a separate bowl and add the chopped cilantro and parsley. As soon as the saffron water has cooled, stir it into the egg and lemon mixture.

VARIATION
Try using different root vegetables, such as rutabaga and turnip, which will subtly vary the flavor of the soup.

5 When the vegetables are tender, transfer the chicken to a plate again. Spoon off any excess fat from the soup, then increase the heat a little and stir in the vermicelli. Cook for 5–6 minutes, until the noodles are tender.

6 Meanwhile, remove the skin from the chicken and, if desired, bone and chop into bite-size pieces. If you prefer, simply skin the chicken and leave the pieces whole.

7 When the vermicelli is cooked, reduce the heat and stir in the chicken pieces and the egg, lemon and saffron mixture. Cook over very low heat for 1–2 minutes, stirring constantly. Adjust the seasoning and serve with rustic bread.

MINESTRONE WITH PASTA AND BEANS

Although minestrone hails originally from northern Italy, it is now found all over that country.
This classic version includes pancetta for a pleasant touch of saltiness.

3 tablespoons olive oil
4 ounces pancetta, any rinds
removed, roughly chopped
2–3 celery stalks, finely chopped
3 medium carrots, finely chopped
1 medium onion, finely chopped
1–2 garlic cloves, crushed
14 ounces canned chopped tomatoes
about 4 cups chicken stock
14 ounces canned cannellini beans,
drained and rinsed
½ cup short-cut macaroni
2–4 tablespoons chopped fresh
flat-leaf parsley, to taste
salt and ground black pepper
shaved Parmesan cheese, to serve

SERVES 4–6

1 Heat the oil in a large saucepan, but do not let the oil smoke, as this will spoil the subtle flavor of the olive oil. Add the pancetta, fry for a moment to release some of the fat, then add the celery, carrots and onion. Cook over low heat for 5 minutes, stirring constantly with a wooden spoon. Continue stirring until the vegetables are tender but not too soft.

2 Add the garlic and tomatoes, breaking them up well with a wooden spoon. Pour in the stock. Add salt and pepper to taste and bring to a boil. Half-cover the pan, reduce the heat and simmer gently for about 20 minutes, until all the vegetables are soft.

3 Add the drained beans to the pan with the macaroni. Bring to a boil again. Cover, lower the heat and continue to simmer for about 20 more minutes. Check the consistency and add more stock if necessary. Stir in the parsley and taste for seasoning.

4 Serve hot, sprinkled with plenty of Parmesan cheese. This hearty soup makes a meal in itself if served with chunks of crusty Italian bread.

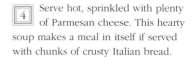

VARIATION
Use long-grain rice instead of pasta, and borlotti beans instead of cannellini beans.

GALICIAN BROTH

This delicious main-dish soup is very similar to the warming, chunky meat and potato broths of cooler climates. For extra color, a few onion skins can be added when cooking the smoked ham, but remember to remove them before serving.

1 pound smoked ham, in one piece
2 bay leaves
2 onions, sliced
2 teaspoons paprika
1½ pounds potatoes, cut into
large chunks
½ pound collard greens
15-ounce can navy beans, drained
salt and ground black pepper

SERVES 4

 1 Soak the smoked ham overnight in cold water. Drain and put in a large saucepan with the bay leaves and sliced onions. Pour in 6¼ cups cold water.

2 Bring to a boil, then reduce the heat and simmer very gently for about 1½ hours, until the meat is tender. Keep an eye on the pan to make sure it doesn't boil over.

3 Drain the meat, reserving the cooking liquid, and let cool slightly. Discard the skin and any excess fat from the meat and cut into small chunks. Return to the pan with the paprika and potatoes. Cover and simmer gently for 20 minutes.

4 Cut away the cores from the greens. Roll up the leaves and cut into thin shreds. Add to the pan with the beans and simmer for about 10 minutes. Season with salt and pepper to taste and serve hot.

COOK'S TIP
Ham hocks can be used instead of the smoked ham. The bones will give the juices a delicious flavor.

ITALIAN LENTIL SOUP WITH TOMATOES

This is a classic rustic soup flavored with rosemary. It is delicious served with garlic bread.

🌿 🌿

1 cup dried green or brown lentils
3 tablespoons extra virgin olive oil
3 strips bacon, diced into small pieces
1 onion, finely chopped
2 celery stalks, finely chopped
2 carrots, finely diced
2 rosemary sprigs, finely chopped
2 bay leaves
14 ounces canned chopped
plum tomatoes
7 cups vegetable stock
salt and ground black pepper
fresh bay leaves and rosemary sprigs,
to garnish

SERVES 4

1 Place the lentils in a bowl and cover with cold water. Leave to soak for 2 hours. Rinse and drain.

2 Heat the oil in a large saucepan. Add the bacon and cook for about 3 minutes, then stir in the onion and cook for 5 minutes, until softened. Stir in the celery, carrots, rosemary, bay leaves and lentils. Toss over the heat for 1 minute, until thoroughly coated in the oil.

3 Add the tomatoes and stock and bring to a boil. Lower the heat, half-cover the pan, and simmer for about 1 hour or until the lentils are perfectly tender. Stir the soup occasionally.

4 Remove the bay leaves, add salt and pepper to taste and serve in heated bowls, garnishing each portion with one or two fresh bay leaves and rosemary sprigs.

SPINACH AND RICE SOUP

Use very fresh, young spinach leaves to prepare this light and fresh-tasting soup.

🌿 🌿

1½ pounds fresh spinach, washed
3 tablespoons extra virgin olive oil
1 small onion, finely chopped
2 garlic cloves, finely chopped
1 small red chile, seeded and
finely chopped
generous ½ cup arborio rice
5 cups vegetable stock
¼ cup grated Pecorino cheese
salt and ground black pepper

SERVES 4

🌿 🌿

1 Place the spinach in a pan with just the water that clings to its leaves. Add salt. Heat until wilted, then drain, reserving any liquid.

2 Chop the spinach finely using a large knife.

3 Heat the oil in a large saucepan and gently cook the onion, garlic and chile for 4–5 minutes, until softened. Stir in the rice until well coated, then pour in the stock and reserved spinach liquid. Bring to a boil, lower the heat and simmer for 10 minutes.

4 Add the spinach, with salt and pepper to taste. Cook for 5–7 more minutes, until the rice is tender. Check the seasoning and serve with the Pecorino cheese.

PISTOU

A delicious vegetable soup from Nice in the south of France, served with a sun-dried tomato pesto and fresh Parmesan cheese.

❦ ❦

1 zucchini, diced
1 small potato, diced
1 shallot, chopped
1 carrot, diced
8-ounce can chopped tomatoes
5 cups vegetable stock
2 ounces green beans, cut into
½-inch pieces
½ cup frozen tiny peas
½ cup small pasta shapes
4–6 tablespoons homemade or
bought pesto
1 tablespoon sun-dried tomato paste
salt and ground black pepper
freshly grated Parmesan cheese,
to serve

SERVES 4–6

1 Place the zucchini, potato, shallot, carrot and tomatoes in a large pan. Add the vegetable stock and season with salt and pepper. Bring to a boil, then cover and simmer for 20 minutes.

2 Add the green beans, peas and pasta. Cook for another 10 minutes, until the pasta is tender. Adjust the seasoning.

3 Ladle the soup into individual bowls. Combine the pesto and sun-dried tomato paste and stir a spoonful into each serving. Serve with grated Parmesan cheese to sprinkle into each bowl.

AVGOLEMONO

*This is the most popular of Greek soups. The name means egg and lemon, the two important ingredients, which
produce a light, nourishing soup. Orzo is a Greek pasta shaped like rice, but you can use any small shape.*

7½ cups flavorful chicken stock
½ cup orzo pasta
3 eggs
juice of 1 large lemon
salt and ground black pepper
lemon slices, to garnish

SERVES 4–6

1. Pour the stock into a large pan
and bring to a boil. Add the
pasta and cook for 5 minutes.

2. Beat the eggs until frothy, then
add the lemon juice and a
tablespoon of cold water. Slowly stir
in a ladleful of the hot chicken stock,
then add one or two more. Return
this mixture to the pan, off the heat,
and stir well. Season with salt and
pepper and serve immediately,
garnished with lemon slices. (Do not
let the soup boil once the eggs have
been added or it will curdle.)

MOROCCAN VEGETABLE SOUP

Creamy parsnip and pumpkin give this soup a wonderfully rich texture.

1 tablespoon olive or sunflower oil
1 tablespoon butter
1 onion, chopped
8 ounces carrots, chopped
8 ounces parsnips, chopped
8 ounces pumpkin
3¾ cups vegetable or chicken stock
lemon juice, to taste
salt and ground black pepper

FOR THE GARNISH
1½ tablespoons olive oil
½ garlic clove, finely chopped
3 tablespoons chopped fresh parsley
and cilantro, mixed
a good pinch of paprika

SERVES 4

2 Cut the pumpkin into chunks, discarding the skin and pith, and stir into the pan. Cover and cook for another 5 minutes, then add the stock and seasoning, and slowly bring to a boil. Cover and simmer very gently for 35–40 minutes, until all the vegetables are tender.

3 Let the soup cool slightly, then purée in a food processor or blender until smooth, adding a little extra water if necessary. Pour back into a clean pan and reheat.

4 To make the garnish, heat the oil in a small pan and add the garlic, parsley and cilantro. Fry over low heat for 1–2 minutes. Add the paprika and stir well.

5 Adjust the seasoning of the soup and stir in just enough lemon juice to taste.

6 Pour into warmed individual soup bowls. Spoon a little garnish on top and carefully swirl it into the soup.

1 Heat the oil and butter in a large pan and fry the onion for about 3 minutes, until softened, stirring occasionally. Add the carrots and parsnips, stir well, cover and cook over low heat for another 5 minutes.

CREAMY ZUCCHINI SOUP

*The beauty of this soup is its delicate color, rich and creamy texture and subtle taste. If you prefer a
more pronounced cheese flavor, use Gorgonzola instead of Dolcelatte.*

2 tablespoons olive oil
1 tablespoon butter
1 medium onion, roughly chopped
2 pounds zucchini,
trimmed and sliced
1 teaspoon dried oregano
2½ cups vegetable or chicken stock
4 ounces Dolcelatte cheese,
rind removed, diced
1¼ cups light cream
salt and ground black pepper
fresh oregano and extra Dolcelatte,
to garnish

SERVES 4–6

1   Heat the oil and butter in a
    large saucepan until foaming.
Add the onion and cook gently for
about 5 minutes, stirring often, until
softened but not browned.

2   Add the zucchini and oregano,
    with salt and pepper to
taste. Cook over medium heat for
10 minutes, stirring frequently.

3   Pour in the stock and bring to
    a boil, stirring. Lower the heat,
half-cover the pan and simmer,
stirring occasionally, for 30 minutes.
Stir in the Dolcelatte until melted.

4   Process the soup in a food
    processor or blender until
smooth, then press through a sieve
into a clean pan.

5   Add two-thirds of the cream
    and stir over low heat until hot,
but not boiling. Check the consistency
and add more stock if the soup is too
thick. Taste for seasoning, then pour
into heated bowls. Swirl in the
remaining cream. Garnish with
oregano and extra cheese, and serve.

COOK'S TIP
To save time, trim off and discard the
ends of the zucchini, cut them into
thirds, then chop them in a food
processor fitted with the metal blade.

SPANISH GARLIC SOUP

This is a simple and satisfying soup, made with one of the most popular ingredients in the Mediterranean—garlic!

2 tablespoons olive oil
4 large garlic cloves, peeled
4 slices French bread, ¼ inch thick
1 tablespoon paprika
4 cups beef stock
¼ teaspoon ground cumin
pinch of saffron strands
4 eggs
salt and ground black pepper
chopped fresh parsley, to garnish

SERVES 4

 1 Preheat the oven to 450°F. Heat the oil in a large pan. Add the whole garlic cloves and cook for a minute or two, until golden. Remove and set aside. Sauté the bread in the oil until golden, then set aside.

2 Add the paprika to the pan and sauté for a few seconds. Stir in the beef stock, cumin and saffron, then add the reserved garlic, crushing the cloves with the back of a wooden spoon. Season with salt and pepper, then cook for about 5 minutes.

3 Ladle the soup into four ovenproof bowls and break an egg into each. Set a slice of bread on top of each egg and place in the oven for 3–4 minutes, until the eggs are set. Sprinkle with parsley and serve immediately.

SPICY PUMPKIN SOUP

Pumpkin is popular all over the Mediterranean, and it's an important ingredient in Middle Eastern cooking, by which this soup is inspired. Ginger and cumin give the soup its spicy flavor.

2 pounds pumpkin, peeled and seeds removed
2 tablespoons olive oil
2 leeks, trimmed and sliced
1 garlic clove, crushed
1 teaspoon ground ginger
1 teaspoon ground cumin
3¾ cups chicken stock
salt and ground black pepper
cilantro leaves, to garnish
4 tablespoons plain yogurt, to serve

SERVES 4

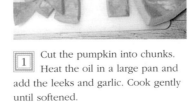

1   Cut the pumpkin into chunks. Heat the oil in a large pan and add the leeks and garlic. Cook gently until softened.

2   Add the ginger and cumin and cook, stirring, for another minute. Add the pumpkin and the chicken stock and season with salt and pepper. Bring to a boil and simmer for 30 minutes, until the pumpkin is tender. Process the soup, in batches if necessary, in a blender or food processor.

3   Reheat the soup and serve in warmed individual bowls, with a swirl of yogurt and a garnish of cilantro leaves.

GREEN SOUP

This is a delicious and nutritious soup, ideal for warming cooler winter evenings.

1 onion, chopped
2 cups leeks (trimmed weight), sliced
8 ounces unpeeled potatoes, diced
3¾ cups vegetable stock
1 bay leaf
8 ounces broccoli florets
1½ cups frozen peas
2–3 tablespoons chopped
fresh parsley
salt and ground black pepper
sprigs of parsley, to garnish

SERVES 4–6

1 Put the onion, leeks, potatoes, stock and bay leaf in a large saucepan and combine. Cover, bring to a boil and simmer for 10 minutes, stirring.

2 Add the broccoli and peas, cover, return to a boil then lower the heat and simmer for another 10 minutes, stirring occasionally.

3 Set aside to cool slightly, and remove and discard the bay leaf. Purée in a blender or food processor until smooth.

4 Add the parsley, season to taste and process briefly. Return to the saucepan and reheat gently until piping hot. Ladle into soup bowls and garnish with parsley sprigs.

ALMOND AND BROCCOLI SOUP

—

The creaminess of the toasted ground almonds combines perfectly with the slight bitterness of the broccoli in this delicious Spanish soup.

½ cup ground almonds
1½ pounds broccoli
3¾ cups vegetable stock
1¼ cups milk
salt and ground black pepper

SERVES 4–6

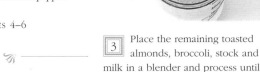

3 Place the remaining toasted almonds, broccoli, stock and milk in a blender and process until smooth. Season to taste.

4 Pour the puréed mixture into a pan and heat to simmering. Serve, sprinkled with the reserved toasted almonds.

1 Preheat the oven to 350°F. Spread the ground almonds evenly on a baking sheet and toast them in the oven for about 10 minutes or until golden. Reserve one-quarter of the almonds and set aside for the garnish.

2 Cut the broccoli into small florets. Steam for 6–7 minutes or until tender.

FRESH TOMATO SOUP

Intensely flavored sun-ripened tomatoes need little embellishment in this fresh-tasting soup. If you buy from the supermarket, choose the ripest-looking ones and add the amount of sugar and vinegar necessary, depending on their natural sweetness. On a hot day, this Italian soup is also delicious chilled.

3–3½ pounds ripe tomatoes
1⅔ cups flavorful chicken or
vegetable stock
3 tablespoons sun-dried tomato paste
2–3 tablespoons balsamic vinegar
2–3 teaspoons sugar
small handful basil leaves
salt and ground black pepper
basil leaves, to garnish
toasted cheese croutons and
sour cream, to serve

SERVES 6

1 Plunge the tomatoes into boiling water for 30 seconds, then refresh in cold water. Peel away the skins and quarter the tomatoes. Put them in a large saucepan and pour in the chicken or vegetable stock. Bring just to a boil, reduce the heat, cover and simmer gently for 10 minutes, until the tomatoes are soft.

2 Stir in the tomato paste, vinegar, sugar and basil. Season with salt and pepper, then cook gently, stirring, for 2 minutes. Process the soup in a blender or food processor, then return to the pan and reheat gently. Serve in bowls topped with one or two toasted cheese croutons and a spoonful of sour cream, garnished with basil leaves.

SPLIT PEA AND ZUCCHINI SOUP

Rich and satisfying—with just the slightest hint of spice—this hearty soup is good to come home to after a long walk.

1 cup yellow split peas
1 medium onion, finely chopped
1 teaspoon sunflower oil
2 medium zucchini, finely diced
3¼ cups chicken stock
½ teaspoon ground turmeric
salt and ground black pepper
crusty bread, to serve

SERVES 4

1 Place the split peas in a bowl, cover with cold water and let soak for several hours or overnight. Drain, rinse in plenty of cold water and drain again.

2 Cook the onion in the oil in a covered pan, shaking occasionally, until soft. Reserve a handful of diced zucchini and add the rest to the pan. Cook, stirring, for 2–3 minutes.

3 Add the stock and turmeric to the pan and bring to a boil. Reduce the heat, then cover and simmer for 30–40 minutes or until the split peas are tender. Season well.

4 When the soup is almost ready, bring a large saucepan of water to a boil, add the reserved diced zucchini and cook for 1 minute, then drain and add them to the soup. Serve hot, with warm crusty bread.

COOK'S TIP
For a quicker alternative, use split red lentils for this soup—they need no presoaking and cook very quickly. Adjust the amount of stock, if necessary.

JERUSALEM ARTICHOKE SOUP

For such an unattractive vegetable, the Jerusalem artichoke has a surprisingly delicate flavor, which makes for a most delicious soup.

2–4 tablespoons butter
1½ cups sliced mushrooms
1 pound Jerusalem artichokes
2 onions, chopped
1¼ cups vegetable stock
1¼ cups milk
salt and ground black pepper

SERVES 4

1 Melt the butter in a saucepan and sauté the mushrooms for 1 minute. Put them on a plate. Peel and slice the artichokes and then sauté them with the onions, adding a little more butter if needed. Do not let the vegetables brown.

2 Add the vegetable stock to the pan and simmer the artichokes until they are soft. Season to taste.

3 Purée in a food processor, adding the milk. Reheat the soup, stir in the mushrooms and serve.

SPINACH AND LEMON SOUP WITH MEATBALLS

Aarshe Saak is standard fare in many parts of the Middle East. In Greece it is normally made without the meatballs and is called Avgolemono.

2 large onions
3 tablespoons oil
1 tablespoon ground turmeric
½ cup yellow split peas
5 cups water
8 ounces ground lamb
1 pound spinach, chopped
½ cup rice flour
juice of 2 lemons
1–2 garlic cloves, very finely chopped
2 tablespoons chopped fresh mint
4 eggs, beaten
salt and ground black pepper

SERVES 6

 1 Chop one of the onions. Heat 2 tablespoons of the oil in a large shallow pan and fry the chopped onion until golden. Add the turmeric and split peas, then pour in the water and bring to the boil. Reduce the heat and simmer for 20 minutes, stirring occasionally.

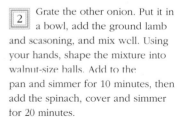

2 Grate the other onion. Put it in a bowl, add the ground lamb and seasoning, and mix well. Using your hands, shape the mixture into walnut-size balls. Add to the pan and simmer for 10 minutes, then add the spinach, cover and simmer for 20 minutes.

3 Mix the rice flour with about 1 cup of cold water into a smooth paste, then slowly add to the pan, stirring constantly to prevent lumps. Stir in the lemon juice, season with salt and pepper and cook over a low heat for 20 minutes.

4 Meanwhile, heat the remaining oil in a small pan and fry the garlic briefly until golden. Stir in the chopped mint.

5 Remove the soup from heat and stir in the beaten eggs. Serve, sprinkled with the garlic and mint garnish.

COOK'S TIP
If preferred, use less lemon juice to begin with and then add more to taste once the soup is cooked.

CHILLED ALMOND SOUP

Unless you want to spend time pounding the ingredients for this dish by hand, a food processor is essential.
Then you'll find that this Spanish soup is very simple to make and refreshing to eat on a hot day.

2 slices fresh white bread
1 cup blanched almonds
2 garlic cloves, sliced
5 tablespoons olive oil
1½ tablespoons sherry vinegar
salt and ground black pepper
toasted sliced almonds and
seedless green and black grapes,
halved and peeled, to garnish

SERVES 6

 Break the bread into a bowl and pour ⅔ cup cold water over it. Let sit for 5 minutes.

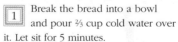

 Put the blanched almonds and garlic in a blender or food processor and process until very finely ground. Blend in the soaked bread.

 Gradually add the olive oil until the mixture forms a smooth paste. Add the sherry vinegar, then 2½ cups cold water, and process until smooth.

4 Transfer to a bowl and season with salt and pepper, adding a little more water if the soup is very thick. Chill for at least 2–3 hours.

5 Ladle the soup into bowls and sprinkle with the toasted almonds and peeled grapes.

GAZPACHO

There are many versions of this refreshingly chilled, pungent soup from southern Spain. All contain an intense blend of tomatoes, peppers, cucumber and garlic, perfect on a hot summer's evening.

2 pounds ripe tomatoes
1 cucumber
2 red bell peppers, seeded and
coarsely chopped
2 garlic cloves, crushed
3 cups fresh white bread crumbs
2 tablespoons white wine vinegar
2 tablespoons sun-dried tomato paste
6 tablespoons olive oil
salt and ground black pepper

TO FINISH
1 slice white bread, crust removed
and cut into cubes
2 tablespoons olive oil
6–12 ice cubes
small bowl of mixed chopped
garnishes, such as tomato, cucumber,
red onion, hard-boiled egg and flat-
leaf parsley or tarragon leaves

SERVES 6

COOK'S TIP
The sun-dried tomato paste has been
added to accentuate the flavor of the
tomatoes. You might not need this if
you use a really flavorful variety.

 1 Plunge the tomatoes into
boiling water for 30 seconds,
then refresh in cold water. Peel away
the skins and quarter. Peel and
coarsely chop the cucumber. Mix the
tomatoes and cucumber in a bowl
with the peppers, garlic, bread
crumbs, vinegar, tomato paste and
olive oil and season lightly with salt
and pepper.

2 Process half the mixture in a
blender or food processor until
fairly smooth. Process the remaining
mixture and combine with the first.

3 Check the seasoning and add a
little cold water if the soup is
too thick. Chill for several hours.

4 To finish, fry the bread in the
oil until golden. Spoon the soup
into bowls, adding one or two ice
cubes to each. Serve accompanied by
the croutons and garnishes.

CHILLED TOMATO AND SWEET PEPPER SOUP

A recipe inspired by the Spanish gazpacho, the difference being that this soup is cooked first,
and then chilled.

2 red bell peppers, halved, cored
and seeded
3 tablespoons olive oil
1 onion, finely chopped
2 garlic cloves, crushed
1½ pounds ripe tomatoes
⅔ cup red wine
2½ cups chicken stock
salt and ground black pepper
snipped fresh chives, to garnish

FOR THE CROUTONS
2 slices white bread, crusts removed
4 tablespoons olive oil

SERVES 4

1 Cut each pepper half into quarters. Place skin side up on a broiler rack and cook until the skins have charred. Transfer to a bowl and cover with a plate.

2 Heat the oil in a large pan. Add the onion and garlic and cook until soft. Meanwhile, remove the skin from the peppers and coarsely chop them. Cut the tomatoes into chunks.

3 Add the peppers and tomatoes to the pan, then cover and cook gently for 10 minutes. Add the wine and cook for another 5 minutes, then add the stock and salt and pepper and continue to simmer for 20 minutes.

4 To make the croutons, cut the bread into cubes. Heat the oil in a small frying pan, add the bread and sauté until golden. Drain on paper towels and store in an airtight box.

5 Process the soup in a blender or food processor until smooth. Pour into a clean glass or ceramic bowl and let cool thoroughly before chilling in the refrigerator for at least 3 hours. When the soup is cold, season to taste.

6 Serve the soup in bowls, topped with the croutons and garnished with snipped chives.

MIDDLE EASTERN YOGURT AND CUCUMBER SOUP

Yogurt is used extensively in Middle Eastern cooking, and it is usually made at home. Sometimes it is added at the end of cooking a dish, so that it won't curdle, but in this cold soup the yogurt is one of the basic ingredients.

1 large cucumber, peeled
1¼ cups light cream
⅔ cup plain yogurt
2 garlic cloves, crushed
2 tablespoons white wine vinegar
1 tablespoon chopped fresh mint
salt and ground black pepper
sprigs of mint, to garnish

SERVES 4

1 Grate the cucumber coarsely. Place in a bowl with the cream, yogurt, garlic, vinegar and mint. Stir well and season to taste.

2 Chill for at least 2 hours before serving. Just before serving, stir the soup again. Pour into individual bowls and garnish with mint sprigs

VEGETABLES

Mediterranean vegetables are a veritable
treasure trove of taste and color that beg to be
transformed into delectable dishes.

A Mediterranean street market is a fascinating vision of color and photo opportunities. The wonderful array of fruit and vegetable stalls in particular gives many vacationers the urge to swap their hotel rooms for a kitchen in which to cook a feast of sweet, juicy local produce. Mediterranean vegetables have an inviting irregularity about them. Uneven colorings, bumpy skins and asymmetrical shapes are a sure indication that the flesh inside will be full of flavor, a far cry from the mass-produced, artificially grown produce of colder climes. The dishes cooked using them are a joy to eat, and even the simplest tossed salad of tomatoes and greens, sprinkled with olive oil and seasoning, is worthy of serving solo—a meal in itself.

All around the Mediterranean, vegetables are the basis of everyday meals. This is due both to the expense of meat and to the religious obligations of fasting before the many festive occasions each year. This austerity has led to the development of many imaginative cooking skills. Deep-fried, roasted, baked, stuffed, marinated, broiled, steamed, added to pies, tarts, omelets, stews and stuffings: Vegetables are very versatile.

BELOW: At a finca—or farm—in Andalusia, vegetables grow alongside the grape-drying beds.

RIGHT: Tomatoes, chiles, potatoes and braids of garlic are just some of the vegetables on sale at this market in southern Turkey.

BELOW: A golden harvest: Pumpkins make delicious soups, pies and casseroles.

A stunning variety of mushrooms appears frequently in Italian and French cooking. In these countries, markets are filled with wild varieties in the spring and autumn. The lovely shapes and flavors make interesting risottos and salads and may even be used to flavor pasta. Many mushroom varieties are dried for year-round availability. A small quantity goes a long way and can be used to liven up the flavor of everyday button mushrooms.

Stuffed vegetables are greatly loved in many countries of the Mediterranean, particularly in Turkey, Greece and the Middle East. Tomatoes, eggplant, peppers, zucchini and onions are filled with couscous, rice, herbs, spices, dried fruits, nuts, cheese and sometimes meat. Large leaves like spinach, grape and cabbage are stuffed with interesting ingredients, packed in a pan and gently cooked so as to mingle all the flavors together.

Even the humble potato takes pride of place at the Mediterranean table. The Spanish make a delicious potato salad in which new potatoes are fried to give a crisp crust. Italian gnocchi is a distinctively shaped, puréed and poached potato dish flavored with a variety of herbs, cheese or mild spices.

In France and Italy, vegetable fritters of zucchini or eggplant, deep-fried in a light crisp batter, make a very enjoyable dish, often served with a ripe tomato sauce or garlicky herb dressing. Even the zucchini flowers are battered and fried, making a visual and interesting garnish. Ratatouille, a wonderful stew of lightly cooked vegetables, is traditionally French, although similar recipes stretch across the Mediterranean.

No vegetable is considered too small to bother with; the smallest artichokes, turnips, eggplant and fava beans are put to good use in many dishes.

MARINATED MUSHROOMS

This Spanish recipe makes a nice change from the classic French mushrooms à la Grecque. Make this dish the day before you eat it; the flavor will improve with keeping.

2 tablespoons olive oil
1 small onion, very finely chopped
1 garlic clove, crushed
1 tablespoon tomato paste
¼ cup dry white wine
2 cloves
pinch of saffron strands
½ pound button mushrooms, trimmed
salt and ground black pepper
chopped fresh parsley, to garnish

SERVES 4

1 Heat the oil in a pan. Add the onion and garlic and cook until soft. Stir in the tomato paste, wine, ¼ cup water, cloves and saffron and season with salt and pepper. Bring to a boil, cover and simmer gently for about 45 minutes, adding more water if the mixture becomes too dry.

2 Add the mushrooms to the pan, then cover and simmer for another 5 minutes. Remove from the heat and, still covered, let cool. Chill overnight. Serve cold, sprinkled with chopped parsley.

POTATO AND ONION TORTILLA

One of the signature dishes of Spain, this delicious, thick potato and onion omelet is eaten at all times of the day, hot or cold.

1¼ cups olive oil
6 large potatoes, peeled and sliced
2 Spanish onions, sliced
6 eggs
salt and ground black pepper
cherry tomatoes, halved, to serve

SERVES 4

1 Heat the oil in a large nonstick frying pan. Stir in the potato, onion and a little salt. Cover and cook gently for 20 minutes, until soft.

2 Beat the eggs in a large bowl. Remove the onion and potato from the pan with a slotted spoon and add to the eggs. Season with salt and pepper to taste. Pour off some of the oil, leaving about 4 tablespoons in the pan. (Reserve the leftover oil for other cooking.) Heat the pan again.

3 When the oil is very hot, pour in the egg mixture. Cook for 2–3 minutes. Cover the pan with a plate and invert the omelet onto it. Slide it back into the pan and cook for 5 more minutes, until golden brown and moist in the middle. Serve in wedges, with the tomatoes.

SWEET BELL PEPPER AND ZUCCHINI FRITTATA

Eggs, cheese and vegetables form the basis of this excellent supper dish. Served cold, in wedges,
it also makes excellent picnic fare.

3 tablespoons olive oil
1 red onion, thinly sliced
1 large red bell pepper, cored and
thinly sliced
1 large yellow bell pepper, cored and
thinly sliced
2 garlic cloves, crushed
1 medium zucchini, thinly sliced
6 eggs
5 ounces Italian cheese, such as
Fontina, Provolone or
Taleggio, grated
salt and ground black pepper
dressed mixed salad leaves, to garnish

SERVES 4

1 Heat 2 tablespoons of the oil in a large heavy frying pan. Fry the onion and pepper slices over low heat for about 10 minutes.

2 Add the remaining oil to the pan. When it is hot, add the garlic and zucchini slices and fry for 5 minutes, stirring constantly.

3 Beat the eggs with salt and pepper in a bowl. Mix in the grated cheese.

4 Pour the egg and cheese mixture over the vegetables in the pan, stirring lightly to mix. Make sure that the bottom of the pan is evenly covered with egg. Cook over low heat until the mixture is just set.

5 Let the frittata rest in the pan for about 5 minutes before cutting. This is delicious served hot or cold, with a salad garnish.

COOK'S TIP
Traditionally, a frittata is inverted on a plate and returned to the pan upside down to cook the top, but it may be easier to brown the top lightly under a hot broiler for a few minutes.

CHILI CHEESE TORTILLA WITH FRESH TOMATO SALSA

Good either warm or cold, this is something like a quiche without the crust.
Cheese and chiles are a great match for each other.

*3 tablespoons sunflower
or olive oil
1 small onion, thinly sliced
2–3 fresh green jalapeño
chiles, sliced
7 ounces cold cooked potato,
thinly sliced
generous 1 cup grated Manchego,
Mexican Queso Blanco
or Monterey Jack cheese
6 eggs, beaten
salt and ground black pepper
fresh herbs, to garnish*

FOR THE SALSA
*1¼ pounds fresh, flavorful tomatoes,
peeled, seeded
and finely chopped
1 fresh mild green chile, seeded
and finely chopped
2 garlic cloves, crushed
3 tablespoons chopped cilantro
juice of 1 lime
½ teaspoon salt
pepper*

SERVES 4

COOK'S TIP
You can brown the top of the
tortilla under a hot broiler, using
a frying pan with a flameproof
handle. If you want to re-heat the
tortilla, place in a hot oven for a
few minutes.

 Make the salsa. Put the chopped
tomatoes in a bowl and add the
chopped chile, garlic, cilantro, lime
juice, salt and pepper. Mix well and
set aside.

2 Heat half the oil in a large
omelet pan and gently fry the
onion and jalapeños for 5 minutes,
stirring once or twice, until softened.
Add the potato and cook for another
5 minutes, until lightly browned,
taking care to keep the slices whole.

3 Using a slotted spoon, transfer
the vegetables to a warm plate.
Wipe the pan with paper towels, and
add the remaining oil. Heat well and
return the vegetable mixture to the
pan. Sprinkle on the cheese.

4 Pour in the beaten eggs, making
sure that they seep under the
vegetables. Cook the tortilla over low
heat until set. Serve in wedges,
garnished with fresh herbs, with the
salsa on the side.

131

STUFFED TOMATOES AND PEPPERS

Colorful bell peppers and tomatoes make perfect containers for various meat and vegetable stuffings.
This rice and herb version uses typically Greek ingredients.

2 large ripe tomatoes
1 green bell pepper
1 yellow or orange bell pepper
4 tablespoons olive oil, plus extra
for sprinkling
2 onions, chopped
2 garlic cloves, crushed
½ cup blanched almonds, chopped
scant ½ cup long-grain rice, cooked
and drained
½ ounce mint, roughly chopped
½ ounce parsley, coarsely chopped
2 tablespoons golden raisins
3 tablespoons ground almonds
salt and ground black pepper
chopped mixed herbs, to garnish

SERVES 4

 Preheat the oven to 375°F. Cut the tomatoes in half and scoop out the pulp and seeds using a teaspoon. Leave the tomatoes to drain on paper towels with cut sides down. Coarsely chop the tomato pulp and seeds and set aside.

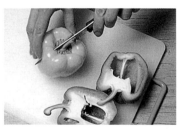

 Halve the peppers, leaving the cores intact. Scoop out the seeds. Brush the peppers with 1 tablespoon of the oil and bake on a baking sheet for 15 minutes. Place the peppers and tomatoes in a shallow ovenproof dish and season with salt and pepper.

3 Sauté the onions in the remaining oil for 5 minutes. Add the garlic and chopped almonds and sauté for another minute.

4 Remove the pan from the heat and stir in the rice, chopped tomatoes, mint, parsley and golden raisins. Season well with salt and pepper and spoon the mixture into the tomatoes and peppers.

5 Pour ⅔ cup boiling water around the tomatoes and peppers and bake, uncovered, for 20 minutes. Scatter the ground almonds over them and sprinkle with a little extra olive oil. Return to the oven and bake for 20 more minutes, or until turning golden. Serve garnished with fresh herbs.

133

RATATOUILLE

A highly versatile vegetable stew from Provence, ratatouille is delicious hot or cold, on its own or with eggs, pasta, fish or meat—particularly roast lamb.

2 pounds ripe tomatoes
½ cup olive oil
2 onions, thinly sliced
2 red bell peppers, seeded and cut into chunks
1 yellow or orange bell pepper, seeded and cut into chunks
1 large eggplant, cut into chunks
2 zucchini, cut into thick slices
4 garlic cloves, crushed
2 bay leaves
1 tablespoon chopped young thyme
salt and ground black pepper

SERVES 6

1 Plunge the tomatoes into boiling water for 30 seconds, then refresh in cold water. Peel and chop coarsely.

2 Heat a little of the oil in a large, heavy pan and sauté the onions for 5 minutes. Add the peppers and sauté for another 2 minutes. Drain. Add the eggplant and more oil and sauté gently for 5 minutes. Add the remaining oil and zucchini and sauté for 3 minutes. Drain.

3 Add the garlic and tomatoes to the pan with the bay leaves and thyme and a little salt and pepper. Cook gently until the tomatoes have softened and are turning pulpy.

4 Return all the vegetables to the pan and cook gently, stirring frequently, for about 15 minutes, until fairly pulpy but retaining a little texture. Season with more salt and pepper to taste.

COOK'S TIP
There are no specific quantities for the vegetables when making ratatouille, so you can, to a large extent, vary the quantities and types of vegetables depending on what you have in the refrigerator. If the tomatoes are a little tasteless, add 2–3 tablespoons tomato paste and a dash of sugar to the mixture along with the tomatoes.

STUFFED PEPPERS

Couscous is a form of pasta used extensively in the Middle East. It makes a good basis for a stuffing, combined with other ingredients.

6 red bell peppers
2 tablespoons butter
1 onion, finely chopped
1 teaspoon olive oil
½ teaspoon salt
1 cup instant couscous
2 tablespoons raisins
2 tablespoons chopped fresh mint
1 egg yolk
salt and ground black pepper
mint leaves, to garnish

SERVES 4

1 Preheat the oven to 400°F. Carefully slit each pepper and remove the core and seeds. Melt the butter in a small pan and add the onion. Cook until soft.

2 To cook the couscous, bring 1 cup water to a boil. Add the olive oil and the salt, then remove the pan from the heat and add the couscous. Stir and let stand, covered, for about 5 minutes. Stir in the cooked onion, raisins and mint, then season well with salt and pepper. Stir in the egg yolk.

3 Using a teaspoon, fill the peppers with the couscous mixture to only about three-quarters full, as the couscous will swell when cooked further. Place in a lightly oiled ovenproof dish and bake, uncovered, for about 20 minutes, until tender. Serve hot or cold, garnished with the mint leaves.

EGGPLANT WITH TZATZIKI

Battered eggplant slices are irresistible with a minted cucumber dip.

2 medium-size eggplant
¾ cup all-purpose flour
1 egg
½–⅔ cup milk
oil for deep-frying
salt

FOR THE TZATZIKI
½ cucumber, peeled and diced
⅔ cup plain yogurt
1 garlic clove, crushed
1 tablespoon chopped fresh mint

SERVES 4

1 To make the tzatziki, place the cucumber in a colander, sprinkle with salt and let sit for 30 minutes. Rinse, drain well and pat dry on paper towels. Mix the yogurt, garlic, mint and cucumber in a bowl. Cover and chill.

2 Slice the eggplant lengthwise. Sprinkle the slices with salt. Let sit for 1 hour to draw out the bitter juices.

3 To make the batter, sift the flour and a pinch of salt into a large bowl, add the egg and milk and beat until smooth.

4 Rinse the eggplant slices and pat dry. Heat ½ inch of oil in a large frying pan. Dip the eggplant slices in the batter and fry them for 3–4 minutes, until golden, turning once. Drain on paper towels and serve with the tzatziki.

EGGPLANT AND ZUCCHINI CASSEROLE

Eggplant and zucchini are classic Mediterranean vegetables which absorb flavors well. They taste delicious when cooked with herbs and cheese.

1 large eggplant
2 tablespoons olive oil
1 large onion, chopped
1–2 garlic cloves, crushed
2 pounds tomatoes, peeled and chopped
a handful of basil leaves, shredded, plus whole leaves, to garnish
1 tablespoon chopped fresh parsley
2 zucchini, sliced lengthwise
all-purpose flour, for coating
5–6 tablespoons sunflower oil
12 ounces mozzarella cheese, sliced
1 ounce Parmesan cheese, grated
salt and ground black pepper

SERVES 4–6

1 Grease a baking dish. Slice the eggplant, sprinkle with salt and set aside for 45–60 minutes. Heat the olive oil in a large frying pan. Fry the onion and garlic for 3–4 minutes, until softened. Stir in the tomatoes, half the basil, the parsley and seasoning. Bring to a boil. Reduce the heat and cook, stirring, for 25–35 minutes, until thickened to a pulp.

2 Rinse and dry the eggplant slices. Dust all the slices with flour. Preheat the oven to 350°F.

3 Heat the sunflower oil in another pan and fry the eggplant and zucchini slices until golden. Spoon half the fried vegetables into the baking dish, pour on half the pulp and scatter with half the mozzarella and remaining basil. Repeat the layers. Sprinkle the Parmesan on top and bake for 30–35 minutes. Serve, garnished with basil.

GREEK SPINACH PIES

*These little horns of phyllo pastry are stuffed with a simple spinach and feta cheese filling
to make a quick and easy main course.*

8 ounces fresh spinach
2 scallions, chopped
6 ounces feta cheese, crumbled
1 egg, beaten
1 tablespoon fresh dill, chopped
ground black pepper
4 large sheets or 8 small sheets
of phyllo pastry
olive oil, for brushing

SERVES 8

1 Preheat the oven to 375°F.
Blanch the spinach in the tiniest
amount of water until just wilted,
then drain very well, pressing it
through a sieve with the back of a
wooden spoon.

2 Chop the spinach finely and
mix with the onions, feta, egg,
dill and ground black pepper. Lay out
a sheet of phyllo pastry and brush
with olive oil. If large, cut the pieces
in half and sandwich them together. If
small, fit another sheet on top and
brush with olive oil.

3 Spread a quarter of the spinach
filling on one corner of the
phyllo, then roll it up firmly, but not
too tightly. Shape into a crescent and
place on a baking sheet.

4 Brush the pastry well with more
oil and bake for 20–25 minutes,
until golden and crisp. Cool slightly,
then remove to a wire rack to
cool completely.

CHUNKY VEGETABLE PAELLA

*This Spanish rice dish has become a family favorite all over the world. There are many versions:
this one uses eggplant and chickpeas.*

good pinch saffron strands
1 eggplant, cut into thick chunks
6 tablespoons olive oil
1 large onion, sliced
3 garlic cloves, crushed
1 yellow bell pepper, sliced
1 red bell pepper, sliced
2 teaspoons paprika
1¼ cups arborio rice
2½ cups stock
1 pound fresh tomatoes, skinned
and chopped
4 ounces sliced mushrooms
4 ounces cut green beans
14-ounce can chickpeas
salt and ground black pepper

SERVES 6

1 Steep the saffron in 3 tablespoons
of hot water. Sprinkle the
eggplant with salt, let drain in a
colander for 30 minutes, then rinse
and drain.

2 In a large paella or frying pan,
heat the oil and fry the onion,
garlic, peppers and eggplant for about
5 minutes, stirring occasionally.
Sprinkle in the paprika and stir again.

3 Mix in the rice, then pour in the
stock, tomatoes, saffron and
seasoning. Bring to a boil, then
simmer for 15 minutes, uncovered,
shaking the pan frequently and
stirring occasionally.

4 Stir in the mushrooms, green
beans and chickpeas (with their
liquid). Continue cooking for
10 minutes, then serve hot from the pan.

VEGETABLE MOUSSAKA

This is a flavorful vegetarian alternative to the classic meat moussaka. Serve it with warm bread and a glass or two of rustic red wine.

1 pound eggplant, sliced
½ cup whole green lentils
2½ cups vegetable stock
1 bay leaf
3 tablespoons olive oil
1 onion, sliced
1 garlic clove, crushed
8 ounces mushrooms, sliced
14-ounce can chickpeas, rinsed
and drained
14-ounce can chopped tomatoes
2 tablespoons tomato paste
2 teaspoons dried herbes de Provence
3 tablespoons water
1¼ cups plain yogurt
3 eggs
½ cup grated aged Cheddar cheese
salt and ground black pepper
flat-leaf parsley sprigs, to garnish

SERVES 6

 1 Sprinkle the eggplant slices with salt and place in a colander. Cover and let sit for about 30 minutes to extract the bitter juices.

2 Meanwhile, place the lentils, stock and bay leaf in a saucepan. Cover, bring to a boil and simmer for about 20 minutes, until the lentils are just tender. Drain well and keep warm.

3 Heat 1 tablespoon of the oil in a large saucepan. Add the onion and garlic and cook for 5 minutes, stirring. Stir in the lentils, mushrooms, chickpeas, tomatoes, tomato paste, herbs and water. Bring to a boil, lower the heat, cover and simmer gently for 10 minutes.

COOK'S TIP
If the eggplant is young, there is no need to salt it.

4 Preheat the oven to 350°F. Rinse all the eggplant slices, drain and pat dry. Heat the remaining oil in a frying pan and fry the slices in batches for 3–4 minutes, turning once.

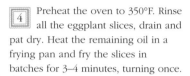

5 Season the lentil mixture with salt and pepper. Arrange a layer of eggplant slices in the bottom of a large, shallow, ovenproof dish or roasting pan, then spoon on a layer of the lentil mixture. Continue the layers until all the eggplant slices and lentil mixture have been used.

6 Beat together the yogurt and eggs, season with salt and pepper, and pour the mixture into the dish. Sprinkle the grated cheese on top and bake for about 45 minutes, until the topping is golden brown and bubbling. Serve immediately, garnished with flat-leaf parsley sprigs.

BROILED EGGPLANT PARCELS

These are delicious little Italian bundles of tomatoes, mozzarella cheese and basil, wrapped in slices of eggplant.

2 large, long eggplant
8 ounces mozzarella cheese
2 plum tomatoes
16 large basil leaves
salt and ground black pepper
2 tablespoons olive oil

FOR THE DRESSING
¼ cup olive oil
1 teaspoon balsamic vinegar
1 tablespoon sun-dried tomato paste
1 tablespoon lemon juice

FOR THE GARNISH
2 tablespoons toasted pine nuts
torn basil leaves

SERVES 4

1 Remove the stems from the eggplant and cut the eggplant lengthwise into thin slices—the aim is to have a total of 16 slices, disregarding the first and last slices (each about ¼ inch thick). (If you have a mandoline, it will cut perfect, even slices for you; otherwise use a sharp, long-bladed knife.)

2 Bring a large pan of salted water to a boil and cook the eggplant slices for about 2 minutes, until just softened. Drain the sliced eggplant, then dry on paper towels.

3 Cut the mozzarella cheese into eight slices. Cut each tomato into eight slices, not counting the first and last slices.

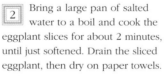

4 Take two eggplant slices and place on an ovenproof baking sheet or dish in a cross. Place a slice of tomato in the center, season with salt and pepper, then add a basil leaf, followed by a slice of mozzarella, another basil leaf, a slice of tomato and more seasoning.

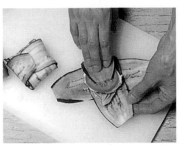

[5] Fold the ends of the eggplant slices around the mozzarella and tomato filling to make a neat parcel (*left*). Repeat with the rest of the assembled ingredients to make eight parcels. Chill the parcels for about 20 minutes.

[6] To make the tomato dressing, whisk together the olive oil, vinegar, sun-dried tomato paste and lemon juice. Season to taste.

[7] Preheat the broiler. Brush the parcels with olive oil and cook for about 5 minutes on each side, until golden. Serve hot, with the dressing, sprinkled with pine nuts and basil.

POTATO AND PUMPKIN SOUFFLE

Serve this savory soufflé with any rich meat dish, or simply with a mixed salad.

3 tablespoons olive oil
1 garlic clove, sliced
1½ pounds pumpkin flesh,
cut into ¾-inch chunks
12 ounces potatoes
2 tablespoons butter
scant ½ cup ricotta cheese
⅓ cup grated Parmesan cheese
pinch of grated nutmeg
4 eggs, separated
salt and ground black pepper
chopped fresh parsley, to garnish

SERVES 4

1 Preheat the oven to 400°F. Lightly grease a 7½-cup shallow, oval baking dish with olive oil or other fat.

2 Heat the oil in a large shallow pan, add the garlic and pumpkin and cook, stirring often to prevent sticking, for 15–20 minutes or until the pumpkin is tender. Meanwhile, cook the potatoes in boiling salted water for 20 minutes, until tender. Drain, let sit until cool enough to handle, then peel off the skins. Place the potatoes and pumpkin in a large bowl and mash well with the butter.

3 Mash the ricotta with a fork until smooth, then add to the potato and pumpkin mixture, stirring well with a wooden spoon.

4 Stir the Parmesan, nutmeg and plenty of seasoning into the potato and pumpkin mixture—it should be smooth and creamy. Add the egg yolks, one at a time, until thoroughly mixed.

5 Whisk the egg whites with an electric whisk until they form stiff peaks, then fold gently into the mixture. Spoon into the prepared baking dish and bake for 30 minutes, until golden and firm. Serve hot, garnished with parsley.

FRIED COLLARD GREENS

This dish can be served as a vegetable accompaniment, or it can be enjoyed simply on its own, with some warm crusty bread.

2 tablespoons olive oil
2 tablespoons butter
3 ounces bacon, chopped
1 large onion, thinly sliced
1 cup dry white wine
2 garlic cloves, finely chopped
2 pounds collard greens, shredded
salt and ground black pepper

SERVES 4

1 Heat the oil and butter in a large frying pan, and fry the bacon for 2 minutes. Then add the onions and fry for another 3 minutes, until the onion is beginning to soften.

2 Add the wine and simmer vigorously for 2 minutes to reduce the liquid.

3 Reduce the heat. Add the garlic, collard greens and seasoning. Cover the pan and cook over low heat for about 15 minutes, until the greens are tender. Serve hot.

COOK'S TIP
Cooking the collard greens in a covered pan helps them to retain their brilliant color.

HOT HALLOUMI WITH ROASTED BELL PEPPERS

*The best-known cheese from Cyprus is the salty, hard halloumi. Delicious served simply sliced or cubed,
it takes on a wonderful texture when broiled or fried. A tumble of roasted sweet bell peppers
makes a fine accompaniment.*

2 red bell peppers
2 green bell peppers
2 yellow bell peppers
olive oil
2 tablespoons balsamic or
red wine vinegar
small handful of raisins (optional)
11 ounces halloumi cheese,
thickly sliced
salt and ground black pepper
flat-leaf parsley, to garnish
sesame seed bread, to serve (optional)

SERVES 4

2 Pour about 2 tablespoons of olive oil over the peppers. Add the vinegar and raisins, if using, with salt and pepper to taste. Toss lightly and let the mixture cool.

3 When you are ready to serve, divide the pepper salad among four plates. Heat olive oil to a depth of about ¼ inch in a large heavy frying pan. Fry the halloumi slices over medium-high heat for 2–3 minutes, until golden, turning them halfway through cooking.

4 Drain the halloumi thoroughly on paper towels and serve with the roasted peppers, a parsley garnish and chunks of sesame seed bread, if desired.

1 Preheat the oven to 425°F. Cut all the peppers in quarters, discard the cores and seeds, then place cut side down on a nonstick baking sheet. Roast for 15–20 minutes, until the skins start to blacken and blister. Remove and cover with several layers of paper towel. Set aside for 30 minutes, then peel off the skins. Slice the flesh into a bowl. Save any roasting juices and mix these with the peppers.

MALFATTI WITH ROASTED BELL PEPPER SAUCE

The Italians use ricotta, which is a rich but light cream cheese, in sweet and savory dishes.
For this recipe, it is beaten into deliciously light spinach dumplings, called malfatti,
which are served with a smoky bell pepper and tomato sauce.

1¼ pounds young spinach
1 onion, finely chopped
1 garlic clove, crushed
1 tablespoon extra virgin olive oil
1½ cups ricotta cheese
3 eggs, beaten
½ cup natural-colored dried
bread crumbs
½ cup all-purpose flour
⅔ cup freshly grated Parmesan cheese
freshly grated nutmeg
2 tablespoons butter, melted
salt and ground black pepper

FOR THE SAUCE
2 red bell peppers,
quartered and cored
2 tablespoons extra virgin olive oil
1 onion, chopped
14-ounce can chopped tomatoes
⅔ cup water

SERVES 4

1   Make the sauce. Broil the pepper quarters, skin side up, until they blister and blacken. Cool slightly, then peel and chop. Heat the oil in a saucepan and lightly sauté the onion and peppers for 5 minutes. Add the tomatoes and water, with salt and pepper to taste. Bring to a boil, then simmer gently for 15 minutes. Purée in a food processor, return to the clean pan and set aside.

2   Trim any thick stalks from the spinach, wash well if necessary, then blanch in a pan of boiling water for about 1 minute. Drain, refresh under cold water and drain again. Squeeze dry, then chop finely.

3   Put the finely chopped onion, garlic, olive oil, ricotta, eggs and bread crumbs in a bowl. Add the spinach and mix well. Stir in the flour and 1 teaspoon of salt with half of the Parmesan, then season to taste with pepper and nutmeg.

4   Roll the mixture into 12 small logs and chill lightly.

5   Bring a large saucepan of water to a boil. Carefully drop in the malfatti in batches and cook for 5 minutes. Remove with a spatula and toss with the melted butter.

6   To serve, reheat the sauce and divide it among four plates. Arrange four malfatti on each and sprinkle on the remaining Parmesan. Serve immediately.

POTATO CAKES

—

Delicious little fried morsels of potato and Greek feta cheese, flavored with dill and lemon juice.

❦ ❦

1¼ pounds potatoes
4 ounces feta cheese
4 scallions, chopped
3 tablespoons chopped fresh dill
1 egg, beaten
1 tablespoon lemon juice
salt and ground black pepper
all-purpose flour for dredging
3 tablespoons olive oil

SERVES 4

❦ ❦

 Boil the potatoes in their skins in lightly salted water until soft. Drain, then peel while still warm. Place in a bowl and mash. Crumble the feta cheese into the potatoes and add the scallions, dill, egg and lemon juice and season with salt and pepper. (The cheese is salty, so taste before you add salt.) Stir well.

 Cover the mixture and chill until firm. Divide the mixture into walnut-size balls, then flatten them slightly. Dredge with flour. Heat the oil in a frying pan and fry the cakes until golden brown on each side. Drain on paper towels and serve immediately.

SQUASH WITH GNOCCHI

*A simple squash preparation, this dish makes an excellent accompaniment to meat,
but it is also good with a vegetarian dish, or simply served with roasted tomatoes.*

*1 small summer squash, cut into
bite-size chunks
2 ounces butter
14-ounce package gnocchi
½ garlic clove, crushed
salt and ground black pepper
chopped fresh basil, to garnish*

SERVES 4

1 Preheat the oven to 350°F.
Butter an oven-proof dish and
place the marrow in a single layer.
Dot with the butter.

2 Place a double layer of buttered
waxed paper on top. Cover with
an ovenproof plate or lid, so that it
presses the squash down, and then
place a heavy, ovenproof weight on
top of that.

3 Bake for about 15 minutes, by
which time the squash should
just be tender. Cook the gnocchi in
a large saucepan of boiling salted
water for 2–3 minutes or according
to the instructions on the package.
Drain well.

4 Stir the garlic and gnocchi into
the squash. Season and then
replace the waxed paper and bake for
another 5 minutes (the weights are not
necessary this time).

5 Just before serving, sprinkle
the mixture with a little
chopped fresh basil.

ZUCCHINI FRITTERS WITH PISTOU

These delicious fritters are a specialty of southern France. The pistou sauce provides a lovely contrast in flavor, but you could substitute other sauces, like a garlicky tomato sauce or an herb dressing.

FOR THE PISTOU
½ ounce basil leaves
4 garlic cloves, crushed
1 cup grated Parmesan cheese
finely grated zest of 1 lemon
⅔ cup olive oil

FOR THE FRITTERS
1 pound zucchini, grated
⅔ cup all-purpose flour
1 egg, separated
1 tablespoon olive oil
oil for shallow-frying
salt and ground black pepper

SERVES 4

1 To make the pistou, crush the basil leaves and garlic with a mortar and pestle to make a fairly fine paste. Transfer the paste to a bowl and stir in the grated cheese and lemon zest. Gradually blend in the oil, a little at a time, until combined, then transfer to a small serving dish.

2 To make the fritters, put the grated zucchini in a strainer over a bowl and sprinkle with plenty of salt. Let sit for 1 hour, then rinse thoroughly. Dry well on paper towels.

3 Sift the flour into a bowl and make a well in the center, then add the egg yolk and oil. Measure 5 tablespoons water and add a little to the bowl.

4 Beat the egg yolk and oil, gradually incorporating the flour and water to make a smooth batter. Season and let sit for 30 minutes.

5 Stir the zucchini into the batter. Beat the egg white until stiff, then fold into the batter.

6 Heat ½ inch of oil in a frying pan. Add spoonfuls of batter to the oil and fry for 2 minutes, until golden. Drain the fritters on paper towels and keep warm while frying the rest. Serve with the sauce.

EGGPLANT PARMIGIANA

A classic Italian dish, this features blissfully tender sliced eggplant layered with melting creamy mozzarella, fresh Parmesan and a good homemade tomato sauce.

🍃 🍃

3 medium eggplant, thinly sliced
olive oil, for brushing
11 ounces mozzarella cheese, sliced
1⅓ cups freshly grated
Parmesan cheese
2–3 tablespoons natural-colored
dried bread crumbs
basil sprigs, to garnish
salt and ground black pepper

FOR THE SAUCE
2 tablespoons olive oil
1 onion, finely chopped
2 garlic cloves, crushed
14-ounce can chopped tomatoes
1 teaspoon sugar
about 8 basil leaves

SERVES 4–6

🍃 🍃

[2] Preheat the oven to 400°F. Spread out the eggplant slices on nonstick baking sheets, brush the tops with olive oil and bake for 10–15 minutes, until softened.

[3] Make the sauce. Heat the oil in a saucepan and sauté the onion and garlic for 5 minutes. Add the canned tomatoes and sugar, with salt and pepper to taste. Bring to a boil, then lower the heat and simmer for about 10 minutes, until reduced and thickened. Tear the basil leaves into small pieces and add them to the tomato sauce.

[4] Layer the eggplant in a greased baking dish with the mozzarella, the tomato sauce and the Parmesan, ending with Parmesan mixed with bread crumbs. Bake for 20–25 minutes, until golden brown and bubbling. Let stand for 5 minutes before serving, garnished with basil.

[1] Layer the eggplant slices in a colander, sprinkling each layer with a little salt. Let the juices drain over a sink for about 20 minutes, then rinse the slices thoroughly under cold running water and pat dry with paper towels.

SPINACH WITH RAISINS AND PINE NUTS

Raisins and pine nuts are frequent partners in Spanish recipes. Here, tossed with wilted spinach and croutons, they make a delicious snack or main-dish accompaniment.

⅓ cup raisins
1 thick slice crusty white bread
3 tablespoons olive oil
⅓ cup pine nuts
1¼ pounds young spinach,
stems removed
2 garlic cloves, crushed
salt and ground black pepper

SERVES 4

[1] Put the raisins in a small bowl with boiling water and let soak for 10 minutes. Drain.

[2] Cut the bread into cubes and discard the crusts. Heat 2 tablespoons of the oil and fry the bread until golden. Drain.

[3] Heat the remaining oil in the pan. Sauté the pine nuts until beginning to color. Add the spinach and garlic and cook quickly, turning the spinach until it has just wilted.

[4] Toss in the raisins and season lightly with salt and pepper. Transfer to a warmed serving dish. Sprinkle croutons on top and serve hot.

VARIATION
Use Swiss chard or beet greens instead of the spinach, cooking them a little longer.

SPICED TURNIPS WITH SPINACH AND TOMATOES

Sweet baby turnips, tender spinach and ripe tomatoes make tempting partners in this simple eastern Mediterranean vegetable stew.

1 pound plum or other
ripe tomatoes
¼ cup olive oil
2 onions, sliced
1 pound baby turnips, peeled
1 teaspoon paprika
½ teaspoon sugar
4 tablespoons chopped cilantro
1 pound fresh young spinach,
stalks removed
salt and ground black pepper

SERVES 6

1 Plunge the tomatoes into a bowl of boiling water for 30 seconds, then refresh in a bowl of cold water. Peel away the tomato skins and chop coarsely. Heat the olive oil in a large frying pan or sauté pan and sauté the onion slices for about 5 minutes until golden.

2 Add the baby turnips, tomatoes and paprika to the pan with ¼ cup water and cook until the tomatoes are pulpy. Cover with a lid and continue cooking until the baby turnips have softened.

3 Stir in the sugar and cilantro, then add the spinach and a little salt and pepper and cook for another 2–3 minutes, until the spinach has wilted. Serve warm or cold.

TUNISIAN FAVA BEANS

Peeling the fava beans is a bit time-consuming, but well worth the effort, and this dish is so delicious that you will never want to eat fava beans any other way.

12 ounces frozen fava beans
1 tablespoon butter
4–5 scallions, sliced
1 tablespoon chopped cilantro
1 teaspoon chopped fresh mint
½–1 teaspoon ground cumin
2 teaspoons olive oil
salt

SERVES 4

1 Simmer the fava beans in water for 3–4 minutes, until tender. Drain and, when cool enough to handle, peel off the outer skin, so you are left with the bright green centers. Put these in a bowl.

2 Melt the butter in a small pan and gently fry the scallions for 2–3 minutes. Add the fava beans and then stir in the cilantro, mint, cumin and a pinch of salt. Stir in the olive oil and serve immediately.

ZUCCHINI WITH MOROCCAN SPICES

The combination of onion and garlic with chile, paprika and cumin gives the zucchini a deliciously spicy flavor.

1¼ pounds zucchini
lemon juice, chopped fresh cilantro
and parsley, to serve

FOR THE SPICY *CHARMOULA*
1 onion
1–2 garlic cloves, crushed
¼ red or green chile,
seeded and finely sliced
½ teaspoon paprika
½ teaspoon ground cumin
3 tablespoons olive oil
salt and ground black pepper

SERVES 4

1 Preheat the oven to 350°F. Cut all the zucchini into quarters lengthwise, and place in a shallow dish.

COOK'S TIP
Buy young zucchini with tender skin—older zucchini may need to be peeled.

2 Finely chop the onion and blend with the other *charmoula* ingredients and 4 tablespoons of water. Pour over the zucchini. Cover and bake for 15 minutes.

3 Baste the zucchini with the *charmoula,* and return to the oven, uncovered, for 5–10 minutes until they are tender. Sprinkle with lemon juice and herbs, and serve.

ROASTED PLUM TOMATOES AND GARLIC

———

These are so simple to prepare yet taste absolutely wonderful. Use a large, shallow earthenware dish that will allow the tomatoes to sear and char in a hot oven.

8 plum tomatoes, halved
12 garlic cloves
¼ cup extra virgin olive oil
3 bay leaves
salt and ground black pepper
3 tablespoons fresh oregano leaves,
to garnish

SERVES 4

1 Preheat the oven to 450°F. Select a shallow flameproof dish which will hold all the tomatoes snugly in a single layer. Place the tomatoes in the dish and push the whole, unpeeled garlic cloves between them.

2 Brush the tomatoes with the oil, add the bay leaves and sprinkle black pepper on top. Bake for about 45 minutes, until the tomatoes have softened and are sizzling in the pan. They should be charred around the edges. Season, garnish and serve.

TAGINE OF ONIONS

This is a typically sweet dish, much appreciated in Morocco, where cooks might even add three or four times the amount of cinnamon and twice the amount of sugar listed here. This recipe is especially good with kebabs.

1½ pounds red or Spanish onions,
finely sliced
6 tablespoons olive or sunflower oil,
or a mixture of both
pinch of saffron
½ teaspoon ground ginger
1 teaspoon ground black pepper
1 teaspoon ground cinnamon
1 tablespoon sugar

SERVES 4

3 Preheat the oven to 325°F and pour the onions and the marinade into an ovenproof dish or casserole.

4 Fold a piece of aluminum foil into thirds and place over the top of the dish, securing with a lid.

5 Cook for 45 minutes or until the onions are very soft. Increase the oven temperature to 400°F, remove the lid and foil and cook for 5–10 more minutes until the onions are lightly glazed. Serve with grilled meats or a vegetarian alternative.

1 Place the onions in a shallow dish. Spread them out evenly.

2 Mix the oil, saffron, ginger, pepper, cinnamon and sugar and pour over the onions. Stir gently to mix and then set aside for 2 hours.

OKRA WITH CORIANDER AND TOMATOES

Okra is frequently combined with tomatoes and mild spices in various parts of the Mediterranean. Buy okra only if it is soft and velvety, not dry and shriveled.

*1 pound tomatoes or 14-ounce can
chopped tomatoes
1 pound fresh okra
3 tablespoons olive oil
2 onions, thinly sliced
2 teaspoons coriander seeds, crushed
3 garlic cloves, crushed
½ teaspoon sugar
finely grated zest and juice
of 1 lemon
salt and ground black pepper*

SERVES 4

1 | If using fresh tomatoes, plunge them into boiling water for 30 seconds, then refresh in cold water. Peel off the skins and chop.

2 | Trim off any stalks from the okra and keep whole. Heat the oil in a sauté pan and sauté the onions and coriander for 3–4 minutes, until beginning to color.

3 | Add the okra and garlic and sauté for 1 minute. Gently stir in the tomatoes and sugar and simmer gently for about 20 minutes, until the okra is tender, stirring once or twice. Stir in the lemon zest and juice and add salt and pepper to taste, adding a little more sugar if necessary. Serve warm or cold.

RADICCHIO AND ENDIVE GRATIN

Salad vegetables such as radicchio and endive take on a different flavor when cooked in this way.
The creamy sauce combines wonderfully with the bitter leaves.

2 heads radicchio, quartered
lengthwise
2 heads endive, quartered lengthwise
¼ cup drained sun-dried tomatoes in
oil, roughly chopped,
plus 2 tablespoons oil from the jar
2 tablespoons butter
1 tablespoon all-purpose flour
1 cup milk
pinch of grated nutmeg
½ cup grated Emmental cheese
salt and ground black pepper
chopped fresh parsley, to garnish

SERVES 4

1 Preheat the oven to 350°F.
Grease a baking dish. Arrange
the radicchio and endive quarters in
the dish. Sprinkle on the tomatoes
and brush the leaves with oil. Season
and cover with aluminum foil. Bake
for 15 minutes, then remove the foil
and bake for another 10 minutes.

2 Make the sauce. Place the butter
in a small saucepan and melt
over medium heat. When the butter is
foaming, add the flour and cook for
1 minute, stirring. Remove from heat
and gradually add the milk, whisking.
Return to the heat and bring to a boil,
still whisking. Simmer for 2–3 minutes
to thicken. Season to taste and add
the nutmeg.

3 Pour the sauce over the
vegetables and sprinkle with
the grated Emmental. Bake for about
20 minutes, until golden. Serve
immediately, garnished with parsley.

BAKED ZUCCHINI

When very small and very fresh zucchini are used in this recipe, it is both simple and delicious.
The creamy, tangy goat cheese contrasts well with the delicate flavor of the young zucchini.

8 small zucchini, about 1 pound
total weight
1 tablespoon olive oil, plus extra
for greasing
3–4 ounces goat cheese,
cut into thin strips
small bunch of fresh mint,
finely chopped
freshly ground black pepper

SERVES 4

3 Insert pieces of goat cheese into the slits. Add a little mint and sprinkle with the remaining olive oil and the ground black pepper.

4 Wrap each zucchini in an aluminum foil rectangle, place on a baking sheet and bake for about 25 minutes, until tender.

1 Preheat the oven to 350°F. Cut out eight rectangles of aluminum foil, each large enough to encase a zucchini. Brush each rectangle with a little olive oil, on one side only.

2 Trim the zucchini. Cut a thin slit along the length of each.

COOK'S TIP
The zucchini can be unwrapped and finished under the broiler.

SPANISH POTATOES

This is an adaptation of a peppery potato dish of which there are several versions. All of them are fried and mildly spiced with the added tang of wine vinegar. Serve with cold meats or as a tapa.

1½ pounds small new potatoes
5 tablespoons olive oil
2 garlic cloves, sliced
½ teaspoon crushed dried chiles
½ teaspoon ground cumin
2 teaspoons paprika
2 tablespoons red or white
wine vinegar
1 red or green bell pepper, seeded
and sliced
coarse sea salt, to serve (optional)

SERVES 4

1 | Cook the potatoes in boiling salted water until almost tender. Drain and, if preferred, peel them. Cut into chunks.

2 | Heat the oil in a large frying or sauté pan and fry the potatoes, turning them frequently, until golden.

3 | Meanwhile, crush together the garlic, chiles and cumin using a mortar and pestle. Mix with the paprika and wine vinegar.

4 | Add the garlic mixture to the potatoes with the sliced pepper and cook, stirring, for 2 minutes. Serve warm, or let sit until cold. Sprinkle with coarse sea salt, if desired, to serve.

ROASTED POTATOES WITH RED ONIONS

These mouthwatering potatoes are a fine accompaniment to just about anything. The key is to use small,
firm potatoes. The smaller they are cut, the quicker they will cook.

1½ pounds small firm potatoes
2 tablespoons butter
2 tablespoons olive oil
2 red onions, cut into chunks
8 garlic cloves, unpeeled
2 tablespoons chopped fresh rosemary
salt and ground black pepper

SERVES 4

COOK'S TIP
Salt the potatoes a few minutes before
the end of cooking; this will help
them maintain their shape.

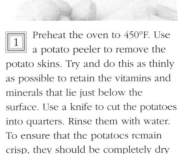

 1 Preheat the oven to 450°F. Use a potato peeler to remove the potato skins. Try and do this as thinly as possible to retain the vitamins and minerals that lie just below the surface. Use a knife to cut the potatoes into quarters. Rinse them with water. To ensure that the potatoes remain crisp, they should be completely dry before cooking. Place the butter and oil in a roasting pan and place in the oven to heat.

2 When the butter has melted and is foaming, add the potatoes, red onions, garlic and rosemary. Toss well and then spread out in one layer.

3 Place the pan in the oven and roast for about 25 minutes, until the potatoes are golden and tender when tested with a fork. Shake the pan occasionally to redistribute the potatoes. When they are cooked, season with salt and pepper.

GREEN BEANS WITH TOMATOES

This is a real summer favorite, using the best ripe plum tomatoes and green beans.

2 tablespoons olive oil
1 large onion, finely sliced
2 garlic cloves, finely chopped
6 large ripe plum tomatoes, peeled,
seeded and coarsely chopped
⅔ cup dry white wine
1 pound green beans,
sliced in half lengthwise
16 pitted black olives
2 teaspoons lemon juice
salt and ground black pepper

SERVES 4

1 Heat the oil in a deep frying pan. Add the onion and garlic and cook for about 5 minutes, until the onion is soft but not brown.

2 Add the chopped tomatoes, white wine, beans, olives and lemon juice. Cook over low heat for another 20 minutes, stirring occasionally, until the liquid is thickened and the beans are tender. Season with salt and pepper to taste and serve immediately.

SALADS

❧❧

*Summer and salads are synonymous, and
nowhere is there a wider variety of these flavorful
dishes than in the Mediterranean.*

The climate of the Mediterranean countries has ensured that salads and cold dishes have always been popular. There is an abundance of wonderful ingredients, particularly vegetables, which are combined to produce delicious results. In its simplest form, a salad in France, Spain or Italy would consist of lettuce, or perhaps a mixture of a few different salad greens, dressed with vinaigrette. A salad may be eaten after the main course, often before the cheese is served. Vinaigrette is the basic salad dressing. Originally a French classic, it is now used worldwide. As its name suggests, vinegar is a main ingredient, combined with three times its quantity of olive

RIGHT: Visiting a Turkish market is more than a mere shopping trip; it's a chance to catch up on local news.

LEFT: Some of these plump Moroccan olives will find their way into salads, but the majority will be pressed for oil.

oil, and seasoned with salt and pepper. There are many variations, using different ingredients such as lemon juice, mustard, herbs, garlic and cream; the types of oils and vinegars can be varied too. Extra virgin olive oil gives the finest flavor of all the olive oils, but a mixture of peanut oil and olive oil will produce a lighter dressing. Nut oils, such as walnut, complement salads containing nuts. The Italians favor a good red wine vinegar, but there is also the sour/sweet flavor of balsamic vinegar to consider—delicious with broiled vegetables. Spanish sherry vinegar is another good flavor to try. Herb-infused vinegars are also useful, particularly if the fresh herbs are unavailable.

There is an abundant variety of salad greens in the Mediterranean, ranging in color, taste and texture. The French favor a mixture of leaves called mesclun, which can be bought at markets by the handful. Dandelion greens are popular too, as well as frisée, Belgian endive, red leaf lettuce and many more. In Italy, radicchio and arugula are preferred, and the Spanish favor romaine lettuce. In

ABOVE: A quiet landscape near Carmona in the beautiful region of Andalusia in southern Spain.

the Middle East, however, green salads are less popular. Salads of cooked or raw vegetables, dressed with a lemony vinaigrette, are more typical of these countries. Fresh herbs also play an important part, sometimes served alone, between courses, to cleanse the palate. These basic salads are spontaneous, depending on what is available in the market, and need no recipes.

The markets of the Mediterranean offer some of the best vegetables and fruit in the world. From huge vine-ripened tomatoes to tiny artichokes, all are lovingly displayed, waiting to be picked up and dropped into a basket to be taken home. The inspiration for salads is endless. Fruit too, is included; grapes and oranges make refreshing additions to some of our recipes.

Apart from the simple salads, there are the composed salads—specific ingredients, with a special dressing, which are dishes on their own, to be eaten as a lunch dish, or perhaps an appetizer. These salads include all sorts of foods: olives, sausage, nuts, cheese, anchovies—morsels chosen for a contrast in taste, texture and color.

This chapter includes some of the classic salads of the region, including Salad Niçoise and Greek Salad, both of which are sure to transport anyone who has eaten them in their native countries straight to a little village on the coast of the Mediterranean. Some salads are substantial enough to be served as a main dish, such as Roasted Peppers with Tomatoes and Anchovies or Fava Bean, Mushroom and Chorizo Salad. Bread and a glass of wine should complete the picture!

PROVENCAL SALAD

There are probably as many versions of this salad as there are cooks in Provence. With good French bread, this regional classic makes a wonderful summer lunch or light supper.

8 ounces green beans
1 pound new potatoes, peeled and cut
into 1-inch pieces
white wine vinegar and olive oil,
for sprinkling
1 small Romaine lettuce, washed
4 ripe plum tomatoes, quartered
1 small cucumber, peeled, seeded
and diced
1 green or red bell pepper,
thinly sliced
4 hard-boiled eggs, peeled
and quartered
24 Niçoise or black olives
8-ounce can tuna, drained
2-ounce can anchovy fillets
in olive oil, drained
basil leaves, to garnish
garlic croûtons, to serve

FOR THE ANCHOVY VINAIGRETTE
¼ cup Dijon mustard
2-ounce can anchovy fillets in olive
oil, drained
1 garlic clove, crushed
¼ cup lemon juice or
white wine vinegar
½ cup sunflower oil
½ cup extra virgin olive oil
ground black pepper

SERVES 4–6

 First, make the anchovy vinaigrette. Place the mustard, anchovies and garlic in a bowl and blend together by pressing the garlic and anchovies against the sides of the bowl. Season generously with pepper.

2 Using a small whisk, blend in the lemon juice or wine vinegar. Slowly whisk in the sunflower oil in a thin stream, followed by the olive oil, whisking until the dressing is smooth and creamy.

 Drop the green beans into a large saucepan of boiling water and boil for 3 minutes, until tender, yet crisp. Transfer the beans to a colander with a slotted spoon, then rinse under cold running water. Drain again and set aside.

COOK'S TIP
To make garlic croûtons, thinly slice a loaf of French bread into 1-inch cubes. Place the bread in a single layer on a baking sheet and bake in a 350°F oven for 7–10 minutes or until golden, turning once. Rub the toast with a garlic clove and serve hot or cool.

4 Cook the potatoes in the same boiling water for 15 minutes, until just tender, then drain. Sprinkle with a little vinegar, olive oil and vinaigrette.

5 Arrange the lettuce on a platter, with the tomatoes, cucumber, pepper, beans and potatoes.

 Arrange the eggs, olives, tuna and anchovies on top and garnish with the basil leaves. Drizzle with the remaining vinaigrette and serve with garlic croûtons.

TOMATO AND FETA CHEESE SALAD

Sweet sun-ripened tomatoes are rarely more delicious than when served with feta cheese and olive oil.
This salad, popular in Greece and Turkey, is enjoyed as a light meal with pieces of crispy bread.

2 Slice the tomatoes thickly and arrange in a shallow dish.

3 Crumble the cheese over the tomatoes, sprinkle with olive oil, then strew with olives and fresh basil sprigs. Season with freshly ground black pepper and serve at room temperature.

2 pounds tomatoes
7 ounces feta cheese
½ cup olive oil, preferably Greek
12 black olives
4 fresh basil sprigs
freshly ground black pepper

SERVES 4

1 Remove the tough cores from the tomatoes with a small knife.

COOK'S TIP
Feta cheese has a strong flavor and can be quite salty. The least salty variety is imported from Greece and Turkey, and is available at specialty delicatessens and markets.

ARUGULA AND GRILLED CHEVRE SALAD

For this recipe, look for a cylinder-shaped goat cheese, or for small individual cheeses with a weight of about 2 ounces, which can be cut into halves.

about 1 tablespoon olive oil
about 1 tablespoon vegetable oil
4 slices of French bread
3 tablespoons walnut oil
1 tablespoon lemon juice
8 ounces goat cheese
generous handful of arugula leaves
about 4 ounces endive
salt and ground black pepper

FOR THE SAUCE
3 tablespoons apricot jam
¼ cup white wine
1 teaspoon Dijon mustard

SERVES 4

3 | Mix the walnut oil and lemon juice and season with a little salt and pepper.

4 | Preheat the broiler for a few minutes before serving the salad. Cut the goat cheese into 2-ounce rounds and place each piece on a French bread croûton, untoasted side up.

5 | Toss the arugula and endive in the walnut oil dressing and arrange on four individual serving plates. Place the croûtons under the broiler for 3–4 minutes, until the cheese melts. When the cheese croûtons are ready, arrange on each salad and pour on a little of the apricot sauce.

1 | Heat both the oils in a frying pan and fry the slices of French bread on one side only, until lightly golden. Drain on paper towels.

2 | To make the sauce, heat the jam in a small saucepan until warm but not boiling. Push through a sieve, into a clean pan, then stir in the wine and mustard. Heat gently and keep warm until ready to serve.

GOAT CHEESE SALAD WITH BUCKWHEAT, FRESH FIGS AND WALNUTS

The robust flavors of goat cheese and buckwheat combine especially well with ripe figs and walnuts. The olive and nut oil dressing contains no vinegar and depends instead on the acidity of the cheese. Enjoy with a gutsy red wine from the south of France.

1 cup couscous
2 tablespoons toasted buckwheat
1 hard-boiled egg
2 tablespoons chopped fresh parsley
¼ cup extra virgin olive oil
3 tablespoons walnut oil
4 ounces arugula
½ frisée lettuce
6 ounces crumbly white goat cheese
½ cup broken walnuts, toasted
4 ripe figs, trimmed and almost cut into fourths
(leave the pieces joined at the base)

SERVES 4

COOK'S TIP
Goat cheeses vary in strength from the youngest, which are soft and mild, to strongly-flavored cheeses, which have a firm and crumbly texture. The crumbly type is best suited to salads and with fruit such as figs.

1 Place the couscous and buckwheat in a bowl, cover with boiling water and let soak for 15 minutes, until softened. Place in a sieve, if necessary, to drain off any remaining water, then spread the couscous and buckwheat on a baking sheet and let cool.

2 Roll the hard-boiled egg on a hard surface to break the shell, then peel the egg. Rinse it under the tap to ensure that no pieces of shell are left on the surface. Carefully grate the egg on the finest side of a cheese grater, ensuring that it does not break up into lumps.

3 Toss the egg, parsley, couscous and buckwheat in a bowl using a spoon or a fork. Combine the two oils and use half the oil to moisten the couscous mixture.

4 Wash the arugula and lettuce leaves in water and spin to dry them. Dress with the remaining walnut and olive oils and distribute the salad between four large plates.

5 Pile the couscous in the center of the leaves, crumble on the goat cheese, sprinkle with toasted walnuts and add the figs. Arrange so that the salad looks attractive.

MOROCCAN FISH SALAD

This salad is similar to the classic Salade Niçoise and uses slightly-spiced fresh tuna or swordfish steaks, along with fava beans and green beans. Olives and hard-boiled eggs make this a very pretty salad.

about 2 pounds fresh tuna or
swordfish, sliced into ¾-inch steaks
olive oil, for brushing

FOR THE SALAD
1 pound green beans
1 pound fava beans
1 Romaine lettuce
1 pound cherry tomatoes,
halved, unless very small
2 tablespoons coarsely
chopped cilantro
3 shelled hard-boiled eggs
3 tablespoons olive oil
2–3 teaspoons lime or lemon juice
1 garlic clove, crushed
1½–2 cups pitted black olives
salt

FOR THE *CHARMOULA*
1 onion
2 garlic cloves
1 bunch fresh parsley
1 bunch cilantro
2 teaspoons paprika
3 tablespoons olive oil
2 tablespoons white wine vinegar
1 tablespoon lime or lemon juice

SERVES 6

[1] First, make the *charmoula*. Place all the ingredients in a food processor, add 3 tablespoons of water and process for 30–40 seconds, until it is all finely chopped.

[2] Prick the tuna or swordfish steaks all over with a fork, place in a shallow dish and pour over the *charmoula*, turning the fish so that each piece is well coated. Cover with plastic wrap and let sit in a cool place for 2–4 hours.

[3] To prepare the salad, cook the green beans and fava beans in boiling salted water until tender. Drain and refresh under cold water. Discard the outer shells from the fava beans and place them in a large serving bowl with the green beans.

[4] Tear the lettuce leaves into pieces. Add to the salad with the tomatoes and cilantro. Cut the eggs into eighths. Mix the olive oil with the citrus juice and garlic.

[5] Brush the steaks with the marinade together with a little olive oil and grill for 5–6 minutes on each side, until the fish is tender. Brush with marinade and more olive oil when turning the fish. Let the fish cool and then break the steaks into large pieces. Toss into the salad with the olives and dressing. Decorate with the eggs and serve.

ROASTED PEPPERS WITH TOMATOES AND ANCHOVIES

This is a Sicilian-style salad, using some typical ingredients from the Italian island. The flavor improves if the salad is made and dressed an hour or two before serving.

1 red bell pepper
1 yellow bell pepper
4 sun-dried tomatoes in oil, drained
4 ripe plum tomatoes, sliced
2 canned anchovies, drained
and chopped
1 tablespoon capers, drained
1 tablespoon pine nuts
1 garlic clove, very thinly sliced

FOR THE DRESSING
5 tablespoons extra virgin olive oil
1 tablespoon balsamic vinegar
1 teaspoon lemon juice
chopped fresh mixed herbs
salt and ground black pepper

SERVES 4

1 Cut the peppers in half and remove the seeds and stems. Cut into quarters and cook, skin side up, under a hot broiler, until the skin chars. Transfer to a bowl and cover with a plate. Let cool. Peel the peppers and cut into strips.

2 Thinly slice the sun-dried tomatoes. Arrange the peppers and fresh tomatoes on a serving dish. Sprinkle the anchovies, sun-dried tomatoes, capers, pine nuts and garlic on top.

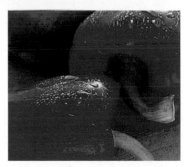

3 To make the dressing, combine the olive oil, vinegar, lemon juice and chopped herbs and season with salt and pepper. Pour over the salad just before serving.

175

SEAFOOD SALAD

—

Squid, mussels and shrimp with a simple dressing make a fresh-tasting salad.

4 ounces prepared squid rings
1 large carrot
6 crisp lettuce leaves, torn
into pieces
4-inch piece cucumber,
finely diced
12 fresh mussels, in their
shells, steamed
4 ounces cooked, peeled shrimp
1 tablespoon drained capers

FOR THE DRESSING
2 tablespoons freshly squeezed
lemon juice
3 tablespoons olive oil
1 tablespoon chopped fresh parsley
sea salt and freshly ground
black pepper

SERVES 6

1   Place the squid in a vegetable steamer or sieve and steam for 3 minutes, until the squid just turns white. Remove the steamer from the pan and cool under cold running water. Drain on paper towels.

2   Using a swivel-style vegetable peeler, cut the carrot into wafer-thin ribbons. Place the lettuce on a serving plate. Sprinkle on the carrot ribbons, followed by the finely diced cucumber.

3   Arrange the mussels, shrimp and squid rings on the salad and sprinkle the capers on top.

4   Whisk the dressing ingredients in a small bowl and drizzle on the salad. Chill before serving.

COOK'S TIP
For a change, use any type of cooked shellfish or fish in this salad—try steamed clams, shrimp in their shells or cubes of firm fish.

AVOCADO, CRAB AND CILANTRO SALAD

The sweet richness of crab combines especially well with ripe avocado, fresh cilantro and tomato.

1½ pounds small new potatoes
1 fresh mint sprig
2 pounds boiled crabs, or
10 ounces frozen crab meat, thawed
1 endive
6 ounces mache or baby spinach
1 large ripe avocado, peeled
and sliced
6 ounces cherry tomatoes
a pinch of ground nutmeg
salt and ground black pepper

FOR THE DRESSING
5 tablespoons olive oil,
preferably Tuscan
1 tablespoon lime juice
3 tablespoons chopped cilantro
½ teaspoon sugar

SERVES 4

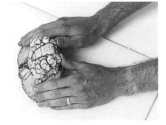

3 Turn the crab on its back and push off the rear leg section with the thumb and forefinger of each hand. Remove the flesh from inside the shell.

4 Discard the soft gills ("dead men's fingers"); the crab uses these gills to filter impurities in its diet. Apart from these and the shell, everything else is edible, both the white and dark meat.

5 Split the central body section open with a knife and remove the white and dark flesh with a toothpick or skewer.

6 Combine all the dressing ingredients in a screw-top jar and shake. Distribute the salad leaves among four plates. Top with avocado, crab, tomatoes and the warm new potatoes. Season with salt, pepper and freshly grated nutmeg, and serve.

1 Scrape or peel the potatoes. Put in a pan with water to cover, and add salt and a sprig of mint. Bring to a boil, then simmer for 20 minutes. Drain, cover and keep warm until needed.

2 Remove the legs and claws from each crab, if necessary. Crack them open with the back of a heavy knife and then remove the white meat and set it aside.

SALAD NIÇOISE

Made with good-quality ingredients, this Provençal salad makes a simple yet unbeatable summer lunch or supper dish. Serve with country-style bread and chilled white wine.

FOR THE DRESSING
6 tablespoons extra virgin olive oil
2 garlic cloves, crushed
1 tablespoon white wine vinegar
salt and ground black pepper

FOR THE SALAD
4 ounces green beans, trimmed
4 ounces mixed salad greens
½ small cucumber, thinly sliced
4 ripe tomatoes, quartered
7-ounce can tuna in oil, drained
2-ounce can anchovies, drained
4 eggs, hard-boiled
½ bunch radishes, trimmed
½ cup small black olives
flat-leaf parsley, to garnish

SERVES 4

1. To make the dressing, whisk together the oil, garlic and vinegar and season to taste with salt and pepper.

2. Halve the green beans and cook in a saucepan of boiling water for 2 minutes, until only just tender; drain.

3. Mix the salad greens, cucumber, tomatoes and green beans in a large, shallow salad bowl. Flake the tuna. Halve the anchovies lengthwise. Shell and quarter the eggs.

4. Sprinkle the radishes, tuna, anchovies, eggs and olives on the salad. Pour the dressing over and toss together lightly. Serve garnished with parsley.

COUSCOUS SALAD

Couscous salad is popular throughout the Mediterranean region. This salad has a delicate flavor and is excellent with grilled chicken or kebabs.

1⅔ cups couscous
2¼ cups boiling vegetable stock
16–20 black olives
2 small zucchini
¼ cup sliced almonds, toasted
¼ cup olive oil
1 tablespoon lemon juice
1 tablespoon chopped cilantro
1 tablespoon chopped fresh parsley
a good pinch of ground cumin
a good pinch of cayenne pepper
salt

SERVES 4

3 Carefully mix the zucchini, olives and toasted almonds into the couscous.

4 Whisk together the olive oil, lemon juice, herbs, spices and a pinch of salt. Stir into the salad.

1 Place the couscous in a bowl and pour in the boiling stock. Stir with a fork and then set aside for 10 minutes for the stock to be absorbed. Fluff up with a fork.

2 Halve the olives, discarding the pits by using the tip of a knife. Trim both the zucchini, cut them into slices along the length, then cut each slice into small strips.

FRISEE SALAD WITH BACON

This country-style salad is popular in France. When they are in season, dandelion leaves often replace the frisée, and the salad is sometimes sprinkled with chopped hard-boiled egg.

8 ounces frisée lettuce
5–6 tablespoons extra virgin
olive oil
6-ounce piece bacon, diced, or
6 thick-cut pancetta strips
cut crosswise into thin strips
2 ounces white bread, cubed
1 small garlic clove, finely chopped
1 tablespoon red wine vinegar
2 teaspoons Dijon mustard
salt and ground black pepper

SERVES 4

3 Add another 2 tablespoons of the oil to the pan and fry the cubes of bread over medium-high heat, turning frequently, until evenly browned. Remove the croûtons with a slotted spoon and drain on paper towels. Wipe the pan clean.

4 Stir the garlic, vinegar and mustard into the pan with the remaining oil and heat until just warm, whisking to combine. Season to taste, then pour the dressing over the salad and sprinkle with the bacon and croûtons.

1 Tear the lettuce into bite-size pieces and put in a salad bowl.

2 Heat 1 tablespoon of the oil in a medium nonstick frying pan over low–medium heat and add the bacon. Fry gently until well browned, stirring occasionally. Remove the bacon with a slotted spoon and drain on paper towels.

FATTOUSH

This simple peasant salad has become a popular dish all over Syria and Lebanon.

1 yellow or red bell pepper
1 large cucumber
4–5 tomatoes
1 bunch scallions
2 tablespoons finely chopped
fresh parsley
2 tablespoons finely chopped
fresh mint
2 tablespoons finely chopped cilantro
2 garlic cloves, crushed
5 tablespoons olive oil
juice of 2 lemons
salt and ground black pepper
2 pita breads

SERVES 4

VARIATION
If you prefer, make this salad in the traditional way. After toasting the pita bread until crisp, crush it in your hand and then sprinkle it on the salad before serving.

COOK'S TIP
Although the recipe calls for only 2 tablespoons of each herb, parsley, mint and cilantro, if you have plenty on hand, then you can add as much as you like to this delicious aromatic salad.

1   Slice the pepper, discarding the seeds and core, then roughly chop the cucumber and tomatoes. Place them in a large salad bowl and combine.

2   Trim and slice the scallions. Add to the cucumber, tomatoes and pepper with the finely chopped parsley, mint and cilantro.

3   To make the dressing, mix the garlic with the olive oil and lemon juice in a pitcher, then season to taste with salt and black pepper. Pour the dressing over the salad and toss lightly to mix.

4   Toast the pita bread in a toaster or under a hot broiler until crisp and then serve it alongside the salad.

TABBOULEH

—

This classic Lebanese salad makes an ideal substitute for a rice dish on a buffet table.
It is excellent served with cold sliced lamb.

🐝 🐝

1 cup fine bulghur wheat
juice of 1 lemon
3 tablespoons olive oil
1½ ounces fresh parsley,
finely chopped
3 tablespoons fresh mint, chopped
4–5 scallions, chopped
1 green bell pepper, seeded and sliced
salt and ground black pepper
2 large tomatoes, diced, and black
olives, to garnish

SERVES 4

🐝 🐝

1 Put the bulghur wheat in a bowl. Add enough cold water to cover the wheat and let it stand for at least 30 minutes and up to 2 hours.

2 Drain in a cloth and squeeze to remove excess water. Spread on paper towels to dry the bulghur wheat completely.

3 Place the bulghur wheat in a large bowl, and add the lemon juice, the oil and a little seasoning. Let stand for 1–2 hours if possible.

4 Add the chopped parsley, mint, scallions and green pepper, and mix well. Garnish with diced tomatoes and olives, and serve.

SWEET-AND-SOUR ONION SALAD

This recipe is primarily from Provence in the south of France, but there are influences from other Mediterranean countries, too.

1 pound baby onions, peeled
¼ cup wine vinegar
3 tablespoons olive oil
3 tablespoons sugar
3 tablespoons tomato paste
1 bay leaf
2 parsley sprigs
½ cup raisins
salt and ground black pepper

SERVES 6

 1 Put all the ingredients in a pan with 1¼ cups water. Bring to a boil and simmer gently, uncovered, for 45 minutes or until the onions are tender and most of the liquid has evaporated.

2 Remove the bay leaf and parsley, check the seasoning and transfer to a serving dish. Serve at room temperature.

PANZANELLA

—

In this lively Italian specialty, a sweet, tangy blend of tomato juice, rich olive oil and red wine vinegar is soaked up in a colorful salad of roasted peppers, anchovies and toasted ciabatta.

8 ounces ciabatta (about ⅔ loaf)
⅔ cup olive oil
3 red bell peppers
3 yellow bell peppers
2-ounce can anchovy fillets
1½ pounds ripe plum tomatoes
4 garlic cloves, crushed
4 tablespoons red wine vinegar
¼ cup caperberries or capers
1 cup pitted black olives
salt and ground black pepper
basil leaves, to garnish

SERVES 4–6

1 Preheat the oven to 400°F. Cut the ciabatta into ¾-inch chunks and drizzle with ¼ cup of the olive oil. Bake lightly until a pale golden color.

2 Put the peppers on a foil-lined baking sheet and bake for about 45 minutes, until the skin begins to char. Remove from the oven, cover with a cloth and let cool slightly.

3 Pull the skin off the peppers and cut them into quarters, discarding the stem ends and seeds. Drain and then coarsely chop the anchovies. Set aside.

4 To make the tomato dressing, peel and halve the tomatoes. Scoop the seeds into a strainer set over a bowl. Using the back of a spoon, press the tomato pulp in the strainer to extract as much juice as possible. Discard the pulp and add the remaining oil, the garlic and vinegar to the juices.

5 Layer the toasted bread, peppers, tomatoes, anchovies, capers and olives in a large salad bowl. Season the tomato dressing with salt and pepper and pour it over the salad. Let stand for about 30 minutes. Serve garnished with plenty of basil leaves.

RADICCHIO, ARTICHOKE AND WALNUT SALAD

—

The distinctive, earthy taste of Jerusalem artichokes makes a lovely contrast to the sharp freshness of radicchio and lemon. Serve warm or cold as an accompaniment to broiled steak or grilled meats.

1 large head radicchio or 5 ounces
radicchio leaves
6 tablespoons walnut pieces
3 tablespoons walnut oil
1¼ pounds Jerusalem artichokes
pared zest and juice of 1 lemon
coarse sea salt and ground
black pepper
flat-leaf parsley, to garnish (optional)

SERVES 4

1 If using a whole radicchio, cut it into 8–10 wedges. Put the wedges or leaves in a flameproof dish. Sprinkle the walnuts on top, then spoon on the oil and season. Broil for 2–3 minutes.

2 Peel the artichokes and cut up any large ones so the pieces are all roughly the same size. Add the artichokes to a pan of boiling salted water with half the lemon juice and cook for 5–7 minutes, until tender. Drain. Preheat the broiler to high.

3 Toss the artichokes into the salad with the remaining lemon juice and the pared zest. Season with coarse salt and pepper. Broil until beginning to brown. Serve immediately garnished with torn pieces of parsley, if desired.

GREEK SALAD

Anyone who has spent a vacation in Greece will have eaten a version of this salad—the Greek equivalent of a mixed salad. Its success relies on using the freshest of ingredients and a good olive oil.

1 small head Romaine lettuce, sliced
1 pound ripe tomatoes, cut into
eighths
1 cucumber, seeded and chopped
7 ounces feta cheese, crumbled
4 scallions, sliced
½ cup black olives, pitted
and halved

FOR THE DRESSING
6 tablespoons good olive oil
1½ tablespoons lemon juice
salt and ground black pepper

SERVES 6

1 | Put all the main salad ingredients into a large bowl. Whisk together the olive oil and lemon juice, then season with salt and pepper, and pour the dressing on the salad. Mix well and serve immediately.

SPICED EGGPLANT SALAD

Serve this Middle Eastern-influenced salad with warm pita bread as an appetizer or to accompany a main-course rice pilaf.

2 small eggplant, sliced
5 tablespoons olive oil
¼ cup red wine vinegar
2 garlic cloves, crushed
1 tablespoon lemon juice
½ teaspoon ground cumin
½ teaspoon ground cilantro
½ cucumber, thinly sliced
2 ripe tomatoes,
thinly sliced
2 tablespoons plain yogurt
salt and ground black pepper
chopped flat-leaf parsley, to garnish

SERVES 4

1 | Preheat the broiler. Brush the eggplant slices lightly with some of the oil and cook under high heat, turning once, until golden and tender. Cut into quarters.

2 | Combine the remaining oil, vinegar, garlic, lemon juice, cumin and cilantro. Season with salt and pepper and mix thoroughly. Add the warm eggplant, stir well and chill for at least 2 hours. Add the cucumber and tomatoes. Transfer to a serving dish and spoon the yogurt on top. Sprinkle with parsley.

WARM FAVA BEAN AND FETA SALAD

This recipe is loosely based on a typical medley of fresh-tasting Greek salad ingredients—fava beans, tomatoes and feta cheese. It's great warm or cold, as an appetizer or main-course accompaniment.

2 pounds fava beans, shelled, or
12 ounces shelled frozen beans
4 tablespoons olive oil
6 ounces plum tomatoes, halved, or
quartered if large
4 garlic cloves, crushed
4 ounces firm feta cheese, cut
into chunks
3 tablespoons chopped fresh dill
12 black olives
salt and ground black pepper
chopped fresh dill, to garnish

SERVES 4–6

1   Cook the fresh or frozen fava beans in boiling salted water until just tender. Drain and set aside.

2   Meanwhile, heat the oil in a heavy frying pan and add the tomatoes and garlic. Cook until the tomatoes are beginning to color.

3   Add the feta to the pan and toss the ingredients together for 1 minute. Mix with the drained beans, dill, olives and salt and pepper. Serve garnished with chopped dill.

HALLOUMI AND GRAPE SALAD

In Eastern Europe, firm, salty halloumi cheese is often served fried for breakfast or supper. Feta cheese makes a good substitute in this recipe.

FOR THE DRESSING
¼ cup olive oil
1 tablespoon lemon juice
½ teaspoon sugar
salt and ground black pepper
1 tablespoon chopped fresh thyme
or dill

FOR THE SALAD
5 ounces mixed salad greens
3 ounces seedless green grapes
3 ounces seedless red grapes
9 ounces halloumi cheese
3 tablespoons olive oil
thyme leaves or dill, to garnish

SERVES 4

1   To make the dressing, combine the olive oil, lemon juice and sugar. Season. Stir in the thyme or dill and set aside.

2   Toss together the salad greens and the green and red grapes, then transfer to a large serving plate.

3   Thinly slice the cheese. Heat the oil in a large frying pan. Add the cheese and sauté briefly until turning golden on the underside. Turn the cheese with a spatula and cook the other side.

4   Arrange the cheese on the salad. Pour on the dressing and garnish with thyme or dill.

TURKISH SALAD

This classic salad is a wonderful combination of textures and flavors. The saltiness of the cheese is perfectly balanced by the refreshing salad vegetables.

1 Romaine lettuce heart
1 green and 1 red bell pepper
½ cucumber
4 tomatoes
1 red onion
8 ounces feta cheese, crumbled
black olives, to garnish

FOR THE DRESSING
3 tablespoons olive oil
3 tablespoons lemon juice
1 garlic clove, crushed
1 tablespoon chopped fresh parsley
1 tablespoon chopped fresh mint
salt and ground black pepper

SERVES 4

1 Chop the lettuce into bite-size pieces. Seed the peppers, remove the cores and cut the flesh into thin strips. Chop the cucumber and slice or chop the tomatoes. Cut the onion in half, then slice finely. Place the chopped lettuce, peppers, cucumber, tomatoes and onion in a large bowl. Sprinkle the feta on top and toss lightly.

2 To make the dressing, whisk together the olive oil, lemon juice and garlic in a small bowl. Stir in the parsley and mint. Season with salt and pepper to taste.

3 Pour the dressing over the salad, toss lightly and serve immediately, garnished with a handful of black olives.

PERSIAN SALAD

This simple salad works very well with baked Italian dishes—don't add the dressing until just before you are ready to serve.

4 tomatoes
½ cucumber
1 onion
1 Romaine lettuce heart

FOR THE DRESSING
2 tablespoons olive oil
juice of 1 lemon
1 garlic clove, crushed
salt and ground black pepper

SERVES 4

1 Cut the tomatoes and cucumber into small cubes. Finely chop the onion and tear the lettuce into pieces. Place the cubed tomatoes, cucumber, onion and lettuce in a large salad bowl and combine.

2 To make the dressing, pour the olive oil into a small bowl. Add the lemon juice, garlic and seasoning and whisk together well. Pour over the salad and toss lightly to mix. Sprinkle with black pepper and serve with meat or rice dishes.

FAVA BEAN, MUSHROOM AND CHORIZO SALAD

Fava beans are used in both their fresh and dried forms in various Mediterranean countries. This Spanish salad could be served as either a first course or a lunch dish.

8 ounces shelled fava beans
6 ounces chorizo sausage
4 tablespoons extra virgin olive oil
8 ounces cremini
mushrooms, sliced
handful of fresh chives
salt and ground black pepper

SERVES 4

1 Cook the fava beans in boiling salted water for about 8 minutes. Drain and refresh under cold water.

2 Remove the skin from the sausage and cut it into small chunks. Heat the oil in a frying pan, add the chorizo and cook for 2–3 minutes. Pour the chorizo and oil into the mushrooms and mix well. Let cool. Chop half the chives. If the beans are large, peel off the tough outer skins. Stir the beans and snipped chives into the mushroom mixture and season to taste. Serve at room temperature, garnished with the remaining chives.

AVOCADO, ORANGE AND ALMOND SALAD

The Mediterranean is not particularly known for its avocados, but the climate is perfect for them and they are grown in many parts of the region. This salad has a Spanish influence.

2 oranges
2 ripe tomatoes
2 small avocados
¼ cup extra virgin olive oil
2 tablespoons lemon juice
1 tablespoon chopped fresh parsley
1 small onion, sliced into rings
salt and ground black pepper
¼ cup sliced almonds and
10–12 black olives, to garnish

SERVES 4

1 Peel the oranges and cut into thick slices. Plunge the tomatoes into boiling water for 30 seconds, then refresh in cold water. Peel off the skins, cut into quarters, remove the seeds and chop coarsely.

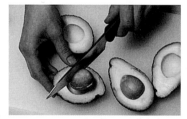

2 Cut the avocados in half, remove the pits and carefully peel off the skin. Cut into chunks.

3 Combine the olive oil, lemon juice and parsley. Season with salt and pepper. Toss the avocados and tomatoes in half of the dressing.

4 Arrange the sliced oranges on a plate and scatter the onion rings over them. Drizzle with the rest of the dressing. Spoon the avocados, tomatoes, almonds and olives on top.

TRICOLORE SALAD

A popular salad, this dish depends for its success on the quality of its ingredients. Mozzarella di bufala is the best cheese to serve uncooked. Whole ripe plum tomatoes release their juices to blend with extra virgin olive oil for a natural dressing.

5 ounces mozzarella di bufala cheese, thinly sliced
4 large plum tomatoes, sliced
sea salt flakes, to season
1 large avocado
about 12 basil leaves or a small handful of flat-leaf parsley leaves
3–4 tablespoons extra virgin olive oil
freshly ground black pepper

SERVES 2

1 Arrange the sliced cheese and tomatoes randomly on two salad plates. Sprinkle on a few good pinches of sea salt flakes. This will help draw out some of the juices from the tomatoes. Set aside in a cool place to marinate for 30 minutes.

2 Just before serving, cut the avocado in half using a large sharp knife and twist to separate. Lift out the pit and remove the peel.

3 Slice the avocado flesh crosswise into half-moons, or cut it into large chunks or cubes if that is easier.

4 Place the avocado on the salad, then sprinkle with the basil or parsley. Drizzle on the olive oil, add a little more salt, if desired, and some black pepper. Serve the salad at room temperature, with chunks of crusty Italian ciabatta.

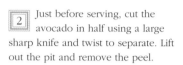

VARIATION
A light sprinkling of balsamic vinegar added just before serving would give this salad a refreshing tang, while a few thinly sliced red onion rings would add extra color and flavor.

SPANISH ASPARAGUS AND ORANGE SALAD

Complicated salad dressings are rarely found in Spain—they simply rely on the wonderful flavor of a good-quality olive oil.

8 ounces asparagus, trimmed and cut
into 2-inch pieces
2 large oranges
2 ripe tomatoes, cut
into eighths
2 ounces Romaine lettuce
leaves, shredded
2 tablespoons extra virgin olive oil
½ teaspoon sherry vinegar
salt and ground black pepper

SERVES 4

COOK'S TIP
Bibb lettuce can be used in place of romaine.

1 Cook the asparagus in boiling, salted water for 3–4 minutes, until just tender. Drain and refresh under cold water.

2 Grate the zest from half an orange and reserve. Peel all the oranges and cut into segments. Squeeze out the juice from the membrane and reserve the juice.

3 Put the asparagus, orange segments, tomatoes and lettuce into a salad bowl. Combine the oil and vinegar and add 1 tablespoon of the reserved orange juice and 1 teaspoon of the zest *(left)*. Season with salt and pepper. Just before serving, pour the dressing over the salad and mix gently to coat.

GLOBE ARTICHOKES WITH GREEN BEANS AND AIOLI

Just like the French aïoli, there are many recipes for the Spanish equivalent. This one is exceptionally garlicky, a perfect partner to freshly cooked vegetables.

FOR THE AIOLI
6 large garlic cloves, sliced
2 teaspoons white wine vinegar
1 cup olive oil
salt and ground black pepper

FOR THE SALAD
8 ounces green beans
3 small globe artichokes
1 tablespoon olive oil
pared zest of 1 lemon
coarse salt for sprinkling
lemon wedges, to garnish

SERVES 4–6

1 To make the aïoli, put the garlic and vinegar in a blender or mini food processor. With the machine switched on, gradually pour in the olive oil until the mixture is thickened and smooth. (Alternatively, crush the garlic to a paste with the vinegar and gradually beat in the oil using a hand whisk.) Season with salt and pepper to taste.

2 To make the salad, cook the beans in boiling water for 1–2 minutes, until slightly softened. Drain.

3 Trim the artichoke stems close to the base. Cook the artichokes in a large pan of salted water for about 30 minutes or until you can easily pull away a leaf from the base. Drain well.

4 Using a sharp knife, halve the artichokes lengthwise and ease out the choke using a teaspoon.

5 Arrange the artichokes and beans on serving plates and drizzle with the oil. Sprinkle on the lemon zest and season with coarse salt and a little pepper. Spoon the aïoli into the artichoke hearts and serve warm, garnished with lemon wedges. To eat artichokes, pull the leaves from the base one at a time and use to scoop a little of the sauce. It is only the fleshy end of each leaf that is eaten, as well as the base or heart of the artichoke.

COOK'S TIP
Mediterranean baby artichokes are sometimes available and are perfect for this kind of salad, as unlike the larger ones, they can be eaten whole. Cook them until just tender, then cut in half to serve.
Canned artichoke hearts, thoroughly drained and sliced, can be substituted when fresh ones are not available.

MOROCCAN COOKED SALAD

A version of a North African favorite, this cooked salad is served as a side dish with a main course.
Make this one the day before serving to improve the flavor.

2 ripe tomatoes, quartered
2 onions, chopped
½ cucumber, halved lengthwise,
seeded and sliced
1 green bell pepper, halved, seeded
and chopped
2 tablespoons lemon juice
3 tablespoons olive oil
2 garlic cloves, crushed
2 tablespoons chopped cilantro
salt and ground black pepper
sprigs of cilantro, to garnish

SERVES 4

1 Put the tomatoes, onions, cucumber and green pepper into a pan, add ¼ cup water and simmer for 5 minutes. Let cool.

2 Combine the lemon juice, olive oil and garlic. Strain the vegetables, then transfer to a bowl. Pour the dressing over them, season with salt and pepper and stir in the chopped cilantro. Serve immediately, garnished with cilantro sprigs.

SCHLADA

Though Schlada is a salad, it is actually the Moroccan cousin of the Spanish soup Gazpacho.
In addition to the usual ingredients, Schlada contains ground cumin
and spicy paprika.

3 green bell peppers, quartered
4 large tomatoes
2 garlic cloves, finely chopped
2 tablespoons olive oil
2 tablespoons lemon juice
good pinch of paprika
pinch of ground cumin
¼ preserved lemon
salt and ground black pepper
cilantro and fresh flat-leaf parsley,
to garnish

SERVES 4

1 Grill the peppers, skin side up, until the skins are blackened, place in a plastic bag and tie the ends. Let sit for about 10 minutes, until the peppers are cool enough to handle, then peel off the skins.

2 Cut the peppers into small pieces, discarding the seeds and core, and place in a serving dish.

3 Peel the tomatoes by placing in boiling water for 1 minute, then plunging into cold water. Peel off the skins, then quarter the tomatoes, discarding the core and seeds. Chop roughly and add to the peppers. Sprinkle the garlic on top and chill for 1 hour.

4 Blend together the olive oil, lemon juice, paprika and cumin and pour over the salad. Season with salt and pepper.

5 Rinse the preserved lemon in cold water and remove the flesh and pith. Cut the peel into slivers and sprinkle over the salad. Garnish with cilantro and flat-leaf parsley.

CACIK

This refreshing yogurt dish is served all over the eastern Mediterranean, whether as part of a mezze with marinated olives and pita bread or as an accompaniment to meat dishes. Greek tzatziki is very similar.

1 small cucumber
1¼ cups thick plain yogurt
3 garlic cloves, crushed
2 tablespoons chopped fresh mint
2 tablespoons chopped fresh dill
or parsley
salt and ground black pepper
mint or parsley and dill, to garnish
olive oil, olives and pita bread,
to serve

SERVES 6

1. Finely chop the cucumber and layer in a colander with plenty of salt. Let sit for 30 minutes. Wash the cucumber in several changes of cold water and drain thoroughly. Pat dry on paper towels.

2. Combine the yogurt, garlic and herbs and season with salt and pepper. Stir in the cucumber. Garnish with herbs, drizzle on a little olive oil and serve with olives and pita bread.

GARDEN SALAD

—

This wonderful salad, which looks just as good as it tastes, is just the thing to eat on a hot sunny day.

1 Romaine lettuce
6 ounces arugula
1 small frisée lettuce
fresh chervil and tarragon sprigs
1 tablespoon snipped fresh chives
handful of mixed edible flower heads,
such as nasturtiums or marigolds

FOR THE DRESSING
3 tablespoons olive oil
1 tablespoon white wine vinegar
½ teaspoon French mustard
1 garlic clove, crushed
a pinch of sugar

SERVES 4

 Combine Romaine, arugula and frisée leaves and herbs.

—

COOK'S TIP
You can use any fresh, edible flowers from your garden in this beautiful, light salad.

2 Make the dressing by whisking all the ingredients together in a large bowl. Toss the salad leaves in the bowl with the dressing, sprinkle on the flower heads decoratively and serve immediately. If you prefer, use only half the dressing initially, and serve the rest separately, in a small pitcher.

Spinach and Roasted Garlic Salad

Don't worry about the amount of garlic in this salad. During roasting, the garlic becomes sweet and subtle and loses its pungent taste.

12 garlic cloves, unpeeled
4 tablespoons extra virgin olive oil
1 pound baby spinach leaves
½ cup pine nuts,
lightly toasted
juice of ½ lemon
salt and ground black pepper

SERVES 4

1 Preheat the oven to 375°F. Place the garlic in a small roasting dish, toss in about 2 tablespoons of the olive oil and bake for about 15 minutes, until the garlic cloves are slightly charred around the edges and have softened.

2 While still warm, put the garlic into a salad bowl. Add the spinach, pine nuts, lemon juice, remaining olive oil and seasoning. Toss well. Serve immediately, inviting guests to squeeze the garlic purée out of the skins to eat.

MOROCCAN DATE, ORANGE AND CARROT SALAD

A colorful and unusual salad with exotic ingredients—fresh dates and orange-flower water—combined with crisp greens, carrots, oranges and toasted almonds.

1 head Bibb lettuce
2 carrots, finely grated
2 oranges
4 ounces fresh dates, pitted and cut
into eighths lengthwise
¼ cup toasted whole
almonds, chopped
2 tablespoons lemon juice
1 teaspoon sugar
¼ teaspoon salt
1 tablespoon orange-flower water

SERVES 4

1. Separate the lettuce leaves and arrange them in the bottom of a salad bowl or on individual serving plates. Place the grated carrot in a mound on top.

2. Peel and segment the oranges and arrange them around the carrot. Pile the dates on top, then sprinkle with the almonds. Combine the lemon juice, sugar, salt and orange-flower water and sprinkle on the salad. Serve chilled.

BLACK AND ORANGE SALAD

———

This dramatic salad is typically north African and contrasts both colors and flavors—the dark black olives with the brightly-fleshed oranges, and the juxtaposition of tastes, sweet and savory. A striking and refreshing salad suitable for any dinner party.

3 oranges
1 cup pitted black olives
1 tablespoon chopped cilantro
1 tablespoon chopped fresh parsley
2 tablespoons olive oil
1 tablespoon lemon juice
½ teaspoon paprika
½ teaspoon ground cumin

SERVES 4

1 Using a knife, cut off the peel and white pith from the oranges, then cut the flesh into thick wedges.

2 Place the oranges in a salad bowl and add the black olives, cilantro and parsley.

3 Whisk together the olive oil, lemon juice, paprika and cumin until it is of one consistency. Pour the dressing over the salad and toss gently. Rearrange the ingredients attractively. Chill for about 30 minutes and serve.

ARUGULA AND CILANTRO SALAD

———

Arugula leaves have a wonderful, peppery flavor and, mixed with cilantro, make a favorite salad. However, unless you grow your own arugula, or have a plentiful supply, you may well have to use extra spinach or another green leaf in order to pad this salad out.

4 ounces or more arugula leaves
4 ounces young spinach leaves
1 large bunch
(about 1 ounce) cilantro
2–3 fresh parsley sprigs
1 garlic clove, crushed
3 tablespoons olive oil
2 teaspoons white wine vinegar,
or herb vinegar
pinch of paprika
salt
cayenne pepper

SERVES 4

1 Wash the arugula and spinach leaves, ensuring that all the grit is washed off, and place in a large salad bowl. Chop the cilantro and parsley and add to the rest of the salad, mixing the different leaves together thoroughly.

2 In a small pitcher, blend together the garlic, olive oil, vinegar, paprika, salt and cayenne pepper.

3 Pour the dressing over the salad, coating all the leaves, and serve immediately.

FISH AND SHELLFISH

*Mediterranean fishermen reap a rich harvest of
fish and shellfish, which are often simply broiled
or fried, or used as the basis of a soup or stew.*

The Mediterranean Sea is tiny in relation to the world's larger seas and oceans. It is also relatively shallow, warm, low in natural food supplies and more polluted. Despite all these factors, the Mediterranean has hundreds of different species of fish and crustacea, marketed in the Mediterranean and beyond. Visit a large fish market in any part of the region and you will be amazed by the fantastic variety of fish, many of which are completely unknown except to the locals and, of course, the fishermen themselves.

ABOVE: *Fishermen in Crete bring home the day's catch, packed in salt.*

LEFT: *Safely back in harbor, a Cretan fishing boat bobs gently on the calm sea.*

A visit to a Mediterranean restaurant, bar or taverna illustrates how this freshly caught fish, cooked simply, can be quite unbeatable. Few of us ever forget the arrival of a hot, steaming bowl of garlicky mussels or crisp shrimp dripping in garlic and olive oil. Perfectly fresh fish, broiled or grilled with a basting of olive oil, garlic and herbs, needs little more embellishment, except perhaps a crisp salad and a light wine.

On a more elaborate scale, fish stews and soups are typically Mediterranean. A varied mixture of fish such as conger eel, gurnard, John Dory, monkfish, bass, bream and red mullet is combined with aromatic flavorings like saffron, herbs, garlic and orange peel and cooked in an intensely flavored fish stock made from fish trimmings. The bourride of France and the brodetto of Italy are classic examples but similar variations can be found all over the Mediterranean.

Small, oily fish thrive in the Mediterranean, and the

ABOVE: A Moroccan cook patiently prepares the family meal of fish kebabs.

freshly broiled or grilled sardines prepared in cafés and tavernas around the region cannot be rivaled anywhere else in the world. Sardines and large anchovies are sometimes stuffed with a slightly tangy mixture of ingredients, such as capers, olives, pine nuts, lemons and dried fruit, that provides a perfect contrast to the rich oiliness of the fish itself. Other interesting preparations are the short-term preserving of fried sardines in olive oil and vinegar or the delicious combination of sardines with fresh herbs and spaghetti or macaroni.

The technique of frying fish in a light batter is typical of the Mediterranean. Fritto Misto is an Italian version in which a medley of seafood, such as mussels, squid, red mullet, shrimp and whitebait, is coated in a light crisp batter and deep-fried. When served piping hot, this is

delicious as a light snack or appetizer with a sprinkling of gremolata (a blend of garlic, parsley and lemon zest), or simply squeezed with lemon. The Spanish also love fried fish and use much the same technique, sometimes simply dredging the fish with seasoned flour before frying in light olive oil.

Taking into consideration the availability of so much fresh produce, it is surprising that salt cod is so well loved in various parts of the Mediterranean; the kite-shaped, leathery pieces are a common sight in many market-places. The Spanish and Portuguese fished for cod in the Atlantic, salted it and sun-dried it at sea as a means of preservation. These familiar stiff, yellow-tinged boards of fish, which once were associated with the frugal eating of Lent, are now a highly esteemed luxury. Perhaps the most famous dish is the brandade of France, a smooth purée of salt cod flavored with garlic and olive oil.

On the eastern side of the Mediterranean the types of fish available are much the same, although the cooking methods vary. Baking fish whole is the most widespread practice, often on a bed of tomatoes, lemons, onions and herbs, and sometimes with slightly sweet and spicy flavorings such as raisins and cinnamon. The Greek plaki is a well-loved example, perfect for fish such as gray mullet, sea bream and bass, which absorb all the wonderful flavors of the accompanying ingredients. Middle Eastern and North African fish dishes emphasize the accompanying sauce—the choice of fish being the pick of the catch. A simple blend of tahini with olive oil and lemon juice is very traditional.

Squid and octopus both play an important role in Mediterranean cooking. Squid, from the tiniest, which are lovely seared in olive oil with garlic and herbs, to huge specimens, rich with stuffings, typify Mediterranean cooking techniques. Octopus, too, is highly esteemed, particularly in the eastern Mediterranean, where it is frequently stewed with red wine or used in salads.

BAKED FISH WITH TAHINI SAUCE

This North African recipe evokes all the color and rich flavors of Mediterranean cuisine. Choose any whole white fish, such as sea bass, hake, bream or snapper.

1 whole fish, about 2½ pounds, scaled
and cleaned
2 teaspoons coriander seeds
4 garlic cloves, sliced
2 teaspoons harissa
6 tablespoons olive oil
6 plum tomatoes, sliced
1 mild onion, sliced
3 preserved lemons or 1 fresh lemon
plenty of fresh herbs, such as bay
leaves, thyme and rosemary
salt and ground black pepper

FOR THE SAUCE
⅓ cup light tahini
juice of 1 lemon
1 garlic clove, crushed
3 tablespoons finely chopped fresh
parsley or cilantro
extra herbs, to garnish

SERVES 4

1 Preheat the oven to 400°F. Grease the bottom and sides of a large, shallow ovenproof dish or roasting pan.

2 Slash the fish diagonally on both sides with a sharp knife. Finely crush the coriander seeds and garlic with a mortar and pestle. Mix with the harissa and about 4 tablespoons of the olive oil.

3 Spread a little of the harissa, coriander and garlic paste inside the cavity of the fish. Spread the remainder over each side of the fish and set aside.

4 Scatter the tomatoes, onion and preserved or fresh lemon into the dish. (Thinly slice the lemon if using fresh.) Sprinkle with the remaining oil and season with salt and pepper. Lay the fish on top and tuck plenty of herbs around it.

5 Bake, uncovered, for about 25 minutes or until the fish has turned opaque—test by piercing the thickest part with a knife.

6 Meanwhile, make the sauce. Put the tahini, lemon juice, garlic and parsley or cilantro in a small saucepan with ½ cup water and add a little salt and pepper. Cook gently until smooth and heated through. Serve in a separate dish.

COOK'S TIP
If you can't get a suitable large fish, use small whole fish such as red snapper or even cod or haddock steaks. Remember to reduce the cooking time slightly.

SEA BASS WITH AN ALMOND CRUST

This is a surprising—and quite delicious—way to cook fish. The almond crust is almost cookie-like, and its sweetness complements the flavor of the sea bass, as well as keeping the fish deliciously moist and succulent. Lime wedges are the perfect garnish.

4   Preheat the oven to 375°F. Grease a shallow ovenproof dish, large enough to hold the whole fish, using about 1 tablespoon of the butter. Sprinkle the sliced onion in the dish. Dissolve the saffron threads in 1 tablespoon of boiling water and add to the dish with some salt and pepper.

5   Stuff the fish with half of the almond mixture and place it on top of the onion. Using a spatula, spread the remaining almond paste evenly on top of the fish.

6   Melt the remaining butter, pour over the fish and then bake, uncovered, for about 45–50 minutes (35–40 minutes if you are cooking 2 smaller fish), until the fish flakes easily and the almond topping is crusty.

7   Transfer the fish to a warmed serving plate and arrange the onion slices around the edge. Garnish with lime wedges and flat-leaf parsley, and serve immediately.

1 large or 2 small sea bass, about
3–3½ pounds total weight, cleaned
and scaled, with head and tail left on
1 tablespoon sunflower oil
1½ cups blanched almonds
about ⅓ cup butter, softened
½–1 teaspoon ground cinnamon
¼ cup confectioners' sugar
1 onion, finely sliced
a good pinch of saffron strands
salt and ground black pepper
lime wedges and sprigs of fresh
flat-leaf parsley, to garnish

SERVES 4

1   Rinse the fish in cold running water and pat dry.

2   Heat the oil in a small frying pan and fry the almonds for 2–3 minutes over brisk heat, until golden, stirring frequently. Drain on paper towels until cool and then grind in a spice or coffee mill.

3   Pour the ground almonds into the bowl of a food processor and blend with 2 tablespoons of the butter, the ground cinnamon, confectioners' sugar and ¼ cup water to make a smooth paste.

GRILLED SEA BASS WITH FENNEL

This dish is served in almost every seafood restaurant on the French Mediterranean coast.
Traditionally, fennel twigs are used, but as they are hard to find, this recipe uses fennel seeds.

1 sea bass, weighing
4–4½ pounds, cleaned
4–6 tablespoons olive oil
2–3 teaspoons fennel seeds
2 large fennel bulbs, trimmed and
thinly sliced (reserve any fronds)
¼ cup Pernod
salt and ground black pepper

SERVES 6–8

1 With a sharp knife, make three
or four deep cuts in both sides
of the fish. Brush the fish with olive
oil and season with salt and pepper.
Sprinkle the fennel seeds in the
stomach cavity and in the cuts. Set
aside while you cook the fennel.

2 Preheat the broiler. Put the slices
of fennel in an ovenproof dish
or on the broiler rack and brush with
oil. Broil for 4 minutes on each side,
until tender. Transfer to a large platter.

3 Place the fish on the oiled
broiler rack and position
4–5 inches away from the heat.
Cook for 10–12 minutes on each side,
brushing with oil occasionally.

4 Transfer the fish to the platter
on top of the fennel. Garnish
with fennel fronds. Heat the Pernod in
a small pan, light it and pour it, flaming,
over the fish. Serve immediately.

PANFRIED RED MULLET WITH BASIL AND CITRUS

Red mullet is popular all over the Mediterranean. This Italian recipe combines it with oranges and lemons, which grow in abundance there.

4 red mullet (or snapper), about 8
ounces each, filleted
6 tablespoons olive oil
10 peppercorns, crushed
2 oranges, one peeled and sliced and
one squeezed
1 lemon
2 tablespoons all-purpose flour
1 tablespoon butter
2 drained canned anchovies, chopped
4 tablespoons shredded fresh basil
salt and ground black pepper

SERVES 4

1. Place the fish fillets in a shallow dish in a single layer. Pour the olive oil over them and sprinkle with the crushed peppercorns. Lay the orange slices on top of the fish. Cover the dish and let marinate in the refrigerator for at least 4 hours.

2. Halve the lemon. Remove the zest and pith from one half using a small sharp knife and slice thinly. Squeeze the juice from the other half.

COOK'S TIP
If you prefer, use other fish fillets for this dish, such as red snapper, lemon sole, haddock or hake.

3. Lift the fish out of the marinade and pat dry on paper towels. Reserve the marinade and orange slices. Season the fish with salt and pepper and dust lightly with flour.

4. Heat 3 tablespoons of the marinade in a frying pan. Add the fish and fry for 2 minutes on each side. Remove from the pan and keep warm. Discard the marinade that is left in the pan.

5. Melt the butter in the pan with any of the remaining original marinade. Add the anchovies and cook until completely softened.

6. Stir in the orange and lemon juice, then check the seasoning and simmer until slightly reduced. Stir in the basil. Pour the sauce on the fish and garnish with the reserved orange slices and the lemon slices.

BAKED FISH WITH NUTS

This specialty comes from Egypt and is as delicious as it is unusual.
Make sure you use good-quality hazelnuts and pine nuts.

3 tablespoons oil
4 small red mullet
1 large onion, finely chopped
¾ cup hazelnuts, chopped
¾ cup pine nuts
3–4 tomatoes, sliced
3–4 tablespoons finely chopped
fresh parsley
1 cup fish stock
salt and ground black pepper
sprigs of parsley, to garnish
new potatoes or rice, and vegetables or
salad, to serve

SERVES 4

2 Heat the remaining oil in a large pan or flameproof casserole and fry the finely chopped onion for 3–4 minutes, until golden. Add the chopped hazelnuts and pine nuts, and stir-fry for a few minutes.

3 Stir in the tomatoes, cook for a few minutes and then add the parsley, stock and seasoning. Simmer for 10–15 minutes, stirring occasionally.

4 Place the fish in an ovenproof dish and spoon on the sauce. Bake for 20 minutes or until the fish is cooked through and flakes easily when pierced with a fork.

5 Serve the fish immediately, garnished with parsley and accompanied by new potatoes or rice, and vegetables or salad.

1 Preheat the oven to 375°F. Heat about 2 tablespoons of the oil in a frying pan and fry the fish, two at a time, until crisp on both sides.

VARIATION
Other small whole fish, such as trout, can be used for this recipe if snapper is unavailable.

MONKFISH DUMPLINGS

Delicate dumplings, with a fish filling, make an elaborate light lunch dish.

1½ cups all-purpose flour,
plus extra for rolling
2 eggs
4 ounces skinless
monkfish fillet, diced
grated zest of 1 lemon
1 garlic clove, chopped
1 small red chile, seeded and sliced
3 tablespoons chopped fresh parsley
2 tablespoons light cream

FOR THE TOMATO OIL
2 tomatoes, peeled, seeded and
finely diced
3 tablespoons extra virgin olive oil
1 tablespoon fresh lemon juice
salt and ground black pepper

SERVES 4

1 Place the flour, eggs and ½ teaspoon of salt in a food processor, pulse until the mixture forms a soft dough. Knead briefly, then wrap in plastic wrap and chill.

2 Process the fish, lemon zest, garlic, chile and parsley until very fine. Add the cream, season and pulse into a thick purée.

3 Make the tomato oil by stirring the diced tomatoes with the olive oil and lemon juice in a bowl. Add salt to taste. Cover and chill.

4 Roll out the dough on a lightly floured surface and cut out 32 rounds with a 1½-inch plain cutter. Divide the monkfish filling among half the rounds, then cover with the remaining rounds. Pinch the edges tightly to seal, trying to exclude as much as air as possible.

5 Bring a large saucepan of water to the simmering point and poach the dumplings, in batches, for about 3 minutes or until they rise to the surface. Drain and serve hot, drizzled with the tomato oil.

STUFFED SWORDFISH ROLLS

This is a very tasty dish, with strong flavors from the tomato, olive and caper sauce—and from the salty Pecorino cheese. If desired, substitute Parmesan cheese, which is milder.

2 tablespoons olive oil
1 small onion, finely chopped
1 celery stalk, finely chopped
1 pound ripe Italian plum
tomatoes, chopped
1 cup pitted green olives, half
chopped, half left whole
3 tablespoons drained bottled capers
4 swordfish steaks, each ¹/₂-inch thick
and 4 ounces in weight
1 egg
²/₃ cup grated Pecorino cheese
¹/₂ cup fresh white bread crumbs
salt and ground black pepper
sprigs of fresh parsley, to garnish

SERVES 4

1 Heat the oil in a large heavy frying pan. Add the onion and celery and cook gently for about 3 minutes, stirring frequently. Stir in the tomatoes, olives and capers, with salt and pepper to taste. Bring to a boil, then lower the heat, cover and simmer for 15 minutes. Stir the sauce occasionally.

2 Remove the fish skin and place each steak between two sheets of plastic wrap. Pound lightly with a rolling pin until each steak is reduced to about ¹/₄-inch thick.

3 Beat the egg in a bowl and add the cheese, bread crumbs and a few spoonfuls of the sauce. Stir well to make a moist stuffing. Spread one-quarter of the stuffing over each swordfish steak, then roll up.

4 Secure the rolls with toothpicks, add them to the sauce and bring to a boil. Lower the heat, cover and simmer for about 30 minutes, turning once. Add a little water as the sauce reduces.

5 Remove the rolls from the sauce and discard the toothpicks. Place on warmed dinner plates and spoon the sauce over and around. Garnish with the parsley and serve.

FISH BOULETTES IN HOT TOMATO SAUCE

This is an unusual dish that needs scarcely any preparation and produces very little mess, as it is all cooked in one pan. It serves four people as a main course, but also makes a great appetizer for eight.

1½ pounds cod, haddock or
white fish fillets
pinch of saffron strands
½ bunch fresh flat-leaf parsley
1 egg
½ cup white bread crumbs
1½ tablespoons olive oil
1 tablespoon lemon juice
salt and ground black pepper
fresh flat-leaf parsley and lemon
wedges, to garnish

FOR THE SAUCE
1 onion, very finely chopped
2 garlic cloves, crushed
6 tomatoes, peeled, seeded
and chopped
1 green or red chile, seeded and
finely sliced
6 tablespoons olive oil
⅔ cup water
1 tablespoon lemon juice

SERVES 4

1 Skin the fish and, if necessary, remove any bones. Cut the fish into large chunks and place in a blender or a food processor.

2 Soak the saffron in 2 tablespoons boiling water for a few minutes and pour into the blender or food processor with the parsley, egg, bread crumbs, olive oil and lemon juice. Season well and process for 10–20 seconds, until the fish is finely chopped and the ingredients are mixed.

3 Mold the mixture into small balls about the size of walnuts. Put them in a single layer on a plate.

4 To make the sauce, place the onion, garlic, tomatoes, chile, olive oil and water in a saucepan. Bring to a boil and then simmer, partially covered, for 10–15 minutes, until the sauce is slightly reduced.

5 Add the lemon juice and then place the fish balls in the simmering sauce. Cover and simmer very gently for 12–15 minutes, until the fish boulettes are cooked through, turning them over occasionally.

6 Serve the boulettes and sauce immediately, garnished with flat-leaf parsley and lemon wedges.

MARINATED SALMON TROUT STEAKS

Marinating the fish in a mixture of saffron, egg yolks and garlic is simplicity itself,
and the results are sensational, especially when served with herb-flavored rice.

2–3 saffron strands
2 egg yolks
1 garlic clove, crushed
4 salmon trout steaks
oil, for deep-frying
salt and ground black pepper
lemon wedges, rice and green salad,
to serve

SERVES 4

 Soak the saffron in 1 tablespoon of boiling water and then beat the mixture into the egg yolks. Season with garlic, salt and pepper.

 Place the fish steaks in a shallow dish and coat with the egg mixture. Cover with plastic wrap and marinate for up to 1 hour.

 Heat the oil in a deep-fryer until very hot and then fry the fish, one steak at a time, for 10 minutes, until they are golden brown. Drain each one on paper towels. Serve with lemon wedges, accompanied by rice and a green salad.

VARIATION
Any type of fish can be used in this recipe. Try a combination of plain and smoked for a delicious change, such as smoked and unsmoked cod or haddock.

PAN-FRIED SARDINES

This delicious fish recipe is a favorite in many countries.

¼ ounce fresh parsley
3–4 garlic cloves, crushed
8–12 sardines, prepared
2 tablespoons lemon juice
½ cup all-purpose flour
½ teaspoon ground cumin
¼ cup vegetable oil
salt and ground black pepper
naan and salad, to serve

SERVES 4

1 Finely chop the parsley and mix in a small bowl with the garlic.

2 Pat the parsley and garlic mixture all over the outsides and insides of the sardines. Sprinkle them with the lemon juice and set aside, covered, in a cool place for about 2 hours to absorb the flavors.

 Place the flour on a large plate and season with cumin, salt and pepper. Roll the sardines in the flour, coating each fish thoroughly.

 Heat the oil in a large frying pan and fry the fish in batches for 5 minutes on each side until crisp. Keep warm in the oven while cooking the remaining fish. Serve with naan and salad.

COOK'S TIP
If you don't have a garlic crusher, you can crush the garlic using the flat side of a large knife blade instead.

COD PLAKI

This is a traditional Greek preparation for fish, using onions, tomatoes, parsley and olive oil. Although cod is an Atlantic fish, it works very well in this recipe.

1¼ cups olive oil
2 onions, thinly sliced
3 large ripe tomatoes, coarsely
chopped
3 garlic cloves, thinly sliced
1 teaspoon sugar
1 teaspoon chopped fresh dill
1 teaspoon chopped fresh mint
1 teaspoon chopped fresh celery leaves
1 tablespoon chopped fresh parsley
6 cod steaks
juice of 1 lemon
salt and ground black pepper
extra dill, mint or parsley, to garnish

SERVES 6

1 Heat the oil in a large sauté pan or flameproof dish. Add the onions and cook until pale golden. Add the tomatoes, garlic, sugar, dill, mint, celery leaves and parsley with 1¼ cups water. Season with salt and pepper, then simmer, uncovered, for 25 minutes, until the liquid has reduced by one-third.

2 Add the fish steaks and cook gently for 10–12 minutes, until the fish is just cooked. Remove from the heat and add the lemon juice (*left*). Cover and let stand for about 20 minutes before serving. Arrange the cod in a dish and spoon the sauce over. Garnish with herbs and serve warm or cold.

SICILIAN SPAGHETTI WITH SARDINES

A traditional dish from Sicily, with ingredients that are common to many parts of the Mediterranean.

12 fresh sardines, cleaned and boned
1 cup olive oil
1 onion, chopped
¼ cup dill sprigs
½ cup pine nuts
2 tablespoons raisins, soaked in water
½ cup fresh bread crumbs
1 pound spaghetti
all-purpose flour for dusting
salt

SERVES 4

 Wash the sardines and pat dry on paper towels. Open them out flat, then cut in half lengthwise.

2 Heat 2 tablespoons of the oil in a pan, add the onion and fry until golden. Add the dill and cook gently for a minute or two. Add the pine nuts and raisins and season with salt. Dry-fry the bread crumbs in a frying pan until golden. Set aside.

3 Cook the spaghetti in boiling salted water according to the instructions on the package until al dente. Heat the remaining oil in a pan. Dust the sardines with flour and fry in the hot oil for 2–3 minutes. Drain on paper towels.

4 Drain the spaghetti and return to the pan. Add the onion mixture and toss well. Transfer the spaghetti mixture to a serving platter and arrange the fried sardines on top. Sprinkle with the toasted bread crumbs and serve immediately.

MONKFISH COUSCOUS

Since fish needs very little cooking, it is quickest and easiest to cook the couscous using this simple method. However, if you prefer to steam couscous, steam it over the onions and bell peppers.

1½ pounds monkfish
2 tablespoons olive oil
1 onion, thinly sliced into rings
3 tablespoons raisins
¼ cup cashews
1 small red bell pepper, cored, seeded
and sliced
1 small yellow bell pepper, cored,
seeded and sliced
4 tomatoes, peeled, seeded and sliced
1½ cups fish stock
1 tablespoon chopped fresh parsley
salt and ground black pepper

FOR THE COUSCOUS
1⅔ cups couscous
2¼ cups boiling vegetable stock
or water

SERVES 4

4 Heat the remaining oil in the pan and add the remaining onion rings. Cook for 4–5 minutes, until golden, and then add the pepper slices. Cook over fairly high heat for 6–8 minutes, until the peppers are soft, stirring occasionally. Add the tomatoes and fish stock, reduce the heat and simmer for 10 minutes, stirring several times.

5 Meanwhile, prepare the couscous. Place in a bowl, pour in the boiling stock or water and stir once or twice. Set aside for 10 minutes so that the couscous can absorb the liquid, then fluff up with a fork. Cover and keep warm.

6 Add the fish to the peppers and onion, partially cover and simmer for 6–8 minutes, until the fish is tender, stirring gently. Season well.

7 Pile the couscous on a large serving plate. Pour on the monkfish mixture, with all of the sauce. Sprinkle with the parsley and the reserved onion rings, raisins and cashews and serve.

1 Bone and skin the monkfish, if necessary, and cut into bite-size chunks using a sharp knife.

2 Heat half the oil in a saucepan and fry a quarter of the onion rings for 5–6 minutes until dark golden brown. Drain on paper towels.

3 Add the raisins to the pan and stir-fry for 30–60 seconds, until they begin to plump up. Add to the plate with the onion rings. Add the cashews to the pan and stir-fry for 30–60 seconds, until golden. Place on the plate with the onion and raisins, and set aside.

MONKFISH WITH TOMATOES AND OLIVES

This makes a really delicious lunch or light supper dish. Alternatively, serve this medley of monkfish,
tomatoes and black olives as an appetizer for six to eight people.

8 tomatoes
1¹/2 pounds monkfish
2 tablespoons all-purpose flour
1 teaspoon ground coriander
¹/2 teaspoon ground turmeric
2 tablespoons butter
2 garlic cloves, finely chopped
1–2 tablespoons olive oil
¹/4 cup pine nuts, toasted
small pieces of preserved lemon
12 black olives, pitted
salt and ground black pepper
whole slices of preserved lemon and
chopped fresh parsley, to garnish

SERVES 4

1 Peel the tomatoes by plunging them briefly in boiling water, then cold water. Quarter them, remove the cores and seeds and chop the flesh roughly.

2 Cut the fish into bite-size chunks. Mix the flour, coriander, turmeric and seasoning in a bowl. Dust the fish with the seasoned flour and set aside.

3 Melt the butter in a medium nonstick frying pan. Fry the tomatoes and garlic over low heat for 6–8 minutes, until most of the liquid has evaporated.

4 Push the tomatoes to the edge of the frying pan, moisten the pan with a little olive oil and fry the monkfish pieces in a single layer over medium heat for 3–5 minutes, turning frequently. You may have to do this in batches, so as the first batch of fish pieces cooks, place them on top of the tomatoes and fry the rest, adding more oil, if needed.

5 When all the fish is cooked, add the pine nuts and stir, scraping the bottom of the pan to incorporate the tomatoes. The sauce should be thick and slightly charred in places.

6 Rinse the preserved lemon in cold water, discard the pulp and cut the peel into strips. Stir into the sauce with the olives. Adjust the seasoning and serve, garnished with whole slices of preserved lemon and a sprinkling of chopped parsley.

FRESH TUNA AND TOMATO STEW

A deliciously simple dish that relies on good basic ingredients. For real Italian flavor, serve with polenta or pasta and an herb salad.

12 baby onions, peeled
2 pounds ripe tomatoes
1½ pounds fresh tuna
3 tablespoons olive oil
2 garlic cloves, crushed
3 tablespoons chopped fresh herbs
2 bay leaves
½ teaspoon sugar
2 tablespoons sun-dried tomato paste
⅔ cup dry white wine
salt and ground black pepper
baby zucchini and fresh herbs,
to garnish

SERVES 4

VARIATION

Two large mackerel make a nice alternative to the tuna. Fillet them and cut them into chunks or simply lay the whole fish on the sauce and cook, covered with a lid, until the mackerel is cooked through.

Sage, rosemary or oregano all go extremely well with this dish. Choose whichever you prefer, or use a mixture of one or two.

1 Leave the onions whole and cook in a pan of boiling water for 4–5 minutes, until softened. Drain.

2 Plunge the tomatoes into boiling water for 30 seconds, then refresh in cold water. Peel off the skins and chop coarsely.

4 Add the onions, garlic, tomatoes, chopped herbs, bay leaves, sugar, tomato paste and wine and bring to a boil, breaking up the tomatoes with a wooden spoon.

5 Reduce the heat and simmer gently for 5 minutes. Return the fish to the pan and cook for another 5 minutes. Season and serve hot, garnished with baby zucchini and fresh herbs.

3 Cut the tuna into 1-inch chunks. Heat the oil in a large frying or sauté pan and quickly sauté the tuna until browned. Drain.

BRANDADE DE MORUE

Salt cod is popular in Spain and France, and it can be found cooked in a number of ways. This recipe is a purée flavored with garlic and olive oil that is made all over southern France.

1½ pounds salt cod
1¼ cups olive oil
1 cup milk
1 garlic clove, crushed
grated nutmeg
lemon juice, to taste
white pepper
parsley sprigs, to garnish

FOR THE CROUTONS
¼ cup olive oil
6 slices white bread, crusts removed
1 garlic clove, halved

SERVES 6

1 Soak the salt cod in cold water for at least 24 hours, changing the water several times. Drain.

2 To make the croutons, heat the oil in a frying pan. Cut the bread slices in half diagonally and fry in the hot oil until golden. Drain on paper towels, then rub both sides with garlic.

3 Put the cod in a large pan with enough cold water to cover. Cover and bring to a boil. Simmer gently for 8–10 minutes, until just tender. Drain and cool. Flake the fish and discard any skin and bones.

4 Heat the oil in a pan until very hot. In a separate pan, scald the milk. Transfer the fish to a blender or food processor and, with the motor running, slowly pour in the hot oil, followed by the milk, until the mixture is smooth and stiff. Transfer to a bowl and beat in the crushed garlic. Season with nutmeg, lemon juice and white pepper. Let the **brandade** cool and then chill until almost ready to serve.

5 Spoon the brandade into a shallow serving bowl and surround with the croutons. Garnish with parsley and serve cold.

SEA BASS AND FENNEL TAGINE

This is a delicious tagine in which the fish is flavored with charmoula, a specially selected blend of herbs and spices used especially in fish dishes.

*1¹/2 pounds sea bass, monkfish or
cod fillets
8 ounces raw Mediterranean shrimp
2 tablespoons olive oil
1 onion, chopped
1 fennel bulb, sliced
8 ounces small new potatoes, halved
2 cups fish stock
lemon wedges, to serve*

FOR THE *CHARMOULA*
*2 garlic cloves, crushed
4 teaspoons ground cumin
4 teaspoons paprika
pinch of chili powder or
cayenne pepper
2 tablespoons chopped fresh parsley
2 tablespoons chopped cilantro
3 tablespoons white vinegar
1 tablespoon lemon juice*

SERVES 4

 First make the *charmoula* by combining the crushed garlic, spices, herbs, vinegar and lemon juice in a bowl.

2 Skin the fish if necessary and remove any bones, then cut into large bite-size chunks. Wash and remove the shells from the shrimp. Using a sharp knife, cut along the back of each shrimp and pull out and discard the dark vein.

3 Place the fish and shrimp in two separate shallow dishes, add half the *charmoula* marinade to each dish and stir well to coat evenly. Cover with plastic wrap and set aside in a cool place for 30 minutes–2 hours.

4 Heat the olive oil in a large flameproof casserole and fry the onion for 2 minutes. Add the sliced fennel and continue cooking over low heat for 5–6 minutes, until the onions and fennel are flecked with brown. Add the potatoes and fish stock and cook for another 10–15 minutes, until the potatoes are tender.

5 Add the marinated fish, stir gently and cook for 4 minutes, then add the shrimp and any remaining marinade and cook for another 5–6 minutes, until the fish is tender and the shrimp are pink. Serve with lemon wedges.

BRODETTO

The different regions of Italy have their own variations of this dish, but all require a good fish stock.
Make sure you buy some of the fish whole so you can simply simmer them, remove the cooked flesh and
strain the deliciously flavored juices to make the stock.

2 pounds mixed fish fillets or steaks,
such as monkfish, cod, haddock,
halibut or hake
2 pounds mixed conger eel, red or
gray mullet, snapper or small
white fish
1 onion, halved
1 celery stalk, coarsely chopped
½ pound squid
½ pound fresh mussels
1½ pounds ripe tomatoes
¼ cup olive oil
1 large onion, thinly sliced
3 garlic cloves, crushed
1 teaspoon saffron strands
⅔ cup dry white wine
6 tablespoons chopped fresh parsley
salt and ground black pepper
croutons, to serve

SERVES 4–5

1 Remove any skin and bones from the fish fillets or steaks, cut the fish into large pieces and reserve. Place the bones in a pan with all the remaining fish.

2 Add the halved onion and the celery and just cover with water. Bring almost to a boil, then reduce the heat and simmer gently for about 30 minutes. Lift out the fish and remove the flesh from the bones. Reserve the stock.

3 To prepare the squid, twist the head and tentacles away from the body. Cut the head from the tentacles. Discard the body contents and peel off the mottled skin. Wash the tentacles and bodies and dry on paper towels.

COOK'S TIP
To make the croutons, cut thin slices from a long thin stick of bread and shallow-fry in a little butter until golden.

4 Scrub the mussels, discarding any that are damaged or open ones that do not close when tapped.

5 Plunge the tomatoes into boiling water for 30 seconds, then refresh in cold water. Peel off the skins and chop coarsely.

6 Heat the oil in a large saucepan or sauté pan. Add the sliced onion and the garlic and sauté gently for 3 minutes. Add the squid and the uncooked fish that you reserved earlier and sauté quickly on all sides. Drain.

7 Add 2 cups strained reserved fish stock, the saffron and tomatoes to the pan. Pour in the wine. Bring to a boil, then reduce the heat and simmer for about 5 minutes. Add the mussels, cover, and cook for 3–4 minutes, until the mussels have opened. Discard any that remain closed.

8 Season the sauce with salt and pepper and put all the fish in the pan. Cook gently for 5 minutes. Sprinkle on the parsley and serve with the croutons.

SARDINE GRATIN

In Sicily and other regions of the western Mediterranean, sardines are filled with a robust stuffing, flavorful enough to compete with the rich oiliness of the fish.

1 tablespoon light olive oil
½ small onion, finely chopped
2 garlic cloves, crushed
6 tablespoons blanched
almonds, chopped
2 tablespoons golden raisins,
coarsely chopped
10 pitted black olives
2 tablespoons capers, coarsely
chopped
2 tablespoons coarsely chopped
fresh parsley
1 cup bread crumbs
16 large sardines, scaled and gutted
⅓ cup grated Parmesan cheese
salt and ground black pepper
flat-leaf parsley, to garnish

SERVES 4

ABOVE: *Brodetto (top) and Sardine Gratin (bottom)*

[1] Preheat the oven to 400°F. Lightly oil a large, shallow ovenproof dish.

[2] Heat the oil in a frying pan and sauté the onion and garlic gently for 3 minutes. Stir in the almonds, raisins, olives, capers, parsley and ¼ cup of the bread crumbs. Season lightly with salt and pepper.

[3] Make 2–3 diagonal cuts on each side of the sardines. Pack the stuffing into the cavities and lay the sardines in the prepared dish.

[4] Mix the remaining bread crumbs with the cheese and sprinkle on the fish. Bake for about 20 minutes, until the fish is cooked through. Test by piercing one sardine through the thickest part with a knife. Garnish with parsley and serve immediately, with a leafy salad.

231

MOROCCAN PAELLA

This is a Moroccan version of the traditional Spanish dish. It is especially popular on the coast.

2 large boneless chicken breasts
about 5 ounces prepared squid
10 ounces cod or haddock fillets
8–10 raw jumbo shrimp, shelled
8 scallops, trimmed and halved
12 ounces raw mussels, in shells
1⅓ cups long grain rice
2 tablespoons sunflower oil
1 bunch scallions, cut into strips
2 small zucchini, cut into strips
1 red bell pepper, cored, seeded and
cut into strips
1⅔ cups chicken stock
1 cup canned puréed tomatoes
salt and ground black pepper
sprigs of cilantro and lemon wedges,
to garnish

FOR THE MARINADE
2 red chiles, seeded
good handful of fresh cilantro
2–3 teaspoons ground cumin
1 tablespoon paprika
2 garlic cloves
3 tablespoons olive oil
¼ cup sunflower oil
juice of 1 lemon

SERVES 6

---

1 First, make the marinade. Place all the ingredients in a food processor with 1 teaspoon salt and process until thoroughly blended.

2 Skin the chicken and cut into bite-size pieces. Place these in a glass or ceramic bowl.

3 Slice the squid into rings. Skin the fish, if necessary, and cut into bite-size chunks. Place the fish and shellfish (apart from the mussels) in a separate glass or ceramic bowl. Divide the marinade between the fish and chicken and stir well. Cover with plastic wrap and let marinate for about 2 hours.

4 Scrub the mussels, discarding any that do not close when tapped sharply, and reserve in a bowl in the refrigerator until ready to use. Place the rice in a bowl, cover with boiling water and set aside for about 30 minutes.

5 Drain the chicken and fish, and reserve the marinade from each separately. Heat the oil in a wok, balti pan or paella pan and fry the chicken pieces for a few minutes, until lightly browned.

6 Add the scallions to the pan, fry for 1 minute and then add the zucchini and red pepper strips and fry for another 3–4 minutes, until slightly softened. Remove the chicken and then the vegetables and place on separate plates.

7 Use a spatula to scrape all the marinade into the pan and cook for 1 minute. Drain the rice, add to the pan and stir-fry for 1 minute. Add the chicken stock, puréed tomatoes and reserved chicken, season with salt and pepper and stir well. Bring the mixture to a boil, then cover the pan with a large lid or foil and simmer very gently for 15–20 minutes, until the rice is almost tender.

8 Add the reserved vegetables to the pan and place all the fish and mussels on top. Cover again with a lid or foil and cook over medium heat for 10–12 minutes, until the fish is cooked and the mussels have opened.

9 Discard any mussels that have not opened during the cooking. Serve, garnished with sprigs of cilantro and lemon wedges.

SEAFOOD RISOTTO

Risotto is one of Italy's most popular rice dishes, and it is made with everything from pumpkin to squid ink. On the Mediterranean shores, seafood is the most obvious addition.

¼ cup sunflower oil
1 onion, chopped
2 garlic cloves, crushed
generous 1 cup arborio rice
7 tablespoons white wine
6¼ cups hot fish stock
12 ounces mixed seafood, such as
raw shrimp, mussels, squid rings
or clams
grated zest of ½ lemon
2 tablespoons tomato paste
1 tablespoon chopped fresh parsley
salt and ground black pepper

SERVES 4

1 Heat the oil in a heavy pan, add the onion and garlic and cook until soft. Add the rice and stir to coat the grains with oil. Add the wine and cook, stirring, over medium heat, for a few minutes until absorbed.

2 Add ⅔ cup of the hot fish stock and cook, stirring constantly, until the liquid is absorbed by the rice. Continue stirring and adding stock in ⅔ cup quantities, until half of the stock is left. This should take about 10 minutes.

3 Stir in the seafood and cook for 2–3 minutes. Add the remaining stock as before, until the rice is cooked. It should be quite creamy and the grains al dente.

4 Stir in the lemon zest, tomato paste and parsley. Season with salt and pepper and serve warm.

ITALIAN SHRIMP SKEWERS

Simple and delicious mouthfuls from the Amalfi Coast.

2 pounds raw shrimp, peeled
¼ cup olive oil
3 tablespoons vegetable oil
1¼ cups very fine dry bread crumbs
1 garlic clove, crushed
1 tablespoon chopped fresh parsley
salt and ground black pepper
lemon wedges, to serve

SERVES 4

1 Slit the shrimp down their backs and remove the dark vein. Rinse in cold water and pat dry.

2 Put the olive oil and vegetable oil in a large bowl and add the shrimp, mixing them to coat evenly. Add the bread crumbs, garlic and parsley and season with salt and pepper. Toss the shrimp thoroughly to give them an even coating of bread crumbs. Cover and let marinate for at least 1 hour.

3 Thread the shrimp onto four metal or wooden skewers, curling them up as you do so, so that the tail is skewered in the middle.

4 Preheat the broiler. Place the skewers in the broiler pan and cook for about 2 minutes on each side, until the bread crumbs are golden. Serve with lemon wedges.

SHELLFISH AND MUSHROOM RISOTTO

The creamy nature of short grain rice, cooked with onions and a simple stock, provides the basis for this delicious combination of shellfish and mushrooms.

3 tablespoons olive oil
1 medium onion, chopped
8 ounces assorted wild and cultivated
mushrooms, trimmed and sliced
2¼ cups arborio or carnaroli rice
5 cups chicken or vegetable
stock, boiling
⅔ cup white wine
4 ounces raw shrimp, peeled
8 ounces live mussels
8 ounces clams
1 medium squid, cleaned, trimmed
and sliced
3 drops truffle oil (optional)
5 tablespoons chopped fresh parsley
and chervil
celery salt and cayenne pepper
bread, to serve

SERVES 4

 Pour in the stock and wine. Add the shrimp, mussels, clams and squid. Stir and simmer for 15 minutes. Discard any mussels that remain shut.

4 Add the truffle oil if using, stir in the herbs, cover and let stand for 10 minutes. Season to taste with celery salt and a pinch of cayenne pepper, and serve with bread.

1 Heat the oil in a large pan and fry the onion for 6–8 minutes, until soft but not brown.

2 Add the mushrooms and soften until their juices begin to run. Stir in the rice and heat through.

TRUFFLE AND LOBSTER RISOTTO

To capture the precious qualities of the fresh truffle, partner it with lobster and serve in a silky smooth risotto. Both truffle shavings and oil are added toward the end of cooking to preserve their flavor.

¼ cup unsalted butter

1 medium onion, chopped

2 cups arborio rice

1 thyme sprig

5 cups chicken stock

⅔ cup dry white wine

1 freshly cooked lobster

3 tablespoons chopped fresh parsley
and chervil, plus sprigs to garnish

3–4 drops truffle oil

2 hard-boiled eggs, sliced

1 fresh black or white truffle

SERVES 4

3 Remove the rice mixture from the heat, and stir in the chopped lobster meat, herbs and truffle oil. Cover the pan with a tight-fitting lid and let stand for 5 minutes.

4 Divide among warmed dishes and arrange the sliced lobster and hard-boiled egg, with shavings of fresh truffle on top. Garnish with herb sprigs and serve immediately.

1 Melt the butter in a large shallow pan, add the onion and fry gently until soft, without letting it color. Add the rice and thyme and stir well to coat evenly with fat. Pour in the stock and wine, stir once and cook uncovered for 15 minutes.

2 Twist off the lobster tail, cut the underside with scissors and remove the white tail meat. Slice half of the meat, then roughly chop the remainder. Break open the claws and remove the flesh in one piece.

STUFFED SQUID

This Greek delicacy is best made with large squid, because they are less ackward to stuff.
If you have to make do with small squid, buy about 1 pound.

❀ ❀

FOR THE STUFFING
2 tablespoons olive oil
1 large onion, finely chopped
2 garlic cloves, crushed
1 cup fresh bread crumbs
4 tablespoons chopped fresh parsley
4 ounces halloumi cheese, grated
salt and ground black pepper

TO FINISH
4 squid tubes, each about
7 inches long
2 pounds ripe tomatoes
3 tablespoons olive oil
1 large onion, chopped
1 teaspoon sugar
½ cup dry white wine
several rosemary sprigs
toasted pine nuts and flat leaf parsley,
to garnish

SERVES 4

❀ ❀

1 To make the stuffing, heat the oil in a frying pan and fry the onion for 3 minutes. Remove the pan from heat and add the garlic, bread crumbs, parsley, cheese and a little salt and pepper. Stir until thoroughly blended.

2 Dry the squid tubes on paper towels and fill with the prepared stuffing using a teaspoon. Secure the ends of the squid with wooden toothsticks.

❀ ❀

VARIATION
If you would prefer a less rich filling, halve the quantity of cheese and bread crumbs in the stuffing and add 8 ounces cooked spinach.

❀ ❀

3 Plunge the tomatoes into boiling water for 30 seconds, then refresh in cold water. Peel away the skins and chop roughly.

4 Heat the oil in a frying pan or sauté pan. Add the squid and fry on all sides. Remove from the pan.

5 Add the onion to the pan and fry gently for 3 minutes. Stir in the tomatoes, sugar and wine and cook rapidly until the mixture becomes thick and pulpy.

6 Return the squid to the pan with the rosemary. Cover and cook gently for 30 minutes. Slice the squid and serve on individual plates with the sauce. Scatter over the pine nuts and garnish with parsley.

OCTOPUS AND RED WINE STEW

Unless you're happy to clean and prepare octopus for this Greek dish, buy one that's ready for cooking.

2 pounds prepared octopus
1 pound onions, sliced
2 bay leaves
1 pound ripe tomatoes
¼ cup olive oil
4 garlic cloves, crushed
1 teaspoon sugar
1 tablespoon chopped fresh oregano
or rosemary
2 tablespoons chopped fresh parsley
⅔ cup red wine
2 tablespoons red wine vinegar
chopped fresh herbs, to garnish
warm bread and pine nuts, to serve

SERVES 4

 Put the octopus in a saucepan of gently simmering water with a quarter of the onions and the bay leaves. Cook gently for 1 hour.

2 While the octopus is cooking, plunge the tomatoes into boiling water for 30 seconds, then refresh in cold water. Peel off the skins and chop coarsely.

3 Drain the octopus and, using a sharp knife, cut it into bite-size pieces. Discard the head.

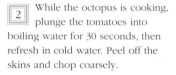

4 Heat the oil in a saucepan and sauté the octopus, the remaining onions and the garlic for 3 minutes. Add the tomatoes, sugar, oregano or rosemary, parsley, wine and vinegar and cook, stirring, for 5 minutes, until pulpy.

5 Cover the pan and cook over the lowest possible heat for about 1½ hours, until the sauce is thickened and the octopus is tender. Garnish with fresh herbs and serve with warm bread and pine nuts to sprinkle on top.

VARIATION
Use white wine instead of red and stir in ½ cup coarsely chopped black olives before serving.

GRILLED JUMBO SHRIMP WITH ROMESCO SAUCE

This sauce, from the Catalan region of Spain, is served with fish and shellfish. Its main ingredients are pimento, tomatoes, garlic and almonds.

1 To make the sauce, immerse the tomatoes in boiling water for about 30 seconds, then refresh them under cold water. Peel off the skins and coarsely chop the flesh.

24 raw jumbo shrimp
2–3 tablespoons olive oil
flat-leaf parsley, to garnish
lemon wedges, to serve

FOR THE SAUCE
2 ripe tomatoes
4 tablespoons olive oil
1 onion, chopped
4 garlic cloves, chopped
1 canned pimiento, chopped
½ teaspoon dried red pepper flakes
5 tablespoons fish stock
2 tablespoons white wine
10 blanched almonds
1 tablespoon red wine vinegar
salt

SERVES 4

2 Heat 2 tablespoons of the oil in a pan, add the onion and three-fourths of the chopped garlic and cook until soft. Add the pimiento, tomatoes, red pepper flakes, fish stock and wine, then cover and simmer for 30 minutes.

3 Toast the almonds under the broiler until golden. Transfer to a blender or food processor and grind coarsely. Add the remaining 2 tablespoons of oil, the vinegar and the remaining chopped garlic and process until evenly combined. Add the tomato and pimiento sauce and process until smooth. Season with salt.

4 Remove the heads from the shrimp, leaving them otherwise unshelled, and, with a sharp knife, slit each one down the back and remove the dark vein. Rinse and pat dry on paper towels. Preheat the broiler. Toss the shrimp in olive oil, then spread out in the broiler pan. Broil for 2–3 minutes on each side, until pink. Arrange on a serving platter with the lemon wedges, and place the sauce in a small bowl. Serve immediately, garnished with parsley.

ZARZUELA

Zarzuela means "light opera" or "musical comedy" in Spanish, and the classic fish stew of the same name should be as lively and colorful as the zarzuela itself. This feast of fish includes lobster and other shellfish, but you can modify the ingredients to suit the occasion and availability.

1 cooked lobster
24 fresh mussels or clams
1 large monkfish tail
8 ounces squid rings
1 tablespoon all-purpose flour
6 tablespoons olive oil
12 large raw shrimp
1 pound ripe tomatoes
2 large mild onions, chopped
4 garlic cloves, crushed
2 tablespoons brandy
2 bay leaves
1 teaspoon paprika
1 fresh red chile, seeded and chopped
1¼ cups fish stock
2 tablespoons ground almonds
2 tablespoons chopped fresh parsley
salt and ground black pepper

SERVES 6

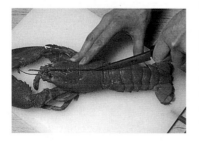

1 Using a large knife, cut the lobster in half lengthwise. Remove the dark intestine that runs down the length of the tail. Crack the claws using a hammer.

2 Scrub the mussels, discarding any that are damaged or open ones that do not close when tapped with a knife. Cut the monkfish fillets away from the central cartilage and cut each fillet into three pieces.

3 Toss the monkfish and squid in seasoned flour. Heat the oil in a large frying pan. Add the monkfish and squid and sauté quickly; remove from the pan. Sauté the shrimp on both sides, then remove from the pan.

4 Plunge the tomatoes into boiling water for 30 seconds, then refresh in cold water. Peel away the skins and chop coarsely.

5 Add the onions and two-thirds of the garlic to the frying pan and, stirring thoroughly, sauté for about 3 minutes. Add the brandy and ignite. When the flames die down, add the tomatoes, bay leaves, paprika, chile and stock.

6 Bring to a boil, reduce the heat and simmer gently for 5 minutes. Add the mussels or clams, cover and cook for 3–4 minutes, until the shells have opened.

7 Remove the mussels or clams from the sauce and discard any that remain closed.

8 Arrange all the fish, including the lobster, in a large flameproof serving dish. Blend the ground almonds to a paste with the remaining garlic and parsley and stir into the sauce. Season with salt and pepper.

9 Pour the sauce over the fish and lobster and cook gently for about 5 minutes, until hot. Serve immediately with a green salad and plenty of warm bread.

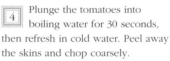

HAKE AND CLAMS WITH SALSA VERDE

Hake (an Atlantic fish) is one of the most popular fish in Spain; here, it is cooked in a sauce flavored with parsley, lemon juice and garlic.

4 hake steaks, about ¾ inch thick
½ cup all-purpose flour for
dusting, plus
2 tablespoons
4 tablespoons olive oil
1 tablespoon lemon juice
1 small onion, finely chopped
4 garlic cloves, crushed
⅔ cup fish stock
⅔ cup white wine
6 tablespoons chopped fresh parsley
3 ounces frozen tiny peas
16 fresh clams
salt and ground black pepper

SERVES 4

1 Preheat the oven to 350°F. Season the fish with salt and pepper, then dust both sides with flour. Heat 2 tablespoons of the oil in a large sauté pan, add the fish and sauté for about 1 minute on each side. Transfer to an ovenproof dish and sprinkle with lemon juice.

2 Clean the pan, then heat the remaining oil. Add the onion and garlic and cook until soft. Stir in 2 tablespoons flour and cook for about 1 minute. Gradually add the stock and wine, stirring until thickened and smooth. Add 5 tablespoons of the parsley and the peas and season with salt and pepper.

3 Pour the sauce over the fish and bake for 15–20 minutes, adding the clams to the dish 3–4 minutes before the end of the cooking time. Discard any clams that do not open, then sprinkle with the remaining parsley before serving.

BLACK PASTA WITH SQUID SAUCE

Tagliatelle flavored with squid ink looks amazing and tastes deliciously of the sea. You'll find it at good Italian food stores.

7 tablespoons olive oil
2 shallots, chopped
3 garlic cloves, crushed
3 tablespoons chopped fresh parsley
1½ pounds cleaned squid, cut
into rings and rinsed
⅔ cup dry white wine
14-ounce can chopped tomatoes
½ teaspoon dried red pepper flakes
1 pound squid ink tagliatelle
salt and ground black pepper

SERVES 4

 Heat the oil in a pan and add the shallots. Cook until pale golden, then add the garlic. When the garlic colors a little, add 2 tablespoons of the parsley, stir, then add the squid and stir again. Cook for 3–4 minutes, then add the wine.

2 Simmer for a few seconds, then add the tomatoes and red pepper flakes (*right*) and season with salt and pepper. Cover and simmer gently for about 1 hour, until the squid is tender. Add more water if necessary.

3 Cook the pasta in plenty of boiling salted water, according to the instructions on the package, or until al dente. Drain and return the tagliatelle to the pan. Add the squid sauce and mix well. Sprinkle each serving with the remaining chopped parsley and serve immediately.

MOUCLADE OF MUSSELS

This recipe is quite similar to Moules Marinière but has the additional flavoring of fennel and mild curry. Traditionally, the mussels are shelled and piled into scallop shells, but nothing beats a bowlful of steaming hot, garlicky mussels, served in their own glistening shells.

4½ pounds fresh mussels
1 cup dry white wine
good pinch of grated nutmeg
3 thyme sprigs
2 bay leaves
1 small onion, finely chopped
4 tablespoons butter
1 fennel bulb, thinly sliced
4 garlic cloves, crushed
½ teaspoon curry paste or powder
2 tablespoons all-purpose flour
⅔ cup heavy cream
ground black pepper
chopped fresh dill, to garnish

SERVES 6

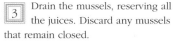 Scrub the mussels, discarding any that are damaged or open ones that do not close when tapped with a knife.

 Put the wine, nutmeg, thyme, bay leaves and onion in a large saucepan and bring just to a boil. Pour in the mussels and cover with a lid. Cook for 4–5 minutes, until the mussels have opened.

 Drain the mussels, reserving all the juices. Discard any mussels that remain closed.

 Melt the butter in a large clean pan and gently sauté the fennel slices and garlic for about 5 minutes, until softened.

 Stir in the curry paste or powder and flour and cook for 1 minute. Remove from the heat and gradually blend in the cooking juices from the mussels. Return to the heat and cook, stirring, for 2 minutes.

 Stir in the cream and a little pepper. Add the mussels to the pan and heat through for 2 minutes. Serve hot, garnished with dill.

VARIATION
Saffron is a popular addition to a mouclade. Soak ½ teaspoon saffron strands in a little boiling water and add to the sauce with the stock.

MEAT

*The Mediterranean style of cooking makes the
most of young lamb and pork, while tougher cuts
are slow-cooked in superb sauces.*

Unlike the vegetable and fish recipes from the Mediterranean, meat recipes do not readily spring to mind. The countryside around the Mediterranean can be quite harsh—no lush, green fields for animals to graze. Beasts are often slaughtered young, and baby lamb and goat are favorite meats. Traditionally, these animals were usually roasted whole on a spit, flavored with wild herbs, and eaten on feast days. The meat of the young kid is particularly popular in certain parts of the Mediterranean, such as Corsica, parts of Greece and the Middle East. Cattle are a rare sight and, in times past, beef was considered a luxury. Many rural families kept a pig, which was slaughtered and the meat preserved, to feed them through the chilly winter months. This, in turn, inspired the many wonderful dry sausages, like salami, and the cured hams, which are still popular today, and appreciated all over the world. Both Jews and Muslims were forbidden by their religion to eat pork, so there are no traditional pork recipes from their countries and regions.

ABOVE: Sunlight dapples the walls of this farmhouse overlooking Lake Trasimeno, in Umbria.

In the Middle East, only lamb and mutton were eaten, although nowadays beef and veal are becoming more popular. The Roman Catholic and Greek Orthodox Churches used to have strict rules concerning "lean" days, when meat could not be consumed, and therefore many special feast dishes using meat were created to celebrate the ends of these regular fasts.

Meat was often of poor quality if the beast had not been properly fed, resulting in tough and stringy cuts. This was remedied by marinating the meat in wine or yogurt and cooking it slowly at a low temperature, to tenderize it and improve the flavor. These methods resulted in some of the most delicious recipes for casseroles and stews. Many are still cooked today, despite the fact that the meat is probably of better quality. Daubes from France, tagines from Morocco, estofados

RIGHT: This French shepherd has a magnificent view of the Provençal countryside.

BELOW: Sacks of spices and grains invite inspection at a Tunisian market.

from Spain—every country has its own version, recipes having been handed down through the generations. As meat was a luxury, beans, rice and potatoes were often added to the pot to make the meal go further.

Another popular method of cooking meat is broiling. Quite often the meat is threaded onto skewers, or sometimes a branch of rosemary or bay, with chunks of onion and other vegetables. This is a basic form of cooking, originating from cooking over the hot embers of an open fire, and it results in succulent, smoky-flavored meat. Greece and the Middle East have mastered this technique, and the smell of meat cooking on a wood fire is one associated with these countries. Using ground meat, in the form of patties, meatballs, sausages, sauces for pasta and fillings for savory pastries, is popular throughout the Mediterranean. This was another way of padding out meat with other ingredients to make a more economical dish. Bread crumbs, rice, bulghur and potatoes are all used to add more bulk, particularly when making meatballs and patties. Onion and tomatoes give flavor and volume to sauces. In the Middle East, spices, nuts and dried fruits are often mixed with ground meat, to make delicious fillings for little parcels of phyllo. Elsewhere, in Italy, garlic, wine, and herbs are added to slow-cooked meat sauces, to eat with pasta. In Greece, ground lamb is layered with eggplant, tomato sauce and béchamel sauce to create Moussaka, and in Turkey, ground lamb is used to stuff halved eggplant, the vegetable flesh being mixed with the ground meat. These versatile dishes are good for feeding a large crowd, often making a little go a long way.

Although there are no recipes for goat in this chapter (as it is not readily available), the selection varies from Sicilian Pork with Marsala to Turkish Lamb Pilaf and Greek Lamb Sausages with Tomato Sauce. As with most recipes in this book, all that is needed to accompany any of them, once cooked and ready to eat, is a glass of wine (in this case red) and some good bread!

MOUSSAKA

—

Like many popular classics, a real moussaka bears little resemblance to the imitations experienced in many Greek tourist resorts. This one is mildly spiced, moist but not dripping in grease, and encased in a golden baked crust.

2 pounds eggplant
½ cup olive oil
2 large tomatoes
2 large onions, sliced
1 pound ground lamb
¼ teaspoon ground cinnamon
¼ teaspoon ground allspice
2 tablespoons tomato paste
3 tablespoons chopped fresh parsley
½ cup dry white wine
salt and ground black pepper

FOR THE SAUCE
4 tablespoons butter
½ cup all-purpose flour
2½ cups milk
¼ teaspoon grated nutmeg
⅓ cup grated Parmesan cheese
3 tablespoons toasted bread crumbs

SERVES 6

1 Cut the eggplant into ¼ inch thick slices. Layer the slices in a colander, sprinkling each layer with plenty of salt. Let stand for 30 minutes.

2 Rinse the eggplant in several changes of cold water. Squeeze gently with your fingers to remove the excess water, then pat them dry on paper towels.

3 Heat some of the oil in a large frying pan. Sauté the eggplant slices in batches until golden on both sides, adding more oil when necessary. Let the eggplant slices drain on paper towels.

4 Plunge the tomatoes into boiling water for 30 seconds, then refresh in cold water. Peel away the skins and chop coarsely.

5 Preheat the oven to 350°F. Heat 2 tablespoons oil in a saucepan. Add the onions and lamb and sauté gently for 5 minutes, stirring and breaking up the lamb with a wooden spoon.

VARIATION
Sliced and sautéed zucchini or potatoes can be used instead of the eggplant in this dish.

6 Add the tomatoes, cinnamon, allspice, tomato paste, parsley, wine and pepper and bring to a boil. Reduce the heat, cover with a lid and simmer gently for 15 minutes.

7 Spoon alternate layers of the eggplant and meat mixture into a shallow ovenproof dish, finishing with a layer of eggplant.

8 To make the sauce, melt the butter in a small pan and stir in the flour. Cook, stirring, for 1 minute. Remove from the heat and gradually blend in the milk. Return to the heat and cook, stirring, for 2 minutes, until thickened. Add the nutmeg, cheese and salt and pepper. Pour the sauce on the eggplant and sprinkle with the bread crumbs. Bake for 45 minutes, until golden. Serve hot, sprinkled with extra black pepper, if desired.

KLEFTIKO

For this Greek recipe, marinated lamb steaks or chops are slow-cooked to develop an unbeatable flavor and meltingly tender texture. The dish is sealed, like a pie, with a flour dough lid to trap succulence and flavor; a tight-fitting foil cover, if less attractive, will serve equally well.

juice of 1 lemon
1 tablespoon chopped fresh oregano
4 lamb leg steaks or loin chops
with bones
2 tablespoons olive oil
2 large onions, thinly sliced
2 bay leaves
⅔ cup dry white wine
2 cups all-purpose flour
salt and ground black pepper

SERVES 4

COOK'S TIP
They are not absolutely essential for this dish, but lamb steaks or chops with bones will provide lots of additional flavor. Boiled potatoes make a delicious accompaniment.

1 Combine the lemon juice, oregano and salt and pepper, and brush onto both sides of the lamb steaks or chops. Let marinate for at least 4 hours or overnight.

3 Transfer the lamb to a shallow baking dish. Scatter the sliced onions and bay leaves around the lamb, then pour on the white wine and the reserved marinade.

2 Preheat the oven to 325°F. Drain the lamb, reserving the marinade, and dry the lamb with paper towels. Heat the olive oil in a large frying pan or sauté pan and sauté the lamb over high heat until browned on both sides.

4 Mix the flour with enough water to make a firm dough. Moisten the rim of the dish. Roll out the dough on a floured surface and use to cover the dish so that it is tightly sealed.

5 Bake for 2 hours, then break open the dough crust and serve the lamb hot with boiled potatoes.

SPICED ROAST LAMB

This is a particularly delicious Turkish version of roast lamb.

6 pound leg of lamb
3–4 large garlic cloves, halved
¼ cup olive oil
2 teaspoons paprika
2 teaspoons Dijon mustard
juice of 1 lemon
½ teaspoon dried thyme
½ teaspoon dried rosemary
½ teaspoon sugar
½ cup white wine
salt and ground black pepper
fresh thyme, to garnish
rice and salad, to serve

SERVES 6–8

1 Trim the fat from the lamb and make several incisions in the meat with a sharp knife. Press the garlic halves into the slits. Combine the olive oil, paprika, mustard, lemon juice, herbs, sugar and seasoning and rub this paste all over the meat. Place the lamb in a shallow dish and let stand in a cool place for 1–2 hours.

2 Preheat the oven to 400°F. Place the lamb in a roasting pan, add the white wine and cook for 20 minutes. Reduce the heat to 325°F and cook for another 2 hours, basting occasionally. Serve garnished with thyme, and accompanied by rice and a salad of young leaves and herbs.

COOK'S TIP
If you can spare the time, it is better to let the meat stand for 15 minutes before carving. This makes the flesh firmer, which in turn makes it easier to carve.

ROAST LEG OF LAMB WITH SAFFRON

Even such a tiny amount of saffron imparts a delicate flavor to the meat.

6 pound leg of lamb
4 garlic cloves, halved
¼ cup olive oil
juice of 1 lemon
2–3 saffron strands, soaked in
1 tablespoon boiling water
1 teaspoon dried mixed herbs
1 pound potatoes
2 large onions
salt and ground black pepper
fresh flat-leaf parsley, to garnish

SERVES 6–8

1 Make several incisions in the meat and press the garlic halves into the slits. Mix the oil, lemon juice, saffron and herbs in a small bowl. Rub this mixture over the meat, then let marinate at room temperature for 2 hours.

2 Preheat the oven to 350°F. Peel all the potatoes and cut them crosswise into thick slices. Cut the onions into thick slices.

3 Layer the potatoes and onions in a large roasting pan. Lift the lamb out of the marinade and place the meat on the top of the potatoes and onions, fat side up.

4 Pour any remaining marinade over the lamb and roast for 2 hours, basting occasionally. Remove the lamb from the oven, cover loosely with foil and let sit in a warm place to rest for about 10–15 minutes before carving. Serve, surrounded by the potatoes and onions, and garnished with parsley.

LAMB WITH RED PEPPERS AND RIOJA

Plenty of garlic, bell peppers, herbs and red wine give this lamb stew a lovely, rich flavor. Slice through the pepper stems, rather than removing them, as this makes it look extra special.

2 pounds lean lamb fillet
1 tablespoon all-purpose flour
¼ cup olive oil
2 red onions, sliced
4 garlic cloves, sliced
2 teaspoons paprika
¼ teaspoon ground cloves
1⅔ cups red Rioja wine
⅔ cup lamb stock
2 bay leaves
2 thyme sprigs
3 red bell peppers, halved and seeded
salt and ground black pepper
bay leaves and thyme sprigs,
to garnish
green beans and saffron rice or boiled
potatoes, to serve

SERVES 4

1. Preheat the oven to 325°F. Cut the lamb into chunks. Season the flour, add the lamb and toss lightly to coat.

2. Heat the oil in a frying pan and sauté the lamb, stirring, until browned. Transfer to an ovenproof dish. Lightly sauté the onions in the pan with the garlic, paprika and cloves.

VARIATION
Use lean cubed pork instead of the lamb and a white Rioja wine instead of the red. A mixture of red, yellow and orange bell peppers looks very effective.

3. Add the Rioja, stock, bay leaves and thyme and bring to a boil, stirring. Pour the contents of the pan onto the meat. Cover with a lid and bake for 30 minutes.

4. Remove the dish from the oven. Stir the red peppers into the stew and season lightly with salt and pepper. Bake for another 30 minutes, until the meat is tender. Garnish the stew with bay leaves and sprigs of thyme and serve with green beans and saffron rice or boiled potatoes.

ROAST LAMB WITH ROSEMARY

In Italy, lamb is traditionally served at Easter. This simple roast with potatoes owes its wonderful flavor to the addition of fresh rosemary and garlic. It makes a perfect Sunday lunch at any time of year, served with one or two lightly-cooked fresh vegetables, such as broccoli, spinach or baby carrots.

½ leg of lamb, about 3 pounds
2 garlic cloves, cut lengthwise into
thin slivers
7 tablespoons olive oil
leaves from 4 sprigs of fresh rosemary,
finely chopped
about 1 cup lamb or vegetable stock
1½ pounds potatoes,
cut into 1-inch cubes
a few fresh sage leaves, chopped
salt and ground black pepper

SERVES 4

 Place the lamb in a roasting pan and rub it all over with 3 table-spoons of the oil. Sprinkle about half of the chopped rosemary, patting it on firmly, and season with plenty of salt and pepper. Roast for 30 minutes, turning once.

 Meanwhile, put the potatoes in a separate roasting pan and toss with the remaining oil and rosemary and the sage. Roast the potatoes on the same rack as the lamb, if possible, for 45 minutes, turning the potatoes several times until golden and tender.

 Preheat the oven to 450°F. Using the point of a sharp knife, make several deep incisions in the lamb, especially near the bone, and insert a sliver of garlic into each.

 Lower the oven temperature to 375°F. Turn the lamb over again. Carefully pour in ½ cup of the stock.

 Roast for another 1¼–1½ hours, until the lamb is tender, turning the lamb two or three more times and adding the rest of the stock in two or three batches. Baste the lamb each time it is turned.

 Transfer the lamb to a carving board, cover with foil and let sit for 10 minutes before carving. Serve with the roast potatoes and accompanied by a green vegetable, baby carrots or roasted Mediterranean vegetables.

VARIATION
Tuck one or two rosemary leaves into each slit in the lamb, as well as the garlic, for a more intense flavor.

COOK'S TIP
If you like, the cooking juices can be strained and used to make a thin gravy with stock and red wine.

LAMB CASSEROLE WITH GARLIC AND FAVA BEANS

This recipe has a Spanish influence and makes a substantial meal, served with potatoes. It's based on stewing lamb with a large amount of garlic and sherry—the addition of fava beans gives color.

3 tablespoons olive oil
3–3½ pounds lamb fillet, cut into
2-inch cubes
1 large onion, chopped
6 large garlic cloves, unpeeled
1 bay leaf
1 teaspoon paprika
½ cup dry sherry
4 ounces shelled fresh or frozen
fava beans
2 tablespoons chopped fresh parsley
salt and ground black pepper

SERVES 6

2 Heat the remaining oil in the pan, add the onion and cook for about 5 minutes, until soft. Return the meat to the casserole.

3 Add the garlic cloves, bay leaf, paprika and sherry. Season with salt and pepper. Bring to a boil, then cover and simmer very gently for 1½–2 hours, until the meat is tender.

1 Heat 2 tablespoons of the oil in a large flameproof casserole. Add half the meat and brown well on all sides. Transfer to a plate. Brown the rest of the meat in the same way and remove from the casserole.

4 Add the fava beans about 10 minutes before the end of the cooking time. Stir in the parsley just before serving.

BRAISED LAMB WITH APRICOTS AND HERB DUMPLINGS

This is a rich and fruity lamb casserole, topped with light, herbed dumplings, which is delicious served with baked potatoes and a green vegetable.

2 tablespoons sunflower oil
1½ pounds lean lamb fillet,
cut into 1-inch cubes
12 ounces pearl onions
1 garlic clove, crushed
3 cups button mushrooms
¾ cup dried apricots
1 cup well-flavored lamb or beef stock
1 cup red wine
1 tablespoon tomato paste
salt and ground black pepper
sprigs of fresh herbs, to garnish

FOR THE DUMPLINGS
1 cup self-rising flour
scant ½ cup chilled shortening,
finely chopped
1–2 tablespoons chopped
fresh mixed herbs

SERVES 6

VARIATIONS
Use lean beef or pork in place of the
lamb, and substitute shallots or
double the amount of caramelized red
and white onions for the pearl
onions, if you prefer. Prunes, dates
or even figs can be used instead
of apricots.

 Preheat the oven to 325°F. Heat
the oil in a large, flameproof
casserole, add the lamb and cook
gently until browned all over, stirring
occasionally. Remove the meat from
the casserole using a slotted spoon,
set aside and keep warm.

 Add the pearl onions, garlic
and mushrooms to the oil
remaining in the casserole. Cook
gently for about 5 minutes, stirring
occasionally to incorporate any
sediment on the bottom.

3 Return all the meat to the
casserole, add the dried apricots,
lamb or beef stock, red wine and
tomato paste. Season to taste with salt
and pepper and stir with a wooden
spoon to mix.

4 Bring to a boil, stirring, then
remove the casserole from heat
and cover. Transfer the casserole to
the oven and cook for 1½–2 hours,
until the lamb is cooked and tender,
stirring once or twice and adding a
little extra stock, if necessary.

5 Meanwhile, make the dumplings.
Place the flour, shortening, herbs
and seasoning in a bowl and stir to
mix. Add enough cold water to make
a soft, elastic dough. Divide the
dough into small, marble-size pieces
and, using lightly floured hands, roll
each piece into a small ball.

6 Remove the lid from the
casserole and place the
dumplings on the top of the braised
lamb and vegetables. Do not place
the dumplings too close together;
they must have room to rise.

7 Increase the oven temperature
to 375°F. Return the casserole
to the oven and cook for another
20–25 minutes, until the herb
dumplings are cooked. Serve straight
from the casserole, garnished with
fresh herb sprigs.

MOROCCAN LAMB STEW

Known locally as Tagine, after the conical-shaped pottery dish in which it is cooked, this colorful, spicy stew combines French colonial and African influences.

1⅓ cups dried chickpeas soaked in
cold water overnight
¼ cup olive oil
2 teaspoons sugar
2 teaspoons ground cumin
1 teaspoon ground cinnamon
1 teaspoon ground ginger
½ teaspoon ground turmeric
½ teaspoon powdered saffron
or paprika
3 pounds lamb shoulder, trimmed of
all fat and cut into 2-inch cubes
2 onions, coarsely chopped
3 garlic cloves, finely chopped
2 tomatoes, peeled, seeded
and chopped
⅔ cup raisins, soaked in warm water
10–24 pitted black olives,
such as Kalamata
2 preserved lemons, thinly sliced, or
grated zest of 1 unwaxed lemon
4–6 tablespoons chopped cilantro
salt and ground black pepper
2⅔ cups couscous, to serve

SERVES 6–8

COOK'S TIP
Preserved lemons are frequently used
in Moroccan cooking. They are
available at delicatessens and
specialty markets but, if you can't find
them, a little grated lemon zest makes
an adequate substitute.
Be sure to use unwaxed lemons,
which are widely available.

1 Drain the chickpeas, rinse under cold running water and place in a large saucepan, then cover with water and boil vigorously for 10 minutes. Drain the chickpeas and return to a clean saucepan. Cover with fresh cold water and bring to a boil over high heat, then reduce the heat and simmer, covered, for 1–1½ hours, until tender. Remove the pan from heat and add a little salt.

2 In a large bowl, combine half of the olive oil with the sugar, cumin, cinnamon, ginger, turmeric, saffron or paprika, 1 teaspoon salt and pepper. Add the lamb, toss to coat well and set aside for 20 minutes.

3 In a large, heavy frying pan, heat the remaining oil and fry the lamb in batches until well browned. Transfer to a large flameproof casserole.

4 Add the onions to the pan and stir them constantly until well browned. Stir in the garlic and tomatoes with 1 cup water, stirring and scraping the bottom of the pan. Pour into the casserole and add enough water to just cover, then bring to a boil over high heat, skimming off any foam that rises to the surface. Reduce the heat to low and simmer for about 1 hour or until the meat is tender when pierced with a sharp knife.

5 Drain the chickpeas, reserving the liquid. Pour onto the lamb in the casserole with about 1 cup of the liquid. Stir in all the raisins with their soaking liquid and simmer for 30 minutes more. Stir in the olives and sliced preserved lemons or lemon zest, and simmer for 20–30 more minutes, then mix in half of the chopped cilantro.

6 About 30 minutes before serving, prepare the couscous according to the instructions on the package. Spoon the couscous onto a warmed serving dish, spoon the lamb stew on top, mounding it up in the center, and sprinkle with the remaining fresh cilantro.

GREEK LAMB SAUSAGES WITH TOMATO SAUCE

The Greek name for these sausages is "soudzoukakia." They are more like elongated meatballs than the sausage shapes we are accustomed to. Passata is strained tomato pulp, which can be bought in cartons or jars.

1 cup fresh bread crumbs
⅔ cup milk
1½ pounds ground lamb
2 tablespoons grated onion
3 garlic cloves, crushed
2 teaspoons ground cumin
2 tablespoons chopped fresh parsley
all-purpose flour for dusting
olive oil for frying
2½ cups passata or tomato purée
1 teaspoon sugar
2 bay leaves
1 small onion, peeled
salt and ground black pepper
flat-leaf parsley, to garnish

SERVES 4

1 Combine the bread crumbs and milk. Add the lamb, onion, garlic, cumin and parsley and season with salt and pepper.

2 Shape the mixture with your hands into little fat sausages, about 2 inches long, and roll them in flour. Heat about ¼ cup olive oil in a frying pan.

3 Fry the sausages for about 8 minutes, turning them until evenly browned. Remove and place on paper towels to drain.

4 Put the passata, sugar, bay leaves and whole onion in a pan and simmer for 20 minutes. Add the sausages and cook for 10 more minutes. Serve garnished with parsley.

TURKISH LAMB PILAF

Here we have a delicious combination of rice, lamb, spices, nuts and fruit—a typical Middle Eastern dish.

3 tablespoons butter
1 large onion, finely chopped
1 pound lamb fillet, cut into
small cubes
½ teaspoon ground cinnamon
2 tablespoons tomato paste
3 tablespoons chopped fresh parsley
½ cup dried apricots, halved
¾ cup pistachios
1 pound long-grain rice, rinsed
salt and ground black pepper
flat-leaf parsley, to garnish

SERVES 4

[1] Heat the butter in a large, heavy pan. Add the onion and cook until soft and golden. Add the cubed lamb and brown on all sides. Add the cinnamon and season with salt and pepper. Cover and cook gently for 10 minutes.

[2] Add the tomato paste and enough water to cover the meat. Stir in the parsley, bring to a boil, cover and simmer very gently for 1½ hours, until the meat is tender. Chop the pistachios.

[3] Add enough water to the pan to measure about 2½ cups liquid. Add the apricots, pistachios and rice, bring to a boil, cover tightly and simmer for about 20 minutes, until the rice is cooked. (You may need to add a little more water.) Transfer to a warmed serving dish and garnish with parsley before serving.

271

LEBANESE KIBBEH

Kibbeh is popular in many parts of the southern and eastern Mediterranean.
This version comes from Lebanon, where it is the national dish.

⅔ cup bulghur wheat
1 pound finely ground lean lamb
1 large onion, grated
1 tablespoon butter, melted
salt and ground black pepper
sprigs of mint, to garnish
rice, to serve

FOR THE FILLING
2 tablespoons oil
1 onion, finely chopped
8 ounces ground lamb or veal
⅔ cup pine nuts
½ teaspoon ground allspice

FOR THE YOGURT DIP
2½ cups plain yogurt
2–3 garlic cloves, crushed
1–2 tablespoons chopped fresh mint

SERVES 6

[1] Preheat the oven to 375°F. Rinse the bulghur wheat in a sieve and squeeze out any excess moisture. Mix the lamb, onion and seasoning, kneading the mixture to make a thick paste. Add the bulghur wheat.

[2] To make the filling, heat the oil in a frying pan and fry the onion until golden. Add the lamb or veal and cook, stirring, until evenly browned, then add the pine nuts, allspice and salt and pepper.

[3] Oil a large baking dish and spread half of the meat and bulghur wheat mixture over the bottom. Spoon the filling over it and top with a second layer of meat and bulghur wheat, pressing down firmly with the back of a spoon.

[4] Pour the melted butter over the top of the *kibbeh* and then bake for 40–45 minutes, until browned on top.

[5] Meanwhile, make the yogurt dip. Combine the yogurt and garlic, spoon into a serving bowl and sprinkle with the chopped mint.

[6] Cut the cooked *kibbeh* into squares or rectangles and serve, garnished with mint and accompanied by the yogurt dip. Serve with rice.

272

LAMB WITH SPLIT PEAS

Khoreshe Ghaimeh is a traditional Persian dish and is always served at parties and religious ceremonies. It is a great favorite with children, too.

2 tablespoons butter or margarine
1 large onion, chopped
1 pound lean lamb, cubed
1 teaspoon ground turmeric
1 teaspoon ground cinnamon
1 teaspoon curry powder
1¼ cups water
2–3 saffron strands
½ cup yellow split peas
3 limu amani (dried limes)
3–4 tomatoes, chopped
2 tablespoons oil
2 large potatoes, chopped
salt and freshly ground black pepper
rice, to serve

SERVES 4

COOK'S TIP
Dried limes are available in all Iranian or Middle Eastern shops. However, if you have difficulty obtaining them, use the juice of either 2 fresh limes, 2 fresh oranges or 1 fresh lemon instead, and reduce the water by the same amount. If you prefer, you can use lean stewing beef in place of the lamb in this traditional dish.

1 Melt the butter or margarine in a large saucepan or flameproof casserole and fry the onion for about 4 minutes, until golden, stirring occasionally. Add the meat and cook over high heat for another 3–4 minutes, until brown.

2 Add the turmeric, cinnamon and curry powder and cook for about 2 minutes, stirring frequently.

3 Stir in the water, season well and bring to a boil, then cover and simmer over low heat for about 30–35 minutes, until the meat is half-cooked. Stir the saffron into about 1 tablespoon of boiling water, then add it to the meat.

4 Stir in the split peas, limes and tomatoes. Simmer, covered, for 35 more minutes, until the meat is tender.

5 Heat the oil in a frying pan and fry the potatoes for 10–15 minutes, until cooked and golden. Lift out the dried limes and discard. Spoon the meat onto a large serving dish and sprinkle the potatoes on top. Serve with rice.

STUFFED KIBBEH

Kibbeh is a tasty North African specialty of ground meat and bulghur. The patties are sometimes stuffed with additional meat and deep-fried. Moderately spiced, they're good with yogurt or cacik sauce.

1 pound lean lamb (or lean ground
lamb or beef)
oil for deep-frying
avocado slices and cilantro sprigs,
to serve

FOR THE KIBBEH
1⅓ cups bulghur
1 red chile, seeded and
coarsely chopped
1 onion, coarsely chopped
salt and ground black pepper

FOR THE STUFFING
1 onion, finely chopped
⅔ cup pine nuts
2 tablespoons olive oil
1½ teaspoons ground allspice
¼ cup chopped cilantro

SERVES 4–6

1 If necessary, coarsely cut up the lamb and process the pieces in a blender or food processor until ground. Divide the ground meat into two equal portions.

2 To make the kibbeh, soak the bulghur for 15 minutes in cold water. Drain well, then process in the blender or food processor with the chile, onion, half the meat and plenty of salt and pepper.

3 To make the stuffing, fry the onion and pine nuts in the oil for 5 minutes. Add the allspice and remaining ground meat and fry gently, breaking up the meat with a wooden spoon, until browned. Stir in the cilantro and a little seasoning.

4 Turn the kibbeh mixture out onto a work surface and shape into a cake. Cut into 12 wedges.

5 Flatten one piece in the palm of your hand and spoon a little stuffing into the center. Bring the edges of the kibbeh up over the stuffing to enclose it. Make into a firm, egg-shaped mold between the palms of your hands, making sure that the filling is completely encased. Repeat with the other kibbeh.

6 Heat oil to a depth of 2 inches in a large pan, until a few kibbeh crumbs sizzle on the surface.

7 Lower half the kibbeh into the oil and fry for about 5 minutes, until golden. Drain on paper towels and keep them hot while cooking the remainder. Serve with avocado slices and cilantro sprigs.

LAMB AND CELERY KHORESH

This unusual stew, known in the Middle East as Khoreshe Karafs, has a lovely fresh taste.

1 large onion, chopped
3 tablespoons butter
1 pound lean lamb, cubed
1 teaspoon ground turmeric
½ teaspoon ground cinnamon
2½ cups water
1 head of celery, chopped
1 ounce fresh parsley, chopped
1 small bunch fresh mint, chopped
juice of 1 lemon
salt and ground black pepper
mint leaves, to garnish

SERVES 4

1 Fry the onion in 2 tablespoons of the butter in a large saucepan or flameproof casserole for 3–4 minutes.

2 Add the meat and cook for 2–3 minutes, until brown, stirring frequently. Then stir in the turmeric, cinnamon and salt and pepper.

3 Add the water and bring a boil, then reduce the heat, cover and simmer for 30 minutes, until the meat is half-cooked. .

4 Melt the remaining butter in a frying pan and fry the celery for 8–10 minutes, until tender, stirring frequently. Add the parsley and mint, and fry for another 3–4 minutes.

5 Stir the celery and herbs into the meat. Add the lemon juice and simmer, covered, for another 25–30 minutes, until the meat is completely tender.

6 Serve in a heated bowl, garnished with mint leaves and accompanied by rice. A salad of dressed cherry tomatoes and pared cucumbers would be the perfect side-dish.

LAMB WITH SPINACH AND PRUNES

If you like fresh spinach you will love this lightly spiced sweet-and-sour dish.
It is traditionally served with rice.

3 tablespoons oil
1 large onion, chopped
1 pound lean lamb, cubed
½ teaspoon grated nutmeg
1 teaspoon ground cinnamon
2½ cups water
5 ounces chives or scallions, green parts included, finely chopped
1 pound fresh spinach, chopped
1¼ cups prunes, soaked
juice of 1 lemon
salt and ground black pepper

SERVES 4

1 Heat 2 tablespoons of the oil in a large pan and fry the onion for 3–4 minutes, until golden. Add the lamb and fry until brown on all sides. Sprinkle with the nutmeg and cinnamon, and stir the mixture well.

2 Add the water, bring to a boil and spoon off any foam that rises to the surface. Season with salt and pepper, cover and simmer over low heat for 40–45 minutes, until the meat is nearly cooked.

3 Heat the remaining oil in another large pan, add the chives or scallions, stir-fry for a few minutes and then add the spinach. Cover and cook over medium heat for 2–3 minutes, until the spinach has wilted, then add this mixture to the meat, with the prunes and lemon juice.

4 Cook, covered, for another 20–25 minutes, until the meat is completely tender. Serve with rice.

MEAT DUMPLINGS WITH YOGURT SAUCE

These Lebanese meat dumplings are braised in yogurt sauce, a specialty known as Shish Barak.
Mint and garlic give the lamb a great flavor.

2 tablespoons oil
1 large onion, chopped
¼ cup pine nuts or
chopped walnuts
1 pound minced lamb
2 tablespoons butter
3 garlic cloves, crushed
1 tablespoon chopped fresh mint
salt and ground black pepper
mint leaves, to garnish

FOR THE DOUGH
2 cups all-purpose flour
1 teaspoon salt

FOR THE YOGURT SAUCE
8 cups yogurt
1 egg, beaten
1 tablespoon cornstarch, blended with
1 tablespoon cold water
salt and white pepper

SERVES 4

1 First, make the dough. Combine the flour and salt and then stir in enough water to bind the dough. Knead lightly, then let stand for 1 hour.

2 Heat the oil in a large frying pan and fry the onion for 3–4 minutes, until soft. Add the pine nuts or walnuts and fry until golden. Stir in the meat and cook until brown. Season, then remove the pan from heat and set it aside.

3 Roll out the dough thinly on a floured board. Cut into small rounds 2–2½ inches in diameter. Place 1 teaspoon of the meat filling on each one, fold the pastry over and firmly press the edges together. It is important not to over-fill the pastries or they may burst. Bring the ends together to form a handle.

4 Make the yogurt sauce. Pour the yogurt into a saucepan and beat in the egg and the cornstarch mixture. Season with salt and white pepper and slowly bring to a boil, stirring constantly. Cook over low heat until the sauce thickens and then carefully drop in the dumplings. Simmer for 20 minutes.

5 Spoon the dumplings and sauce onto warmed serving plates. Melt the butter in a small frying pan and fry the garlic until golden. Stir in the mint, cook briefly and then pour over the dumplings. Garnish with mint leaves. Serve with rice and a salad.

KOFTAS IN TOMATO SAUCE

There are many varieties of kofta in the Mediterranean and Middle East. This is a popular version from Turkey.

12 ounces ground lamb or beef
½ cup fresh bread crumbs
1 onion, grated
3 tablespoons chopped fresh parsley
1 tablespoon chopped fresh mint
1 teaspoon ground cumin
1 teaspoon ground turmeric
3 tablespoons oil for frying
salt and ground black pepper
noodles, to serve
mint leaves, to garnish

FOR THE TOMATO SAUCE
1 tablespoon olive oil
1 onion, chopped
14-ounce can plum tomatoes
1 tablespoon tomato paste
juice of ½ lemon
salt and ground black pepper

SERVES 4

2 Meanwhile, place the ground lamb or beef in a large bowl and mix in the bread crumbs, grated onion, herbs and spices and a little salt and pepper.

COOK'S TIP
Instead of using either ground lamb or beef, use a mixture of the two, or add a little chopped bacon.

3 Knead the mixture by hand until thoroughly blended and then shape it into walnut-size balls and place on a plate.

4 Heat the oil in a frying pan and fry the meatballs, in batches if necessary, until evenly browned. Transfer them to the pan of tomato sauce. Cover the pan and simmer gently for about 30 minutes. Serve with noodles and garnish with mint leaves.

1 First, make the tomato sauce. Heat the oil in a large saucepan or flameproof casserole and fry the onion until golden. Stir in the canned tomatoes, tomato paste, lemon juice and seasoning, bring to a boil and then reduce the heat and simmer for about 10 minutes.

SKEWERED LAMB WITH CILANTRO YOGURT

Although lamb is the most commonly used meat for Turkish kebabs, lean beef or pork work equally well.
For color you can alternate pieces of bell pepper, lemon or onions, although this is not traditional.

2 pounds lean boneless lamb
1 large onion, grated
3 bay leaves
5 thyme or rosemary sprigs
grated zest and juice of
1 lemon
½ teaspoon sugar
⅓ cup olive oil
salt and ground black pepper
sprigs of rosemary, to garnish
broiled lemon wedges, to serve

FOR THE CORIANDER YOGURT
⅔ cup thick plain yogurt
1 tablespoon chopped fresh mint
1 tablespoon chopped cilantro
2 teaspoons grated onion

SERVES 4

1 To make the cilantro yogurt, combine the yogurt, mint, cilantro and grated onion and transfer to a small serving dish.

2 To make the kebabs, cut the lamb into small chunks and put in a bowl. Combine the grated onion, herbs, lemon zest and juice, sugar and oil, then add salt and pepper and pour over the lamb.

3 Combine the ingredients and let marinate in the refrigerator for several hours or overnight.

4 Drain the meat and thread onto skewers. Arrange on a broiler rack and cook under a preheated broiler for about 10 minutes, until browned, turning occasionally. Transfer to a plate and garnish with rosemary. Serve with the broiled lemon wedges and the cilantro yogurt.

COOK'S TIP
Cover the tips of wooden skewers with foil so they don't char.

GROUND MEAT KEBABS

These kebabs are often served with rice, into which is stirred raw egg yolk and melted butter.
Traditionally, the kebabs are barbecued over open fires, but they can also be cooked
under a very hot broiler.

1 pound lean lamb
1 pound lean beef
1 large onion, grated
2 garlic cloves, crushed
1 tablespoon sumac *(optional)*
2–3 saffron strands, soaked in
1 tablespoon boiling water
2 teaspoons baking soda
6–8 tomatoes, halved
1 tablespoon melted butter
salt and ground black pepper

SERVES 4

1 Grind the lamb and beef two or three times until very finely ground, place in a large bowl and add the grated onion, garlic, *sumac*, if using, soaked saffron, baking soda, and salt and pepper. Knead by hand until the mixture becomes glutinous.

COOK'S TIP

2 Take a small handful of meat and roll it into a ball. If the ball seems crumbly, knead the mixture in the bowl for a few minutes.

3 Shape the ball around a flat skewer, molding it around the skewer. Repeat until you have three or four balls on each skewer, pressing them tightly to prevent the meat from falling off.

4 Thread the tomatoes onto separate skewers. Cook the meat and the tomato kebabs on a grill or under a hot broiler for about 10 minutes, basting them with melted butter and turning them occasionally.

CORIANDER LAMB KEBABS WITH AN ALMOND CHANTERELLE SAUCE

The delicate sweetness of lamb combines well with chanterelles, which are used here to make this especially delicious almond sauce.

8 lamb cutlets, trimmed
8 ounces chanterelle
mushrooms, trimmed
2 tablespoons unsalted butter
¼ cup whole almonds, toasted
2 ounces white bread, crusts removed
1 cup milk
3 tablespoons olive oil
½ teaspoon sugar
2 teaspoons lemon juice
salt and cayenne pepper, to taste

FOR THE MARINADE
3 tablespoons olive oil
1 tablespoon lemon juice
2 teaspoons ground coriander
½ garlic clove, crushed
2 teaspoons honey

SERVES 4

1 Put the lamb in a shallow dish. Make the marinade. Mix the oil, lemon juice, ground coriander, garlic and honey in a bowl. Spoon over the lamb, coating each cutlet, then cover and let sit for at least 30 minutes.

2 Fry the chanterelles gently in butter for 3–4 minutes without coloring. Set aside.

3 Place the almonds in a food processor and grind finely. Add half of the chanterelles, the bread, milk, oil, sugar and lemon juice, then process together well.

4 Thread the lamb cutlets onto four metal skewers, and cook under a medium hot broiler for 6–8 minutes on each side. Season the almond mixture with salt and cayenne, then spoon this over the kebabs. Top with the remaining chanterelles and serve with new potatoes and dressed green leaves.

SKEWERED LAMB WITH RED ONION SALSA

This summery tapas dish is ideal for outdoor eating, but if the weather fails, the skewers can be cooked under a conventional broiler. The simple salsa makes a refreshing accompaniment—make sure that you use a mild-flavored red onion, which is fresh and crisp, and a tomato that is ripe and full of flavor.

8 ounces lean lamb
½ teaspoon ground cumin
1 teaspoon ground paprika
1 tablespoon olive oil
salt and ground black pepper

FOR THE SALSA
1 red onion, finely sliced
1 large tomato, seeded and chopped
1 tablespoon red wine vinegar
3–4 fresh basil or mint leaves,
roughly torn
small mint leaves, to garnish

SERVES 4

COOK'S TIP
To make an alternative sauce to the red onion salsa, stir chopped fresh mint or basil and a little lemon juice into a small carton of plain yogurt. Drizzle the mixture over the cooked kebabs before serving.

VARIATION
For a more fiery flavor, prepare the salsa the day before and spike it with a chopped red chile.

1 Cut the lamb into cubes, removing some of the fat, but leaving a little on the meat to prevent it from drying out too much when grilled or broiled. Place the lamb cubes in a bowl with the cumin, paprika, olive oil and plenty of salt and pepper. Toss well until the lamb is coated with spices.

2 Cover the bowl with plastic wrap and let sit in a cool place for several hours, or in the fridge overnight, so that the lamb absorbs the spicy flavors. Stir the meat cubes occasionally, if convenient.

3 Spear the lamb cubes onto four small skewers—if using wooden skewers, soak them first in cold water for at least 30 minutes to prevent them from burning. Do not pack the cubes too closely.

4 To make the salsa, put the sliced onion, tomato, vinegar and basil or mint leaves in a small bowl, and stir together until thoroughly blended. Season to taste with salt, garnish with mint, then set the salsa aside while you cook the skewered lamb.

5 Cook the skewered lamb over hot coals or under a preheated broil for 5–10 minutes, turning the skewers frequently, until the lamb is well browned but still slightly pink in the center. Serve hot, with the red onion salsa.

LAMB KOUTLETS

Koutlets are very tasty and are equally popular served hot at a buffet or cold on a picnic.

3 eggs
1 onion, grated
2 tablespoons chopped fresh parsley
1 pound new potatoes, peeled
1 pound finely minced lean lamb
1 cup dried bread crumbs
oil, for frying
salt and ground black pepper
mint leaves, to garnish

MAKES 12–15

1 Beat the eggs in a large bowl, add the onion and parsley, season with salt and pepper, and beat together well.

2 Cook the potatoes in a large saucepan of boiling salted water for 20 minutes, until tender, then drain and let cool. When the potatoes are cold, grate them coarsely and stir into the egg mixture together with the ground lamb. Knead by hand for 3 minutes until thoroughly mixed.

3 Take a handful of meat and roll it into a ball. Next, roll each ball in the bread crumbs and then mold into triangles, about 5 inches long. Cover with the bread crumbs again, patting them on firmly.

4 Heat the oil in a frying pan and fry the *koutlets* over medium heat for 8–12 minutes, until golden brown, turning occasionally. Garnish with mint and serve hot, with pita bread and a salad.

DILL AND FAVA BEAN MEATBALLS

This is another recipe for kofta, this time using lean ground beef instead of the more common lamb.

generous ½ cup long grain rice
1 pound ground lean beef
1 cup all-purpose flour
3 eggs, beaten
1 cup fava beans, skinned
2 tablespoons chopped fresh dill
2 tablespoons butter or margarine
1 large onion, chopped
½ teaspoon ground turmeric
5 cups water
salt and ground black pepper
chopped fresh parsley, to garnish
naan, to serve

SERVES 4

1 Put the rice in a saucepan, cover with water and boil for about 4 minutes, until half-cooked. Drain and place in a bowl with the meat, flour, eggs and seasoning. Knead thoroughly by hand until well blended.

2 Add the skinned fava beans and dill, and knead again thoroughly until the mixture resembles a firm paste. Shape the mixture into large balls and set aside on a plate. This is easier to do if you wet your hands first.

3 Melt the butter or margarine in a large saucepan or flameproof casserole and fry the onion for about 4 minutes until golden. Stir in the turmeric, cook for 30 seconds and then add the water and bring to a boil over high heat.

4 Add the meatballs to the pan, reduce the heat and simmer for 45–60 minutes, until the meatballs are cooked through and the sauce is reduced to about 1 cup. Garnish with parsley and serve with warm naan.

LAMB TAGINE WITH ARTICHOKES AND PRESERVED LEMON

You can also use stewing or braising beef for this tagine, if you prefer.

1½ pounds leg of lamb, trimmed and
cut into cubes
2 onions, very finely chopped
2 garlic cloves, crushed
¼ cup chopped fresh parsley
¼ cup chopped cilantro
a good pinch of ground ginger
1 teaspoon ground cumin
6 tablespoons olive oil
1½–1⅔ cups water or stock
1 preserved lemon
14-ounce can artichoke hearts,
drained and halved
1 tablespoon chopped fresh mint
1 egg, beaten (optional)
salt and ground black pepper
couscous and mint, to serve

SERVES 4–6

1 Place the meat in a shallow dish. Stir together the onions, garlic, parsley, cilantro, ginger, cumin, seasoning and olive oil. Stir into the meat, cover with plastic wrap and set aside to marinate for at least 3 hours or preferably overnight.

2 Heat a large heavy saucepan and stir in the meat with all the marinade. Cook for 5–6 minutes, until the meat is evenly brown, then stir in enough water or stock to just cover the meat. Bring to a boil, cover and simmer for 45–60 minutes, until the meat is just tender.

3 Rinse the preserved lemon under cold water, discard the flesh and cut the peel into pieces. Stir into the meat and simmer for another 15 minutes, then add the artichoke hearts and mint.

4 Simmer for a few more minutes to warm through. If you want to thicken the sauce, remove the pan from heat and stir in some or all of the beaten egg. Garnish with mint and serve with couscous.

BEEF ROLLS WITH GARLIC AND TOMATO SAUCE

Italy has many regional variations on the technique of wrapping thin slices of beef around a richly flavored stuffing. This recipe incorporates some classic ingredients. Serve with polenta, if desired.

🍃 🍃

4 thin slices of sirloin steak (about
4 ounces each)
4 slices smoked ham
5 ounces Pecorino cheese, grated
2 garlic cloves, crushed
5 tablespoons chopped fresh parsley
2 eggs, soft boiled and peeled
3 tablespoons olive oil
1 large onion, finely chopped
⅔ cup passata or tomato purée
⅓ cup red wine
2 bay leaves
⅔ cup beef stock
salt and ground black pepper
flat-leaf parsley, to garnish

SERVES 4

1. Preheat the oven to 325°F. Lay the steak slices on a sheet of waxed paper. Cover the steak with another sheet of waxed paper or plastic wrap and beat with a mallet or rolling pin until the slices are very thin.

2. Lay a ham slice over each. Mix the cheese in a bowl with the garlic, parsley, eggs and a little salt and pepper. Stir well until all the ingredients are evenly mixed.

3. Spoon the stuffing onto the ham and steak slices. Fold two opposite sides of the meat over the stuffing, then roll up the meat to form neat parcels. Secure with string.

4. Heat the oil in a frying pan. Add the parcels and sauté quickly on all sides to brown. Transfer to an ovenproof dish.

5. Add the onion to the frying pan and sauté for 3 minutes. Stir in the passata, wine, bay leaves and stock and season with salt and pepper. Bring to a boil, then pour the sauce over the meat in the dish.

6. Cover the dish and bake for 1 hour. Drain the meat and remove the string. Spoon onto warmed serving plates. Taste the sauce, adding extra salt and pepper if necessary, and spoon it over the meat. Serve garnished with flat-leaf parsley.

CORSICAN BEEF STEW WITH MACARONI

Pasta is eaten in many parts of the Mediterranean. In Corsica, it's often served with gravy as a sauce and, in this case, in a rich beef stew.

1 ounce dried mushrooms
(cèpes or porcini)
6 garlic cloves
2 pounds stewing beef, cut into
2-inch cubes
4 ounces lardons, or thick bacon
cut into strips
3 tablespoons olive oil
2 onions, sliced
1¼ cups dry white wine
2 tablespoons passata
or tomato purée
pinch of ground cinnamon
sprig of rosemary
1 bay leaf
2 cups large macaroni
⅔ cup freshly grated
Parmesan cheese
salt and ground black pepper

SERVES 4

1 Soak the dried mushrooms in warm water for 30 minutes. Drain, set the mushrooms aside and reserve the liquid. Cut three of the garlic cloves into thin strips and insert into the pieces of beef by making little slits with a sharp knife. Push the lardons or pieces of bacon into the beef with the garlic. Season the meat with salt and pepper.

3 Stir in the white wine, passata, mushrooms, cinnamon, rosemary and bay leaf and season with salt and pepper. Cook gently for about 30 minutes, stirring often. Strain the mushroom liquid and add to the stew with enough water to cover. Bring to a boil, cover and simmer very gently for 3 hours, until the meat is very tender.

2 Heat the oil in a heavy pan, add half the beef and brown well on all sides. Repeat with the remaining beef. Transfer to a plate. Add the sliced onions to the pan and cook until lightly browned. Crush the remaining garlic and add to the onions with the meat.

4 Cook the macaroni in a large pan of boiling salted water for 10 minutes or until al dente Lift the pieces of meat out of the gravy and transfer to a warmed serving platter. Drain the pasta and layer in a serving bowl with the gravy and cheese. Serve with the meat.

PROVENÇAL BEEF AND OLIVE DAUBE

A daube is a French method of braising meat with wine and herbs. This version from the Nice area in the south of France also includes black olives and tomatoes.

3–3½ pounds top round roast
½ pound lardons, or thick bacon
cut into strips
½ pound carrots, sliced
1 bay leaf
1 thyme sprig
2 parsley sprigs
3 garlic cloves
2 cups pitted black or
green olives
14-ounce can chopped tomatoes
crusty bread, flageolet beans or pasta,
to serve

FOR THE MARINADE
½ cup extra virgin olive oil
1 onion, sliced
4 shallots, sliced
1 celery stalk, sliced
1 carrot, sliced
⅔ cup red wine
6 peppercorns
2 garlic cloves, sliced
1 bay leaf
1 thyme sprig
2 parsley stalks
salt

SERVES 6

1. To make the marinade, heat the oil in a large shallow pan and add the onion, shallots, celery and carrot. Cook for 2 minutes, then lower the heat and add the red wine, pepper-corns, garlic, bay leaf, thyme and parsley. Season with salt, then cover and let simmer gently for 15–20 minutes. Set aside.

2. Place the beef in a large glass or earthenware dish and pour the cooled marinade over. Cover the dish and let marinate in a cool place or in the refrigerator for 12 hours, turning the meat once or twice.

3. Preheat the oven to 325°F. Lift the meat out of the marinade and fit snugly into an ovenproof casserole. Add the lardons or bacon and carrots, along with the herbs and garlic. Strain in all the marinade. Cover the casserole with waxed paper, then the lid, and bake for 2½ hours.

4. Remove the casserole from the oven and stir in the olives and tomatoes. Re-cover the casserole, return to the oven and cook for another 30 minutes. Serve the meat cut into thick slices, accompanied by crusty bread, beans or pasta.

BEEF STEW WITH TOMATOES, WINE AND PEAS

There are as many versions of this Italian recipe as there are cooks. This one is very traditional,
perfect for a winter lunch or dinner. Serve it with boiled or mashed potatoes
to soak up the deliciously rich sauce.

2 tablespoons all-purpose flour
2 teaspoons chopped fresh thyme or
1 teaspoon dried thyme
2¼ pound braising or stewing beef,
cut into large cubes
3 tablespoons olive oil
1 medium onion, roughly chopped
2 cups passata or tomato purée
1 cup beef stock
1 cup red wine
2 garlic cloves, crushed
2 tablespoons tomato paste
2 cups shelled fresh peas
1 teaspoon sugar
salt and ground black pepper
sprigs of fresh thyme, to garnish

SERVES 4

3 Add the onion to the pan, scraping the bottom of the pan to mix in any sediment. Cook gently for about 3 minutes, until softened, then add the passata, stock, wine, garlic and tomato paste. Bring to a boil, stirring. Return the beef to the pan and coat with the sauce. Cover and cook for 1½ hours.

1 Preheat the oven to 325°F. Put the flour in a shallow dish and season with the thyme and salt and pepper. Add the beef cubes and turn them in the mixture to coat evenly.

2 Heat the olive oil in a large flameproof casserole, add the beef and brown on all sides over medium to high heat. Remove with a slotted spoon and drain on paper towels. It may be necessary to cook the beef in batches.

4 Stir in the peas and sugar. Return the casserole to the oven and cook for 30 more minutes, or until the beef is tender. Check the seasoning and garnish with fresh thyme before serving.

CALF'S LIVER WITH BALSAMIC VINEGAR

This sweet-and-sour liver dish is a specialty of Venice. Serve it very simply, with a side vegetable such as lightly cooked green beans.

🔪 🔪

1 tablespoon all-purpose flour
½ teaspoon finely chopped fresh sage
4 thin slices of calf's liver, cut into serving pieces
3 tablespoons olive oil
2 tablespoons butter
2 small red onions, sliced and separated into rings
⅔ cup dry white wine
3 tablespoons balsamic vinegar
a pinch of sugar
salt and ground black pepper
fresh sage sprigs, to garnish

SERVES 2

1 Spread out the flour in a shallow bowl. Season it with the sage and plenty of salt and pepper. Turn the liver in the flour until well coated.

2 Heat 2 tablespoons of the oil with half of the butter in a wide heavy saucepan or frying pan until foaming.

3 Add the onion rings and cook gently, stirring frequently, for about 5 minutes, until softened but not colored. Remove the onion rings with a spatula and set them aside on a plate.

4 Heat the remaining oil and butter in the pan until foaming, add the liver and cook over medium heat for 2–3 minutes on each side.

Transfer to warmed dinner plates and keep hot.

5 Add the wine and vinegar to the pan, then stir to mix with the pan juices and any sediment. Return the onions and add the sugar, and heat through, stirring. Spoon the sauce over the liver, garnish with sage and serve immediately.

CALF'S LIVER WITH HONEY

Liver is prepared in many ways all over the Mediterranean—this is a quick and easy, slightly contemporary treatment from France. Cook the liver until it is browned on the outside but still rosy pink in the center.

4 slices calf's liver, each about
6 ounces and ½ inch thick
all-purpose flour, for dusting
2 tablespoons butter
2 tablespoons vegetable oil
2 tablespoons sherry vinegar or
red wine vinegar
2–3 tablespoons chicken stock
1 tablespoon honey
salt and ground black pepper
watercress sprigs, to garnish

SERVES 4

1 Wipe the liver slices with damp paper towels, then season both sides with a little salt and pepper, and dust the slices lightly with flour, shaking off any excess. Place the floured slices on a board.

2 In a large, heavy frying pan, melt half of the butter with the oil over high heat and swirl the pan to combine them.

3 Add the liver slices to the pan and cook for 1–2 minutes, until browned on one side, then turn and cook for another 1 minute. Transfer to heated plates and keep warm.

4 Stir the vinegar, stock and honey into the pan and boil for about 1 minute, stirring constantly, then add the remaining butter, stirring until melted and smooth. Spoon the liquid over the liver slices, garnish with watercress and serve.

COOK'S TIP
Use a mild-flavored honey, such as acacia, for the sauce.

POLPETTINI WITH FONTINA

In this Italian dish, meatballs are filled with Fontina cubes, then rolled in crumbs and fried.
They are delicious served with noodles and a rich tomato sauce.

1¼ pounds lean ground beef
1¼ pounds lean ground pork
3 garlic cloves, crushed
grated zest and juice of 1 lemon
2 slices of day-old bread, crumbed
½ cup freshly grated Parmesan cheese
½ teaspoon ground cinnamon
1 teaspoon dried oregano
2 eggs, beaten
1 teaspoon salt
5 ounces Fontina cheese, cut into
16 cubes
1–1¼ cups dried bread crumbs
olive oil, for shallow frying
ground black pepper
fresh herbs and freshly grated
Parmesan cheese, to garnish

SERVES 6–8

1 Preheat the oven to 350°F. Put the lean ground beef and pork into a bowl. Add the garlic, lemon rind and juice, bread crumbs, Parmesan, cinnamon and oregano and stir. Beat in the eggs, salt and plenty of pepper.

2 Using clean hands occasionally dipped into cold water, knead the mixture to ensure that all the ingredients are well distributed, then shape it into 16 balls. Cup each ball in turn in your hand and press a piece of Fontina into the center. Reshape each ball, making sure the cheese is well covered.

3 Roll the meatballs in the dried bread crumbs. Heat the olive oil in a large frying pan. Add the meatballs in batches and cook them quickly all over, until lightly browned and sealed. Transfer them to a roasting pan and bake for 20 minutes or until cooked through. Garnish with fresh herbs and Parmesan, and serve.

297

MEATBALLS WITH MOZZARELLA AND TOMATO

These Italian meatballs are made with beef and topped with mozzarella cheese and tomato.

½ slice white bread, crusts removed
3 tablespoons milk
1½ pounds ground beef
1 egg, beaten
⅔ cup dry bread crumbs
vegetable oil for frying
2 beefsteak or other large
tomatoes, sliced
1 tablespoon chopped fresh oregano
1 mozzarella cheese, cut into 6 slices
6 drained canned anchovies, cut in
half lengthwise
salt and ground black pepper

SERVES 6

1 Preheat the oven to 400°F. Put the bread and milk in a small saucepan and heat very gently over low heat until the bread absorbs all the milk. Mash it to a pulp and let cool.

2 Put the beef into a bowl with the bread mixture and the egg and season with salt and pepper. Mix well, then shape the mixture into six patties. Sprinkle the bread crumbs on a plate and dredge the patties, coating them thoroughly.

3 Heat about ¼ inch oil in a large frying pan. Add the patties and fry for 2 minutes on each side, until brown. Transfer to a greased ovenproof dish in a single layer.

4 Lay a slice of tomato on top of each patty, sprinkle with oregano and season with salt and pepper. Place the mozzarella slices on top. Arrange two strips of anchovy placed in a cross on top of each slice of mozzarella.

5 Bake for 10–15 minutes, until the mozzarella has melted. Serve hot, straight from the dish.

BELL PEPPERS STUFFED WITH GROUND BEEF

This lunch or buffet dish makes a pleasant change from vegetables stuffed with rice or wheat.

 Sauté the ground beef in a nonstick. frying pan for a few minutes, stirring until it is no longer red. Transfer to a plate. Pour half of the oil into the frying pan and sauté the onion and celery over high heat until the onion starts to brown. Trim the mushrooms and stir in the partly-cooked beef. Season with the cinnamon, salt and pepper. Cook over low heat for about 30 minutes.

1 onion
2 celery stalks
4 red bell peppers
1 pound ground lean beef
¼ cup olive oil
2 ounces button mushrooms
pinch of ground cinnamon
salt and ground black pepper
chervil or flat-leaf parsley, to garnish
green salad, to serve

SERVES 4

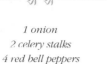 Dice the onion and celery. Cut the tops off the peppers and remove the seeds and membranes.

Preheat the oven to 375°F. Cut a sliver off the bottom of each pepper to make sure that they stand level, spoon in the beef and vegetable mixture and then replace the lids. Arrange in an oiled baking dish, drizzle the remaining oil on top, and bake for 30 minutes. Garnish with herbs, then serve with a green salad.

TANGY BEEF AND HERB KHORESH

Lamb, beef or poultry stews with herbs, spices and vegetables or fruit are all called khoresh and are among the best-loved Persian dishes. Like this beef stew, Khoreshe Gormeh Sabzi, they are mildly spiced and are ideal to serve as a simple but delicious dish for a dinner party.

3 tablespoons oil
1 large onion, chopped
1 pound lean stewing beef, cubed
1 tablespoon fenugreek leaf
2 teaspoons ground turmeric
½ teaspoon ground cinnamon
2½ cups water
1 ounces fresh parsley, chopped
1 ounces fresh chives, snipped
15-ounce can red kidney beans
juice of 1 lemon
salt and ground black pepper

SERVES 4

1 Heat 2 tablespoons of the oil in a large saucepan or flameproof casserole and fry the onion for 3–4 minutes, until light golden. Add the beef and fry for 5–10 more minutes, until brown, stirring so that the meat is colored on all sides.

2 Add the fenugreek, turmeric and cinnamon and cook for about 1 minute, stirring, then add the water and bring to a boil. Cover and simmer over low heat for 45 minutes, stirring occasionally with a wooden spoon.

3 Heat the remaining oil in a small frying pan and fry the parsley and chives over medium heat for 2–3 minutes, stirring the mixture frequently.

4 Drain the kidney beans and stir them into the beef with the fried herbs and lemon juice. Season with salt and pepper.

5 Simmer the stew for another 30–35 minutes, until the meat is tender. Serve with rice.

BEEF TAGINE WITH SWEET POTATOES

This warming dish is eaten during the winter in Morocco, where, especially in the mountains, the weather can be surprisingly cold. Tagines, by definition, are cooked on the stove (or, more often in Morocco, over coals). However, this also works well cooked in the oven.

1½–2 pounds braising or
stewing beef
2 tablespoons sunflower oil
a good pinch of ground turmeric
1 large onion, chopped
1 red or green chile, seeded
and chopped
1½ teaspoons paprika
a good pinch of cayenne pepper
½ teaspoon ground cumin
1 pound sweet potatoes
1 tablespoon chopped fresh parsley
1 tablespoon chopped cilantro
1 tablespoon butter
salt and ground black pepper

SERVES 4

3 Add the onion, chile, paprika, cayenne pepper and cumin to the casserole, with just enough water to cover the meat. Cover tightly and cook for 1–1½ hours, until the meat is very tender, checking occasionally and adding a little extra water to keep the stew moist.

4 Meanwhile, peel the sweet potatoes and slice them straight into a bowl of salted water. Transfer to a pan, bring to a boil and simmer for 3 minutes, until just tender. Drain.

5 Stir the herbs into the meat. Arrange the potato slices over the meat and dot with the butter. Cover. Bake for 10 more minutes.

6 Increase the oven temperature to 400°F or heat the broiler. Remove the lid of the casserole and cook under the broiler for another 5–10 minutes, until the potatoes are golden.

1 Cube the beef. Heat the oil in a flameproof casserole and fry the meat, with the turmeric and seasoning, for 3–4 minutes, until evenly brown, stirring frequently.

2 Cover the pan tightly and cook for 15 minutes over low heat, without lifting the lid. Preheat the oven to 350°F.

PORK WITH MARSALA WINE AND JUNIPER

Although most frequently used in desserts, Sicilian marsala gives savory dishes a rich, fruity tang.
Use good quality butcher's pork that won't be drowned out by the flavor of the sauce.

🌿 🌿

1 ounce dried cèpes or porcini
mushrooms
4 pork cutlets
2 teaspoons balsamic vinegar
8 garlic cloves
1 tablespoon butter
3 tablespoons marsala wine
several rosemary sprigs
10 juniper berries, crushed
salt and ground black pepper
noodles and green vegetables,
to serve

SERVES 4

🌿 🌿

1. Put the dried mushrooms in a bowl and just cover with hot water. Let stand.

2. Brush the pork with 1 teaspoon of the vinegar and season with salt and pepper. Put the garlic cloves in a small pan of boiling water and cook for 10 minutes, until soft. Drain and set aside.

3. Melt the butter in a large frying pan. Add the pork and cook quickly until browned on the underside. Turn the meat over and cook for another minute.

4. Add the marsala, rosemary, mushrooms, 4 tablespoons of the mushroom juices, the garlic cloves, juniper and remaining vinegar.

5. Simmer gently for about 3 minutes, until the pork is cooked through. Season lightly and serve hot with noodles and green vegetables.

CASSOULET

Cassoulet is a classic French dish in which a feast of various meats is baked slowly with beans under a golden crumb crust. It is hearty and rich, perfect for a winter gathering.

3½ cups dried navy or
Great Northern beans
2 pounds salt pork or
pork pieces
4 large duck breasts
4 tablespoons olive oil
2 onions, chopped
6 garlic cloves, crushed
2 bay leaves
¼ teaspoon ground cloves
4 tablespoons tomato paste
8 good-quality sausages
4 tomatoes
1½ cups dried bread crumbs
salt and ground black pepper

SERVES 6–8

 Put the beans in a large
bowl and cover with plenty
of cold water. Let soak overnight.
If using salt pork, soak it overnight
in water.

2 Drain the beans thoroughly and
put them in a large saucepan
with fresh water to cover. Bring to a
boil and boil rapidly for 10 minutes.
Drain and set the beans aside.

3 Cut the pork into large pieces,
discarding the rind. Halve the
duck breasts.

4 Heat 2 tablespoons of the oil in
a frying pan and sauté the pork
in batches until browned.

5 Put the beans in a large, heavy
saucepan with the onions,
garlic, bay leaves, ground cloves and
tomato paste. Stir in the browned
pork and just cover with water. Bring
to a boil, then reduce the heat to the
lowest setting and simmer, covered,
for about 1½ hours, until the beans
are tender.

 Preheat the oven to 350°F.
Heat the rest of the oil in a
frying pan and sauté the duck breasts
and sausages until browned. Cut the
sausages into pieces.

7 Plunge the tomatoes into
boiling water for 30 seconds,
then refresh in cold water. Peel away
the skins and cut them into quarters.

8 Transfer the bean mixture to a
large earthenware pot or
ovenproof dish and stir in the
sausages, duck breasts and chopped
tomatoes with salt and pepper
to taste.

9 Sprinkle with an even layer
of bread crumbs and bake for
45 minutes to 1 hour, until the crust is
golden. Serve hot.

VARIATION
You can easily alter the proportions
and types of meat and vegetables in a
cassoulet. Turnips, carrots and celery
root make suitable vegetable
substitutes, while cubed lamb and
goose can replace the pork and duck.

SPANISH PORK AND SAUSAGE CASSEROLE

Another pork dish from the Catalan region of Spain, which uses the spicy butifarra sausage. You can find these sausages in some Spanish food stores but, if not, sweet Italian sausages will do.

2 tablespoons olive oil
4 boneless pork chops, about
1 pound
4 butifarra or sweet Italian sausages
1 onion, chopped
2 garlic cloves, chopped
½ cup dry white wine
4 plum tomatoes, chopped
1 bay leaf
2 tablespoons chopped fresh parsley
salt and ground black pepper
green salad and baked potatoes,
to serve

SERVES 4

1 Heat the oil in a large, deep frying pan. Cook the pork chops over high heat until browned on both sides, then transfer to a plate.

2 Add the sausages, onion and garlic to the pan and cook over medium heat until the sausages are browned and the onion softened, turning the sausages two or three times during cooking. Return the chops to the pan.

3 Stir in the wine, tomatoes and bay leaf, and season with salt and pepper. Add the parsley. Cover the pan and cook for 30 minutes.

4 Remove the sausages from the pan and cut them into thick slices. Return them to the pan and heat through. Serve hot, accompanied by a green salad and baked potatoes.

COOK'S TIP
Vine tomatoes, which are making a welcome appearance in supermarkets, can be used instead of plum tomatoes.

BLACK BEAN STEW

This simple Spanish stew uses a few robust ingredients to create a deliciously intense flavor, something like a French cassoulet.

🌿 🌿

1⅓ cups black beans
1½ pounds bacon
¼ cup olive oil
12 ounces baby onions
2 celery stalks, thickly sliced
2 teaspoons paprika
5 ounces chorizo sausage, cut into chunks
2½ cups light chicken or vegetable stock
2 green bell peppers, seeded and cut into large pieces
salt and ground black pepper

SERVES 5–6

🌿 🌿

 1 Put the beans in a bowl and cover with plenty of cold water. Let soak overnight. Drain the beans in a saucepan and cover with fresh water. Bring to a boil and boil rapidly for 10 minutes. Drain.

2 Preheat the oven to 325°F. Cut the bacon into chunks.

3 Heat the oil in a large frying pan and sauté the onions and celery for 3 minutes. Add the bacon and sauté for 5–10 minutes, until the bacon is browned.

4 Add the paprika and chorizo and cook for another 2 minutes. Transfer to an ovenproof dish with the beans and combine.

5 Add the stock to the pan and bring to a boil. Season lightly, then pour over the meat and beans. Cover and bake for 1 hour.

6 Stir the green peppers into the stew and return to the oven for 15 minutes more. Serve hot.

🌿 🌿

COOK'S TIP
This is the sort of stew to which you can add a variety of winter vegetables, such as chunks of leek, turnip, celery root and even little potatoes.

🌿 🌿

AFELIA

This lightly spiced pork stew makes a delicious supper dish served simply, as it would be in Cyprus, with warm bread, a leafy salad and a few olives.

3 Preheat the oven to 325°F. Heat 2 tablespoons of the oil in a frying pan over high heat. Brown the meat quickly, then transfer to an ovenproof dish.

1½ pounds pork fillet, boneless leg or loin chops
4 teaspoons coriander seeds
½ teaspoon sugar
3 tablespoons olive oil
2 large onions, sliced
1¼ cups red wine
salt and ground black pepper
cilantro, to garnish

SERVES 4

COOK'S TIP
A clean coffee grinder can also be used to grind the coriander seeds. Alternatively, use 1 tablespoon ground coriander.

---

1 Cut the pork into small chunks, discarding any excess fat. Crush the coriander seeds with a mortar and pestle until fairly finely ground.

2 Mix the coriander seeds with the sugar and salt and pepper and rub all over the meat. Let marinate for up to 4 hours.

4 Add the remaining oil to the pan and sauté the onions until beginning to color. Stir in the wine and a little salt and pepper and bring just to a boil.

5 Pour the onion and wine mixture over the meat and cover with a lid. Bake for 1 hour or until the meat is very tender. Serve sprinkled with cilantro.

ROAST LOIN OF PORK STUFFED WITH FIGS, OLIVES AND ALMONDS

Pork is a popular meat in Spain, and this recipe using fruit and nuts in the stuffing is inspired by Catalan cooking, where the combination of meat and fruit is quite common.

2 Remove any string from the pork and unroll the belly flap, cutting away any excess fat or meat to enable you to do so. Spread half the stuffing on the flat piece and roll up, starting from the thick side. Tie at intervals with string.

3 Pour the remaining oil into a small roasting pan and put in the pork. Roast for 1 hour and 15 minutes. Form the remaining stuffing mixture into balls and add to the roasting pan around the meat 15–20 minutes before the end of cooking time.

4 tablespoons olive oil
1 onion, finely chopped
2 garlic cloves, chopped
1½ cups fresh bread crumbs
4 dried figs, chopped
8 pitted green olives, chopped
¼ cup sliced almonds
1 tablespoon lemon juice
1 tablespoon chopped fresh parsley
1 egg yolk
2 pounds boned loin of pork
salt and ground black pepper

SERVES 4

1 Preheat the oven to 400°F. Heat 3 tablespoons of the oil in a pan, add the onion and garlic, and cook gently until softened. Remove the pan from the heat and stir in the bread crumbs, figs, olives, almonds, lemon juice, parsley and egg yolk. Season to taste.

COOK'S TIP
Keep a container of bread crumbs in the freezer. They can be used frozen.

4 Remove the pork from the oven and let it rest for 10 minutes. Carve into thick slices and serve with the stuffing balls and any juices from the pan. This is also good served cold.

POULTRY
AND GAME

❦❦

*Poultry and game play key roles in the cuisines of
all Mediterranean countries, and the addition of
fruits creates sensational flavor combinations.*

Poultry and game have always played an important role in Mediterranean cooking. This is largely due to the dry, rugged and, in some places, mountainous land that does not provide good pasture. Chickens and ducks are more accessible to the poorer people of the Mediterranean, who often raise them on their own land.

Chicken is without doubt the most popular type of poultry and is used creatively for Mediterranean dishes. Traditionally corn-fed, the poultry's flesh is rich in color and full of flavor, despite the fact that individual birds might look quite thin. The cooking methods are varied and interesting, but they have many similarities. In both the east and west Mediterranean cooks have acknowledged the fact that chicken is perfectly complemented by the tang of fresh, dried or preserved fruits, the rich earthiness of nuts and the lively warmth of spices.

In the Middle East, chickens were traditionally kept mainly for their eggs rather than meat, and generally only the older birds were cooked. This meant long, slow braising with highly flavored stuffings and sauces to add flavor. These recipes are now perfectly suited to improving the

BELOW: Verdant farmland rimmed by mountains in southern Spain.

316

RIGHT: Lord of all he surveys, this Greek cockerel patrols his perimeter wall.

BELOW: Lemons are a favorite flavoring for chicken dishes, notably in Chicken with Lemons and Olives.

mild taste of our mass-produced chickens. Preserved lemons tucked in or around a whole chicken impart a fresh, aromatic flavor that lacks the acidity of fresh lemons, although these can also be used successfully, adding a little sugar or honey for sweetness. Another popular flavoring for chicken is provided by glassy, jewellike segments of pomegranates, crushed and blended to a juice or made into a canned preserve, having been mixed with lemon, sugar and seasoning.

From the simplest roast, served with a raisin, pine nut and sherry sauce, to chorizo-flavored casseroles, Spain has numerous excellent chicken and rabbit recipes that are popular favorites throughout the country. Duck and goose feature prominently, cooked with pears, apples or figs to counteract the richness of the meat.

Small game birds are typically Mediterranean but are used more in winter, when the tourists have left. Squab and small game birds such as partridge and quail take their migratory route across the sea, and hunters from all quarters of the Mediterranean take full advantage of this. Italians are particularly fond of small game and prepare some delicious squab dishes, lightly cooked in rich sauces and accompanied by broiled or soft polenta.

OLIVE OIL-ROASTED CHICKEN WITH MEDITERRANEAN VEGETABLES

This is a delicious French alternative to a traditional roast chicken. Use a corn-fed or free-range bird, if available. This recipe also works well with guinea fowl.

4½-pound roasting chicken
⅔ cup extra virgin olive oil
½ lemon
few sprigs of fresh thyme
1 pound small new potatoes
1 eggplant, cut into 1-inch cubes
1 red bell pepper, seeded and quartered
1 fennel bulb, trimmed and quartered
8 large garlic cloves, unpeeled
coarse salt and ground black pepper

SERVES 4

2 Remove the chicken from the oven and season with salt. Turn the chicken right side up and baste with the drippings from the pan. Surround the bird with the potatoes, roll them in the pan drippings and return the roasting pan to the oven to continue roasting.

1 Preheat the oven to 400°F. Rub the chicken all over with olive oil and season with pepper. Place the lemon half inside the bird with a sprig or two of thyme. Put the chicken breast side down in a large roasting pan. Roast for about 30 minutes.

3 After 30 minutes, add the eggplant, red pepper, fennel and garlic cloves to the pan. Drizzle with the remaining oil and season with salt and pepper. Add any remaining thyme to the vegetables. Return to the oven and cook for 30–50 more minutes, basting and turning the vegetables occasionally.

4 To find out if the chicken is cooked, push the tip of a sharp knife between the thigh and breast. If the juices run clear, it is done. The vegetables should be tender and just beginning to brown. Serve the chicken and vegetables from the pan, or transfer the vegetables to a serving dish, cut up the chicken and place it on top. Serve the skimmed juices in a gravy boat.

ROAST CHICKEN WITH ALMONDS

———

Despite the wide availability of alternatives, roast chicken remains a family favorite all over the Mediterranean. It is delectable with a fruited almond stuffing.

3–3½-pound chicken
pinch of ground ginger
pinch of ground cinnamon
pinch of saffron, dissolved in
2 tablespoons boiling water
2 onions, chopped
1¼ cups chicken stock
3 tablespoons sliced almonds
1 tablespoon all-purpose flour
salt and ground black pepper
lemon wedges and cilantro,
to garnish

FOR THE STUFFING
⅓ cup couscous
½ cup chicken stock
1½ tablespoons butter
1 shallot, finely chopped
½ small apple
1½ tablespoons sliced almonds
2 tablespoons ground almonds
2 tablespoons chopped cilantro
a good pinch of paprika
pinch of cayenne pepper

SERVES 4

1 Preheat the oven to 350°F. First, prepare the almond stuffing. Place the couscous in a bowl, bring the chicken stock to a boil and pour it over the couscous. Stir with a fork and then set aside for 10 minutes for the couscous to swell. Meanwhile, melt the butter in a small frying pan and fry the shallot for 2–3 minutes, until soft.

2 Fluff up the couscous and stir in the shallot and all the butter from the pan. Peel, core and chop the apple and add to the couscous with the remaining stuffing ingredients. Season and stir well.

3 Loosely push the couscous mixture into the neck end of the chicken. Truss the chicken.

4 Mix the ginger and cinnamon with the saffron water. Rub the chicken with salt and pepper, and then pour on the spiced water.

5 Place the chicken in a small roasting pan or dish so that it fits snugly. Spoon the chopped onions and stock around the chicken. Cover the dish with an aluminum foil tent.

6 Cook for 1¼ hours and then increase the oven temperature to 400°F. Transfer the chicken to a plate and strain the cooking liquid into a pitcher, reserving the onions. Return the chicken to the roasting pan with the onions, baste with a little of the cooking liquid and sprinkle the sliced almonds on top. Return to the oven and cook for about 30 minutes, until the chicken is golden brown and cooked through.

7 Remove and discard the fat from the reserved cooking liquid, and pour into a small saucepan. Mix the flour with 2 tablespoons cold water, stir into the pan of cooking liquid and heat gently, stirring, to make a smooth sauce. Garnish the chicken and serve with the sauce.

CHICKEN WITH LEMONS AND OLIVES

Preserved lemons and limes are frequently used in Mediterranean cooking, particularly in North Africa, where their gentle flavor enhances all kinds of meat and fish dishes.

½ teaspoon ground cinnamon
½ teaspoon ground turmeric
3½-pound chicken
2 tablespoons olive oil
1 large onion, thinly sliced
2-inch piece fresh ginger
root, grated
2½ cups chicken stock
2 preserved lemons or limes, or fresh,
cut into wedges
½ cup pitted black olives
1 tablespoon honey
¼ cup chopped cilantro
salt and ground black pepper
cilantro sprigs, to garnish

SERVES 4

1 Preheat the oven to 375°F. Mix the ground cinnamon and turmeric in a small bowl with a little salt and pepper and rub all over the chicken skin to give an even coating.

2 Heat the oil in a large sauté or shallow frying pan and sauté the chicken on all sides until it turns golden. Transfer the chicken to an ovenproof dish.

3 Add the sliced onion to the pan and sauté for 3 minutes. Stir in the grated ginger and the chicken stock and bring just to a boil. Pour over the chicken, cover with a lid and bake for 30 minutes.

4 Remove the chicken from the oven and add the lemons or limes, olives and honey. Bake, uncovered, for another 45 minutes, until the chicken is tender.

5 Stir in the cilantro and season to taste. Garnish with cilantro sprigs and serve immediately.

CHICKEN IN A SALT CRUST

Cooking food in a casing of salt gives a deliciously moist, tender flavor that, surprisingly, is not too salty.
The technique is used in both Italy and France for chicken and whole fish, although chicken is easier to
deal with.

4½-pound chicken
about 5 pounds coarse sea salt

FOR THE GARLIC PUREE
1 pound onions, quartered
2 large heads of garlic
½ cup olive oil
salt and ground black pepper

FOR THE ROASTED TOMATOES
AND PEPPERS
1 pound plum tomatoes
3 red bell peppers, seeded and
quartered
1 red chile, seeded and finely chopped
6 tablespoons olive oil
flat-leaf parsley, to garnish

SERVES 6

1 Preheat the oven to 425°F. Choose a deep ovenproof dish into which the whole chicken will fit snugly. Line the dish with a double layer of heavy foil, allowing plenty of excess foil to overhang the top edge of the ovenproof dish.

2 Truss the chicken tightly so that the salt cannot fall into the cavity. Sprinkle a thin layer of salt in the foil-lined dish, then place the chicken on top.

3 Pour the remaining salt all around and on the top of the chicken until it is completely encased. Sprinkle the top with a little water.

4 Cover tightly with the foil and bake the chicken on the lower oven shelf for 1¾ hours. Meanwhile, put the onions in a small, heavy saucepan. Break up the heads of garlic, but leave the skins on. Add to the pan with the olive oil and a little salt and pepper.

5 Cover and cook over the lowest possible heat for about 1 hour or until the garlic is completely soft.

COOK'S TIP
This recipe makes a stunning main course when you want to serve something a little different. Take the salt-crusted chicken to the table garnished with plenty of fresh mixed herbs. Once you've scraped off the salt, transfer the chicken to a clean plate to carve it.

6 Plunge the tomatoes into boiling water for 30 seconds, then refresh in cold water. Peel off the skins and quarter the tomatoes. Put the red peppers, tomatoes and chile in a shallow ovenproof dish and sprinkle with the oil. Bake on the shelf above the chicken for 45 minutes, or until the peppers are slightly charred.

7 Squeeze the garlic out of the skins. Process the onions, garlic and pan juices in a blender or food processor until smooth. Return the purée to the clean saucepan.

8 To serve the chicken, open up the foil and ease it out of the dish. Place on a large serving platter. Transfer the roasted pepper mixture to a serving dish and garnish with parsley. Reheat the garlic purée. Crack open the salt crust on the chicken and brush off the salt before carving and serving with the garlic purée and pepper mixture.

CHICKEN WITH RED WINE

The robust red wine and red pesto give this sauce a rich color and an almost spicy flavor, while the grapes add a delicious suggestion of sweetness. Serve the stew with grilled polenta or warm crusty bread, and accompany with greens, such as arugula or watercress, tossed in a well-flavored dressing.

3 tablespoons olive oil
4 part-boned chicken breasts, skinned
1 medium red onion
2 tablespoons red pesto
1¼ cups red wine
1¼ cups water
4 ounces red grapes, halved lengthwise and seeded, if necessary
salt and ground black pepper
fresh basil leaves, to garnish

SERVES 4

VARIATIONS
Use green pesto instead of red, and substitute a dry white wine for the red, then finish with seedless green grapes. A few spoonfuls of mascarpone cheese can be added at the end, if desired, to enrich the sauce.

1 Heat 2 tablespoons of the oil in a large frying pan, add the chicken breasts and sauté over medium heat for about 5 minutes, until they have changed color on all sides. Remove with a slotted spoon and drain on paper towels.

2 Cut the onions in half, through the root. Trim off the root, then slice the onion halves lengthwise to create thin wedges.

3 Heat the remaining oil in the pan, add the onion wedges and red pesto, and cook gently, stirring constantly, for about 3 minutes, until the onion is softened, but not browned.

4 Add the red wine and water to the pan and bring to a boil, stirring constantly. Then return the sautéed chicken breasts to the pan and add salt and freshly ground black pepper to taste.

5 Reduce the heat, then cover the pan and simmer gently for about 20 minutes or until the chicken is tender, stirring occasionally to stop it from sticking to the bottom of the pan.

6 Add the grapes to the pan and cook over low to medium heat until heated through. Check the seasoning, then add more salt and pepper if necessary. Serve the chicken hot, garnished with fresh basil leaves.

CHICKEN WITH MORELS

Morels are among the best-flavored dried mushrooms and, although they are expensive, a little goes a long way. You can, of course, use fresh mushrooms if you prefer.

1¹/2 ounces dried morels
1 cup chicken stock
4 tablespoons butter
5 or 6 shallots, finely sliced
3¹/2 ounces button mushrooms,
finely sliced
¹/2 teaspoon dried thyme
2–3 tablespoons brandy
³/4 cup heavy cream
4 skinless boneless chicken breasts,
about 7 ounces each
1 tablespoon vegetable oil
³/4 cup dry sparkling wine
salt and ground black pepper

SERVES 4

1 Put the morels in a strainer and rinse well under cold running water, shaking to remove as much sand as possible. Place in a saucepan with the stock and bring to a boil over medium-high heat. Remove pan from heat and let stand for 1 hour.

2 Remove the morels from the cooking liquid and strain the liquid through a fine sieve or muslin-lined strainer and reserve for the sauce. Reserve a few whole morels and slice the rest.

3 Melt half of the butter in a frying pan over medium heat. Add the shallots and cook for 2 minutes, until softened. Add the sliced morels and button mushrooms and cook, stirring frequently, for 2–3 more minutes. Season and add the thyme, brandy and 7 tablespoons of the cream. Reduce the heat and simmer gently for 10–12 minutes, until any liquid has evaporated, stirring occasionally. Remove the morel mixture from the pan and set aside.

4 Pull off the fillets from the chicken breasts (the finger-shaped pieces on the underside) and reserve for another use. Make a pocket in each chicken breast by cutting a slit along the thicker edge with a sharp knife, taking care not to cut all the way through. Using a small spoon, fill each pocket with one-quarter of the mushroom mixture and then, if necessary, close with a toothpick.

5 Melt the remaining butter with the oil in a heavy frying pan over medium-high heat and cook the chicken breasts on one side for 6–8 minutes, until golden. Transfer the chicken breasts to a plate. Add the sparkling wine to the pan and boil to reduce by half. Add the strained morel cooking liquid and boil to reduce by half again.

6 Add the remaining cream and cook over medium heat for 2-3 minutes, until the sauce thickens just enough to coat the back of a spoon. Adjust the seasoning. Return the chicken to the pan with any accumulated juices and the reserved whole morels, and simmer for about 5 minutes over medium heat until the chicken breasts are hot and the juices run clear when the meat is pierced with a knife. Serve immediately.

CHICKEN WITH TOMATOES AND SHRIMP

This Piedmontese dish was created for Napoleon after the battle of Marengo.
Versions of it appear in both Italian and French recipe books.

½ cup olive oil
8 chicken thighs on the bone, skinned
1 onion, finely chopped
1 celery stalk, finely chopped
1 garlic clove, crushed
12 ounces ripe Italian plum tomatoes,
    peeled and roughly chopped
1 cup dry white wine
½ teaspoon finely chopped
    fresh rosemary
6 ounces raw large shrimp, shelled
1 tablespoon butter
8 small triangles of thinly sliced white
    bread, without crusts
salt and ground black pepper
finely chopped flat-leaf parsley,
    to garnish

SERVES 4

1   Heat about 2 tablespoons of the oil in a frying pan, add the chicken thighs and sauté over medium heat for about 5 minutes, until they have changed color on all sides. Transfer the chicken to a flameproof casserole.

2   Add the onion and celery to the frying pan and cook gently, stirring frequently, for about 3 minutes, until softened. Add the garlic, tomatoes, wine and rosemary to the pan. Season well with salt and pepper. Add the shrimp to the tomato sauce and heat until the shrimp are cooked.

3   Pour the tomato sauce over the chicken. Cover and cook gently for 40 minutes or until the chicken is tender when pierced.

4   About 10 minutes before serving, add the remaining oil and the butter to the frying pan and heat until the mixture is hot but not smoking. Add the triangles of white bread and shallow-fry for about 2 minutes on each side or until they are crisp and golden. Drain on paper towels. Season.

5   Dip one of the tips of each fried bread triangle in parsley to garnish. Serve the dish piping hot, decorated with the bread triangles.

MOROCCAN ROAST CHICKEN

In Morocco, a whole chicken is commonly cooked on a spit over hot charcoal. However, it is still excellent roasted in a hot oven and can be cooked whole, halved or in quarters.

Thoroughly rub the paste onto the skin of the chicken and then let it stand for 1–2 hours. **3**

Preheat the oven to 400°F and place the chicken in a roasting pan. Quarter the lemon, if using, place one or two quarters around the chicken pieces (or in the body cavity if the chicken is whole) and squeeze a little juice over the skin. Roast for 1–1¼ hours (2–2½ hours for a whole bird), until the chicken is cooked through and the meat juices run clear. Baste occasionally with the juices in the roasting pan. If the skin browns too quickly, cover the chicken loosely with aluminum foil. **4**

4–4½-pound chicken
2 small shallots
1 garlic clove
1 fresh parsley sprig
1 cilantro sprig
1 teaspoon salt
1½ teaspoons paprika
pinch of cayenne pepper
1–1½ teaspoons ground cumin
about 3 tablespoons butter
½–1 lemon (optional)
sprigs of fresh parsley or cilantro,
to garnish

SERVES 4–6

1 Unless cooking whole, cut the chicken in half or into quarters using poultry shears or a sharp knife.

2 Place the shallots, garlic, herbs, salt and spices in a food processor or blender and process until the shallots are finely chopped. Add the butter and process to make a smooth paste.

5 Let the chicken stand for 5–10 minutes, covered in aluminum foil, before carving, and then serve garnished with sprigs of fresh parsley or cilantro.

PAN-FRIED CHICKEN

The essence of this dish is to cook it quickly over high heat. It therefore works best with small amounts, as larger amounts would have less contact with the pan and would braise rather than fry.

🌿 🌿

2 skinless, boneless chicken breasts
1 small red or green chile, seeded and
finely sliced
2 garlic cloves, finely sliced
3 scallions, sliced
4–5 wafer-thin slices
fresh ginger root
$1/2$ teaspoon ground coriander
$1/2$ teaspoon ground cumin
2 tablespoons olive oil
$1^1/2$ tablespoons lemon juice
2 tablespoons pine nuts
1 tablespoon raisins (optional)
oil, for frying
1 tablespoon chopped cilantro
1 tablespoon chopped fresh mint
salt and ground black pepper
sprigs of fresh mint and lemon
wedges, to garnish

SERVES 2 AS A MAIN COURSE,
4 AS AN APPETIZER

🌿 🌿

1 Cut the chicken breasts horizontally into three or four thin pieces: this will speed up the cooking. Place in a shallow bowl until they are needed.

2 Combine the chile, garlic, scallions, spices, olive oil, lemon juice, pine nuts and raisins, if using. Season with salt and pepper, and then pour onto the chicken pieces, stirring gently so that each piece is coated. Cover and let sit in a cool place for 1–2 hours.

3 Brush a wok, balti pan or cast-iron frying pan with oil and heat. Add the chicken slices and stir-fry them over fairly high heat for 3–4 minutes, until the chicken is browned on both sides.

4 Add the remaining marinade and continue to cook over high heat for 6–8 minutes, until the chicken is cooked through. (The timing will depend on the thickness of the chicken, but make sure that it is completely cooked.)

5 Reduce the heat and stir in the cilantro and mint. Cook for 1 minute and serve immediately, garnished with mint sprigs and lemon wedges. Serve with bread as an appetizer or, if preferred, with rice or couscous as a main course.

HUNTER'S CHICKEN

This traditional dish sometimes has strips of green bell pepper in the sauce for extra color and flavor instead of the fresh mushrooms.

1 cup dried porcini mushrooms
2 tablespoons olive oil
1 tablespoon butter
4 chicken pieces, on the bone, skinned
1 large onion, finely sliced
14-ounce can chopped tomatoes
2/3 cup red wine
1 garlic clove, crushed
leaves of 1 sprig of fresh rosemary,
finely chopped
1 3/4 cups fresh field mushrooms,
finely sliced
salt and ground black pepper
fresh rosemary sprigs, to garnish

SERVES 4

3 Add the onion and chopped porcini to the pan. Cook gently, stirring frequently, for about 3 minutes, until the onion has softened but not browned. Stir in the chopped tomatoes, wine and reserved mushroom soaking liquid, then add the crushed garlic and chopped rosemary, with salt and ground black pepper to taste. Bring to a boil over medium heat, stirring constantly with a wooden spoon.

4 Return the chicken to the pan and spoon the sauce on top. Cover the pan and simmer gently for 30 minutes.

5 Add the fresh mushrooms and stir well to mix into the sauce. Continue simmering gently for about 10 minutes, until the chicken is tender. Taste for seasoning. Serve hot, with creamed potato or polenta, if desired. Garnish with rosemary.

1 Put the porcini mushrooms in a bowl, add 1 cup warm water and soak for 20–30 minutes. Squeeze the porcini over the bowl. Strain the liquid and reserve. Finely chop the porcini.

2 Heat the oil and butter in a flameproof casserole. Sauté the chicken over medium heat for 5 minutes. Drain on paper towels.

CHICKEN KDRA WITH CHICKPEAS AND ALMONDS

A kdra is a type of tagine that is traditionally cooked with smen, a strong Moroccan butter, and a lot of onions. The almonds in this recipe are precooked until soft, adding an interesting texture and flavor.

3/4 cup blanched almonds
1/2 cup chickpeas,
soaked overnight
4 part-boned chicken breasts, skinned
1/4 cup butter
1/2 teaspoon saffron strands
2 Spanish onions, finely sliced
3 3/4 cups
chicken stock
1 small cinnamon stick
1/4 cup chopped fresh flat-leaf parsley,
plus extra to garnish
lemon juice, to taste
salt and ground black pepper

SERVES 4

1 Simmer the almonds in a pan of water for 2 hours until soft. Drain. Cook the chickpeas for 1 1/2 hours until soft. Drain. Place the chickpeas in a bowl of cold water and rub off the skins. Put the chicken pieces, butter, half the saffron and seasoning in a pan. Heat until the butter melts.

2 Add the onions and stock, bring to a boil and then add the chickpeas and cinnamon stick. Cover the pan and cook very gently for 45–60 minutes, until the chicken is completely tender.

3 Transfer the chicken to a serving plate and keep warm. Bring the sauce to a boil, then simmer until well reduced, stirring frequently. Add the almonds, parsley and remaining saffron, and cook for another 2–3 minutes. Sharpen the sauce with a little lemon juice, then pour over the chicken and serve, garnished with the extra parsley.

CHICKEN WITH TOMATOES AND HONEY

Honey is surprisingly good in savory dishes such as this one, making it rich rather than sweet.

2 tablespoons sunflower oil
2 tablespoons butter
4 chicken quarters or 1 whole
chicken, quartered
1 onion, grated or finely chopped
1 garlic clove, crushed
a good pinch of ground ginger
1 teaspoon ground cinnamon
3–3 1/2 pounds tomatoes, peeled, cored
and roughly chopped
2 tablespoons honey
1/2 cup blanched almonds
1 tablespoon sesame seeds
salt and ground black pepper

SERVES 4

1 Heat the oil and butter in a large casserole. Add the chicken pieces and cook over medium heat for about 3 minutes, until the chicken is lightly browned.

2 Add the onion, garlic, ginger, cinnamon, tomatoes and seasoning, and heat gently until the tomatoes begin to bubble.

3 Lower the heat, cover and simmer gently for 1 hour, stirring and turning the chicken occasionally, until it is completely cooked through.

4 Transfer the chicken pieces to a plate. Increase the heat and cook the tomato mixture, stirring frequently, until the sauce is reduced to a thick purée. Stir in the honey, cook for 1 minute and then return the chicken to the pan and cook for 2–3 minutes to heat through. Dry-fry the almonds and sesame seeds until golden, or toast them under the broiler.

5 Transfer the chicken and sauce to a warmed serving dish and sprinkle with the almonds and sesame seeds. Serve immediately, with crusty bread.

CHICKEN WITH CHORIZO

—

The addition of chorizo sausage and sherry gives a warm, interesting flavor to this simple Spanish casserole. Serve with rice or boiled potatoes.

*1 medium chicken, cut up, or
4 chicken legs, halved
2 teaspoons ground paprika
4 tablespoons olive oil
2 small onions, sliced
6 garlic cloves, thinly sliced
5 ounces chorizo sausage,
thickly sliced
14-ounce can chopped tomatoes
12–16 bay leaves
5 tablespoons medium sherry
salt and ground black pepper
rice or potatoes, to serve*

SERVES 4

1 Preheat the oven to 375°F. Coat the chicken pieces in the paprika, making sure they are evenly covered, then season with salt. Heat the olive oil in a frying pan and sauté the chicken until brown.

2 Transfer to an ovenproof dish. Add the onions to the pan and sauté quickly. Add the garlic and chorizo and sauté for 2 minutes.

3 Add the tomatoes, two of the bay leaves and the sherry and bring to a boil. Pour over the chicken and cover with a lid. Bake for 45 minutes. Remove the lid and season to taste. Cook for another 20 minutes, until the chicken is tender and golden. Serve with rice or potatoes, garnished with bay leaves.

CIRCASSIAN CHICKEN

This is a Turkish dish that is popular all over the Middle East. The chicken is poached and served cold with a flavorful walnut sauce.

3½-pound chicken
2 onions, quartered
1 carrot, sliced
1 celery stalk, trimmed and sliced
6 peppercorns
3 slices bread, crusts removed
2 garlic cloves, coarsely chopped
3½ cups chopped walnuts
1 tablespoon walnut oil
salt and ground black pepper
chopped walnuts and paprika,
to garnish

SERVES 6

1 Place the chicken in a large pan with the onions, carrot, celery and peppercorns. Add enough water to cover and bring to a boil. Simmer for about 1 hour, uncovered, until the chicken is tender. Let cool in the stock. Drain the chicken, reserving the stock.

2 Tear up the bread and soak in 6 tablespoons of the chicken stock. Transfer to a blender or food processor with the garlic and walnuts and add 1 cup of the remaining stock. Process until smooth, then transfer to a pan.

3 Over low heat, gradually add more chicken stock to the sauce, stirring constantly, until it is a thick pouring consistency. Season with salt and pepper, remove from the heat and let cool in the pan. Skin and bone the chicken, and cut into bite-size chunks.

4 Place in a bowl and add a little of the sauce. Stir to coat the chicken, then arrange on a serving dish. Spoon the remaining sauce over the chicken and drizzle with the walnut oil. Sprinkle with walnuts and paprika and serve immediately.

PAN-FRIED CHICKEN WITH PESTO

Pan-fried chicken, served with warm pesto, makes a deliciously quick main course. Serve with boiled pasta or rice noodles and braised vegetables, such as baby carrots and celery.

1 tablespoon olive oil
4 skinless, boneless chicken breasts
fresh basil leaves, to garnish

FOR THE PESTO
6 tablespoons olive oil
1/2 cup pine nuts
2/3 cup freshly grated Parmesan cheese
1 cup fresh basil leaves
1/4 cup fresh parsley
2 garlic cloves, crushed
salt and ground black pepper

SERVES 4

1. Heat the 1 tablespoon oil in a frying pan. Add the chicken breasts and cook gently for about 15 minutes, turning several times, until the chicken is tender, lightly browned and thoroughly cooked.

2. Meanwhile, make the pesto. Place the olive oil, pine nuts, Parmesan cheese, basil leaves, parsley, garlic, salt and pepper in a blender or food processor, and process until smooth and well mixed.

3. Remove the chicken from the pan, cover and keep hot. Reduce the heat slightly, then add the pesto to the pan and cook gently for a few minutes, stirring constantly, until the pesto has warmed through.

4. Pour the warm pesto over the chicken, then garnish with basil leaves. Serve with braised baby carrots and celery, if desired.

CHICKEN CASSEROLE WITH SPICED FIGS

*The Spanish Catalans have various recipes for fruit with meat. This is quite an unusual one, but it uses
one of the fruits most strongly associated with the Mediterranean—the fig.*

FOR THE FIGS
⅔ cup sugar
½ cup white wine vinegar
1 lemon slice
1 cinnamon stick
1 pound fresh figs

FOR THE CHICKEN
½ cup medium-sweet white wine
pared zest of ½ lemon
3½-pound chicken, cut into
eight pieces
2 ounces lardons, or thick bacon
cut into strips
1 tablespoon olive oil
¼ cup chicken stock
salt and ground black pepper

SERVES 4

1 Put the sugar, vinegar, lemon slice and cinnamon stick in a pan with ½ cup water. Bring to a boil, then simmer for 5 minutes. Add the figs, cover, and simmer for 10 minutes. Remove from heat, cover, and let sit for 3 hours.

2 Preheat the oven to 350°F. Drain the figs and place in a bowl. Add the wine and lemon zest. Season the chicken. In a large frying pan, cook the lardons or bacon strips until the fat melts and they turn golden. Transfer to a shallow ovenproof dish, leaving any fat in the pan. Add the oil to the pan and brown the chicken pieces all over.

3 Drain the figs, adding the wine to the pan with the chicken. Boil until the sauce has reduced and is syrupy. Transfer the contents of the frying pan to the ovenproof dish and bake, uncovered, for about 20 minutes. Add the figs and chicken stock, cover and return to the oven for another 10 minutes. Serve with a green salad.

PERSIAN CHICKEN WITH WALNUT SAUCE

This distinctive dish is traditionally served on festive occasions in Iran.

2 tablespoons olive oil
4 chicken pieces (leg or breast)
1 large onion, grated
1 cup water
1 cup finely chopped walnuts
5 tablespoons pomegranate purée
1 tablespoon tomato paste
2 tablespoons lemon juice
1 tablespoon sugar
3–4 saffron strands, dissolved in
1 tablespoon boiling water
salt and freshly ground black pepper

SERVES 4

[2] Heat the remaining oil in a frying pan and fry the rest of the onion for 2–3 minutes, until soft. Add the chopped walnuts and fry for another 2–3 minutes over low heat, stirring frequently so that the walnuts do not burn.

[3] Stir in the pomegranate purée and tomato paste, lemon juice, sugar and the dissolved saffron. Season to taste and simmer over low heat for 5 minutes.

[4] Pour the walnut sauce over the chicken, ensuring that all the pieces are well coated. Cover and simmer for 30–35 minutes, until the meat is cooked and the oil from the walnuts has risen to the surface.

[5] Serve immediately with Persian rice and lettuce leaves such as baby Romaine.

[1] Heat 1 tablespoon of the oil in a large frying pan and sauté the chicken pieces until golden brown. Add half of the grated onion and fry until slightly softened, then add the water and seasoning, and bring to a boil. Cover the pan, reduce the heat and simmer for 15 minutes.

COOK'S TIP
Pomegranate purée is available at Middle Eastern food stores.

CHICKEN WITH OLIVES

Olives and lemon make a wonderful combination, one which is used traditionally in the Middle East and north Africa.

2 tablespoons olive oil
3–3½-pound chicken
1 large onion, sliced
1 tablespoon fresh ginger root, grated
3 garlic cloves, crushed
1 teaspoon paprika
1 cup chicken stock
2–3 saffron strands, soaked in
1 tablespoon boiling water
4–5 scallions, chopped
15–20 pitted black and green olives
juice of ½ lemon
salt and ground black pepper

SERVES 4

1 Heat the oil in a large saucepan and sauté the chicken on all sides until golden.

2 Add the onion, ginger, garlic, paprika and seasoning, and continue frying over medium heat, coating the chicken with the mixture.

3 Add the chicken stock and saffron, and bring to a boil. Cover and simmer for 45 minutes, until the chicken is almost done.

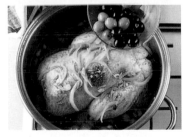

4 Add the scallions and cook for another 15 minutes, until the chicken is well cooked and the surrounding sauce is reduced to about half. Add the olives.

5 Stir in the lemon juice. Cook over medium heat for another 5 minutes. Place the chicken on a large, deep plate and pour on the sauce. Serve with rice or flat bread and a salad of mixed leaves and cherry tomatoes, if desired.

CHICKEN THIGHS WITH LEMON AND GARLIC

This recipe uses classic flavorings for chicken. Versions of it can be found in Spain and Italy.
This particular recipe, however, is of French origin.

2½ cups chicken stock
20 large garlic cloves
2 tablespoons butter
1 tablespoon olive oil
8 chicken thighs
1 lemon, peeled, pith removed and
thinly sliced
2 tablespoons all-purpose flour
⅔ cup dry white wine
salt and ground black pepper
chopped fresh parsley or basil,
to garnish
new potatoes or rice, to serve

SERVES 4

1 Put the stock into a pan and bring to a boil. Add the garlic cloves, cover and simmer gently for 40 minutes. Heat the butter and oil in a sauté or frying pan, add the chicken thighs and cook gently on all sides until golden. Transfer them to an ovenproof dish. Preheat the oven to 375°F.

2 Strain the stock and reserve it. Distribute the garlic and lemon slices among the chicken pieces. Add the flour to the fat in the pan in which the chicken was browned and cook, stirring, for 1 minute. Add the wine, stirring constantly and scraping the bottom of the pan, then add the stock. Cook, stirring, until the sauce has thickened and is smooth. Season with salt and pepper.

3 Pour the sauce over the chicken, cover and bake for 40–45 minutes. If a thicker sauce is required, lift out the chicken pieces and reduce the sauce by boiling rapidly until it reaches the desired consistency. Sprinkle the chopped parsley or basil on top and serve with boiled new potatoes or rice.

CHICKEN AND APRICOT PHYLLO PIE

The filling for this pie has a Middle Eastern flavor—chopped chicken combined with apricots, bulghur, nuts and spices.

½ cup bulghur
6 tablespoons butter
1 onion, chopped
1 pound chopped chicken
¼ cup dried apricots, finely chopped
¼ cup blanched almonds, chopped
1 teaspoon ground cinnamon
½ teaspoon ground allspice
¼ cup strained plain yogurt
1 tablespoon snipped fresh chives
2 tablespoons chopped fresh parsley
6 large sheets phyllo pastry
salt and ground black pepper
chives, to garnish

SERVES 6

1 Preheat the oven to 400°F. Put the bulghur in a bowl with ½ cup boiling water. Soak for 5–10 minutes, until the water is absorbed.

2 Heat 2 tablespoons of the butter in a pan and gently sauté the onion and chicken until pale golden.

3 Stir in the apricots, almonds and bulghur and cook for 2 more minutes. Remove from heat and stir in the cinnamon, allspice, yogurt, chives and parsley. Season to taste with salt and pepper.

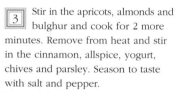

4 Melt the remaining butter. Unroll the phyllo pastry and cut into 10-inch circles. Keep the pastry circles covered with a clean, damp dish towel to prevent drying.

5 Line a 9-inch quiche pan with a removable bottom with three of the pastry circles, brushing each one with butter as you layer them. Spoon in the chicken mixture and cover with three more pastry rounds, brushed with melted butter as before.

6 Crumple the remaining circles and place them on top of the pie, then brush on any remaining melted butter. Bake the pie for about 30 minutes, until the pastry is golden brown and crisp. Serve Chicken and Apricot Phyllo Pie hot or cold, cut into wedges and garnished with chives.

BISTEEYA

Bisteeya is one of the most elaborate and intriguing dishes in Moroccan cuisine. It is often the centerpiece at feasts and banquets, and is normally made using squab, which is then layered with a wafer-thin pastry known as ouarka and cooked in a pan over hot coals. This simplified version uses chicken and phyllo.

2 tablespoons sunflower oil, plus extra
for brushing
2 tablespoons butter
3 chicken quarters, preferably breasts
1½ Spanish onions, grated or
finely chopped
a good pinch of ground ginger
a good pinch of saffron strands
2 teaspoons ground cinnamon, plus
extra for dusting
¼ cup sliced almonds
1 large bunch cilantro,
finely chopped
1 large bunch fresh parsley,
finely chopped
3 eggs, beaten
about 6 ounces phyllo pastry
1–2 teaspoons confectioners' sugar
(optional), plus extra for dusting
salt and ground black pepper

SERVES 4

1 | Heat the oil and butter in a large saucepan or flameproof casserole and brown the chicken pieces for about 4 minutes. Add the onions, ginger, saffron, ½ teaspoon of the cinnamon and enough water so that the chicken braises, rather than boils (about 1¼ cups). Season well.

2 | Bring to a boil, cover and simmer for 45–55 minutes over low heat, until the chicken is tender and completely cooked. Meanwhile, dry-fry the almonds until golden and set aside.

3 | Transfer the chicken to a plate and, when cool enough to handle, remove the skin and bones and cut the flesh into pieces.

4 | Stir the cilantro and parsley into the pan and simmer the sauce until well-reduced and thick. Add the beaten eggs and cook over low heat until the eggs are lightly scrambled.

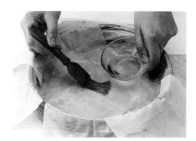

5 | Preheat the oven to 350°F. Oil a round shallow flameproof dish, about 10 inches in diameter. Place one or two sheets of phyllo pastry in a single layer over the bottom of the dish, so that it is completely covered and the edges of the pastry sheets hang over the sides. Brush lightly with oil and add two more layers of phyllo, brushing each layer lightly with oil.

6 | Place the chicken on the pastry and then spoon the egg and herb mixture on top.

7 | Place a single layer of phyllo pastry on top of the filling (you may need to use more than one sheet of phyllo pastry) and sprinkle with the almonds. Sift the remaining cinnamon and the confectioners' sugar, if using, on top.

8 | Fold the edges of the phyllo over the almonds and then make four more layers of phyllo (using one or two sheets per layer, depending on size), brushing each layer with a little oil. Tuck the phyllo edges under the pie (as if you were making a bed!) and brush the top layer with oil.

9 | Bake the pie for 40–45 minutes, until golden. Dust the top with confectioners' sugar, if using, and use the extra cinnamon to make criss-cross or diagonal lines. Serve immediately.

CHICKEN AND EGGPLANT KHORESH

*This eggplant and bell pepper stew is often served on festive occasions in Iran
and is believed to have been a favorite with royalty.*

2 Add the crushed garlic, chopped tomatoes and their liquid, water and seasoning. Bring to a boil, then reduce the heat and simmer slowly, covered, for 10 minutes.

3 Meanwhile, heat the remaining oil and fry the eggplant in batches until light golden. Transfer to a plate with a spatula. Add the peppers to the pan and fry for a few minutes, until slightly softened.

4 Place the eggplant slices on the chicken or chicken pieces and then add the peppers. Sprinkle the lemon juice and cinnamon on top, then cover and continue cooking over low heat for about 45 minutes or until the chicken is cooked through.

5 Transfer the chicken to a serving plate and spoon the eggplant and peppers around the edge. Reheat the sauce if necessary, adjust the seasoning and pour onto the chicken. Serve with rice.

*4 tablespoons oil
1 whole chicken or 4 large
chicken pieces
1 large onion, chopped
2 garlic cloves, crushed
14-ounce can chopped tomatoes
1 cup water
3 eggplant, sliced
3 bell peppers (preferably red, green
and yellow), seeded and sliced
2 tablespoons lemon juice
1 tablespoon ground cinnamon
salt and ground black pepper*

SERVES 4

1 Heat 1 tablespoon of the oil in a large saucepan or flameproof casserole, and fry the chicken or chicken pieces on all sides for about 10 minutes or until golden all over. Add the onion and fry for 4–5 more minutes, until the onion is golden brown.

VARIATION
Substitute zucchini for some or all of the eggplant, if desired.

YOGURT CHICKEN AND RICE

This rice dish is very unusual, but tastes absolutely superb.

🌾 🌾

3 tablespoons butter
3 3½-pound chicken
1 large onion, chopped
1 cup chicken stock
2 eggs
2 cups plain yogurt
2–3 saffron strands, dissolved in
1 tablespoon boiling water
1 teaspoon ground cinnamon
2⅓ cups basmati rice, soaked in water
for 20 minutes
3 ounces zereshk (small dried berries)
salt and ground black pepper

SERVES 6

🌾 🌾

1 Melt 2 tablespoons of the butter and fry the chicken and onion for 4–5 minutes, until the onion is softened and the chicken browned.

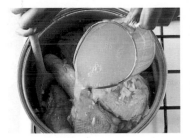

2 Add the chicken stock, salt and pepper, and bring to a boil. Then reduce the heat and simmer for about 45 minutes, or until the chicken is cooked and the stock reduced by half. Skin and bone the chicken. Cut the flesh into large pieces and place in a bowl. Reserve the stock.

3 Beat the eggs and mix with the yogurt. Add the saffron water and cinnamon and season with more salt and black pepper. Pour over the chicken and let marinate for up to 2 hours.

4 Drain the rice, then boil in salted water for 5 minutes. Reduce the heat and simmer very gently for 10 minutes, until half-cooked. Drain and rinse in lukewarm water, then drain again.

5 Transfer the chicken from the yogurt mixture to a dish and mix half the rice into the yogurt.

6 Preheat the oven to 325°F and grease a large 4-inch-deep flameproof dish.

7 Place the rice and yogurt mixture in the bottom of the dish, arrange the chicken pieces in a layer on top and then add the plain rice. Sprinkle with the *zereshk*.

8 Mix the remaining butter with the chicken stock and pour over the rice. Cover tightly with aluminum foil and a lid. Bake for 35–45 minutes.

9 Let the dish cool for a few minutes. Place on a cold, damp cloth (which will help lift the rice from the bottom of the dish), then run a knife around the edges of the dish. Place a large flat plate over the dish and turn out. You should have a rice "cake," which can be cut into wedges. Serve hot with a salad.

MUSHROOM PICKER'S CHICKEN PAELLA

A good paella is based on a few well-chosen ingredients. Here, wild mushrooms are combined with chicken and vegetables.

3 tablespoons olive oil
1 medium onion, chopped
1 small bulb fennel, sliced
3 cups assorted wild and cultivated
mushrooms, such as cèpes, bay
boletus, chanterelles and oyster
mushrooms, trimmed and sliced
1 garlic clove, crushed
3 large chicken legs, chopped through
the bone
1¾ cups short grain Spanish or
Italian rice
3¾ cups chicken stock, boiling
pinch of saffron strands or 1 envelope
of saffron powder
1 thyme sprig
14-ounce can lima beans, drained
¾ cup frozen peas

SERVES 4

 Heat the olive oil gently in a 14-inch paella pan or a large frying pan. Add the onion and fennel and fry, stirring, over low heat, for 3–4 minutes.

Add the mushrooms and garlic, and cook until the juices begin to run, then increase the heat to evaporate the juices. Push the onion and mushrooms to one side. Add the chicken pieces and fry briefly.

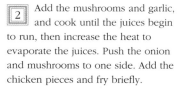

Stir in the rice, pour in the stock, then stir in the saffron, thyme, lima beans and peas. Bring to a simmer and then cook gently for 15 minutes without stirring.

Remove from heat and cover the surface of the paella with a circle of oiled waxed paper. Cover the paper with a clean dish towel and let sit for about 5 minutes before serving the paella.

COOK'S TIP
For a vegetarian mushroom paella, omit the chicken, replace the chicken stock with vegetable stock and, if you can, include chicken-of-the-woods in your choice of mushrooms.

CHICKEN WITH PIMIENTOS

"Pimiento" is the Spanish word for the sweet bell-shaped pepper, which is a favorite ingredient in many Mediterranean recipes.

2 Heat half the oil in a large frying pan and sauté the onion, garlic and peppers for 3 minutes. Transfer to an ovenproof dish. Add the chicken pieces to the pan. Fry them until browned on all sides, then add them to the dish.

3 Add the remaining oil to the pan and, when it is hot, fry the tomatoes for a few minutes. Stir in seasoning, sugar and 1 tablespoon water, then spoon the mixture over the chicken. Bake, uncovered, for 30 minutes.

4 Remove the chicken from the oven and carefully pour the free juices from the dish into a small pan. Return the chicken to the oven and bake for 30 more minutes, covering the dish with aluminum foil if the chicken starts to get too brown.

🌿 🌿

4½-pound roasting chicken
3 ripe tomatoes
2 large red bell peppers
4–6 tablespoons olive oil
1 large onion, sliced
2 garlic cloves, crushed
1 tablespoon sugar
salt and ground black pepper
½ cup pitted black olives
flat-leaf parsley, to garnish

SERVES 6

1 Preheat the oven to 375°F. Bone the chicken, then cut it into eight pieces and set aside. Peel and chop the tomatoes and seed and slice the red peppers.

5 When the chicken is almost cooked, skim the fat from the juices in the saucepan and reheat. Stir the olives into the vegetables surrounding the chicken mixture, garnish with flat-leaf parsley and serve with rice. Pour the pan juices into a pitcher and pass around as extra gravy.

POUSSINS WITH BULGHUR WHEAT AND DRY VERMOUTH

Vermouth is a valuable asset in the kitchen. It appears twice in this recipe, first to flavor the bulghur wheat stuffing and then in the glaze for the poussins.

2   Heat half of the oil and fry the onion and carrots for 10 minutes, then remove the pan from heat and stir in the nuts, celery seeds and well-drained bulghur wheat.

3   Stuff the poussins with the bulghur wheat mixture. Place them in a roasting pan, brush with oil and sprinkle with salt and pepper. Roast for 45–55 minutes, until cooked.

4   Meanwhile, spread out the red onions, eggplant, squash and baby carrots on a baking sheet.

¹⁄₃ cup bulghur wheat
²⁄₃ cup dry white vermouth
4 tablespoons olive oil
1 large onion, finely chopped
2 carrots, finely chopped
1 cup pine nuts, chopped
1 teaspoon celery seeds
4 poussins
3 red onions, quartered
4 baby eggplant, halved
4 patty pan squashes
12 baby carrots
3 tablespoons corn or golden syrup
salt and ground black pepper

SERVES 4

1   Preheat the oven to 400°F. Put the bulghur wheat in a heatproof bowl, pour in half of the vermouth and cover with boiling water. Set aside until needed.

5   Mix the corn syrup with the remaining vermouth and oil in a small bowl. Season with salt and pepper. Brush the syrup mixture onto the vegetables and roast them for 35–45 minutes, until golden. Cut each poussin in half and serve with the roasted vegetables.

CITRUS GLAZED POUSSINS

This recipe is suitable for many kinds of small birds, including squab and partridges.
It would also work with quail, but in such a case decrease the cooking time and spread the citrus mixture
over, rather than under, the fragile skin.

2 poussins (about 1½ pounds each)
¼ cup butter, softened
2 tablespoons olive oil
2 garlic cloves, crushed
½ teaspoon dried thyme
¼ teaspoon cayenne pepper,
or to taste
grated zest and juice of
1 unwaxed lemon
grated zest and juice of
1 unwaxed lime
2 tablespoons honey
salt and ground black pepper
fresh dill, to garnish

SERVES 4

1   Using kitchen scissors, cut along both sides of the backbone of each bird; remove and discard the spine. Cut the birds in half along the breast bone, and then press down firmly with a rolling pin to flatten.

2   Place the butter in a small bowl, then beat in 1 tablespoon of the olive oil, the garlic, thyme, cayenne, salt and black pepper, half the lemon and lime zest, and 1 tablespoon each of the lemon and lime juice.

3   Carefully loosen the skin of each poussin breast with your fingertips. Using a round-bladed knife or small spatula, spread the butter mixture evenly between the skin and the breast meat.

4   Preheat the broiler and line a broiler pan with foil. In a small bowl, combine the remaining olive oil, lemon and lime juices, and the honey. Place the bird halves, skin side up, on the broiler pan and brush with the citrus juice mixture.

5   Broil on one side for 10–12 minutes, basting once or twice with the juices. Turn over and broil for 7–10 minutes, basting once, or until the meat juices run clear when the thigh is pierced with a knife. Garnish with the dill. Serve with broiled tomatoes and a salad.

POUSSINS WITH ZUCCHINI AND APRICOT STUFFING

If possible, buy very small or baby poussins for this recipe. If these are not available, buy slightly larger poussins and serve half a poussin per person.

4 small poussins
about 3 tablespoons butter
1–2 teaspoons ground coriander
1 large red bell pepper
1 red chile
1–2 tablespoons olive oil
1/2 cup chicken stock
2 tablespoons cornstarch
salt and ground black pepper
fresh flat-leaf parsley, to garnish

FOR THE STUFFING
2 1/4 cups chicken or vegetable stock
1 2/3 cups couscous
2 small zucchini
8 ready-to-eat dried apricots
1 tablespoon chopped fresh
flat-leaf parsley
1 tablespoon chopped cilantro
juice of 1/2 lemon

SERVES 4

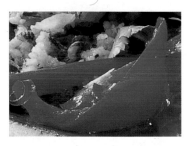

1 First, make the stuffing. Bring the stock to a boil and pour it over the couscous in a large bowl. Stir once, then set aside for 10 minutes so that the couscous absorbs the liquid.

2 Meanwhile, trim the zucchini and then grate them coarsely. Roughly chop the apricots and add to the zucchini. Preheat the oven to 400°F.

3 When the couscous has swollen, fluff up with a fork and then spoon 6 tablespoons into a separate bowl and add the zucchini and chopped apricots. Add the herbs, seasoning and lemon juice, and stir to make a fairly loose stuffing. Set aside the remaining couscous for serving.

4 Spoon the stuffing loosely into the body cavities of the poussins and secure with string or toothpicks. Place the birds in a medium to large roasting pan, so that they fit comfortably but not too closely. Rub the butter into the skins and sprinkle with ground coriander and a little salt and pepper.

5 Cut the red pepper into medium-size strips and finely slice the chile, discarding the seeds and core from both. Place in the roasting pan, around the poussins, and spoon on the olive oil.

6 Roast for 20 minutes, then reduce the oven temperature to 350°F. Pour the chicken stock around the poussins and baste each bird with the stock and red pepper/chile mixture. Return the pan to the oven and cook for another 30–35 minutes, basting occasionally with the stock, until the poussins are cooked through and the meat juices run clear.

7 When the poussins are cooked, transfer them to a warmed serving plate. Mix the cornstarch with 3 tablespoons cold water, and stir into the stock and peppers in the roasting pan.

8 Heat gently, stirring constantly, until the sauce is slightly thickened. Check the seasoning and transfer to a pitcher, or pour directly over the poussins. Garnish the birds with fresh flat-leaf parsley and serve immediately with the reserved couscous.

DUCK BREASTS WITH A WALNUT AND POMEGRANATE SAUCE

This is an extremely exotic sweet-and-sour dish that originally came from Persia.

4 tablespoons olive oil
2 onions, very thinly sliced
½ teaspoon ground turmeric
3½ cups walnuts, coarsely chopped
4 cups duck or chicken stock
6 pomegranates
2 tablespoons sugar
¼ cup lemon juice
4 duck breasts, about 8 ounces each
salt and ground black pepper

SERVES 6

COOK'S TIP
Choose pomegranates with shiny, brightly colored skins. The juice stains, so be careful when cutting them. Only the seeds are used in cooking; the pith is discarded.

1 Heat half the oil in a frying pan. Add the onions and turmeric and cook gently until soft. Transfer to a pan, add the walnuts and stock, then season with salt and pepper. Stir, then bring to a boil and simmer the mixture, uncovered, for 20 minutes.

2 Cut the pomegranates in half and scoop out the seeds into a bowl, reserving the seeds of one pomegranate. Transfer the remaining seeds to a blender or food processor and process to break them up. Put through a strainer to extract the juice and stir in the sugar and lemon juice.

3 Score the skin of the duck breasts in a lattice fashion with a sharp knife. Heat the remaining oil in a frying pan or grill pan and place the duck breasts in it, skin side down.

4 Cook gently for 10 minutes, pouring off the fat from time to time, until the skin is dark golden and crisp. Turn the duck breasts over and cook for another 3–4 minutes. Transfer to a plate and allow to rest.

5 Deglaze the frying pan or grill pan with the pomegranate juice mixture, stirring with a wooden spoon, then add the walnut and stock mixture and simmer for 15 minutes, until the sauce has thickened slightly. Serve the duck breasts sliced, drizzled with a little sauce, and garnished with the reserved pomegranate seeds. Serve the remaining sauce separately.

354

APPLE-STUFFED DUCK

Stuffing the duck breasts with whole apples keeps the slices moist and gives an attractive appearance when they are served cold.

¼ cup raisins
2 tablespoons brandy
3 large onions
2 tablespoons oil
3 cups fresh bread crumbs
2 small apples
2 large duck breasts, including
the skin
salt and ground black pepper
mixed leaf salad, to serve

SERVES 4 AS A HOT DISH; MORE WHEN
SERVED COLD AS PART OF A BUFFET

1 Soak the dried fruit in the brandy. Preheat the oven to 425°F.

2 Chop 1 of the onions finely and sauté in the oil until golden. Season with salt and pepper, and add ¼ cup water. Bring to a boil, add the bread crumbs and enough extra water to make a moist but not sloppy stuffing.

3 Core and peel the apples. Drain the raisins and press them into the centers of the apples. Flatten the duck breasts and spread out, skin down.

4 Divide the stuffing between them and spread it onto the meat. Place an apple at one end of each duck breast and carefully roll up to enclose the apple and stuffing. Secure with a length of cotton string. Quarter the remaining onions. Prick the duck skin in several places to release the fat.

5 Arrange on a rack in a roasting pan with the onions underneath. Roast for about 35 minutes. Pour off the fat, reduce the oven temperature to 325°F and roast for another 30–45 minutes.

6 Serve hot with mixed, roasted vegetables or, to serve cold, chill and then cut each breast into 5 or 6 thin slices. Arrange on a platter and bring to room temperature before serving. Serve with a mixed leaf salad.

DUCK STEW WITH OLIVES

This method of preparing duck has its roots in Provence. The sweetness of the onions
balances the saltiness of the olives.

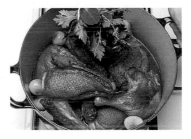

2 Heat 1 tablespoon of the duck fat in a large flameproof casserole and cook the onions, covered, over low-medium heat until evenly browned, stirring frequently. Sprinkle with flour and continue cooking, uncovered, for 2 minutes, stirring frequently.

3 Stir in the wine and bring to a boil, then add the duck pieces, stock and bouquet garni. Bring to a boil, then simmer, covered, for about 40 minutes, stirring occasionally.

4 Rinse the olives in several changes of cold water. If they are very salty, put in a saucepan, cover with water and bring to a boil, then drain and rinse. Add the olives to the casserole and continue cooking for another 20 minutes, until the duck is very tender.

2 ducks, each about 3–3½ pounds,
quartered, or 8 duck leg quarters
8 ounces baby onions
2 tablespoons all-purpose flour
1½ cups dry red wine
generous 2¼ cups duck or
chicken stock
bouquet garni
⅔ cup pitted green or black olives,
or a combination
salt and freshly ground
black pepper

SERVES 6–8

1 Put the duck pieces, skin side down, in a large frying pan over medium heat and cook for about 12 minutes, until well browned, turning to color evenly. Cook in batches if necessary. Pour off and reserve the fat from the pan.

5 Transfer the duck pieces, onions and olives to a plate. Strain the cooking liquid, skim off all the fat and return the liquid to the pan. Boil to reduce by about one-third, then adjust the seasoning and return the duck and vegetables to the casserole. Simmer gently for a few minutes to heat through. Serve.

SPICED DUCK WITH PEARS

This delicious casserole is based on a Catalan dish that uses goose or duck. The sautéed pears are added toward the end of cooking, along with picarda sauce, a pounded pine-nut and garlic paste that both flavors and thickens.

6 duck portions, either breast or
leg pieces
1 tablespoon olive oil
1 large onion, thinly sliced
1 cinnamon stick, halved
2 thyme sprigs
2 cups chicken stock

TO FINISH
3 firm, ripe pears
2 tablespoons olive oil
2 garlic cloves, sliced
⅓ cup pine nuts
½ teaspoon saffron strands
2 tablespoons raisins
salt and ground black pepper
young thyme sprigs or parsley,
to garnish

SERVES 6

1 Preheat the oven to 350°F. Sauté the duck portions in the olive oil for about 5 minutes, until the skin is golden. Transfer the duck to an ovenproof dish and drain off all but 1 tablespoon of the fat left in the pan.

2 Add the onion to the pan and sauté for 5 minutes. Add the cinnamon stick, thyme and stock and bring to a boil. Pour over the duck and bake for 1¼ hours.

3 Meanwhile, peel, core and halve the pears and sauté quickly in the oil until beginning to turn golden on the cut sides. Pound the garlic, pine nuts and saffron in a mortar with a pestle to make a thick, smooth paste.

4 Add the paste to the casserole along with the raisins and pears. Bake for another 15 minutes, until the pears are tender.

5 Season to taste with salt and pepper and garnish with parsley or thyme. Serve with mashed potatoes and a green vegetable, if desired.

COOK'S TIP
A good stock is essential for this dish. Buy a large duck (plus two extra duck breasts if you want portions to be generous) and cut it up yourself, using the giblets and carcass for stock. Alternatively, buy duck portions and canned chicken stock.

QUAIL WITH FRESH FIGS

The fig trees in the south of France are laden with ripe purple fruit in early autumn,
coinciding with the quail-shooting season.

 Melt the butter in a deep frying pan or heavy flameproof casserole over medium-high heat. Cook the quail for 5–6 minutes, turning to brown all sides evenly; cook in batches if necessary.

 Add the sherry and boil for 1 minute, then add the stock, garlic, thyme and bay leaf. Bring to a boil, reduce the heat and simmer gently, covered, for 20 minutes.

Add the remaining fig quarters and continue cooking for another 5 minutes, until the meat juices run clear when the thigh of a quail is pierced with a knife. Transfer the quail and figs to a warmed serving dish, cut off the trussing string and cover to keep warm.

Bring the cooking liquid to a boil, then stir in the cornstarch paste. Cook gently for 3 minutes, stirring frequently, until the liquid is thickened, then strain into a sauce boat. Serve the quail and figs with the sauce and a green salad.

8 oven-ready quail
6 firm ripe figs, quartered
1 tablespoon butter
6 tablespoons dry sherry
1¼ cups chicken stock
1 garlic clove, finely chopped
2–3 thyme sprigs
1 bay leaf
1½ teaspoons cornstarch, mixed to a
paste with 1 tablespoon water
salt and ground black pepper
green salad, to serve

SERVES 4

 Season the quail inside and out. Put a fig quarter in the cavity of each quail and tie the legs with string.

COOK'S TIP
Farmed quail are available all year
and are an excellent buy.

DUCK BREASTS WITH ENDIVE

A plum and sherry purée is the perfect accompaniment for glazed duck breasts with chicory.

---

1 tablespoon lemon juice
4 heads of endive
4 duck breasts,
about 4–6 ounces each
1 tablespoon honey
1 tablespoon sunflower oil
salt and ground black pepper

FOR THE PURÉE
1 apple, peeled, cored and sliced
6 ounces plums, halved and pitted
1 tablespoon light brown sugar
2/3 cup vegetable stock
3 tablespoons sherry
2 teaspoons balsamic vinegar

SERVES 4

---

2 Stir the lemon juice into a saucepan of lightly salted water and bring to a boil. Cut the heads of endive lengthwise into quarters and add to the pan. Cook for 3 minutes, then drain and set aside.

3 Score the duck breasts, brush with honey and sprinkle with a little salt. Transfer to a baking sheet and bake for 6–9 minutes, depending on weight.

4 Brush the endive pieces with oil and place them alongside the duck. Bake for 6 more minutes.

5 Stir the sherry and balsamic vinegar into the purée and season to taste with salt and pepper. Arrange the endive pieces on a platter. Slice the duck breasts and fan them out on top of the endive. Spoon the purée on top and serve.

1 Preheat the oven to 425°F. Make the plum purée. Put the apple, plums, sugar and stock into a saucepan. Bring to a boil, lower the heat and simmer for 10 minutes, until the fruit is soft. Press the fruit through a strainer into a bowl and set it aside.

SQUAB BREASTS WITH PANCETTA

*Mild, succulent squab breasts are easy to cook and make an impressive main course for a special dinner.
Serve this Italian-style dish with polenta and some simple green vegetables.*

4 whole squabs
2 large onions
2 carrots, coarsely chopped
1 celery stalk, trimmed and
coarsely chopped
1 ounce dried porcini mushrooms
2 ounces pancetta
2 tablespoons butter
2 tablespoons olive oil
2 garlic cloves, crushed
⅔ cup red wine
salt and ground black pepper
flat-leaf parsley, to garnish
cooked oyster mushrooms, to serve

SERVES 4

2 Put the squab carcasses in a large saucepan. Halve one of the onions, leaving the skin on. Add to the pan with the carrots and celery and just cover with water. Bring to a boil, reduce the heat and simmer very gently, uncovered, for about 1½ hours, to make a dark, rich stock. Let cool slightly, then strain into a bowl.

3 Cover the porcini mushrooms with ⅔ cup hot water and let soak for at least 30 minutes. Chop the pancetta.

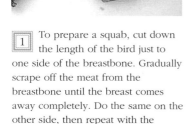

1 To prepare a squab, cut down the length of the bird just to one side of the breastbone. Gradually scrape off the meat from the breastbone until the breast comes away completely. Do the same on the other side, then repeat with the remaining squabs.

4 Peel and finely chop the remaining onion. Melt half the butter with the oil in a large frying pan. Add the onion and pancetta and sauté very gently for 3 minutes. Add the squab breasts, skin side down, and sauté for 2 minutes, until browned. Turn over and sauté for another 2 minutes.

5 Add the mushrooms with their soaking liquid, garlic, wine and 1 cup of the stock. Bring just to a boil, then reduce the heat and simmer gently for 5 minutes, until the squab breasts are tender but still a little pink in the center.

6 Lift out the squab breasts and keep them hot. Return the sauce to a boil and boil rapidly to reduce slightly. Gradually whisk in all the remaining butter and season with salt and pepper to taste.

7 Transfer the squab breasts to warmed serving plates and pour on the sauce. Serve immediately, garnished with sprigs of parsley and accompanied by oyster mushrooms.

COOK'S TIP
If buying squab from a butcher, order them in advance and ask him to remove the breasts for you. You can also cut off the legs and sauté these with the breasts, although there is little meat on them and you might prefer to let them flavor the stock.

MOROCCAN PIGEON PIE

This recipe is based upon a classic Moroccan dish called Pastilla, which is a phyllo pastry pie filled with an unusual but delicious mixture of squab, eggs, spices and nuts. If squab is unavailable, chicken makes a good substitute.

3 squabs
4 tablespoons butter
1 onion, chopped
1 cinnamon stick
½ teaspoon ground ginger
2 tablespoons chopped fresh cilantro
3 tablespoons chopped parsley
pinch of ground turmeric
1 tablespoon sugar
¼ teaspoon ground cinnamon
1 cup toasted almonds, finely chopped
6 eggs, beaten
salt and ground black pepper
cinnamon and confectioners' sugar,
to garnish

FOR THE PASTRY
12 tablespoons (1½ sticks) butter,
melted
16 sheets phyllo pastry
1 egg yolk

SERVES 6

1 Wash the squabs and place in a pan with the butter, onion, cinnamon stick, ginger, cilantro, parsley and turmeric. Season with salt and pepper. Add just enough water to cover and bring to a boil. Cover and simmer gently for about 1 hour, until the squab is very tender.

2 Strain off the stock and reserve. Skin and bone the squabs, and shred the flesh into bite-size pieces. Preheat the oven to 350°F. Combine the sugar, cinnamon and almonds, and set aside.

3 Measure ⅔ cup of the reserved stock into a small pan. Add the eggs and mix well. Stir over low heat until creamy and very thick and almost set. Season with salt and pepper.

4 Brush a 12-inch diameter ovenproof dish with some of the melted butter and lay the first sheet of pastry in the dish. Brush this with butter and continue with five more sheets of pastry. Cover with the almond mixture, then half the egg mixture. Moisten with a little stock.

5 Layer four more sheets of phyllo pastry, brushing with butter as before. Lay the squab meat on top. Add the remaining egg mixture and more stock. Cover with the remaining pastry, brushing each sheet with butter, and tuck in any overlapping edges.

6 Brush the pie with egg yolk and bake for 40 minutes. Raise the oven temperature to 400°F and bake for 15 minutes more, until the pastry is crisp and golden. Garnish with a lattice design of cinnamon and confectioners' sugar. Serve hot.

SQUAB AND CHESTNUT CASSEROLE WITH PORT

Relish the flavors of autumn in this delicious, warming casserole.

2 tablespoons oil
4 squabs, halved
1 onion, chopped
6 strips bacon, chopped
2 tablespoons all-purpose flour
1⅔ cups game or chicken stock
⅔ cup orange juice
2 tablespoons port
2 cups shelled chestnuts
2 tablespoons butter
2 oranges, sliced
salt and ground black pepper
watercress sprigs, to garnish

SERVES 4

COOK'S TIP
To shell fresh chestnuts, make a cross
with a sharp knife on each nut. Cook
in a hot oven for 15 minutes, until the
shells crack, then peel.

 Add the chopped onion and
bacon to the pan and sauté
until golden. Stir in the flour and cook
for 1 minute, until it begins to brown.
Pour in the stock, orange juice and
port, with salt and pepper to taste.
Bring to a boil, stirring constantly,
then return the pigeons to the
casserole. Cover, place in the oven
and cook for 30 minutes.

3 Stir the chestnuts into the
casserole, return to the oven
and cook for 30 more minutes.

4 Just before serving, melt the
butter in a frying pan. Fry the
orange slices until golden on both
sides. Garnish the pigeon casserole
with the orange slices and watercress
sprigs. Serve immediately.

1 Preheat the oven to 350°F. Heat
the oil in a shallow flameproof
casserole and sauté the squabs until
browned. Transfer them to a bowl.

RABBIT WITH PUY LENTILS AND PORT

Port gives this rustic dish from France a wonderfully warm and rich flavor.

1 tablespoon all-purpose flour
1 pound diced boneless rabbit
1 tablespoon olive oil
2 onions, sliced
1 garlic clove, crushed
3 cups mushrooms, sliced
3 tablespoons port
1²/₃ cups chicken or vegetable stock
1 teaspoon red wine vinegar
2 tablespoons chopped fresh parsley,
plus extra to garnish
1 tablespoon tomato paste
³/₄ cup Puy lentils
12 slices French bread
2 tablespoons olive paste
1 tablespoon butter
salt and ground black pepper

SERVES 4

 Preheat the oven to 350°F. Put the flour into a plastic bag, season with salt and pepper, and add the rabbit. Shake until evenly coated in flour.

2 Heat the oil in a flameproof casserole and fry the rabbit until all the pieces are browned.

3 Stir in the sliced onions, garlic and mushrooms. Add the port, stock, vinegar, parsley and tomato paste. Stir well, then bring the mixture to a boil.

4 Cover the casserole with a lid, transfer it to the oven and cook for 40 minutes. Meanwhile, bring a saucepan of lightly salted water to a boil. Add the lentils and cook for 35 minutes, until tender.

5 Spread the French bread with the olive paste. Drain the lentils, stir them into the casserole and put the bread on top, with the topping facing up. Dot with butter.

6 Return the casserole to the oven and cook, uncovered, for another 10 minutes. Serve garnished with lots of chopped parsley.

367

RABBIT SALMOREJO

Small pieces of rabbit, conveniently sold in packages at some supermarkets, make an interesting alternative to chicken in this light, spicy sauté from Spain. Serve with a simple dressed salad.

1½ pounds rabbit pieces
1¼ cups dry white wine
1 tablespoon sherry vinegar
several oregano sprigs
2 bay leaves
6 tablespoons olive oil
6 ounces baby onions, peeled and left whole
1 red chile, seeded and finely chopped
4 garlic cloves, sliced
2 teaspoons paprika
⅔ cup chicken stock
salt and ground black pepper
flat-leaf parsley sprigs, to garnish

SERVES 4

1 Put the rabbit in a bowl. Add the wine, vinegar, oregano and bay leaves and toss together lightly. Cover and let marinate for several hours or overnight.

2 Drain the rabbit, reserving the marinade, and pat dry on paper towels. Heat the oil in a large sauté or frying pan. Add the rabbit and sauté on all sides until golden, then remove with a slotted spoon. Sauté the onions until beginning to color.

3 Remove the onions from the pan and add the chile, garlic and paprika. Cook, stirring, for about a minute. Add the reserved marinade, with the stock. Season lightly.

4 Return the rabbit to the pan with the onions. Bring to a boil, then reduce the heat and cover with a lid. Simmer very gently for about 45 minutes, until the rabbit is tender. Serve garnished with a few sprigs of flat-leaf parsley, if desired.

COOK'S TIP
If more convenient, rather than cooking on top of the stove, transfer the stew to an ovenproof dish and bake at 350°F for about 50 minutes.

GRAINS AND BEANS

Mediterranean countries deserve thanks for the creation of risotto, paella, pizzas and pasta, and the many salads and stews based on dried peas and beans.

The countries surrounding the Mediterranean produce a seemingly inexhaustible quantity and variety of grains, peas and beans. Wheat, the most ancient cereal grown in the region, predominates. It is the staple that provides for traditional and specialized local dishes, but from centuries of trading and travel come a great number of dishes that, although originally associated with one country, are often made using slightly different techniques and ingredients in many different areas of the Mediterranean.

Pasta, for example, although most widely consumed in Italy, is also made in the eastern Mediterranean under the name of **rishta**; it is known in Spain as **fideos**, and in Egypt as **macaroni or koshari**.

Bread is a staple food all over the Mediterranean. When you consider that it is made using the same basic ingredients, it is remarkable that there is such a variety of flavors and textures. There are the Italian olive breads—focaccia and ciabatta—and the dry breads like grissini and crostini, as well as a feast of soft breads, richly flavored with sun-dried tomatoes and herbs. Visit

BELOW: Spain produces a wide range of grains of all types, seen here at a typical market.

any part of France and see how important freshly baked breads, from rich brioches to crisp baguettes, are to the French. Bakeries stay open all through the day, turning out batch after batch of hot loaves. French bakers do not depend on preservatives, so bread has to be prepared fresh for every meal. Festive breads are also still widely enjoyed. The most elaborate is the braided Greek Easter Bread, flavored with nuts and fruit and adorned with hard-boiled eggs that are dyed red. According to legend, the eggs will keep those who eat them safe from harm.

The unleavened or slightly leavened flat breads of the eastern Mediterranean and North Africa are eaten with every meal. The most common of these is the pita, which varies in shape and size. The Turks bake a huge, flat loaf that inflates like a balloon during baking. This is carried ceremoniously to the table, where it is shared by the diners; its soft, chewy dough is perfect for mopping up spicy sauces. Pita bread is often used instead of knives and forks; when slit, the empty pocket makes a perfect container for salads, bean dishes, falafel and meats.

Wheat flour is also used to make the highly popular phyllo pastries of North Africa, Lebanon, Greece and Turkey. It is skillfully shaped and stretched to form a transparent sheet, which is then brushed with olive oil or melted butter and folded into layers. When cooked, it is extremely flaky, light and crisp. Phyllo is used in many sweet or savory classics, such as the Moroccan pastilla, a spicy squab pie with cloves and cinnamon.

Regional classics like North African couscous are also made with wheat. Couscous is a kind of wheat pasta that gives its name to the traditional dish of either a spiced meat or vegetable sauce that covers the steamed pasta. At its most splendid it is served as a finale to a special feast when guests have already enjoyed several delicate courses. The couscous is piled high on a large platter and topped with meat or vegetables smothered in a delectable sweet, spicy sauce.

ABOVE. The fertile Guadalquivir valley near Carmona, in Spain.

Rice has been central to Mediterranean cooking for as long as twelve thousand years. The Moors brought rice to Europe in the eighth century through the eastern Mediterranean from Persia and Asia. With its strong Moorish tradition, southern Spain, particularly Valencia, remains the country's main producer of rice. The national dish, paella, originated in the coastal cities and fishing ports of Andalusia. But the uses for rice extend much further than one national dish. Many other rich, saffron-flavored risottos are widely popular and are good with zarzuela, an extravagant feast of fish and crustacea. Italians also consume a lot of rice, predominantly arborio, a short-grain, starchy rice that cooks down to a soft, creamy consistency. Arborio supplies the authentic taste of the classic subtle accompaniment Risotto alla Milanese, which is enriched with saffron, wine and Parmesan. In contrast, the fiery, dry pilafs of Turkey and the Middle East are heavily spiced and mixed with numerous herbs, dried fruits, nuts and vegetables.

Chickpeas are perhaps the most popular of the Mediterranean peas and form the basis of creamy pastes like hummus. Along with other peas and beans they are widely used in cold, garlicky dressed salads and as the base of many soups.

Traditionally a peasant food, beans are given long, slow cooking, and their taste is enhanced with cheap but flavorful meats or garlic-cured sausages. Served with locally produced vegetables, beans are the heart of many delicious soups and stews—for example, the traditional cassoulet of France. Before cooking dried beans, soak them in water overnight. Drain, cover with fresh water, then boil them rapidly for ten minutes to eliminate the sugars that cause indigestion. Reduce the heat and simmer for the rest of the recommended cooking time. Only add salt toward the end of the cooking time—if added too soon, salt will toughen the beans.

PERSIAN RICE

Plain rice in Iran is called Chelo. The rice is soaked in salted water before cooking, and it is important not to skimp on this process. The longer it is soaked, the better the flavor of the finished rice.

1¾ cups long grain rice
about 4 teaspoons salt
3 tablespoons butter, melted
2–3 saffron strands, soaked in
1 tablespoon boiling water (optional)

SERVES 4

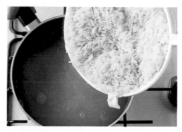

 Soak the rice in lukewarm water, salted with 3 teaspoons of the salt, for at least 2 hours.

 When the rice has soaked and you are ready to cook, fill a nonstick pan with fresh water, add 1 teaspoon salt and bring to a boil.

3 Drain the rice well and stir it into the boiling water. Boil for 5 minutes, then reduce the heat and simmer for about 10 minutes, until half-cooked. Drain and rinse in lukewarm water. Wash and dry the pan.

4 Heat 2 tablespoons of the melted butter in the saucepan. Keep the heat low so that it does not brown. Add about 1 tablespoon water and stir in the rice. Cook the rice over very low heat for 10 minutes, then pour on the remaining butter.

5 Cover the pan with a clean dish towel and secure with a tight-fitting lid, lifting back the corners of the cloth over the lid.

6 Steam for 30–40 minutes. The dish towel will absorb the excess steam and will turn the bottom of the rice into a crisp, golden crust known as *tahdiq*. Many regard this as the best part of the rice. If desired, mix 2–3 tablespoons of the rice with the saffron water and sprinkle on top. Serve.

PLAIN RICE

This is a simplified and slightly quicker version of Persian rice (Chelo).

3 cups water
1 teaspoon salt
1¾ cups basmati rice
3 tablespoons butter

SERVES 4

1 Place the water and salt in a nonstick saucepan and pour in the rice. Set aside to soak for at least 30 minutes and for up to 2 hours.

2 Bring the water and rice to a boil, then reduce the heat and simmer for 10–15 minutes, until all the water has been absorbed.

3 Add the butter to the rice, cover the pan with a tight-fitting lid and steam over very low heat for about 30 minutes.

SPICED RICE

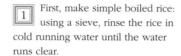

In the countries that border the eastern Mediterranean, rice is served at everyday meals and feasts.
Spices, nuts and dried fruit can be used to turn boiled rice into a special dish.

generous 1 cup basmati rice
2 tablespoons oil
1-inch piece cinnamon stick
¼ teaspoon ground turmeric
¼ teaspoon tomato paste
1 tablespoon raisins
¼ teaspoon toasted almonds,
to serve
salt and freshly ground black pepper

SERVES 4-6

1 First, make simple boiled rice: using a sieve, rinse the rice in cold running water until the water runs clear.

2 Add the rice to a saucepan of fast boiling water, add 1 teaspoon salt and boil for 5–7 minutes or until the grains are tender. Drain and rinse with a little boiling water.

3 To make fried rice, heat the oil in a large frying pan. Add the cinnamon stick and the turmeric and then the boiled rice. Stir well and heat thoroughly. Mix in the tomato paste and the raisins, and taste to check the seasoning.

4 Remove the cinnamon stick, spoon the rice into a dish and serve, sprinkled with the almonds.

COOK'S TIP
Pouring water through the boiled rice removes the excess starch.

BULGHUR PILAF

Bulghur—or cracked wheat—is much easier to cook than rice. For every 1 cup of grain, you simply
need 2 cups of liquid. Then you can add herbs, nuts or dried fruits to make the pilaf more interesting.

about ¼ cup oil
2 onions, finely chopped
2 cups bulghur wheat
4 cups hot chicken or vegetable stock
2–3 fresh mint or flat-leaf
parsley sprigs
3–4 dried apricots, sliced
3 tablespoons pine nuts, toasted
salt and ground black pepper
1 fresh mint sprig, to garnish

SERVES 8

1 Heat the oil in a large frying pan. When it is hot, toss in the onions. Stir over medium to high heat until the onions have browned slightly.

2 Wash the bulghur wheat and drain it thoroughly, squeezing out any excess moisture. Add the bulghur wheat to the sautéed onion and stir for a few minutes to coat the grains with the oil, adding a little more if necessary.

3 Add the stock. Bring to a boil, switch off the heat and cover.

4 Let stand for 10 minutes. Meanwhile, chop the herbs. Check the pilaf seasoning and add the apricots. To serve, spoon the hot bulghur wheat into a large dish and sprinkle on the herbs and toasted pine nuts. Garnish with mint.

SWEET RICE

In Iran, sweet rice (Shirin Polo) is always served at wedding banquets and on other traditional special occasions.

3 oranges
6 tablespoons sugar
5–6 carrots, cut into julienne strips
3 tablespoons butter, melted
1/2 cup mixed chopped pistachios,
   almonds and pine nuts
3 1/2 cups basmati rice, soaked in
   salted water for 2 hours
2–3 saffron strands, soaked in
   1 tablespoon boiling water
salt, to taste

SERVES 8-10

 Cut the peel from the oranges. Scrape off any pith. Cut the peel into thin shreds and place in a pan.

 Simmer the peel in water for 10 minutes, drain and repeat until the bitterness of the peel has gone.

3 Add 3 tablespoons of sugar and 1/4 cup water to the peel. Boil until the water is reduced by half. Set aside. Fry the carrots in 1 tablespoon of butter for 3 minutes. Add the remaining sugar and 1/4 cup water, and simmer for 10 minutes, until the water has evaporated.

4 Stir the carrots and half of the nuts into the orange peel mixture and set aside. Drain the rice, boil in salted water for 5 minutes, then reduce the heat and simmer for 10 minutes. Drain and rinse.

5 Heat 1 tablespoon of the butter in the pan and add 3 tablespoons water. Fork in a little rice and spoon on some carrot mixture. Make layers until the mixture has been used up.

6 Cook gently for 10 minutes. Pour on the remaining butter and cover with a clean dish towel. Secure the lid and steam for 30–45 minutes. Serve garnished with the remaining nuts and the saffron water.

RICE WITH FRESH HERBS

Chives and scallions give this easy rice dish a lovely fresh flavor.

1 3/4 cups basmati rice, soaked in salted
   water for 2 hours
2 tablespoons chopped fresh parsley
2 tablespoons chopped cilantro
2 tablespoons finely snipped
   fresh chives
1 tablespoon finely chopped fresh dill
3–4 scallions, finely chopped
2–3 saffron strands (optional)
1/4 cup butter
1 teaspoon ground cinnamon
salt

1 Drain the rice, then boil in a pan of salted water for 5 minutes. Reduce the heat and simmer for 10 minutes.

2 Stir in the herbs and scallions, and mix well with a fork. Simmer for a few more minutes, then drain but do not rinse. Wash and dry the pan. If using the saffron, soak the strands in 1 tablespoon boiling water and set aside.

3 Heat half of the butter in the pan, add 1 tablespoon of water, then stir in the rice. Cook over very low heat for 10 minutes, by which time it will be half-cooked. Add the remaining butter, the cinnamon and saffron water, if using, and cover with a clean dish towel. Secure with a tight-fitting lid, and steam over low heat for 30–40 minutes. Serve immediately.

SWEET-AND-SOUR RICE

Persian Zereshk Polo is flavored with fruit and spices and is usually served with chicken dishes.

❧ ❧

2 ounces zereshk
3 tablespoons butter, melted
⅓ cup raisins
2 tablespoons sugar
1 teaspoon ground cinnamon
1 teaspoon ground cumin
1¾ cups basmati rice, soaked in salted
water for 2 hours
2–3 saffron strands, soaked in
1 tablespoon boiling water
pinch of salt

SERVES 4

❧ ❧

 Thoroughly wash the *zereshk* in cold water at least 4–5 times to rinse off any bits of grit.

2 Heat 1 tablespoon of the butter in a small frying pan and stir-fry the raisins for 1–2 minutes.

3 Add the *zereshk*, fry for a few seconds, then add the sugar, and half of the ground spices. Cook briefly and then set aside.

4 Drain the rice. Boil in salted water for 5 minutes. Reduce the heat and simmer for 10 minutes.

 Drain the rice again; rinse well, then wash and dry the pan. Heat half of the remaining butter in the pan, add 1 tablespoon water and fork in half of the rice.

❧ ❧

COOK'S TIP
Zereshk are very small dried berries that are delicious mixed with rice. They are available at most Persian and Middle Eastern food stores.

6 Sprinkle with half of the raisin and *zereshk* mixture, and top with all but 3 tablespoons of the rice. Sprinkle the remaining raisin mixture evenly on top.

7 Mix the reserved rice with the remaining cinnamon and cumin and sprinkle on top of the rice mixture. Drizzle on the remaining butter and then cover the pan with a clean dish towel. Secure with a tight-fitting lid, lifting back the corners of the cloth over the lid. Steam the sweet-and-sour rice over low heat for 30–40 minutes.

8 Just before serving, 3 tablespoons of the rice with the saffron water. Spoon the rice onto a large flat serving dish and sprinkle the saffron rice on top to decorate.

RICE WITH DILL AND FAVA BEANS

With its delicate colors and wonderful flavors, this dish is perfect for spring.

1½ cups basmati rice, soaked in salted
water for 2 hours
1½ cups fava beans,
fresh or frozen
6 tablespoons finely chopped fresh dill
3 tablespoons butter, melted
1 teaspoon ground cinnamon
1 teaspoon ground cumin
2–3 saffron strands, soaked in
1 tablespoon boiling water
salt

SERVES 4

1. Drain the rice and then boil in salted water for 5 minutes. Reduce the heat and simmer very gently for 10 minutes, until partially cooked. Drain, rinse and drain again. Mix the fava beans and dill.

2. Put 1 tablespoon of the melted butter in a nonstick saucepan, then add enough rice to cover the bottom of the pan. Add a quarter of the fava bean and dill mixture in an even layer.

3. Add another layer of rice, followed by a layer of fava beans and dill, and continue making layers until all the beans and dill are used, finishing with a layer of rice.

4. Cook over low heat for 10 minutes. Pour the remaining melted butter over the rice.

5. Sprinkle the cinnamon and cumin evenly on top of the rice. Cover the pan with a clean dish towel and secure with a tight-fitting lid, lifting back the corners of the cloth over the lid, and then steam over low heat for 30–45 minutes.

6. Mix 3 tablespoons of the rice with the saffron water. Spoon the remaining rice onto a large serving dish and sprinkle on the saffron rice to decorate. Serve with either a lamb or a chicken dish.

RISOTTO WITH SPRING VEGETABLES

This is one of the prettiest risottos, especially when made with yellow summer squash.

1 cup shelled fresh peas
1 cup green beans,
cut into short lengths
2 tablespoons olive oil
6 tablespoons butter
2 small yellow summer squash,
cut into matchsticks
1 onion, finely chopped
1½ cups arborio rice
½ cup Italian dry
white vermouth
about 4 cups boiling chicken stock
1 cup grated Parmesan cheese
a small handful of fresh basil leaves,
finely shredded, plus a few whole
leaves, to garnish
salt and ground black pepper

SERVES 4

[1] Blanch the peas and beans in a large saucepan of lightly salted boiling water for 2–3 minutes, until just tender. Drain, refresh under cold running water, drain again and set aside for later.

[2] Heat the oil and 2 tablespoons of the butter in a medium saucepan until foaming. Add the squash and cook gently for about 3 minutes, until just softened. Remove with a slotted spoon and set aside. Add the onion to the pan and cook gently for about 3 minutes, stirring frequently, until softened.

[3] Stir in the rice until the grains start to swell and burst, then add the vermouth. Stir until the vermouth stops sizzling and most of it has been absorbed by the rice, then ladle in a little of the stock, with salt and pepper to taste. Stir over low heat until the stock has been absorbed.

[4] Continue cooking and stirring for 20–25 minutes, adding the remaining stock, a few ladles at a time. The rice should be *al dente* and the risotto should have a moist and creamy appearance.

[5] Gently stir in the peas, beans, remaining butter and about half the grated Parmesan. Heat through, then stir in the shredded basil and taste for seasoning. Garnish with a few whole basil leaves and serve hot, with the remaining Parmesan.

RISOTTO WITH FOUR CHEESES

*Risotto was originally a northern Italian dish, but it is now found all over Italy. Serve this rich risotto
for a dinner-party first course, with sparkling white wine.*

3 tablespoons butter
1 small onion, finely chopped
4 cups boiling chicken stock
1¾ cups arborio rice
scant 1 cup sparkling dry white wine
½ cup grated Gruyère cheese
½ cup diced Fontina cheese
½ cup crumbled Gorgonzola cheese
⅔ cup grated Parmesan cheese
salt and ground black pepper
fresh flat-leaf parsley, to garnish

SERVES 6

1 Melt the butter in a saucepan until foaming. Add the onion and cook gently, stirring frequently, for about 3 minutes, until softened. Have the hot stock ready in an adjacent pan.

2 Add the rice to the onions and stir until the grains start to swell and burst, then add the sparkling wine. Stir until it stops sizzling and most of it has been absorbed by the rice, then pour in a little of the hot stock. Add salt and pepper to taste.

3 Stir over low heat until the stock has been absorbed. Add more stock, a little at a time, allowing the rice to absorb it before adding more. Stir constantly.

4 After 20–25 minutes the rice will be *al dente* and the risotto creamy. Turn off the heat under the pan, then add the Gruyère, Fontina, Gorgonzola and 2 tablespoons of the Parmesan. Stir gently until the cheeses have melted, then taste for seasoning. Transfer into a serving bowl and garnish with parsley. Spoon the remaining Parmesan into a bowl and serve it separately.

PORCINI AND PARMESAN RISOTTO

The success of a good risotto depends on the quality of the rice used and the technique. For this variation on the classic Risotto alla Milanese, saffron, porcini mushrooms and Parmesan cheese are stirred into the creamy cooked rice.

2 tablespoons dried porcini
mushrooms
1¼ cups warm water
5 cups vegetable stock
a generous pinch of saffron strands
2 tablespoons olive oil
1 onion, finely chopped
1 garlic clove, crushed
1⅓ cups arborio or carnaroli rice
⅔ cup dry white wine or
3 tablespoons dry vermouth
2 tablespoons butter
⅔ cup freshly grated Parmesan cheese
salt and ground black pepper

SERVES 4

2 Put about 3 tablespoons of the hot stock in a cup and stir in the saffron strands. Set aside.

3 Finely chop the mushrooms. Heat the oil in a separate pan and lightly sauté the onion, garlic and mushrooms for 5 minutes. Gradually add the rice, stirring. Cook for 2 minutes, stirring. Season generously.

4 Pour in the wine or vermouth. Cook, stirring, until it has been absorbed, then ladle in a quarter of the stock. Bring to a boil, stirring. Cook, stirring constantly with a wooden spoon, until most of the liquid has been absorbed.

5 Continue to add the stock, a ladle at a time, stirring after each addition. The secret of a good risotto is to add the stock gradually and to stir frequently to encourage a creamy texture.

6 After about 20 minutes, when all the stock has been absorbed and the rice is cooked but still has a "bite," stir in the butter, saffron water and strands, and half of the Parmesan cheese. Serve, sprinkled with the remaining Parmesan.

1 Soak the dried mushrooms in the warm water for 20 minutes. Lift out with a slotted spoon. Filter the soaking water through a layer of paper towels in a sieve, then place it in a saucepan with the stock. Bring the liquid to a gentle simmer.

VARIATIONS

There are endless variations on this delectable dish. The proportion of stock to rice, onions, garlic and butter must remain constant, but you can make changes with the flavorings and cheese. Try Pecorino with lightly blanched baby vegetables to make risotto primavera.

PILAF WITH SAFFRON AND PICKLED WALNUTS

Pickled walnuts have a warm, tangy flavor that is delicious in rice and bulghur dishes. This eastern Mediterranean pilaf is interesting enough to serve on its own or with broiled lamb or pork.

1 teaspoon saffron strands
½ cup pine nuts
3 tablespoons olive oil
1 large onion, chopped
3 garlic cloves, crushed
¼ teaspoon ground allspice
1½-inch piece fresh ginger root, grated
generous 1 cup long-grain rice
1¼ cups vegetable stock
½ cup pickled walnuts, drained and coarsely chopped
¼ cup raisins
3 tablespoons coarsely chopped parsley or cilantro
salt and ground black pepper
parsley or cilantro, to garnish
plain yogurt, to serve

SERVES 4

1 Put the saffron in a bowl with 1 tablespoon boiling water and let stand. Heat a large frying pan and dry-fry the pine nuts until they turn golden. Set them aside.

2 Heat the oil in the pan and sauté the onion, garlic and allspice for 3 minutes. Stir in the ginger and rice and cook for 1 more minute.

3 Add the stock and bring to a boil. Reduce the heat, cover and simmer gently for 15 minutes, until the rice is just tender.

4 Stir in the saffron and liquid, the pine nuts, pickled walnuts, raisins and parsley or cilantro. Season to taste with salt and pepper. Heat through gently for 2 minutes. Garnish with parsley or cilantro leaves and serve with plain yogurt.

VARIATION
Use one small eggplant, chopped and sautéed in a little olive oil, instead of the pickled walnuts, if you prefer.

EGYPTIAN RICE WITH LENTILS

Lentils are cooked with spices in many ways in the Middle East. Two important staples come together in this dish, which can be served hot or cold.

❦ ❦

1½ cups large brown lentils, soaked
overnight in water
2 large onions
3 tablespoons olive oil
1 tablespoon ground cumin
½ teaspoon ground cinnamon
generous 1 cup long-grain rice
salt and ground black pepper
flat-leaf parsley, to garnish

SERVES 6

❦ ❦

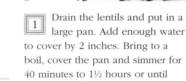

 Drain the lentils and put in a
large pan. Add enough water
to cover by 2 inches. Bring to a
boil, cover the pan and simmer for
40 minutes to 1½ hours or until
tender. Drain thoroughly.

 Finely chop one onion and slice
the other. Heat 1 tablespoon oil
in a pan, add the chopped onion and
sauté until soft. Add the lentils, salt,
pepper, cumin and cinnamon.

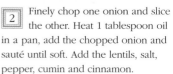 Measure out the rice and add it,
with the same volume of water,
to the lentil mixture. Cover and
simmer for about 20 minutes, until
both the rice and lentils are tender.
Heat the remaining oil in a frying pan
and cook the sliced onion until very
dark brown. Pour the rice mixture
into a serving bowl, sprinkle with the
onion and serve hot or cold,
garnished with flat-leaf parsley.

BROWN BEAN SALAD

Brown beans, sometimes called "ful medames," are widely used in Egyptian cooking and are occasionally seen in health-food stores here. Dried fava beans or black or red kidney beans make a good substitute.

1½ cups dried brown beans
3 thyme sprigs
2 bay leaves
1 onion, halved
4 garlic cloves, crushed
1½ teaspoons cumin seeds, crushed
3 scallions, finely chopped
6 tablespoons coarsely chopped
fresh flat-leaf parsley
4 teaspoons lemon juice
6 tablespoons olive oil
3 hard-boiled eggs, shelled and
coarsely chopped
1 dill pickle, roughly chopped
salt and ground black pepper

SERVES 6

1   Put the beans in a bowl with plenty of cold water and let soak overnight. Drain, transfer to a saucepan and cover with fresh water. Bring to a boil and boil rapidly for 10 minutes.

2   Reduce the heat and add the thyme, bay leaves and onion. Simmer very gently for about 1 hour, until tender. Drain and discard the herbs and onion.

COOK'S TIP
The cooking time for dried beans can vary considerably. They may need only 45 minutes or a lot longer.

3   Combine the garlic, cumin, scallions, parsley, lemon juice, oil and add a little salt and pepper. Pour over the beans and toss the ingredients together lightly.

4   Gently stir in the eggs and pickle and serve immediately.

SPICED VEGETABLE COUSCOUS

Couscous, a cereal processed from semolina, is used throughout North Africa, mostly in Morocco, where it is served with meat, poultry and vegetable stews or tagines.

3 tablespoons vegetable oil
1 large onion, finely chopped
2 garlic cloves, crushed
1 tablespoon tomato paste
½ teaspoon ground turmeric
½ teaspoon cayenne pepper
1 teaspoon ground coriander
1 teaspoon ground cumin
1½ cups cauliflower florets
8 ounces baby carrots, trimmed
1 red bell pepper, seeded and diced
4 beefsteak tomatoes
8 ounces zucchini, thickly sliced
14-ounce can chickpeas, drained
and rinsed
3 tablespoons chopped cilantro
salt and ground black pepper
cilantro sprigs, to garnish

FOR THE COUSCOUS
1 teaspoon salt
2⅔ cups couscous
2 tablespoons butter

SERVES 6

1 | Heat 2 tablespoons of the oil in a large pan, add the onion and garlic, and cook until soft. Stir in the tomato paste, turmeric, cayenne, ground coriander and cumin. Cook, stirring, for 2 minutes.

2 | Add the cauliflower, carrots and pepper, with enough water to come halfway up the vegetables. Bring to a boil, then lower the heat, cover and simmer for 10 minutes.

COOK'S TIP
Beefsteak tomatoes have excellent flavor and are ideal for this recipe, but you can substitute six ordinary tomatoes or two 14-ounce cans chopped tomatoes.

3 | Plunge the tomatoes into boiling water for 30 seconds, then refresh in cold water. Peel away the skins and chop. Add the sliced zucchini, chickpeas and tomatoes to the other vegetables and cook for another 10 minutes. Stir in the cilantro and season with salt and pepper. Keep hot.

4 | To cook the couscous, bring 2 cups water to a boil in a large saucepan. Add the remaining oil and the salt. Remove from the heat and add the couscous, stirring. Let swell for 2 minutes, then add the butter and heat through gently, stirring to separate the grains.

5 | Turn the couscous out onto a warm serving dish and spoon the vegetables on top, pouring any liquid over. Garnish and serve.

SPICY CHICKPEA AND EGGPLANT STEW

This is a Lebanese dish, but similar dishes are found all over the Mediterranean.

3 large eggplant, cubed
1 cup chickpeas, soaked overnight
¼ cup olive oil
3 garlic cloves, chopped
2 large onions, chopped
½ teaspoon ground cumin
½ teaspoon ground cinnamon
2½ teaspoons ground coriander
3 14-ounce cans chopped tomatoes
salt and ground black pepper
cooked rice, to serve

FOR THE GARNISH
2 tablespoons olive oil
1 onion, sliced
1 garlic clove, sliced
sprigs of cilantro

SERVES 4

1   Place the eggplant pieces in a colander and sprinkle them with salt. Set the colander in a bowl and let sit for 30 minutes, to allow the bitter juices to escape. Rinse with cold water and dry on paper towels.

2   Drain the chickpeas and put in a pan with enough water to cover. Bring to a boil and simmer for 30 minutes or until tender. Drain.

3   Heat the oil in a large pan. Add the garlic and onions and cook gently, until soft. Add the spices and cook, stirring, for a few seconds. Add the eggplant and stir to coat with the spices and onion. Cook for 5 minutes. Add the tomatoes and chickpeas and season with salt and pepper. Cover and simmer for 20 minutes.

4   To make the garnish, heat the oil in a frying pan and, when very hot, add the sliced onion and garlic. Fry until golden and crisp. Serve the stew with rice, topped with the onion and garlic and garnished with cilantro.

CHICKPEA TAGINE

One of the wonderful things about the tagine is its versatility. This vegetarian version is delicious with a chunk of crusty bread.

3/4 cup chickpeas, soaked overnight, or
2 14-ounce cans chickpeas, drained
2 tablespoons sunflower oil
1 large onion, chopped
1 garlic clove, crushed
14-ounce can chopped tomatoes
1 teaspoon ground cumin
1 1/2 cups vegetable stock
1/4 preserved lemon
2 tablespoons chopped cilantro

SERVES 4

1 If using dried, soaked chickpeas, cook in plenty of boiling water for 1 1/2–2 hours, until tender. Drain thoroughly.

2 Skin the chickpeas. Put them in a bowl of cold water and rub them between your palms; the skins will rise to the surface.

3 Heat the oil in a saucepan or flameproof casserole and fry the onion and garlic for 8–10 minutes, until golden.

4 Add the chickpeas, tomatoes, cumin and stock, and stir well. Bring to a boil, then simmer for 30–40 minutes, until the chickpeas are soft and fairly dry.

5 Rinse the preserved lemon and cut off the flesh and pith. Cut the peel into slivers and stir into the chickpeas with the cilantro. Serve.

SEMOLINA AND PESTO GNOCCHI

These gnocchi are cooked rounds of semolina paste, which are brushed with melted butter and then topped with cheese and baked. When they are carefully cooked, they taste wonderful, especially when served with a homemade tomato sauce.

3 cups milk
generous 1 cup semolina
3 tablespoons pesto
¼ cup finely chopped sun-dried tomatoes, patted dry if oily
¼ cup butter
1 cup freshly grated Pecorino cheese
2 eggs, beaten
freshly grated nutmeg, to taste
salt and ground black pepper
tomato sauce, to serve
fresh basil sprigs, to garnish

SERVES 4

1 Heat the milk in a large nonstick saucepan. When it is on the point of boiling, sprinkle in the semolina, stirring constantly, until the mixture is smooth and very thick. Lower the heat and simmer for 2 minutes, until the paste starts to come away from the sides of the pan.

2 Remove from heat and stir in the pesto and sun-dried tomatoes, with half of the butter and half of the Pecorino. Add the eggs, with nutmeg, salt and pepper to taste. Spoon onto a clean shallow baking dish or pan to a depth of ½ inch, and level the surface. Let cool, then chill.

3 Preheat the oven to 375°F. Lightly grease a shallow baking dish, then, using a 1½-inch cookie cutter or a glass, stamp out as many rounds as possible from the semolina paste.

4 Place the leftover semolina paste on the bottom of the greased dish and arrange the rounds on top in overlapping circles.

5 Melt the remaining butter and brush it over the gnocchi. Sprinkle on the remaining Pecorino. Bake for 30–40 minutes, until golden. Garnish with basil and serve with tomato sauce.

PUMPKIN GNOCCHI WITH A CHANTERELLE PARSLEY CREAM

Gnocchi is an Italian pasta dumpling, usually made from potatoes. In this special recipe, pumpkin is added, too. A chanterelle sauce provides both richness and flavor.

1 pound peeled potatoes
1 pound peeled pumpkin, chopped
2 egg yolks
1¾ cups all-purpose flour,
plus more if necessary
pinch of ground allspice
¼ teaspoon ground cinnamon
pinch of grated nutmeg
finely grated zest of ½ orange
salt and ground black pepper
2 ounces Parmesan cheese, shaved,
to garnish

FOR THE SAUCE
2 tablespoons olive oil
1 shallot, chopped
2¼ cups fresh chanterelles, sliced, or
¼ cup dried, soaked for 20 minutes
in warm water
2 teaspoons almond butter
⅔ cup crème fraîche
a little milk or water
3 tablespoons chopped fresh parsley

SERVES 4

1 Cover the potatoes with cold salted water, bring to a boil and cook for 20 minutes. Drain and set aside. Place the pumpkin in a bowl, cover and microwave on full power for 8 minutes. Alternatively, wrap the pumpkin in aluminum foil and bake at 350°F for 30 minutes. Drain, add to the potato and pass through a vegetable mill into a bowl.

2 Add the egg yolks, flour, spices, orange zest and seasoning to the pumpkin and mix into a soft dough, adding more flour if needed. Spoon the mixture into a piping bag fitted with a ½-inch nozzle. Pipe onto a floured surface to make a 6-inch sausage. Roll in the flour and cut into 1-inch pieces. Repeat the process, making more sausage shapes.

3 Bring a large pan of salted water to a boil. Mark the gnocchi lightly with a fork and cook for 3–4 minutes in the boiling water.

4 Meanwhile, make the sauce. Heat the oil in a nonstick frying pan, add the shallot and fry until soft without coloring. Add the chanterelles and cook briefly, then add the almond butter. Stir to melt, and stir in the creme fraiche. Simmer briefly and adjust the consistency with milk or water. Add the parsley and season to taste.

5 Lift the gnocchi out of the water with a slotted spoon, turn into bowls and spoon the sauce over the top. Sprinkle on the Parmesan.

SPINACH AND RICOTTA GNOCCHI

The success of this Italian dish lies in not overworking the mixture, to achieve delicious, light mouthfuls.

2 pounds fresh spinach
1½ cups ricotta cheese
¼ cup freshly grated
Parmesan cheese, plus extra to serve
3 eggs, beaten
¼ teaspoon grated nutmeg
3–4 tablespoons all-purpose flour
8 tablespoons butter, melted
salt and ground black pepper

SERVES 4

1 Place the spinach in a large pan and cook for 5 minutes, until wilted. Let cool, then squeeze the spinach as dry as possible. Process in a blender or food processor, then transfer to a bowl.

2 Add the ricotta, Parmesan, eggs and nutmeg. Season with salt and pepper and combine. Add enough flour to make the mixture into a soft dough. Using your hands, shape the mixture into 3-inch sausages, then dust lightly with flour.

3 Bring a large pan of salted water to a boil. Gently slide the gnocchi into the water and cook for 1–2 minutes, until they float to the surface. Remove the gnocchi with a slotted spoon and transfer to a warmed dish. Pour the melted butter over them and sprinkle with Parmesan cheese. Serve immediately.

POLENTA WITH MUSHROOM SAUCE

In Italy, polenta often fulfills the same function as rice, bread or potatoes in providing the starchy base for a meal. Here, it is cooked until it forms a soft dough, then flavored with Parmesan. Its subtle taste works well with this rich mushroom sauce.

5 cups vegetable stock
3 cups polenta
²/₃ cup grated Parmesan cheese
salt and ground black pepper
fresh thyme sprigs, to garnish

FOR THE SAUCE
1 cup dried porcini mushrooms
1 tablespoon olive oil
¹/₄ cup butter
1 onion, finely chopped
1 carrot, finely chopped
1 celery stalk, finely chopped
2 garlic cloves, crushed
6 cups mixed chestnut and
large flat mushrooms,
roughly chopped
¹/₂ cup red wine
14-ounce can chopped tomatoes
1 teaspoon tomato paste
1 tablespoon chopped fresh
thyme leaves

SERVES 4

1 Make the sauce. Put the dried mushrooms in a bowl, add ²/₃ cup hot water and soak for 20 minutes. Drain the mushrooms, reserving the liquid, and chop them roughly.

2 Heat the oil and butter in a saucepan. Fry the onion, carrot, celery and garlic over low heat until the vegetables are beginning to soften, then raise the heat and add the fresh and soaked, dried mushrooms. Cook for 8–10 minutes, until the mushrooms are soft and golden

3 Pour in the wine and cook rapidly for 2–3 minutes, until reduced, then add the tomatoes and the reserved mushroom liquid. Stir in the tomato paste, thyme and plenty of salt and pepper. Lower the heat and simmer for 20 minutes.

4 Meanwhile, heat the stock in a large, heavy saucepan. Add a generous pinch of salt. As soon as the stock simmers, pour in the polenta in a fine stream, whisking until the mixture is smooth. Cook for 30 minutes, stirring constantly, until the polenta comes away from the sides of the pan. Remove from heat and stir in half of the Parmesan and some black pepper.

5 Divide among four heated bowls and top each with the mushroom sauce. Sprinkle with the remaining grated Parmesan cheese, and garnish with thyme.

BAKED CHEESE POLENTA WITH TOMATO SAUCE

Polenta, or cornmeal mush, is a staple food in Italy. It is cooked like a sort of porridge, and eaten soft, or set, cut into shapes, then baked or broiled.

🌾 🌾

1 teaspoon salt
2¼ cups instant polenta
1 teaspoon paprika
½ teaspoon ground nutmeg
2 tablespoons olive oil
1 large onion, finely chopped
2 garlic cloves, crushed
2 14-ounce cans chopped tomatoes
1 tablespoon tomato paste
1 teaspoon sugar
salt and ground black pepper
3 ounces Gruyère cheese, grated

SERVES 4

1 Preheat the oven to 400°F. Line an 11 x 7-inch baking pan with plastic wrap. Put 4 cups water into a pan and bring to a boil with the salt.

2 Pour in the polenta in a steady stream and cook, stirring constantly, for 5 minutes. Beat in the paprika and nutmeg, then pour into the prepared pan and smooth the surface. Let cool.

3 Heat the oil in a pan and cook the onion and garlic until soft. Add the tomatoes, paste and sugar. Season. Simmer for 20 minutes.

4 Turn out the polenta onto a cutting board and cut into 2-inch squares. Place half the squares in a greased ovenproof dish. Spoon on half the tomato sauce, and sprinkle with half the cheese. Repeat the layers. Bake for about 25 minutes, until golden.

POLENTA ELISA

This dish comes from the valley around Lake Como, in Italy. Serve it solo as an appetizer, or with a mixed salad and some sliced salami or prosciutto for a midweek supper.

1 cup milk
2 cups quick-cook polenta
1 cup Gruyère cheese
1 cup torta di Dolcelatte cheese,
crumbled
¼ cup butter
2 garlic cloves, roughly chopped
a few fresh sage leaves, chopped
salt and freshly ground black pepper
prosciutto, to serve

SERVES 4

1 In a large pan, bring the milk and 3 cups water to a boil, add 1 teaspoon salt, then add the polenta. Cook for about 8 minutes.

2 Preheat the oven to 400°F. Lightly grease a 8–10-inch baking dish.

3 Spoon half of the polenta into the baking dish and level. Cover with half of the grated Gruyère and crumbled Dolcelatte. Spoon the remaining polenta on top and sprinkle with the remaining cheeses.

4 Melt the butter in a small pan until foaming, then fry the garlic and sage, stirring, until the butter turns golden brown.

5 Drizzle the butter mixture onto the polenta and cheese and grind black pepper liberally over the top. Bake for 5 minutes. Serve hot, with slices of prosciutto.

COOK'S TIP
Pour the polenta into the boiling liquid in a continuous stream, stirring constantly. If using a whisk, change to a wooden spoon once the polenta starts to thicken, and keep stirring until it is very thick.

CALZONE

—

A calzone looks a lot like a folded pizza, and consists of bread dough wrapped around a cheese and vegetable filling. The traditional tomato and garlic can be enlivened with chunks of melting cheese, olives, crumbled bacon, slices of pepperoni or anchovy fillets.

2 tablespoons extra virgin olive oil
1 small red onion, thinly sliced
2 garlic cloves, crushed
14-ounce can chopped tomatoes
2 ounces sliced chorizo sausage
¹/₂ cup pitted black olives
1¹/₄ pound bread dough mix
7 ounces mozzarella or other semi-soft cheese, diced
1 teaspoon dried oregano
salt and freshly ground black pepper
oregano sprigs, to garnish

MAKES 4

1 Heat the oil in a frying pan and sauté the onion and garlic for 5 minutes. Add the tomatoes and cook for 5 more minutes or until slightly reduced. Add the sliced chorizo and pitted black olives. Season with plenty of salt and pepper.

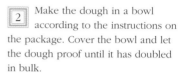

2 Make the dough in a bowl according to the instructions on the package. Cover the bowl and let the dough proof until it has doubled in bulk.

3 Punch down the dough and divide it into four portions. Roll out each portion to a circle measuring about 8 inches. Preheat the oven to 400°F. Lightly grease two baking sheets.

4 Spread the tomato filling on half of each dough circle, leaving a margin around the edge. Sprinkle the cheese on top. Sprinkle the filling with the dried oregano.

5 Dampen the edges of the dough with cold water. Fold the dough in half and press the edges together to seal.

6 Place two calzones on each baking sheet. Bake for 12–15 minutes, until risen and golden. Cool for 2 minutes, then loosen with a spatula and transfer to serving plates. Serve immediately, garnished with oregano.

RADICCHIO PIZZA

This unusual pizza topping consists of chopped radicchio, leeks, tomatoes, and Parmesan and mozzarella cheeses. The base is a scone dough, making this a quick and easy supper dish to prepare. Serve with a crisp green salad.

🌿 🌿

1²/₃ cups passata or tomato purée
pinch of dried basil
2 garlic cloves, crushed
1¹/₂ tablespoons olive oil, plus extra
for dipping
2 leeks, sliced
3¹/₂ ounces radicchio,
roughly chopped
³/₄ ounce Parmesan cheese, grated
4 ounces mozzarella cheese, sliced
10–12 pitted black olives
fresh basil leaves, to garnish
salt and ground black pepper

FOR THE DOUGH
2 cups self-rising flour
¹/₂ teaspoon salt
¹/₄ cup butter
about ¹/₂ cup milk

SERVES 2

🌿 🌿

1 Preheat the oven to 425°F and grease a baking sheet. Mix the flour and salt in a bowl, rub in the butter, and stir in enough milk to make a soft dough. Roll it out on a lightly floured surface to a 10–11-inch round. Place on the baking sheet.

2 Mix the passata, basil and half of the garlic in a small pan. Season, then simmer over medium heat until the mixture is thick and has reduced by about half.

3 Heat the olive oil in a large frying pan and fry the leeks and remaining garlic for 4–5 minutes, until slightly softened. Add the radicchio and cook, stirring constantly for a few minutes, then cover and simmer gently for 5–10 minutes. Stir in the Parmesan cheese and season with salt and pepper.

4 Cover the crust with the passata mixture and then spoon on the leek and radicchio mixture. Arrange the mozzarella slices on top and sprinkle on the black olives. Dip a few basil leaves in olive oil, arrange on top and bake the pizza for 15–20 minutes, until the scone crust and top are golden brown.

RICOTTA AND FONTINA PIZZAS

The earthy flavors of the mixed mushrooms are delicious with the creamy cheeses.

½ teaspoon active dry yeast
pinch of sugar
4 cups all-purpose flour
1 teaspoon salt
2 tablespoons olive oil

FOR THE TOPPING
14-ounce can chopped tomatoes
⅔ cup passata or tomato purée
1 teaspoon dried oregano
1 bay leaf
2 teaspoons malt vinegar
2 large garlic cloves, finely chopped
2 tablespoons olive oil, plus extra
for brushing
4 cups mixed mushrooms
(chestnut, flat or button), sliced
2 tablespoons chopped fresh oregano,
plus whole leaves, to garnish
generous 1 cup ricotta cheese
8 ounces Fontina cheese, sliced
salt and ground black pepper

SERVES 4

1 First, make the dough. Put 1¼ cups warm water in a measuring cup. Add the yeast and sugar and let sit for 5–10 minutes, until frothy. Sift the flour and salt into a large bowl and make a well in the center. Gradually pour in the yeast mixture and the olive oil. Mix to make a smooth dough. Knead on a lightly floured surface for about 10 minutes. Place the dough in a floured bowl, cover and let rise in a warm place for 1½ hours.

2 Make the tomato sauce. Place the tomatoes, passata, herbs, vinegar and half of the garlic in a pan, cover and bring to a boil. Lower the heat, remove the lid and simmer for 20 minutes, stirring occasionally, until reduced.

3 Make the topping. Heat the oil in a frying pan. Add the mushrooms and remaining garlic. Season to taste. Cook, stirring, for about 5 minutes or until the mushrooms are tender. Set aside.

4 Preheat the oven to 425°F. Knead the dough for 2 minutes, then divide into four equal pieces. Roll out each piece to a 10-inch round and place onto four lightly oiled baking sheets.

5 Spoon the tomato sauce onto each dough round. Brush the edges with a little olive oil. Add the mushrooms, fresh oregano and cheeses. Bake for about 15 minutes until golden brown and crisp. Sprinkle the oregano leaves on top.

MARRAKESH PIZZAS

In Morocco, cooks tend to place flavorings inside the pizza rather than on top of the bread.
The results are surprising—and quite delicious.

1 teaspoon sugar
2 teaspoons active dry yeast
4 cups all-purpose flour
(or a mixture of all-purpose and
whole-wheat flour,
according to preference)
salt
melted butter, for brushing
arugula salad and black olives,
to serve

FOR THE FILLING
1 small onion, very finely chopped
2 tomatoes, peeled, seeded
and chopped
1½ tablespoons chopped fresh parsley
1½ tablespoons chopped cilantro
1 teaspoon paprika
1 teaspoon ground cumin
2 ounces chilled shortening,
finely chopped
1½ ounces Cheddar cheese, grated

SERVES 4

1 First, prepare the yeast. Place
⅔ cup warm water in a small
bowl, stir in the sugar and then
sprinkle with the yeast. Stir once or
twice, then set aside in a warm place
for about 10 minutes, until frothy.

2 Meanwhile, make the filling.
Combine the onion, tomatoes,
parsley, cilantro, paprika, cumin,
shortening and cheese, then season
with salt and set aside.

3 In a large bowl, combine the
flour and 2 teaspoons salt. Add
the yeast mixture and enough warm
water (about 1 cup) to make a fairly
soft dough.

4 Knead the mixture into a ball
and then knead on a floured
work surface for 10–12 minutes, until
the dough is firm and elastic.

5 Break the dough into four pieces.
Shape each piece into a ball. On
the floured surface, roll each into a
rectangle, measuring 8 × 12 inches.
Spread the filling down the center of
each rectangle, then fold into thirds,
to make 8 × 4-inch rectangles.

6 Roll out the dough again, until
it is the same size as before and
again fold into thirds to make a
smaller rectangle. (The filling will be
squeezed out in places, but don't
worry—just push it back inside.)

7 Place the pizzas on a buttered
baking sheet, cover with oiled
plastic wrap and let sit in a warm place
for about 1 hour, until slightly risen.

8 Heat a griddle and brush with
butter. Prick the pizzas with a
fork, five or six times on both sides,
and then cook for about 8 minutes on
each side until crisp and golden.
Serve immediately, accompanied by
arugula salad and black olives.

MUSHROOM AND PESTO PIZZA

—

Home-made Italian-style pizzas are a little time-consuming to make, but the results are well worth the effort.

FOR THE PIZZA CRUST
3 cups all-purpose flour
¼ teaspoon salt
½ ounce active dry yeast
1 tablespoon olive oil

FOR THE FILLING
2 ounces dried porcini mushrooms
¾ cup fresh basil
⅓ cup pine nuts
1½ ounces Parmesan cheese,
thinly sliced
7 tablespoons olive oil
2 onions, thinly sliced
8 ounces cremini mushrooms, sliced
salt and ground black pepper

SERVES 4

1 To make the pizza crust, put the flour in a bowl with the salt, yeast and olive oil. Add 1 cup warm water and mix to a dough using a round-bladed knife.

2 Turn out onto a work surface and knead for 5 minutes, until smooth. Place in a clean bowl, cover with plastic wrap and let rise in a warm place until doubled in bulk.

3 Meanwhile, make the filling. Soak the dried mushrooms in hot water for 20 minutes. Place the basil, pine nuts, Parmesan and 5 tablespoons of the olive oil in a blender or food processor and process to make a smooth paste. Set the paste aside.

4 Fry the onions in the remaining olive oil for 3–4 minutes, until beginning to color. Add the cremini mushrooms and fry for 2 minutes. Stir in the drained porcini mushrooms and season lightly.

5 Preheat the oven to 425°F. Lightly grease a large baking sheet. Turn out the pizza dough onto a floured surface and roll out to a 12-inch circle. Place the dough on the baking sheet.

6 Spread the pesto mixture to within ½ inch of the edges. Spread the mushroom mixture on top.

7 Bake the pizza for 35–40 minutes, until risen and golden.

BUTTERNUT SQUASH AND SAGE PIZZA

The combination of the sweet butternut squash, sage and sharp goat cheese works wonderfully on this pizza. Pumpkin and winter squashes are popular vegetables in Italy.

1 tablespoon butter
2 tablespoons olive oil
2 shallots, finely chopped
1 butternut squash, peeled, seeded
and cubed
16 sage leaves
1 batch prepared pizza dough,
kneaded and proved
2½ cups thick homemade
or bottled tomato sauce
4 ounces mozzarella cheese, sliced
4 ounces firm goat cheese
salt and ground black pepper

SERVES 4

1. Preheat the oven to 400°F. Oil four baking sheets. Put the butter and oil in a roasting pan and heat in the oven for a few minutes. Add the shallots, squash and half of the sage leaves. Toss to coat. Roast for 15–20 minutes, until tender, turning the mixture several times.

2. Raise the oven temperature to 425°F. Divide the pizza dough into four equal pieces and roll out each piece on a lightly floured surface to a 10-inch round.

3. Transfer each round to a baking sheet and spread with the tomato sauce, leaving a ½-inch border all around. Spoon the squash and shallot mixture on top.

4. Arrange the slices of mozzarella on the squash mixture and crumble the goat cheese on top. Sprinkle the remaining sage leaves over that, and season with plenty of salt and pepper. Bake for 15–20 minutes until the cheese has melted and the crust on each pizza is golden.

SPINACH AND BELL PEPPER PIZZAS

The topping on these pizza is an unusual one, but delicious.

1 pound fresh spinach
¼ cup light cream
1 ounce Parmesan cheese, grated
1 tablespoon olive oil
1 large onion, chopped
1 garlic clove, crushed
½ green bell pepper,
seeded and thinly sliced
½ red bell pepper,
seeded and thinly sliced
¾–1 cup passata or tomato purée
½ cup pitted black olives, chopped
1 tablespoon chopped fresh basil
6 ounces mozzarella, grated
6 ounces Gruyère cheese, grated
salt

FOR THE DOUGH
1 ounce fresh yeast or
1 tablespoon active dry yeast and
1 teaspoon sugar
about scant 1 cup
warm water
3 cups all-purpose flour
1 teaspoon salt
2 tablespoons olive oil

SERVES 2–4

1 To make the dough, cream together the fresh yeast and ⅔ cup of the water and set aside until frothy. If using active dry yeast, stir the sugar into ⅔ cup water, sprinkle on the yeast and let sit until frothy.

2 Place the flour and salt in a large bowl, make a well in the center and pour in the olive oil and the yeast mixture. Add the remaining water. Mix to make a stiff but pliable dough. Knead on a lightly floured surface for about 10 minutes.

3 Shape the dough into a ball and place in a lightly oiled bowl. Cover with plastic wrap and let sit in a warm place for about 1 hour, until doubled in bulk.

4 To prepare the topping, cook the spinach over medium heat for 4–5 minutes, until the leaves have wilted. Strain and press out the excess liquid. Place in a bowl and mix with the cream, Parmesan cheese and salt to taste.

5 Heat the oil in a frying pan and fry the onion and garlic over medium heat for 3–4 minutes, until the onion has softened slightly. Add the peppers and continue to cook until the onion is lightly golden.

6 Preheat the oven to 425°F. Knead the dough briefly on a lightly floured surface. Divide the dough and roll out into two 12-inch rounds.

7 Spread each crust with passata or puréed tomatoes. Add the onions and peppers, then spread on the spinach mixture. Sprinkle the olives, basil, mozzarella and Gruyère on top. Bake for 15–20 minutes or until the crusts are lightly browned. Cool slightly before serving.

SPANISH ONION AND ANCHOVY PIZZA

This pizza has flavors and ingredients brought to Spain by the Moors and still used today in many classic Spanish recipes.

2½ cups all-purpose flour
½ teaspoon salt
½ ounce rapid-rise yeast
½ cup olive oil
⅔ cup milk and water, in equal quantities, combined
3 large onions, thinly sliced
2-ounce can anchovies, drained and coarsely chopped
2 tablespoons pine nuts
2 tablespoons golden raisins
1 teaspoon red pepper flakes
salt and ground black pepper

SERVES 6–8

1. Sift the flour and salt together into a large bowl. Stir in the yeast. Make a well in the center, and add half of the olive oil and a little of the milk and water. Bring the flour mixture and liquid together, gradually adding the remaining milk and water, until a dough is formed. Knead on a floured surface for about 10 minutes. Return to the bowl, cover with a cloth, and set in a warm place to rise for about 1 hour.

2. Heat the remaining oil in a large frying pan, add the onions and cook until soft. Preheat the oven to 475°F.

3. Punch down the dough and roll out to a rectangle about 12 x 15 inches. Place on an oiled baking sheet. Cover with the onions. Sprinkle on the anchovies, pine nuts, golden raisins and red pepper flakes. Season. Bake for 10–15 minutes, until the edges are beginning to brown. Serve hot.

GRILLED VEGETABLE PIZZA

Grilled or broiled vegetables are good at any time, but are particularly tasty when teamed with melted

1 zucchini, sliced
2 baby eggplant or
1 small eggplant, sliced
2 tablespoons olive oil
1 yellow bell pepper, seeded and
thickly sliced
1 cup cornmeal
$^{1}/_{2}$ cup potato flour
$^{1}/_{2}$ cup soy flour
1 teaspoon baking powder
$^{1}/_{2}$ teaspoon salt
$^{1}/_{4}$ cup butter or soft margarine
about 7 tablespoons milk
4 plum tomatoes, peeled and chopped
2 tablespoons chopped fresh basil
4 ounces mozzarella cheese, sliced
salt and ground black pepper
fresh basil leaves, to garnish

SERVES 4

 1 Preheat the broiler. Brush the zucchini and eggplant slices with a little oil and place on a broiler rack with the pepper slices. Cook under the broiler until lightly browned, turning once.

2 Meanwhile, preheat the oven to 400°F. Place the cornmeal, potato flour, soy flour, baking powder and salt in a mixing bowl and stir to mix. Lightly rub in the butter or margarine until the mixture resembles coarse bread crumbs, then stir in enough of the milk to make a soft but not sticky dough.

3 Place the dough on a sheet of nonstick baking parchment on a baking sheet and roll or press it out to form a 10-inch round, pushing up the edges so that they are slightly thicker than the center.

4 Brush the pizza dough with any remaining oil, then spread the chopped tomatoes on the dough.

5 Sprinkle with the chopped basil and season with salt and pepper. Arrange the grilled vegetables on the tomatoes and top with the sliced mozzarella cheese.

6 Bake for 25–30 minutes, until crisp and golden brown. Garnish the pizza with fresh basil and serve, cut into slices.

ONION FOCACCIA

This pizza-like flat bread is characterized by its soft, dimpled surface, sometimes dredged simply with coarse salt or with onions, herbs or olives. It tastes delicious served warm with soups and stews.

6 cups all-purpose flour
½ teaspoon salt
½ teaspoon sugar
1 tablespoon rapid-rise yeast
4 tablespoons extra virgin olive oil
2 cups warm water

TO FINISH
2 red onions, thinly sliced
3 tablespoons extra virgin olive oil
1 tablespoon coarse salt

MAKES TWO 10-INCH BREADS

1 Sift the flour, salt and sugar into a large bowl. Stir in the yeast, oil and water and mix to a dough using a round-bladed knife. (Add a little extra water if the dough is dry.)

2 Turn out onto a lightly floured surface and knead for about 10 minutes, until smooth and elastic.

3 Put the dough in a clean, lightly oiled bowl and cover with plastic wrap. Let rise in a warm place until doubled in bulk.

4 Place two 10-inch plain metal baking rings on baking sheets. Oil the insides of the rings and the baking sheets.

5 Preheat the oven to 400°F. Halve the dough and roll out each piece to a 10-inch circle. Press into the rings, cover with a dampened dish towel and let rise for 30 minutes.

6 Make deep holes, about 1 inch apart, in the dough. Cover and let rest for another 20 minutes.

7 Sprinkle the onions on top and drizzle with the oil. Sprinkle with the salt, then a little cold water, to prevent a crust from forming.

8 Bake for about 25 minutes, sprinkling with water again during cooking. Cool on a wire rack.

409

FOCACCIA

This is a flattish bread, originating in Genoa, Italy, made with flour, olive oil and salt. There are many variations from many regions, including stuffed varieties and versions topped with onions, olives or herbs.

1 package active dry yeast
3½ cups all-purpose flour
2 teaspoons salt
5 tablespoons olive oil
2 teaspoons coarse sea salt

MAKES 1 ROUND 10-INCH LOAF

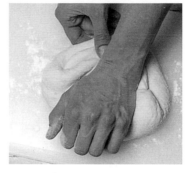

1 Dissolve the yeast in ½ cup warm water. Let stand for 10 minutes. Sift the flour into a large bowl, make a well in the center, and add the yeast mixture, salt and 2 tablespoons oil. Mix in the flour and add more water to make a dough.

2 Turn out onto a floured surface and knead the dough for about 10 minutes, until smooth and elastic. Return to the bowl, cover with a cloth, and let rise in a warm place for 2–2½ hours, until the dough has doubled in bulk.

3 Punch down the dough and knead again for a few minutes. Press into an oiled 10-inch tart pan and cover with a damp cloth. Let rise for 30 minutes.

4 Preheat the oven to 400°F. Poke the dough all over with your fingers to make little dimples in the surface. Pour the remaining oil over the dough, using a pastry brush to take it to the edges. Sprinkle with the salt.

5 Bake for 20–25 minutes, until the bread is pale gold. Carefully remove from the pan and let cool on a rack. The bread is best eaten on the same day, but it also freezes very well.

SUN-DRIED TOMATO BREAD

In the south of Italy, tomatoes are often dried in the hot sun. They are then preserved in oil, or hung up on strings in the kitchen, to use in the winter. This recipe uses the former type.

6 cups all-purpose flour
2 teaspoons salt
2 tablespoons sugar
1 package active dry yeast
1⅔–2 cups warm milk
1 tablespoon tomato paste
5 tablespoons oil from the jar of sun-dried tomatoes
5 tablespoons extra virgin olive oil
¾ cup drained sun-dried tomatoes, chopped
1 large onion, chopped

MAKES 4 SMALL LOAVES

 2 Mix the tomato paste into the remaining milk until evenly blended, then add to the flour with the tomato oil and olive oil.

3 Gradually mix the flour into the liquid ingredients until you have a dough. Turn out onto a floured surface and knead for about 10 minutes, until smooth and elastic. Return to the clean bowl, cover with a cloth and let rise in a warm place for about 2 hours.

4 Punch down, and add the tomatoes and onion. Knead until evenly distributed through the dough. Shape into four loaves and place on a greased baking sheet. Cover with a dish towel and let rise again for about 45 minutes.

5 Preheat the oven to 375°F. Bake the bread for 45 minutes or until the loaves sound hollow when you tap them with your fingers. Let cool on a wire rack. Eat warm, or toasted with grated mozzarella cheese sprinkled on top.

1 Sift the flour, salt and sugar into a bowl, and make a well in the center. Mix the yeast with ⅔ cup of the warm milk and add to the flour.

COOK'S TIP
Use a pair of sharp kitchen scissors to cut up the sun-dried tomatoes.

OLIVE BREAD

Olive breads are popular all over the Mediterranean. For this Greek recipe use rich, oily olives or those marinated in herbs rather than canned ones.

🌿 🌿

2 red onions, thinly sliced
2 tablespoons olive oil
1⅓ cups pitted black or green olives
7 cups all-purpose flour
1½ teaspoons salt
4 teaspoons rapid-rise yeast
3 tablespoons each coarsely-chopped
parsley and cilantro or mint

MAKES TWO 1½-POUND LOAVES

🌿 🌿

 Sauté the onions in the oil until soft. Coarsely chop the olives.

 Put the flour, salt, yeast, parsley and cilantro or mint in a large bowl with the olives and onions and pour in 2 cups warm water.

🌿 🌿

VARIATION
Shape the dough into 16 small rolls. Slash the tops as above and reduce the cooking time to 25 minutes.

🌿 🌿

 Mix to a dough using a round-bladed knife, adding a little more water if the mixture feels dry.

 Turn out onto a lightly floured surface and knead for about 10 minutes. Put in a clean bowl, cover with plastic wrap and let sit in a warm place until doubled in bulk.

⑤ Preheat the oven to 425°F. Lightly grease two baking sheets. Turn the dough out onto a floured surface and cut in half. Shape into two loaves and place on the baking sheets. Cover loosely with lightly oiled plastic wrap and let rise until doubled in size.

⑥ Slash the tops of the loaves with a knife, then bake for about 40 minutes or until the loaves sound hollow when tapped on the bottom. Transfer to a wire rack to cool.

MOROCCAN BREAD

Warm this bread in the oven and cut it into thick slices to serve with any classic Moroccan savory dish.
It is just the thing for mopping up a really good sauce.

2¹/₂ cups all-purpose flour
1¹/₂ cups whole-wheat flour
2 teaspoons salt
1 cup warm milk and water, mixed
2 teaspoons sesame seeds

FOR THE YEAST STARTER
²/₃ cup warm milk and water, mixed
1 teaspoon sugar
2 teaspoons dried yeast

MAKES 2 LOAVES

1 First, prepare the yeast. Place the warm milk mixture in a small bowl or pitcher, stir in the sugar and then sprinkle the yeast on top. Stir, then set aside in a warm place for about 10 minutes, until frothy.

2 In a large bowl, combine the two flours and salt. Add the yeast mixture and enough diluted warm milk to make a fairly soft dough. Knead the mixture into a ball and then knead on a floured surface for 10–12 minutes, until firm and elastic.

3 Break the dough into two pieces and shape into flattened ball shapes. Place on floured baking sheets and press down with your hand to make round breads about 5–6 inches in diameter.

4 Cover the breads with oiled plastic wrap or a clean, damp cloth and set aside for 1–1¹/₂ hours in a warm place until risen. The breads are ready to bake when the dough springs back if gently pressed.

5 Preheat the oven to 400°F. Sprinkle the risen loaves with the sesame seeds and bake for 12 minutes. Reduce the oven temperature to 300°F and bake for 20–30 more minutes, until the loaves sound hollow when tapped on the bottom.

SEED BREAD

This bread is quite delicious—just the thing to make for special occasions.

3 cups all-purpose flour
1 cup cornmeal
2 teaspoons salt
2/3 cup warm milk and water, mixed
1 1/2 tablespoons pumpkin seeds
1 1/2 tablespoons sunflower seeds
1 tablespoon sesame seeds

FOR THE YEAST STARTER
2/3 cup warm water
1 teaspoon sugar
2 teaspoons active dry yeast

MAKES 2 LOAVES

1 First, prepare the yeast. Place the warm water in a small bowl or pitcher, stir in the sugar and then sprinkle the yeast on top. Stir, then set aside in a warm place for about 10 minutes, until frothy.

2 In a large bowl, combine the flour, cornmeal and salt. Add the yeast mixture and enough of the diluted warm milk to make a fairly soft dough. Knead the mixture into a ball and then knead on a floured surface for 5 minutes.

3 Add the pumpkin, sunflower and sesame seeds, and knead them into the dough. Continue kneading for 5–6 minutes, until the dough is firm and elastic.

4 Break the dough into two pieces and shape into balls, flattening them to make two round frisbee shapes. Place on floured baking sheets and press down with your hand to make round breads measuring 5–6 inches in diameter.

5 Cover with oiled plastic wrap or a damp dish towel and set aside for 1–1 1/2 hours in a warm place, until risen. The bread is ready to bake when it springs back if gently pressed.

6 Preheat the oven to 400°F and bake the breads for 12 minutes. Reduce the oven temperature to 300°F and continue cooking for 20–30 minutes, until the loaves are golden and sound hollow when tapped on the bottom.

417

SESAME BREADSTICKS

*Breadsticks are one of the most versatile snack foods. Try serving them with eggplant dip,
or with shrimp and a bowl of garlic mayonnaise and a glass of red wine.*

2 cups all-purpose flour
1 teaspoon salt
¼ ounce active dry yeast
2 tablespoons sesame seeds
2 tablespoons olive oil

MAKES 30

 Preheat the oven to 450°F. Sift the flour into a bowl. Stir in the salt, yeast and sesame seeds. Using a wooden spoon, make a well in the center of the mixture.

 Rub a little oil onto the surface of the dough. Return it to the clean bowl and cover with a clean dish towel or oiled plastic bag. Let the dough rise in a warm place for about 40 minutes, until it has doubled in bulk.

 Punch down the dough, then knead lightly until smooth. Pull off small balls of dough then, using your hands, roll out each ball on a lightly floured surface to a thin sausage about 10 inches long.

COOK'S TIP

Breadsticks can be made with many different flavorings—try using fennel seeds, poppy seeds or finely grated Parmesan cheese instead of sesame seeds. They are best eaten fresh, so don't make them more than a day or two in advance. Store them in an airtight container until ready to eat.

 Place the breadsticks on baking sheets and bake for 15 minutes, until crisp and golden. Cool the breadsticks on a wire rack, then store them in an airtight container until ready to serve.

 Add the olive oil to the flour mixture and enough warm water to make a firm dough. Transfer the dough to a lightly floured surface and knead for 5–10 minutes, until smooth and elastic.

VARIATION
Try using whole-wheat flour for a rich nutty flavor. You may find that a little water, or more oil, is required to achieve the same consistency as the all-purpose-flour breadsticks.

FRIED DOUGH BALLS WITH FIERY SALSA

These crunchy dough balls are accompanied by a hot and spicy tomato salsa. You may prefer to serve them with a juicy tomato salad.

4 cups all-purpose flour
1 teaspoon active dry yeast
1 teaspoon salt
2 tablespoons chopped fresh parsley
2 garlic cloves, finely chopped
2 tablespoons olive oil, plus extra
for greasing
vegetable oil, for frying

FOR THE SALSA
6 hot red chiles, seeded and roughly
chopped
1 onion, roughly chopped
2 garlic cloves, quartered
1-inch piece fresh ginger root,
roughly chopped
1 pound tomatoes, roughly chopped
2 tablespoons olive oil
a pinch of sugar
salt and ground black pepper

MAKES 40 DOUGH BALLS

1 Sift the flour into a large bowl. Stir in the yeast and salt and make a well in the center. Add the parsley, garlic, olive oil and enough warm water to make a firm dough.

2 Gather the dough together, then transfer to a lightly floured surface or board. Knead for about 10 minutes, until the dough feels very smooth and elastic.

3 Rub a little oil into the surface of the dough. Return it to the clean bowl, cover with plastic wrap or a clean dish towel and let sit in a warm place to rise for about 1 hour, or until doubled in bulk.

COOK'S TIP
These dough balls can be deep-fried
for 3–4 minutes or baked at
400°F for 15–20 minutes.

4 Meanwhile, make the salsa. Combine the chiles, onion, garlic and ginger in a food processor and process until very finely chopped. Add the tomatoes and olive oil, and process until smooth.

5 Sieve the mixture into a saucepan. Add the sugar, salt and pepper to taste, and simmer gently for 15 minutes. Do not let the salsa boil.

6 Roll the dough into 40 balls. Shallow-fry them in batches in hot vegetable oil for 4–5 minutes, until crisp and golden. Drain on paper towels and serve hot, with the fiery salsa in a separate bowl for dipping.

GOLDEN RAISIN AND WALNUT BREAD

This bread is delicious with soup for a first course, or with salami, cheese and salad for lunch.
It also tastes good with jam, and toasts extremely well when it is a day or two old.

2¾ cups all-purpose flour
½ teaspoon salt
1 tablespoon butter
1½ teaspoons active dry yeast
⅔ cup golden raisins
¾ cup walnuts,
roughly chopped
melted butter, for brushing

MAKES 1 LOAF

1 Sift the flour and salt into a bowl, cut in the butter with a knife, then stir in the yeast.

2 Gradually add ¾ cup tepid water to the flour mixture, stirring with a spoon at first, then gathering the dough together with your hands.

3 Turn the dough out onto a floured surface and knead for about 10 minutes, until elastic.

4 Knead the golden raisins and walnuts into the dough until they are evenly distributed. Shape into a rough oval, place on a lightly oiled baking sheet and cover with oiled plastic wrap. Let rise in a warm place for 1–2 hours, until doubled in bulk. Preheat the oven to 425°F.

5 Remove the plastic wrap from the loaf. Bake for 10 minutes, then reduce the oven temperature to 375°F and bake for another 20–25 minutes.

6 Transfer to a wire rack, brush with melted butter and cover with a dish towel. Let cool before slicing and serving.

LITTLE SPICED BREADS

These rich breads are delicious served with butter and honey.

🌾 🌾

1 teaspoon sugar
2 teaspoons active dry yeast
6 tablespoons butter, melted,
plus extra for greasing
1 tablespoon orange flower water or
almond extract (optional)
3½ cups all-purpose flour
¾ cup confectioners' sugar
1 teaspoon salt
2 tablespoons sesame seeds
1 tablespoon fennel seeds
1 egg, beaten with 1 tablespoon water

MAKES 12

1 First, start the yeast. Place ½ cup warm water in a bowl, stir in the sugar and sprinkle the yeast on top. Stir and then set aside for about 10 minutes, until frothy.

2 Place the butter, orange flower water or almond extract, if using, in a separate bowl. Stir in ¾ cup warm water.

3 Put the flour, confectioners' sugar, salt, sesame seeds and fennel seeds in the bowl of a food processor fitted with the dough blade.

4 Add the yeast and half of the butter and water mixture to the flour, and process so that they combine slowly. Continue processing, adding the remaining butter and water, to make a smooth and glossy dough. (You may need to add extra flour or warm water.)

5 Continue to process the dough for 1–2 minutes, then transfer it to a floured board and knead by hand for a few minutes until it is smooth and elastic.

6 Place in a clean, lightly oiled bowl, cover with plastic wrap and let sit in a warm place for 1–1½ hours, until doubled in bulk. Knead again for a few minutes and then break into 12 small balls and flatten slightly with oiled hands. Place on a greased baking sheet, cover with oiled plastic wrap and let rise for 1 hour.

7 Preheat the oven to 375°F. Brush the breads with the beaten egg and water, then bake for 12–15 minutes or until golden brown. Serve warm or cold.

GREEK EASTER BREAD

In Greece, Easter celebrations are very important and involve much preparation in the kitchen. This bread is sold in all the bakers' shops and also made at home. It is traditionally decorated with eggs dyed red.

🐝 🐝

1 package active dry yeast
½ cup warm milk
6 cups bread flour
2 eggs, beaten
½ teaspoon caraway seeds
1 tablespoon sugar
1 tablespoon brandy
4 tablespoons butter, melted
1 egg white, beaten
2–3 hard-boiled eggs, dyed red
½ cup split almonds

MAKES 1 LOAF

🐝 🐝

1 Mix the yeast with one or two tablespoons of warm water and set aside until it bubbles. Add the milk and 1 cup of the flour and mix to a creamy consistency. Cover with a cloth and let rest in a warm place to rise for 1 hour.

🐝 🐝

COOK'S TIP
For a nontraditional but festive variation, dye the eggs in different, spring-like colors.

2 Sift the remaining flour into a large bowl and make a well in the center. Pour the risen yeast mixture into the well and draw in a little of the flour from the sides. Add the eggs, caraway seeds, sugar and brandy. Incorporate the remaining flour until the mixture begins to form a dough.

3 Mix in the melted butter. Turn out onto a floured surface and knead for about 10 minutes, until the dough becomes smooth. Return to the bowl and cover with a cloth. Let rise in a warm place for 3 hours.

4 Preheat the oven to 350°F. Punch down the dough, turn out onto a floured surface and knead for a minute or two. Divide the dough into three pieces and roll each piece into a long sausage. Make a braid, as shown above, and place the loaf on a greased baking sheet.

5 Tuck the ends under, brush with the egg white and decorate with the eggs and split almonds. Bake for about 1 hour, until the loaf sounds hollow when tapped on the bottom. Cool on a wire rack.

DESSERTS
AND PASTRIES

*Mediterranean meals are often finished simply with
fresh fruit. Sweet pastries, ices and other confections
are usually served separately, with black coffee.*

A peep in the glass display cabinets of any pâtisserie, confectioner or coffeehouse just about anywhere around the Mediterranean will reveal an absolute feast of sweet treats. From highly decorated cakes and tortes, lavishly finished with sugared decorations, to the painstakingly stuffed and glazed or candied fruits, all Mediterranean sweets offer an abundance of fabulous flavors. Many desserts, pastries and confections involve complex cooking techniques and need specialized ingredients, and they are perhaps best left to the skills of professional pastry chefs. These include some of the lavish, multi-flavored ice cream gâteaux of Italy and a number of the specialized pastries of the Arab world.

On a domestic level, most Mediterranean desserts take full advantage of the glorious abundance of fresh fruits. For a special occasion, a colorful selection of seasonal fruits such as figs, plums, apricots, peaches, melons and cherries makes a stunning finale. These can be arranged on a platter lined with grape or fig leaves with some of the fruits cut open decoratively, and the whole platter scattered with crushed ice. On a simpler scale, pomegranate seeds or sweet juicy oranges can be arranged in bowls, sprinkled with sugar and rose water or orange-

BELOW: Orange groves abound in this fertile valley near Jaén in Spain.

ABOVE: Plump, rosy and ready for picking, peaches make a perfect dessert, alone or with a delicious amaretto stuffing.

ABOVE: Pyramids of gorgeous fruit await the shopper at the covered market in Florence.

flower water and served iced. Fresh fruits can also be lightly poached in sugar- or honey-sweetened syrups, sometimes with the addition of mild spices. They'll store well for several days as the syrup becomes impregnated with the flavors of the fruit and spices. Pears, quinces, apricots and figs are typical examples. Other refreshing desserts are the smooth sorbets of France and the granitas of Italy, or the broiled or baked fruits that are so full of flavor. Sometimes these are sugared or topped with a scoop of mascarpone or ricotta and laced with a little liqueur. A selection of dried fruits, available in abundance and of good quality, makes an ideal end to a meal when served with dessert wine or liqueurs.

In Turkey, Greece, Lebanon and Egypt, small sweet pastries and confections are enjoyed as a between-meal snack with good strong coffee. These include the rich pastries, doughnuts, and semolina and nut cakes, drenched in spiced syrup and featuring flavors like honey, almonds, pistachios, sesame, pine nuts, rose water and orange-flower water. Served in small pieces, they make a wonderful contrast to the bitterness of the coffee. The Semolina and Nut Halva is a light version of a syrupy steeped cake which that is perfect with coffee or as a dessert with cream.

Other prominent Mediterranean desserts are the sweet milk-based puddings of both the east and the west. In North Africa and the Middle East these are made with ground or short-grain rice and spiced with cinnamon, cloves, anise or fennel. They are usually served cold, sometimes drizzled with a honey-and-orange-flavored syrup. One of Spain's classic desserts is the elegant Crema Catalana, a sweet, creamy custard that is absolutely delicious either on its own or accompanied by fresh or sweetened fruits.

RUBY ORANGE SHERBET IN GINGER BASKETS

This superb frozen dessert is perfect for people who do not have ice cream makers and who cannot be bothered with the freezing and stirring that homemade ices normally require. It is also ideal for serving at a special dinner party, as both the sherbet and the ginger baskets can be made in advance.

grated zest and juice of
2 blood oranges
1¹/₂ cups confectioners' sugar
1¹/₄ cups heavy cream
scant 1 cup plain yogurt
blood orange segments, to
decorate (optional)

FOR THE GINGER BASKETS
2 tablespoons unsalted butter, plus
extra for greasing
1 tablespoon golden syrup
2 tablespoons sugar
¹/₄ teaspoon ground ginger
1 tablespoon finely chopped mixed
citrus peel
1 tablespoon all-purpose flour

SERVES 6

1 Place the orange zest and juice in a bowl. Sift the confectioners' sugar on top and set aside for about 30 minutes, then stir until smooth.

2 Whisk the heavy cream in a large bowl until the mixture forms soft peaks, then fold in the yogurt with a metal spoon.

3 Gently stir in the orange juice mixture, and pour into a freezerproof container. Cover and freeze until firm.

4 Make the baskets. Preheat the oven to 350°F. Place the butter, syrup and sugar in a heavy saucepan and heat gently until melted.

COOK'S TIP
When making the ginger baskets, it is essential to work quickly. Have the greased molds ready before you start.

5 Add the ground ginger, mixed citrus peel and flour, and stir until the mixture is smooth.

6 Lightly grease two baking sheets. Using about 2 teaspoons of the mixture at a time, drop three portions of the ginger dough onto each baking sheet, spacing them well apart. Spread out each one to make a 2-inch circle, then bake for 12–14 minutes or until the cookies are a dark golden color.

7 Remove the cookies from the oven and let stand on the baking sheets for 1 minute to firm slightly. Lift off with a spatula and drape over six greased upturned mini pudding basins or upturned cups. Flatten the top (which will become the bottom), and quickly flute the edge of each to form a basket shape.

8 When cool, lift the baskets off the basins or cups and place on individual dessert plates. Arrange small scoops of the frozen orange sherbet in each basket. Decorate each portion with a few blood orange segments, if desired.

FRESH ORANGE GRANITA

*A granita is like an Italian ice, but coarser and grainier in texture—hence its name. It makes a
refreshing dessert after a rich main course, or a cooling treat on a hot summer's day.*

*4 large oranges
1 large lemon
⅔ cup sugar
2 cups water
cookies, to serve*

SERVES 6

1 Thinly pare the zest from the
oranges and lemon, taking care
to avoid the bitter white pith, and set
aside. Cut the fruit in half and
squeeze the orange and lemon juice
into a bowl. Set aside.

2 Heat the sugar and water in a
heavy saucepan, stirring over
low heat until the sugar dissolves.
Bring to a boil, then boil without
stirring for about 10 minutes, until
a syrup forms.

3 Remove the syrup from heat and
add most of the reserved pieces
of orange and lemon zest, but keep
a few for decoration. Shake the pan.
Cover and let cool.

4 Strain the sugar syrup into a
shallow freezer container and
add the fruit juice. Stir well to mix,
then freeze, uncovered, for about
4 hours, until slushy.

5 Remove the half-frozen mixture
from the freezer and mix with a
fork, then return to the freezer and
freeze again for another 4 hours or
until frozen hard.

6 To serve, transfer to a bowl and
let soften for about 10 minutes,
then break up into small pieces with a
fork again and pile the granita into
long-stemmed glasses. Blanch the
reserved strips of orange and lemon
zest, and serve with cookies.

COFFEE GRANITA

Granitas are like semi-frozen sherbets, but consist of larger particles of ice. Served in Italian cafés,
they are very refreshing, particularly in the summer. Some are made with fruit, but the coffee version is
perhaps the most popular and is often served with a spoonful of whipped cream on top.

1½ cups hot strong
espresso coffee
2 tablespoons granulated sugar
1 cup heavy cream
2 teaspoons superfine sugar

SERVES 6–8

1 Stir the sugar into the hot coffee until dissolved. Let cool, then chill. Pour into a shallow plastic or metal freezer container, cover and freeze for about 1 hour.

2 The coffee should have formed a frozen crust around the rim of the container. Scrape this off with a spoon and mix with the rest of the coffee. Repeat this process every 30 minutes, using the spoon to break up the clumps of ice.

3 After about 2½ hours, the granita should be ready. It will have the appearance of small, fairly uniform ice crystals. Whip the cream with the superfine sugar until stiff. Serve the granita in tall glasses, each topped with a spoonful of cream.

ICED ORANGES

These little sherbets served in the fruit shell were originally sold in the beach cafés in the south of France. They are pretty and easy to eat—a good picnic treat to store in the cooler.

⅔ cup sugar
juice of 1 lemon
14 medium oranges
8 fresh bay leaves, to decorate

SERVES 8

1   Put the sugar in a heavy pan. Add half the lemon juice and ½ cup water. Cook over low heat until the sugar has dissolved completely. Bring to a boil and boil for 2–3 minutes, until the syrup is clear. Let cool.

2   Slice the tops off eight of the oranges to make "hats." Scoop out the flesh of the oranges and reserve. Put the empty orange shells and "hats" on a tray and place in the freezer until needed.

3   Grate the zest of the remaining oranges and add to the syrup. Squeeze the juice from the oranges and from the reserved flesh. There should be 3 cups. Squeeze another orange or add bought orange juice, if necessary.

4   Stir the orange juice and remaining lemon juice, with 6 tablespoons water, into the syrup. Taste, adding more lemon juice or sugar, as desired. Pour the mixture into a shallow freezer container and freeze for 3 hours.

5   Transfer the mixture into a bowl and whisk to break down the ice crystals. Freeze for 4 more hours, until firm but not solid.

6   Pack the mixture into the orange shells, piling it up, and set the "hats" on top. Freeze until ready to serve. Just before serving, push a skewer into the tops of the "hats" and push a bay leaf into each one.

COOK'S TIP
Use crumpled paper towels to keep the shells upright.

PISTACHIO HALVA ICE CREAM

Halva is made from sesame seeds and is available in several flavors. This ice cream, studded with chunks of pistachio-flavored halva, is as unusual as it is irresistible.

🍃 🍃

3 egg yolks
1/2 cup sugar
1 1/4 cups light cream
1 1/4 cups heavy cream
4 ounces pistachio halva
chopped pistachios, to decorate

SERVES 6

3 Whisk the heavy cream lightly, then whisk in the cooled custard. Crumble the halva into the mixture and stir in gently.

4 Pour the mixture into a freezerproof container. Cover and freeze for 3 hours or until half set. Stir well, breaking up any ice crystals, then return to the freezer until frozen solid.

5 About 15 minutes before serving, remove the ice cream from the freezer so that it softens enough for scooping and to let the full flavor develop. Decorate with chopped pistachios.

🍃 🍃

1 Turn the freezer to its lowest setting. Whisk the egg yolks with the sugar in a bowl until the mixture is thick and pale. Pour the light cream into a small saucepan and bring to a boil, then remove from heat. Stir the hot cream into the egg yolk mixture.

2 Transfer the mixture to a double boiler or a heatproof bowl placed over a pan of boiling water. Cook, stirring continuously, until the custard is thick enough to coat the back of a spoon. Strain into a bowl and let cool.

TURKISH DELIGHT ICE CREAM

Not strictly a traditional Middle Eastern recipe, but a delicious way of using Turkish delight.
Serve scattered with rose petals, if you can find them.

4 egg yolks
½ cup sugar
1¼ cups milk
1¼ cups heavy cream
1 tablespoon rose water
6 ounces rose-flavored Turkish
delight, chopped

SERVES 6

1 Beat the egg yolks and sugar until light. In a pan, bring the milk to a boil. Add to the egg and sugar, stirring, then return to the pan.

2 Continue stirring over low heat until the mixture coats the back of a spoon. Do not boil, or it will curdle. Let cool, then stir in the cream and rose water.

3 Put the Turkish delight in a pan with 2–3 tablespoons water. Heat gently, until almost completely melted, with just a few small lumps. Remove from the heat and stir into the cooled custard mixture.

4 Let the mixture cool completely, then pour into a shallow freezer container. Freeze for 3 hours, until just frozen all over. Spoon the mixture into a bowl.

5 Using a whisk, beat the mixture well, return it to the freezer container and freeze for 2 hours more. Repeat the beating process, then return to the freezer for about 3 hours or until firm. Remove the ice cream from the freezer 20–25 minutes before serving. Serve with thin almond cookies or meringues.

436

COFFEE AND CHOCOLATE BOMBE

In Italy, the commercial ice cream is so good that no one would dream of making their own for this dessert. Assembling the bombe is impressive enough in itself.

15–18 savoiardi (Italian ladyfingers)
about ¾ cup sweet Marsala
3 ounces amaretti cookies
about 2 cups coffee ice cream, softened
about 2 cups vanilla ice cream, softened
2 ounces bittersweet chocolate, grated
chocolate curls and unsweetened cocoa powder or confectioners' sugar, to decorate

SERVES 6–8

1 Line a 4-cup-pudding basin with a large piece of damp muslin, letting it hang over the top edge. Trim the ladyfingers to fit the basin, if necessary. Pour the Marsala into a shallow dish. Dip a ladyfinger in the Marsala, turning it quickly so that it becomes saturated but does not disintegrate. Stand it against the side of the basin, sugared-side out. Repeat with the remaining ladyfingers until the basin is fully lined.

2 Fill in the base and any gaps around the side with any trimmings of ladyfinger, cut to fit. Chill for about 30 minutes.

3 Put the amaretti cookies in a bowl and crush them with a rolling pin. Then transfer the crushed cookies to a larger bowl, add the coffee ice cream and any remaining Marsala, and beat until thoroughly mixed. Spoon into the ladyfinger-lined basin.

4 Press the ice cream against the cookies to form an even layer with a hollow in the center. Freeze for 2 hours.

5 Put the vanilla ice cream and grated chocolate in a bowl and beat together until evenly mixed. Spoon into the hollow in the center of the mold. Smooth the top, then cover with the overhanging muslin. Place in the freezer overnight.

6 To serve, run a spatula between the muslin and the basin, then unfold the top of the muslin. Invert a chilled serving plate on top of the pudding basin, then invert the two and lift off the bowl. Decorate with the chocolate curls, then sift the cocoa powder or confectioners' sugar over the top. Serve immediately.

CHOCOLATE SALAMI

This after-dinner treat resembles a salami in shape, hence its intriguing name. It is very rich and will serve a lot of people. Slice it thinly and serve with espresso coffee and amaretto liqueur.

24 Petit Beurre cookies, broken
12 ounces bittersweet or semisweet
chocolate, broken into squares
1 cup unsalted butter,
softened
¼ cup amaretto liqueur
2 egg yolks
½ cup sliced almonds,
lightly toasted and thinly
shredded lengthwise
¼ cup ground almonds

SERVES 8–12

 Remove the bowl from the heat, let the chocolate cool for a minute or two, then stir in the egg yolks followed by the remaining butter, a little at a time. Add most of the crushed cookies, reserving a good handful, and stir well to mix. Stir in the sliced almonds. Let the mixture sit in a cold place for about 1 hour, until it begins to stiffen.

 Turn the chocolate and cookie mixture onto a sheet of lightly oiled waxed paper. Shape into a 14-inch sausage using a spatula, tapering the ends slightly so that the roll looks like a salami. Wrap in the paper and freeze for at least 4 hours, until solid.

To serve, unwrap the "salami." Spread out the finely ground cookie and almonds on a clean sheet of waxed paper, and roll the salami in them until evenly coated. Transfer to a board and let stand for about 1 hour before cutting into thin slices to serve.

Place the cookies in a food processor or blender fitted with a metal blade and process until coarsely chopped.

Place the chocolate in a large heatproof bowl. Place the bowl over a saucepan of barely simmering water, add a small chunk of the butter and all of the liqueur, and heat until the chocolate melts, stirring the mixture occasionally.

Process the reserved crushed cookies in the food processor until they are very finely ground. Put in a bowl and mix with the ground almonds. Cover and set aside until you are ready to serve.

COOK'S TIP
Take care when melting chocolate that it does not overheat, or it will form a hard lump. The bottom of the bowl containing the chocolate must not touch the water, and the chocolate must be melted very slowly. If you think the mixture is getting too hot, remove the pan from heat.

APPLE SLUSH

This simple dessert is easy to make and perfect after a rich meal.

4 apples
2 tablespoons lemon juice
2 tablespoons rose water
3–4 tablespoons confectioners' sugar
crushed ice, to serve

SERVES 4

COOK'S TIP
Pears can also be used to make this delicious dessert. Choose ripe pears, which yield when pressed gently.

1 Carefully and thinly peel the apples, using a swivel peeler. Discard the peel. Work quickly, otherwise the apples will begin to brown. If necessary, place the peeled apples in a bowl of acidulated water while you peel the others.

2 Grate the apples coarsely into a bowl, discarding the cores. Stir in the lemon juice and rose water, and add confectioners' sugar to taste. Chill for at least 30 minutes. Mound on a platter and serve with crushed ice.

PINEAPPLE ICE CREAM

Light, refreshing and slightly tangy, pineapple ice cream is always an excellent choice.

8 eggs, separated
1/2 cup sugar
1/2 teaspoon vanilla extract
2 1/2 cups whipping cream
1/4 cup confectioners' sugar
15-ounce can pineapple chunks
3/4 cup pistachios, chopped
wafer cookies, to serve

SERVES 8–10

1 Place the egg yolks in a bowl, add the sugar and vanilla extract and beat until thick and pale.

2 In a separate bowl, whip the cream and confectioners' sugar to soft peaks, then add to the egg-yolk mixture and mix well.

3 Whisk the egg whites in a separate large bowl until they are firm and hold stiff peaks. Gently fold the whipped egg whites into the cream mixture and mix gently so that the ingredients are combined with no loss of volume.

4 Cut the pineapple into very small pieces, add the pistachios and stir into the cream mixture. Mix well with a spoon.

5 Pour the mixture into an ice-cream container and place in the freezer for a few hours until it is set and firm, stirring it occasionally.

6 Serve in scoops or slices, with wafer cookies.

RICOTTA PUDDING

—

*This rich, creamy dessert is easy to make and, as it can be made up to 24 hours ahead, it is ideal for a
dinner party. The combination of ricotta cheese and candied fruits is a popular one in Sicily,
where this recipe originated.*

🌾 🌾

1 cup ricotta cheese
¹/₃ cup candied fruits
4 tablespoons sweet Marsala
1 cup heavy cream
¹/₄ cup sugar, plus extra, for dusting
finely grated zest of 1 orange
2 cups fresh raspberries
strips of thinly pared orange zest,
to decorate

SERVES 4–6

🌾 🌾

 Press the ricotta through a sieve into a bowl to remove any lumps. Finely chop the candied fruits and stir into the sieved ricotta with half of the Marsala. Put the cream, sugar and grated orange zest in another bowl and whip until the cream is standing in soft peaks.

2. Fold the whipped cream into the ricotta mixture. Spoon into individual glass serving bowls and top with the raspberries. Chill until serving time. Sprinkle with the remaining Marsala and dust the top of each bowl liberally with sugar just before serving. Decorate with the pared orange zest.

TIRAMISU

—

*The name of this popular dessert translates as "pick me up," which is said to derive from the fact that it is
so good that it literally makes you swoon when you eat it. There are many, many versions, and the recipe
can be adapted to suit your own taste—you can vary the amounts of mascarpone, eggs, ladyfingers,
coffee and liqueur.*

3 eggs, separated
2 cups mascarpone cheese,
at room temperature
1 tablespoon of vanilla sugar
¾ cup cold, very strong, black coffee
½ cup Kahlúa or other
coffee-flavored liqueur
18 savoiardi (Italian ladyfingers)
sifted unsweetened cocoa powder
and grated bitter-sweet chocolate,
to decorate

SERVES 6–8

1. Put the egg whites in a grease-free bowl and whisk with an electric mixer until stiff and standing in peaks. You should be able to tilt the bowl without losing any of the mixture.

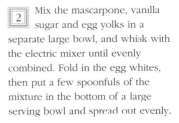

2. Mix the mascarpone, vanilla sugar and egg yolks in a separate large bowl, and whisk with the electric mixer until evenly combined. Fold in the egg whites, then put a few spoonfuls of the mixture in the bottom of a large serving bowl and spread out evenly.

3. Combine the coffee and liqueur in a shallow dish. Dip one of the ladyfingers in the mixture, turn it quickly so that it becomes saturated but does not disintegrate, and place it on top of the mascarpone mixture in the bowl. Add five more dipped ladyfingers in this way, placing them side by side.

4. Spoon in about one-third of the remaining mixture and spread out. Make more layers in the same way, ending with mascarpone. Level the surface, then sift the cocoa powder on top. Cover and chill overnight. Before serving, sprinkle grated chocolate on top, to decorate.

LEMON COEUR A LA CREME WITH COINTREAU ORANGES

This zesty dessert is the ideal choice to follow a rich main course.

1 cup cottage cheese
generous 1 cup mascarpone cheese
¼ cup sugar
grated zest and juice of 1 lemon
spirals of pared orange zest,
to decorate

FOR THE COINTREAU ORANGES
4 oranges
2 teaspoons cornstarch
1 tablespoon confectioners' sugar
¼ cup Cointreau

SERVES 4

1 Put the cottage cheese in a food processor or blender and process until the mixture is smooth and of one consistency.

2 Add the mascarpone cheese, sugar, lemon zest and juice, and process briefly to combine all the ingredients.

3 Line four coeur à la crème molds with damp muslin, then divide the mixture among them. Level the surface of each, then place the molds on a plate to catch any liquid that drains from the cheese. Cover all the molds and chill overnight.

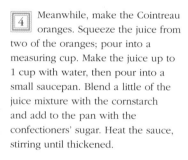

4 Meanwhile, make the Cointreau oranges. Squeeze the juice from two of the oranges; pour into a measuring cup. Make the juice up to 1 cup with water, then pour into a small saucepan. Blend a little of the juice mixture with the cornstarch and add to the pan with the confectioners' sugar. Heat the sauce, stirring until thickened.

5 Using a sharp knife, peel and segment the remaining oranges. Add the segments to the pan, stir to coat, then set aside. When cool, stir in the Cointreau. Pour into a bowl, cover and chill overnight.

6 Turn the coeur à la crème molds out onto plates and lift off the muslin. Surround with the oranges and sauce. Decorate with spirals of orange zest and serve immediately.

CREMA CATALANA

———

This delicious Spanish dessert is a cross between a crème caramel and a crème brûlée. It is not as rich as crème brûlée, but has a similar caramelized sugar topping.

2 cups milk
pared zest of ½ lemon
1 cinnamon stick
4 egg yolks
7 tablespoons sugar
1½ tablespoons cornstarch
ground nutmeg

SERVES 4

1 Put the milk in a pan with the lemon zest and cinnamon stick. Bring to a boil, then simmer for 10 minutes. Remove the lemon zest and cinnamon. Place the egg yolks and 3 tablespoons of the sugar in a bowl and whisk until pale yellow. Add the cornstarch and mix well.

2 Stir in a few tablespoons of the hot milk, then add this mixture to the remaining milk. Return to the heat and cook gently, stirring, for about 5 minutes, until thickened and smooth. Do not let it boil. There should be no cornstarch taste.

3 Pour into 4 shallow ovenproof dishes, about 5 inches in diameter. Let cool, then chill for a few hours or overnight if possible, until firm. Before serving, sprinkle each custard with a tablespoon of sugar and a little of the ground nutmeg. Preheat the broiler to high.

4 Place the custards under the broiler, on the highest shelf, and cook until the sugar caramelizes. This will only take a few seconds. Let cool for a few minutes before serving. (The caramel will only stay hard for about 30 minutes.)

BANANA AND MASCARPONE CREAMS

If you like cold banana custard, you will love this recipe. It is a grown-up version of an old favorite.
No one will guess that the secret is instant pudding.

generous 1 cup mascarpone cheese
1¼ cups vanilla instant
pudding (made)
⅔ cup plain yogurt
4 bananas
juice of 1 lime
½ cup pecans,
coarsely chopped
½ cup maple syrup

SERVES 4–6

 1 Combine the mascarpone, pudding and yogurt in a large bowl, and beat together until smooth. Make this mixture several hours ahead, if desired. Cover and chill, then stir before using.

2 Peel the bananas, slice diagonally and place in a separate bowl. Pour the lime juice on top, and toss until the bananas are coated in the juice.

3 Divide half of the pudding mixture among four to six dessert glasses and top each portion with some of the banana slices, until you have used half of them.

4 Spoon the remaining pudding mixture into the glasses and top with the remaining bananas. Sprinkle the nuts on top. Drizzle maple syrup onto each portion and chill for 30 minutes before serving.

BANANAS WITH LIME AND CARDAMOM SAUCE

Serve these bananas solo, with vanilla ice cream, or spoon them onto folded crêpes.

6 small bananas
¼ cup butter
seeds from 4 cardamom pods, crushed
½ cup sliced almonds
thinly pared zest and juice of 2 limes
⅓ cup light brown sugar
2 tablespoons dark rum
vanilla ice cream, to serve (optional)

SERVES 4

1 Peel the bananas and cut them in half lengthwise. Heat half the butter in a large frying pan. Add half the bananas, and cook until the undersides are golden. Turn carefully, using a spatula. Cook until golden.

2 As they cook, transfer the bananas to a heatproof serving dish. Cook the remaining bananas in the same way.

3 Melt the remaining butter, then add the cardamom and almonds. Cook, stirring until golden.

4 Stir in the lime zest and juice, then the sugar. Cook, stirring, until the mixture is smooth, bubbling and slightly reduced. Stir in the rum. Pour the sauce over the bananas and serve immediately, with vanilla ice cream, if desired.

COOK'S TIP
If you prefer not to use alcohol in your cooking, replace the rum with orange juice or even pineapple juice.

STUFFED PEACHES WITH MASCARPONE CREAM

Mascarpone is a thick, velvety Italian cream cheese made from cow's milk. It is often used in desserts or eaten with fresh fruit.

🌿 🌿

4 large peaches, halved and pitted
1½ ounces amaretti cookies, crumbled
2 tablespoons ground almonds
3 tablespoons sugar
1 tablespoon cocoa powder
⅔ cup sweet wine
2 tablespoons butter

FOR THE MASCARPONE CREAM
2 tablespoons sugar
3 egg yolks
1 tablespoon dessert wine
1 cup mascarpone cheese
⅔ cup heavy cream

SERVES 4

🌿 🌿

3. Place the peaches in a buttered ovenproof dish and fill them with the stuffing. Dot with the butter, then pour the remaining wine into the dish. Bake for 35 minutes.

4. To make the mascarpone cream, beat the sugar and egg yolks until thick and pale. Stir in the wine, then fold in the mascarpone. Whip the heavy cream to soft peaks and fold into the mixture. Remove the peaches from the oven and let them cool. Serve at room temperature, with the mascarpone cream.

1. Preheat the oven to 400°F. Using a teaspoon, scoop some of the flesh from the cavities in the peaches, to make a reasonable space for stuffing. Chop the scooped-out peach flesh.

2. Combine the amaretti, ground almonds, sugar, cocoa and peach flesh. Add enough wine to make the mixture into a thick paste.

FRESH FRUIT SALAD

When peaches and strawberries are out of season, use other fruits, such as bananas and grapes.

※ ※

2 apples
2 oranges
16–20 strawberries
2 peaches
2 tablespoons lemon juice
1–2 tablespoons orange flower water
confectioners' sugar, to taste
(optional)
a few fresh mint leaves, to decorate

SERVES 4

※ ※

1   Peel and core the apples and slice finely. Peel the oranges with a sharp knife, removing all the pith, and segment them, catching any juice in a bowl.

2   Hull the strawberries and halve or quarter them, depending on size. Blanch the peaches for about 1 minute in boiling water, then peel off the skin and cut the flesh into thick slices. Discard the pits. Place all the fruit in a large serving bowl. Toss lightly to mix.

3   Combine the lemon juice, orange flower water and any leftover orange juice. Taste and add a little confectioners' sugar to sweeten, if desired. Pour the fruit juice mixture over the salad and serve, decorated with fresh mint leaves.

※ ※

VARIATION
There are no rules with this fruit salad, and you can use almost any fruit that you like. Oranges, however, should form the base and are available all year round. Apples give a welcome contrast in texture.

DRIED FRUIT SALAD

This is a wonderful combination of fresh and dried fruit, and makes an excellent dessert throughout the year. Use frozen raspberries or blackberries in winter.

※ ※

1/2 cup dried apricots
1/2 cup dried peaches
1 fresh pear
1 fresh apple
1 fresh orange
2/3 cup mixed raspberries and
blackberries
1 cinnamon stick
1/4 cup sugar
1 tablespoon honey
2 tablespoons lemon juice

SERVES 4

1   Soak the apricots and peaches in water for 1–2 hours, until plump, then drain. Cut into halves, quarters or thin slices.

2   Peel and core the pear and apple and cut them into cubes. Peel the orange with a sharp knife, removing all the pith, and cut into wedges.

3   Place all the fruit in a large saucepan with the raspberries and the blackberries.

4   Add 2 cups water, the cinnamon, sugar and honey and bring to a boil. Cover and simmer very gently for 10–12 minutes, then remove the pan from the heat. Stir in the lemon juice. Let cool, then pour into a bowl and chill for 1–2 hours before serving.

※ ※

VARIATION
To vary the flavor of the fruit salad, try using cloves or ginger.

CHAROSET

This is an unusual Israeli recipe. Variations of it go back at least two thousand years.

1 large apple
¾ cup blanched almonds
2 teaspoons ground cinnamon
2 tablespoons kosher sweet red wine

MAKES ENOUGH TO FILL A
12-OUNCE JAR

1 Peel, quarter and chop the apple. Chop it finely with the blanched almonds. If using a food processor, make sure that you don't process the mixture too finely—it should still be crunchy.

2 Stir in the cinnamon and sweet wine, and spoon the mixture into a jar. Cover and set aside. The color and flavor will develop after 1–2 hours. Serve the mixture as a topping for Israeli unleavened bread.

RED FRUIT SALAD

Cut fruit usually deteriorates quickly, but the juices from lightly-cooked mixed berries make a brilliant red coating, so this salad can be made the day before. It is also one of the quickest ways of making fruit salad for a crowd.

1⅓ cup raspberries
or blackberries
½ cup red currants
or black currants
2–4 tablespoons sugar
8 ripe plums
8 ripe apricots
2 cups seedless red grapes
1 cup strawberries

SERVES 8

VARIATION
Use dried apricots instead of fresh, if you prefer, or even dried mango.

3 Let cool slightly and then add the reserved plums and apricots, and the grapes. Taste for sweetness and add more sugar if the fruit is too tart. Let the fruit salad cool, then cover and chill.

1 Mix the berries and currants with 2 tablespoons sugar. Pit the plums and apricots, cut them into pieces and put half of them into a pan with all of the berries.

2 Cook over very low heat with about 3 tablespoons water until the fruit is just beginning to soften and the juices are starting to run.

4 Just before serving, transfer the fruit to a serving bowl. Hull and slice the strawberries, and arrange them over the fruit in the bowl.

452

FRESH FIGS WITH HONEY AND WINE

Any variety of figs can be used in this recipe, their ripeness determining the cooking time. Choose ones that are plump and firm, and use them quickly because they don't keep well.

🌾 🌾

2 cups dry white wine
⅓ cup honey
¼ cup sugar
1 small orange
8 whole cloves
1 pound fresh figs
1 cinnamon stick
mint sprigs or bay leaves, to decorate

FOR THE CREAM
1¼ cups heavy cream
1 vanilla bean
1 teaspoon sugar

SERVES 6

1   Put the wine, honey and sugar in a heavy saucepan and heat gently until the sugar dissolves.

2   Stud the orange with the cloves and add to the syrup with the figs and cinnamon. Cover and simmer very gently for 5–10 minutes, until the figs are softened. Transfer to a serving dish and let cool.

3   Put ⅔ cup of the cream in a small saucepan with the vanilla bean. Bring almost to a boil, then let cool and infuse for 30 minutes. Remove the vanilla bean and mix with the remaining cream and sugar in a bowl. Whip lightly. Transfer to a serving dish. Decorate the figs, then serve with the cream.

APRICOTS STUFFED WITH ALMOND PASTE

Almonds, whether whole, sliced or ground, are a favorite Moroccan ingredient. They have a delightful affinity with apricots, making this a popular—and delicious—dessert.

scant ½ cup sugar
2 tablespoons lemon juice
1 cup ground almonds
½ cup confectioners' sugar
or sugar
a little orange flower water (optional)
2 tablespoons melted butter
½ teaspoon almond extract
2 pounds fresh apricots
fresh sprigs of mint, to decorate

SERVES 6

1 Preheat the oven to 350°F. Place the sugar, lemon juice and 1¼ cups water in a small, heavy-based pan and bring to a boil, stirring until all the sugar has dissolved. Simmer gently for 5–10 minutes.

2 In a bowl, combine the ground almonds, confectioners' sugar (or sugar, if preferred), orange flower water, if using, butter and almond extract to make a smooth paste.

3 Wash the apricots, then make a slit in the flesh and ease out the pit. Take small pieces of the almond paste, roll into balls and press one into each of the apricots.

4 Arrange the stuffed apricots in a shallow ovenproof dish and carefully pour the sugar syrup around them. Cover with aluminum foil and bake for 25–30 minutes.

5 Serve the apricots with a little of the syrup, if desired, and decorate with sprigs of mint.

CARAMEL BANANAS

Although the method for this recipe sounds simple, it can, in fact, be a bit tricky to master. You need to work fast, especially when dipping the fruit in the caramel, as it will cool and set quite quickly. The luscious results, however, are worth the effort.

4 firm bananas
3/4 cup all-purpose flour
1/2 cup cornstarch
2 teaspoons baking powder
3/4 cup water
1 teaspoon sesame oil
oil, for deep-frying
ice water

FOR THE CARAMEL
1 cup sugar
2 tablespoons sesame seeds
4 tablespoons water

SERVES 4

1 Peel the bananas, then slice them thickly, at an angle, into a bowl. Sift the flour, cornstarch and baking powder into a separate large bowl. Quickly beat in the water and sesame oil, taking care not to overmix. Stir in the bananas until evenly coated.

2 Heat the frying oil in a deep pan until it registers 350°F or until a cube of bread, added to the oil, turns pale brown in 45 seconds.

3 Using a fork, remove a piece of banana from the batter, letting the excess batter drain back into the bowl. Gently lower the piece of banana into the hot oil. Add more pieces of battered banana in the same way, but do not overcrowd the pan. Fry for about 2 minutes or until the coating is golden brown.

4 As they are cooked, remove the banana fritters from the oil with a slotted spoon and place on paper towels to drain. Cook the remaining battered bananas in the same way.

5 When all the banana pieces have been fried, make the caramel. Combine the sugar, sesame seeds and water in a heavy-based pan. Heat gently, stirring occasionally, until the sugar has dissolved. Raise the heat slightly and continue cooking, without stirring, until the syrup becomes a light caramel. Remove from the heat.

6 Have a bowl of ice water ready. Working quickly, drop one fritter at a time into the hot caramel. Flip over with a fork, remove immediately and plunge the piece into the ice water, taking care not to burn yourself. Quickly remove from the water and drain on a wire rack while you coat the rest. Serve.

CITRUS FRUIT FLAMBE WITH PISTACHIO PRALINE

A fruit flambé makes a dramatic finale for a dinner party. Top this refreshing citrus fruit dessert with crunchy pistachio praline to make it extra-special.

4 oranges
2 ruby grapefruit
2 limes
1/4 cup butter
1/3 cup light brown sugar
3 tablespoons Cointreau
fresh mint sprigs, to decorate

FOR THE PRALINE
oil, for greasing
1/2 cup sugar
1/2 cup pistachios

SERVES 4

 First, make the pistachio praline. Brush a baking sheet lightly with oil. Place the sugar and pistachios in a small heavy saucepan and swirl over low heat until the sugar has melted.

2 Continue to cook over fairly low heat until the nuts start to pop and the sugar turns a dark golden color. Pour onto the oiled baking sheet and set aside to harden. Chop the praline into rough chunks.

3 Peel and remove pith from all the citrus fruit. Holding each fruit in turn over a large bowl, cut between the membranes so that the segments fall into the bowl, with any juice.

4 Heat the butter and brown sugar together in a heavy frying pan until the sugar has melted and the mixture is golden. Strain the citrus juices into the pan and continue to cook, stirring occasionally, until the juice has reduced and is syrupy.

5 Add the fruit segments and warm through without stirring. Pour on the Cointreau and set it on fire. As soon as the flames die down, spoon the fruit flambé into serving dishes. Sprinkle some praline on each portion and decorate with mint. Serve immediately.

BERRY BRULEE TARTS

This amount of pastry is enough to make 8 tartlets, so freeze half of it for another day.
The brûlée topping is best added no more than 2 hours before serving the tarts.

2¼ cups all-purpose flour
a pinch of salt
¼ cup ground almonds
1 tablespoon confectioners' sugar
⅔ cup unsalted butter,
chilled and diced
1 egg yolk
about 3 tablespoons cold water

FOR THE FILLING
4 egg yolks
1 tablespoon cornstarch
¼ cup sugar
a few drops of pure vanilla extract
1¼ cups milk
2 cups mixed berries, such as small
strawberries, raspberries,
black currants
and red currants
½ cup confectioners' sugar

MAKES 4

3 Use the pastry rounds to line four individual tartlet pans, letting the excess pastry hang over the edges. Chill for 30 minutes.

4 Preheat the oven to 400°F. Line the pastry with nonstick baking paper and baking beans. Bake blind for 10 minutes. Remove the paper and beans and return the tartlet shells to the oven for 5 minutes until golden. Let the pastry cool, then carefully trim off the excess pastry.

5 Beat the egg yolks, cornstarch, sugar and vanilla in a bowl.

COOK'S TIP
A culinary blow torch can be used to melt and caramelize the brûlée topping.

6 Warm the milk in a heavy pan, pour it onto the egg yolks, whisking constantly, then return the mixture to the clean pan.

7 Heat, stirring, until the custard thickens, but do not let it boil. Remove from heat. Press a piece of plastic wrap directly on the surface of the custard and let it cool.

8 Sprinkle the berries in the tartlet shells and spoon on the custard. Chill the tarts on a baking sheet for 2 hours.

9 To serve, sift confectioners' sugar generously on the tops of the tartlets. Preheat the broiler to the highest setting. Place the tartlets under the hot broiler until the sugar melts and caramelizes. Let the topping cool and harden for about 10 minutes before serving the tarts.

1 Mix the flour, salt, ground almonds and confectioners' sugar in a bowl. Rub in the butter by hand or in a food processor until the mixture resembles fine bread crumbs. Add the egg yolk and enough cold water to form a dough. Knead the dough gently, then cut it in half and freeze half for use later.

2 Cut the remaining pastry into four equal pieces and roll out thinly on a lightly floured surface.

BAKED LATTICE PEACHES

—

If you would rather use nectarines for the recipe, there is no need to peel them first.

❧ ❧

3 peaches
juice of ¹/₂ lemon
scant ¹/₂ cup white marzipan
13 ounces ready-rolled puff pastry,
thawed if frozen
a large pinch of ground cinnamon
beaten egg, to glaze
sugar, for sprinkling

FOR THE CARAMEL SAUCE
¹/₄ cup sugar
2 tablespoons cold water
²/₃ cup heavy cream

MAKES 6

❧ ❧

3 Unroll the puff pastry and cut it in half. Set one half aside, then cut out six rounds from the rest, making each round slightly larger than a peach half. Sprinkle a little cinnamon on each pastry round, then place a peach half, marzipan side down, on the pastry.

5 Dampen the edges of the pastry rounds with a little water, then drape a lattice pastry square over each peach half. Press around the edge to seal, then trim off the excess pastry and decorate with small peach leaves made from the trimmings.

6 Transfer the peach pastries to a baking sheet. Brush with the beaten egg and sprinkle with the sugar. Bake for 20 minutes or until the pastries are golden.

1 Preheat the oven to 375°F. Place the peaches in a large bowl and pour in boiling water to cover. Let sit for 60 seconds, then drain the peaches and peel off the skins. Toss the skinned fruit in the lemon juice to stop it from turning brown.

2 Divide the marzipan into six pieces and shape each to form a small round. Cut the peaches in half and remove their pits. Fill the cavity in each with a marzipan round.

4 Cut the remaining pastry into lattice pastry, using a special cutter if you have one. If not, simply cut small slits in rows all over the pastry, starting each row slightly lower than the last. Cut the lattice pastry into six equal squares.

❧ ❧

COOK'S TIP
Take care when adding the cream to the hot caramel, as the mixture is liable to spit. Pour it from a pitcher, protecting your hand with an oven mitt.

7 Meanwhile, make the caramel sauce. Heat the sugar with the water in a small pan until it dissolves. Bring to a boil and continue to boil until the syrup turns a dark golden brown. Stand back and add the cream carefully. Heat gently, stirring until smooth. Serve the peach pastries with the sauce.

APRICOT PARCELS

Apricots, mincemeat and marzipan layered with phyllo pastry make a delicious end to a meal.

12 ounces phyllo pastry, thawed
if frozen
¼ cup butter, melted
8 apricots, halved and pitted
4 tablespoons mincemeat
12 ratafia cookies, crushed
2 tablespoons grated marzipan
confectioners' sugar, for dusting

MAKES 8

1   Preheat the oven to 400°F.
Spread the phyllo pastry onto a
flat surface. Cut into 7-inch squares.
Brush four of the squares with a little
melted butter and stack them one on
top of the other, giving each layer a
quarter turn so that the stack acquires
a star shape. Repeat the process to
make eight stars.

2   Place an apricot half, hollow
up, in the center of each pastry
star. Combine the mincemeat, crushed
ratafia cookies and marzipan, and
spoon a little of the mixture into the
hollow in each apricot.

3   Top with another apricot half,
then bring the corners of each
pastry together and squeeze to make
a gathered purse. Place the purses
on a baking sheet and brush each
with a little melted butter. Bake for
15–20 minutes or until the pastry is
golden and crisp.

4   Lightly dust with confectioners'
sugar to serve. Whipped cream,
flavored with a little brandy, makes
an ideal accompaniment.

COOK'S TIP
Phyllo pastry dries out quickly, so
keep any squares that are not
currently being used covered under a
clean damp dish towel, and work as
quickly as possible. If the phyllo
should turn dry and brittle, simply
brush it with melted butter to moisten.

OMM ALI

This is an Egyptian version of a traditional bread-and-butter pudding.

🌿 🌿

10–12 sheets phyllo pastry
2½ cups milk
1 cup heavy cream
1 egg, beaten
2 tablespoons rose water
½ cup each chopped pistachios,
almonds and hazelnuts
⅔ cup raisins
1 tablespoon ground cinnamon,
for dusting
light cream, to serve

SERVES 4

1   Preheat the oven to 325°F. Bake the phyllo pastry, on one or two baking sheets, for 15–20 minutes, until crisp. Remove from the oven and raise the temperature to 400°F.

2   Scald the milk and cream by pouring into a pan and heating very gently until hot but not boiling. Slowly add the beaten egg and the rose water. Cook over low heat until the mixture begins to thicken, stirring.

3   Crumble the pastry, using your hands, and then spread in layers with the nuts and raisins in a shallow baking dish.

4   Pour the custard mixture over the nut and pastry shell and bake for 20 minutes, until golden. Dust with cinnamon and serve with cream.

YELLOW PLUM TART

In this tart, glazed yellow plums are arranged on a delectable almond filling in a crisp pastry shell.
When they are in season, greengage plums make an excellent alternative to the yellow plums.

1½ cups all-purpose flour
pinch of salt
6 tablespoons butter, chilled
2 tablespoons sugar
a few drops of pure vanilla extract
3 tablespoons ice water
cream or custard, to serve

FOR THE FILLING
6 tablespoons sugar
6 tablespoons butter, softened
¾ cup ground almonds
1 egg, beaten
2 tablespoons all-purpose flour
1 pound yellow plums or
greengage plums,
halved and pitted

FOR THE GLAZE
3 tablespoons apricot jam, sieved
1 tablespoon water

SERVES 8

1 Sift the flour and salt into a bowl, then rub in the chilled butter until the mixture resembles fine bread crumbs. Stir in the sugar, vanilla extract and enough of the ice water to form a soft dough.

2 Knead the dough gently on a lightly floured surface until smooth, then wrap in plastic wrap and chill for 10 minutes.

3 Preheat the oven to 400°F. Roll out the pastry and line a 9-inch fluted flan pan, letting any excess pastry overhang the top. Prick the bottom with a fork and line with nonstick baking paper and baking beans.

COOK'S TIP
Ceramic baking beans are ideal for baking blind, but any dried beans will do. You can use them over and over again, but make sure you keep them in a special jar, separate from the rest of your dried beans, as they cannot be used for conventional cooking after being used for baking blind.

4 Bake blind for 10 minutes, remove the paper and beans, then return the pastry shell to the oven for 10 minutes. Remove and let cool. Trim off any excess pastry with a sharp knife.

5 To make the filling, whisk or beat together all the ingredients except the plums. Spread on the bottom of the pastry shell. Arrange the plums on top, placing them cut side down. Make a glaze by heating the jam with the water. Stir well, then brush a little of the glaze on top of the fruit.

6 Bake the plum tart for about 50 minutes, until the almond filling is cooked and the plums are tender. Warm any remaining jam glaze and brush it on top. Cut into slices and serve with cream or custard.

DATE AND ALMOND TART

Fresh dates make an unusual but delicious filling for a tart. The influences here are French and Middle Eastern—a true Mediterranean fusion!

FOR THE PASTRY
1½ cups all-purpose flour
6 tablespoons butter
1 egg

FOR THE FILLING
scant 8 tablespoons (1 stick) butter
7 tablespoons sugar
1 egg, beaten
scant 1 cup ground almonds
2 tablespoons all-purpose flour
2 tablespoons orange-flower water
12–13 fresh dates, halved
and pitted
¼ cup apricot jam

SERVES 6

 Preheat the oven to 400°F. Place a baking sheet in the oven. Sift the flour into a bowl, add the butter and work with your fingertips until the mixture resembles fine bread crumbs. Add the egg and a tablespoon of cold water, then work to a smooth dough.

2 Roll out the pastry on a lightly floured surface and use to line an 8-inch tart pan. Prick the bottom with a fork, then chill until needed.

3 To make the filling, cream the butter and sugar until light, then beat in the egg. Stir in the ground almonds, flour and 1 tablespoon of the orange-flower water, mixing well.

4 Spread the mixture evenly over the bottom of the pastry shell. Arrange the dates, cut side down, on the almond mixture. Bake on the hot baking sheet for 10–15 minutes, then reduce the heat to 350°F. Bake for another 15–20 minutes, until light golden and set.

5 Transfer the tart to a rack to cool. Gently heat the apricot jam, then strain. Add the remaining orange-flower water.

6 Brush the tart with the jam and serve at room temperature.

HONEY AND PINE NUT TART

Wonderful tarts of all descriptions are to be found throughout France. This recipe recalls the flavors of the south.

FOR THE PASTRY
2 cups all-purpose flour
8 tablespoons (1 stick) butter
2 tablespoons confectioners' sugar
1 egg

FOR THE FILLING
¾ pound (3 sticks) unsalted butter, diced
½ cup granulated sugar
3 eggs, beaten
⅔ cup sunflower or other flower honey
grated zest and juice of 1 lemon
2⅔ cups pine nuts
pinch of salt
confectioners' sugar for dusting

SERVES 6

1   Preheat the oven to 350°F. Sift the flour into a bowl, add the butter and work with your fingertips until the mixture resembles fine bread crumbs. Stir in the confectioners' sugar. Add the egg and 1 tablespoon of water and work to a firm dough that leaves the bowl clean.

3   Cream together the butter and sugar until light. Beat in the eggs one by one. Gently heat the honey in a small saucepan until runny, then add to the butter mixture with the lemon zest and juice. Stir in the pine nuts and salt, then pour the filling into the pastry shell.

2   Roll out the pastry on a floured surface and use to line a 9-inch tart pan. Prick the bottom with a fork and chill for 10 minutes. Line with foil or waxed paper and fill with dried beans or rice, or baking beans if you have them. Bake the pastry shell for 10 minutes.

4   Bake for about 45 minutes, until the filling is lightly browned and set. Let cool slightly in the pan, then dust generously with confectioners' sugar. Serve warm or at room temperature, with sour cream or vanilla ice cream.

GLAZED PRUNE TART

Generously glazed, creamy custard tarts are a pâtisserie favorite all over France. Plump prunes, heavily laced with brandy or kirsch, add a wonderful taste and texture to this deliciously sweet and creamy filling.

1 cup pitted prunes
¼ cup brandy or kirsch

FOR THE SWEET PASTRY
1½ cups all-purpose flour
pinch of salt
8 tablespoons (1 stick) unsalted butter
2 tablespoons sugar
2 egg yolks

FOR THE FILLING
⅔ cup heavy cream
⅔ cup milk
1 vanilla bean
3 eggs
¼ cup sugar

TO FINISH
¼ cup apricot jam
1 tablespoon brandy or kirsch
confectioners' sugar for dusting

SERVES 8

1 Put the prunes in a bowl with the brandy or kirsch and let sit for about 4 hours, until most of the liqueur has been absorbed.

2 To make the pastry, sift the flour and salt into a bowl. Add the butter, cut into small pieces, and rub in with the fingertips. Stir in the sugar and egg yolks and mix to a dough using a round-bladed knife.

3 Turn the dough out onto a lightly floured surface and knead to a smooth ball. Wrap tightly and chill for 30 minutes.

4 Preheat the oven to 400°F. Roll out the pastry on a lightly floured surface and use to line a 10-inch springform tart pan.

5 Line with waxed paper and fill with dried beans or rice, or baking beans if you have them. Bake for 15 minutes. Remove the beans and paper and bake for another 5 minutes.

6 Arrange the prunes, evenly spaced, in the pastry shell, reserving any liqueur left in the bowl.

7 For the filling, put the cream and milk in a saucepan with the vanilla bean and bring to a boil. Turn off the heat and let the mixture infuse for 15 minutes.

8 Whisk together the eggs and sugar in a bowl. Remove the vanilla bean from the cream and return the cream to a boil. Pour on the eggs and sugar, whisking to make a smooth custard.

9 Cool slightly, then pour the custard over the prunes. Bake the tart for about 25 minutes, until the filling is lightly set and turning golden around the edges.

10 Strain the apricot jam into a small pan. Add the liqueur and heat through gently. Use to glaze the tart. Serve warm or cold, dusted with confectioners' sugar.

COOK'S TIP
The vanilla bean can be washed and dried, ready for use another time. Alternatively, use 1 teaspoon vanilla or almond extract.

LEMON TART

This is one of the classic French desserts, and it is hard to beat—a rich lemon curd is encased in flaky pastry. Crème fraîche is an optional accompaniment.

FOR THE PASTRY
2 cups all-purpose flour
8 tablespoons (1 stick) butter
2 tablespoons confectioners' sugar
1 egg
1 teaspoon vanilla extract

FOR THE FILLING
6 eggs, beaten
1½ cups sugar
8 tablespoons (1 stick) unsalted butter
grated zest and juice of 4 lemons
confectioners' sugar, for dusting

SERVES 6

1 Preheat the oven to 400°F. Sift the flour into a bowl, add the butter and work with your fingertips until the mixture resembles fine bread crumbs. Stir in the 2 tablespoons of confectioners' sugar.

2 Add the egg, vanilla extract and a scant tablespoon of cold water, then work to a dough.

3 Roll the pastry out on a floured surface and use to line a 9-inch tart pan. Line with foil or waxed paper and fill with dried beans or rice, or baking beans if you have them. Bake for 10 minutes.

4 To make the filling, put the eggs, sugar and butter into a pan and stir over low heat until the sugar has dissolved completely. Add the lemon zest and juice and continue cooking, stirring constantly, until the lemon curd has thickened slightly.

5 Pour the mixture into the pastry shell. Bake for 20 minutes, until just set. Transfer the tart to a wire rack to cool. Dust with confectioners' sugar just before serving.

RICOTTA AND MARSALA TARTS

These sweet, melt-in-your-mouth tarts have crisp puff-pastry crusts. The light cheese filling is flavored in the Italian way with Marsala.

13-ounce package ready-rolled puff
pastry, thawed if frozen
generous 1 cup ricotta cheese
1 egg, plus 2 egg yolks
3–4 tablespoons sugar
2 tablespoons Marsala
grated zest of 1 lemon
⅓ cup golden raisins

MAKES 12

1 Cut out 3½-inch rounds of pastry and line a tray of deep muffin cups. Set the tray aside for 20 minutes. Meanwhile preheat the oven to 375°F.

2 Put the ricotta cheese in a bowl and add the egg, extra yolks, sugar, Marsala and lemon zest. Whisk until smooth, then stir in the raisins.

3 Spoon the mixture into the lined pans. Bake the tarts for about 20 minutes or until the filling has risen in each and the pastry is crisp and golden.

4 Cool the tarts slightly before easing each one out with a small spatula. Serve warm.

FRESH FIG PHYLLO TART

Figs cook wonderfully well and taste superb in this tart—the riper the figs, the better.

2 tablespoons butter, melted, plus
extra for greasing
5 sheets of phyllo pastry, each
14 × 10 inches, thawed if frozen
6 fresh figs, cut into wedges
3/4 cup all-purpose flour
1/2 cup sugar
4 eggs
1 3/4 cups milk
1/2 teaspoon almond extract
1 tablespoon confectioners' sugar,
for dusting
whipped cream or plain yogurt,
to serve

SERVES 6–8

1. Preheat the oven to 375°F. Grease a 10 × 6¼-inch baking pan with butter. Brush each phyllo sheet in turn with melted butter and use the phyllo sheet to line the prepared pan.

2. Using scissors, cut off any excess pastry, leaving a little overhanging the edge. Arrange the figs in the phyllo shell.

3. Sift the flour into a bowl and stir in the sugar. Add the eggs and a little of the milk, then whisk until smooth. Slowly whisk in the remaining milk and the almond extract. Pour the mixture over the figs and bake for 1 hour.

4. Remove the tart from the oven and let it cool in the pan on a wire rack for 10 minutes. Dust with the confectioners' sugar and serve with whipped cream or yogurt.

475

RICOTTA CHEESECAKE

Ricotta cheese is excellent for cheesecake fillings because it has a firm texture. Here, it is enriched with
eggs and cream and enlivened with tangy orange and lemon zest to make a Sicilian-style dessert
that would make an impressive finale for a dinner party.

2 cups ricotta cheese
½ cup heavy cream
2 eggs
1 egg yolk
6 tablespoons sugar
finely grated zest of 1 orange
finely grated zest of 1 lemon
pared orange and lemon zest,
to decorate

FOR THE PASTRY
1½ cups all-purpose flour
3 tablespoons sugar
pinch of salt
½ cup chilled butter, diced
1 egg yolk

SERVES 8

2. Gather the dough together, reserving about a quarter for the lattice, then press the rest into a 9-inch fluted tart pan with a removable bottom. Chill the pastry shell for 30 minutes.

4. Prick the bottom of the pastry shell, then line with aluminum foil and fill with baking beans. Bake blind for 15 minutes, then transfer to a wire rack, remove the foil and beans and let the tart shell cool in the pan.

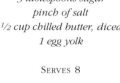

3. Meanwhile, preheat the oven to 375°F and make the filling. Put the ricotta, cream, eggs, egg yolk, sugar and orange and lemon zests in a large bowl, and beat together until evenly mixed.

5. Spoon the cheese and cream filling into the pastry shell and level the surface. Roll out the reserved dough and cut into strips. Arrange the strips on the top of the filling in a lattice pattern, sticking them in place with water.

1. Make the pastry. Sift the flour, sugar and salt onto a cold work surface. Make a well in the center and add the diced butter and egg yolk. Gradually work the flour into the diced butter and egg yolk, using your fingertips.

VARIATIONS
Add ⅓–⅔ cup finely chopped candied peel to the filling in Step 3, or ⅓ cup chocolate chips. For a really rich dessert, you can add both candied peel and some grated chocolate.

6. Bake for 30–35 minutes, until golden and set. Transfer to a wire rack and let cool, then carefully remove the side of the pan, leaving the cheesecake on the pan bottom. Serve in slices, decorated with pared orange and lemon zest.

CHERRY CLAFOUTI

When fresh cherries are in season this makes a deliciously simple dessert for any occasion. Serve warm with a little cream.

1½ pounds fresh cherries
½ cup all-purpose flour
pinch of salt
4 eggs, plus 2 egg yolks
½ cup sugar
2½ cups milk
4 tablespoons butter, melted
sugar for dusting

SERVES 6

1 Preheat the oven to 375°F. Lightly butter the bottom and sides of a shallow ovenproof dish. Pit the cherries and place in the dish.

2 Sift the flour and salt into a bowl. Add the eggs, egg yolks, sugar and a little of the milk and whisk to a smooth batter.

3 Gradually whisk in the rest of the milk and the rest of the butter, then strain the batter over the cherries. Bake for 40–50 minutes, until golden and just set. Serve warm, dusted with sugar, if desired.

VARIATION

Use two 15-ounce cans pitted black cherries, thoroughly drained, if fresh cherries are not available. For a special dessert, add 3 tablespoons kirsch to the batter.

MOROCCAN RICE PUDDING

A simple and delicious alternative to a traditional rice pudding. The rice is cooked in almond-flavored milk and delicately flavored with cinnamon and orange-flower water.

🍚 🍚

¼ cup blanched almonds, chopped
2¼ cups short-grain rice
¼ cup confectioners' sugar
3-inch cinnamon stick
4 tablespoons butter
pinch of salt
¼ teaspoon almond extract
¾ cup milk
¾ cup sweetened condensed milk
2 tablespoons orange-
flower water
toasted sliced almonds and ground
cinnamon, to decorate

SERVES 6

1 Put the chopped almonds in a food processor or blender with ¼ cup of very hot water. Process, then strain into a bowl. Return the almonds to the food processor or blender, add another ¼ cup very hot water, and process again. Strain into a saucepan.

2 Add 1¼ cups of water to the almond "milk" and bring to a boil. Combine the other milks. Add the rice, sugar, cinnamon and half the butter, the salt, the almond extract, and half the mixed milks.

3 Bring to a boil, then simmer, covered, for about 30 minutes, adding more milk if necessary. Continue to cook the rice, stirring and adding the remaining milk, until it becomes thick and creamy. Stir in the orange-flower water, then taste the rice pudding for sweetness, adding extra sugar, if necessary.

4 Pour the rice pudding into a serving bowl and sprinkle with the sliced almonds. Dot with the remaining butter and dust with ground cinnamon. Serve hot.

HAZELNUT SPONGE CAKE

This is an interesting cake, which does not contain any flour. The fruit coulis and the vanilla sauce make a delicious combination, or they can be served separately.

6 large eggs, separated
3/4 cup sugar
juice and grated zest of 1 lemon
1 1/2 cups ground hazelnuts
1 ounce cornmeal
oil, for greasing

FOR THE FRUIT COULIS
2 cups blackberries
or strawberries
2 tablespoons sugar
1–2 tablespoons water

FOR THE VANILLA SAUCE
2 teaspoons potato flour
2 tablespoons vanilla sugar
3 egg yolks (or 2 small eggs)
1 1/4 cups milk

SERVES 6–8

| 1 | Preheat the oven to 350°F. Whisk the egg yolks with the sugar until the mixture is pale, thick and mousse-like. Add the lemon juice and grated zest, and fold these into the mixture.

| 2 | Whisk the egg whites until stiff. Add a quarter of the whisked whites to the yolk mixture and then fold in the hazelnuts, cornmeal and remaining whites. Take care to fold these in gently so as not to deflate the mixture.

| 3 | Pour the mixture into a greased 10-inch cake pan and bake for 30–40 minutes. The center should be dry when tested with a toothpick or thin skewer.

| 4 | Meanwhile, make the fruit coulis and vanilla sauce. To make the coulis, put the berries in a pan with the sugar and water. Cook over low heat until the berries collapse. Then, strain the fruit and juice through a nylon sieve into a pitcher.

| 5 | To make the vanilla sauce, mix the potato flour, vanilla sugar and egg yolks until they form a smooth paste. Add the milk a little at a time; stir thoroughly. Put the mixture in a pan over low heat and bring slowly to a boil, stirring constantly. It will thicken after about 5 minutes. Take it off the heat, strain and cool.

| 6 | When the cake is cool, take it out of the pan and sift confectioners' sugar on top. Cut the cake into six or eight wedges, depending on the number of servings required. Spoon the vanilla sauce onto dessert plates, swirl a little fruit coulis through each portion and top with a slice of cake.

COOK'S TIP
To make your own vanilla sugar, store a cut vanilla bean in a jar of sugar. The sugar will absorb the vanilla flavor.

WALNUT AND RICOTTA CAKE

Soft, tangy ricotta cheese is widely used in Italian desserts. Here, it is included along with walnuts and orange to flavor a sponge cake. Don't worry if it sinks slightly after baking—this gives it an authentic appearance.

1 cup walnut pieces
10 tablespoons unsalted butter, softened
⅔ cup sugar
5 eggs, separated
finely grated zest of 1 orange
⅔ cup ricotta cheese
6 tablespoons all-purpose flour

TO FINISH
¼ cup apricot jam
2 tablespoons brandy
2 ounces unsweetened or semisweet chocolate, coarsely grated

MAKES 10 SLICES

1 Preheat the oven to 375°F. Grease and line the bottom of a deep 9-inch round, removable-bottomed cake pan. Coarsely chop and lightly toast the walnuts.

2 Cream together the butter and ½ cup of the sugar until light and fluffy. Add the egg yolks, orange zest, ricotta cheese, flour and walnuts and combine.

3 Beat the egg whites in a large bowl until stiff. Gradually beat in the remaining sugar. Using a large metal spoon, fold a quarter of the beaten whites into the ricotta mixture. Carefully fold in the rest of the beaten whites.

4 Turn the mixture out into the prepared pan and level the surface. Bake for about 30 minutes, until risen and firm. Let the cake cool in the pan.

5 Transfer the cake to a serving plate. Heat the apricot jam in a small saucepan with 1 tablespoon water. Strain and stir in the brandy. Use to coat the top and sides of the cake. Scatter grated chocolate generously over the cake.

VARIATION
Use toasted and chopped almonds in place of the walnuts.

SICILIAN RICOTTA CAKE

*In most of Italy, the word cassata is often used to describe a layered ice-cream cake. In Sicily,
however, it is a traditional cake made of layers of sponge cake, ricotta cheese and candied peel, imbibed
with alcohol. It both looks and tastes truly delicious.*

3 cups ricotta cheese
finely grated zest of 1 orange
2 tablespoons vanilla sugar
5 tablespoons orange-flavored liqueur
2/3 cup candied peel
8 slices sponge cake
4 tablespoons freshly squeezed
orange juice
extra candied peel, to decorate

SERVES 8–10

1 Push the ricotta cheese through
a sieve into a bowl, add the
orange zest, vanilla sugar and
1 tablespoon of liqueur, and beat well.
Transfer one-third of the mixture to
another bowl and chill until needed.

COOK'S TIP
If the cake has become an uneven
shape, this can be disguised by
covering with chilled ricotta.

2 Finely chop the candied peel
and beat into the remaining
ricotta cheese mixture until evenly
mixed. Set aside while you prepare
the loaf pan.

3 Carefully line the bottom of a
5-cup loaf pan with nonstick
baking paper. Cut the pieces of cake
in half vertically. Arrange four pieces
of cake side by side in the bottom
of the loaf pan and sprinkle with
1 tablespoon of the remaining liqueur
and 1 tablespoon orange juice.

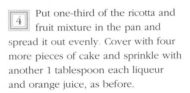

4 Put one-third of the ricotta and
fruit mixture in the pan and
spread it out evenly. Cover with four
more pieces of cake and sprinkle with
another 1 tablespoon each liqueur
and orange juice, as before.

5 Repeat the alternate layers of
ricotta mixture and cake until
all the ingredients have been used,
soaking the cake pieces with liqueur
and orange juice each time, and
ending with soaked cake. Cover with
a piece of nonstick baking paper
which has been cut to fit the loaf pan.

6 Cut a piece of cardboard to fit
inside the pan, place on top of
the nonstick baking paper and weight
down evenly. Chill for 24 hours.

7 To serve, remove the weights,
cardboard and paper, and run a
spatula between the sides of the
filling and the pan. Invert a serving
plate on top of the pan, then invert
the two so that the cake is on the
plate. Lift off the pan and peel off the
lining paper.

8 Spread the chilled ricotta
mixture over the cake to
cover it completely, then decorate
the top with the extra candied peel.
Serve chilled.

YOGURT AND FIG CAKE

———

Baked fresh figs, thickly sliced, make a delectable base for a featherlight cake.
Figs that are on the firm side work best for this particular recipe.

6 firm fresh figs, thickly sliced
3 tablespoons honey, plus extra for
glazing the cooked figs
scant 1 cup butter, softened
¾ cup sugar
grated zest of 1 lemon
grated zest of 1 orange
4 eggs, separated
2 cups all-purpose flour
1 teaspoon baking powder
1 teaspoon baking soda
1 cup plain yogurt

SERVES 6–8

2 In a large mixing bowl, cream together the butter and sugar with the lemon and orange zests until the mixture is pale and fluffy, then beat in the egg yolks, a little at a time.

3 Sift together the flour, baking powder and baking soda. Add a little to the creamed mixture, beat well, then beat in a spoonful of plain yogurt. Repeat this process until all the dry ingredients and yogurt have been incorporated.

4 Whisk all the egg whites in a grease-free bowl until they form stiff peaks. Stir half of the whites into the cake mixture to slacken it slightly, then fold in the rest. Pour the mixture over the figs in the pan, then bake for 1¼ hours until golden and a skewer inserted in the center of the cake comes out clean.

1 Preheat the oven to 350°F. Lightly grease a 9-inch cake pan and line the bottom with nonstick baking paper. Arrange the figs on the bottom of the pan and drizzle on the honey.

5 Turn out the cake onto a wire rack, peel off the lining paper and cool. Drizzle the figs with extra honey before serving.

MOROCCAN SERPENT CAKE

This is perhaps the most famous of all Moroccan pastries, filled with lightly fragrant almond paste.

8 sheets of phyllo pastry
¼ cup butter, melted
1 egg, beaten
1 teaspoon ground cinnamon
confectioners' sugar, for dusting

FOR THE ALMOND PASTE
¼ cup butter, melted
2 cups ground almonds
½ teaspoon almond extract
½ cup confectioners' sugar
egg yolk, beaten
1 tablespoon rose water or orange
flower water (optional)

SERVES 8

1 First, make the almond paste. Blend the melted butter with the ground almonds and almond extract. Add the confectioners' sugar, egg yolk and rose or orange flower water, if using, mix well and knead until soft and pliable. Chill the paste for about 10 minutes.

2 Break the almond paste into 10 balls. Roll them into 4-inch "sausages." Chill again.

3 Preheat the oven to 350°F, then place two sheets of phyllo pastry on a work surface so that they overlap to form an 7 × 22-inch rectangle. Brush the overlapping pastry to secure and then brush all over with butter. Cover with another two sheets of phyllo and brush again with butter.

4 Place five "sausages" of almond paste along the lower edge of the phyllo sheet and roll up the pastry tightly, tucking in the ends. Shape the roll into a loose coil. Repeat with the remaining phyllo and almond paste, so that you have two coils.

5 Brush a large baking sheet with butter and place the coils together to make a coiled "serpent."

6 Beat together the egg and half of the cinnamon. Brush onto the pastry snake and then bake for 20–25 minutes, until golden brown. Carefully invert the snake onto another baking sheet and return to the oven for 5–10 minutes, until the side now on top is golden.

7 Place on a serving plate. Dust with confectioners' sugar and then sprinkle with the remaining cinnamon. Serve warm.

CASSATA

—

Another version of a world-famous dessert. Unlike Sicilian Ricotta Cake,
this one flavors the ricotta with chocolate and uses coffee and rum for soaking the cookie layer.
Try to track down authentic Savoiardi cookies.

2½ cups ricotta cheese
¾ cup confectioners' sugar,
plus extra for dusting
½ teaspoon pure vanilla extract
grated zest and juice of
1 small orange
2 ounces dark chocolate, grated
1½ cups mixed candied fruits, such
as orange, pineapple, citron, cherries
and angelica
1 cup freshly brewed
strong black coffee
½ cup rum
24 Savoiardi cookies
geranium leaves, to decorate

SERVES 8

1 Line the base and sides of an 8-inch round cake pan with plastic wrap. Put the ricotta in a bowl. Sift in the confectioners' sugar, then add the vanilla extract with the orange zest and juice. Beat until smooth, then stir in the chocolate.

2 Cut the candied fruits into small pieces and stir into the ricotta.

3 Mix the coffee and rum. Line the bottom of the pan with cookies, dipping each cookie in the coffee mixture first. Cut the remaining cookies in half, dip them in the liquid and arrange around the sides.

4 Spoon the cassata mixture into the center and level the top. Cover with more plastic wrap, then place a plate on top that fits exactly inside the rim of the pan. Weight this with a bag of dried beans or sugar, then chill overnight until firm.

5 Turn out to serve, shaking the pan firmly if necessary and tugging the plastic wrap gently. Lift the plastic wrap off. Dust the top of the cassata with a little sifted confectioners' sugar and serve in wedges, decorated with geranium leaves.

SPICY FRUIT CAKE FROM SIENA

This is a delicious flat cake, known as panforte, with a wonderful spicy flavor. It is very rich, so it should be cut into small wedges. Offer a glass of sparkling wine to go with it.

butter, for greasing
1 cup hazelnuts,
roughly chopped
$^{1}/_{2}$ cup whole almonds,
roughly chopped
$1^{1}/_{3}$ cups mixed candied fruits, diced
$^{1}/_{4}$ teaspoon ground coriander
$^{3}/_{4}$ teaspoon ground cinnamon
$^{1}/_{4}$ teaspoon ground cloves
$^{1}/_{4}$ teaspoon grated nutmeg
$^{1}/_{2}$ cup all-purpose flour
$^{1}/_{2}$ cup honey
generous 1 cup sugar
confectioners' sugar, for dusting

SERVES 12–14

1 Preheat the oven to 350°F. Grease an 8-inch round cake pan. Line the bottom with nonstick baking paper.

2 Spread the nuts on a baking sheet and lightly toast in the oven for about 10 minutes. Remove and set aside. Lower the oven temperature to 300°F.

3 In a large mixing bowl, mix the candied fruits with all the spices and the flour, and stir with a wooden spoon. Add the nuts and stir in thoroughly.

4 In a small heavy saucepan, stir together the honey and sugar, and bring to a boil. Cook the mixture until it reaches 280°F on a candy thermometer or when a small amount spooned into ice water forms a hard ball when pressed between the fingertips. Take care when doing this.

5 At this stage, immediately pour the sugar syrup into the dry ingredients and stir in well until evenly coated. Pour into the prepared cake pan. Dip a spoon into water and use the back of the spoon to press the mixture firmly into the pan. Bake for 1 hour.

6 When ready, the cake will still feel quite soft, but will harden as it cools. Cool completely in the pan and then turn out on to a serving plate. Cut into wedges and dust with confectioners' sugar before serving.

BISCOTTI

These Italian cookies are baked, sliced to reveal a feast of mixed nuts and then baked again until crisp and golden. Traditionally they're served dipped in vin santo, a sweet dessert wine—perfect for rounding off a Mediterranean meal.

4 tablespoons unsalted butter,
softened
½ cup sugar
1½ cups self-rising flour
¼ teaspoon salt
2 teaspoons baking powder
1 teaspoon ground coriander
finely grated zest of 1 lemon
½ cup polenta
1 egg, lightly beaten
2 teaspoons brandy or orange-
flavored liqueur
½ cup unblanched almonds
½ cup pistachios

MAKES 24

1 Preheat the oven to 325°F. Lightly grease a baking sheet. Cream together the butter and sugar in a bowl.

2 Sift all the flour, salt, baking powder and coriander into the bowl. Add the lemon zest, polenta, egg and brandy or liqueur and combine to make a soft dough.

3 Stir in the nuts until evenly combined. Halve the mixture. Shape each half into a flat sausage about 9 inches long and 2½ inches wide. Bake for about 30 minutes, until risen and just firm. Remove from oven.

4 When cool, cut each sausage diagonally into 12 thin slices. Return to the baking sheet and cook for another 10 minutes, until crisp.

5 Transfer to a wire rack to cool completely. Store in an airtight jar for up to 1 week.

COOK'S TIP
Use a sharp, serrated knife to slice the cooled cookies, otherwise they will crumble.

CINNAMON ROLLS

—

These delicately spicy rolls are delicious served fresh for breakfast or a snack, spread with butter.

FOR THE DOUGH
$3^{1}/_{2}$ cups all-purpose flour
$^{1}/_{2}$ teaspoon salt
2 tablespoons sugar
1 teaspoon active dry yeast
3 tablespoons oil
$^{1}/_{2}$ cup warm milk
$^{1}/_{2}$ cup warm water

FOR THE FILLING
3 tablespoons butter, softened
2–3 tablespoons dark brown sugar
$^{1}/_{2}$–1 teaspoon ground cinnamon
1 tablespoon raisins

MAKES 24 SMALL ROLLS

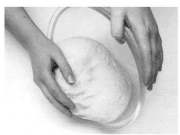

1 | Preheat the oven to 400°F. Sift together the flour, salt and sugar, and sprinkle onto the yeast. Mix the oil, egg, milk and water, and add to the flour. Mix into a dough, then knead until smooth. Let rise in a covered bowl until doubled in bulk, then punch down again.

2 | Roll out the dough into a large rectangle and cut in half vertically. Spread on the softened butter, reserving 1 tablespoon for brushing. Combine the brown sugar and cinnamon, and sprinkle this over the top. Dot the surface with the raisins.

3 | Roll each piece into a long Swiss roll shape, to enclose the filling. Cut into 1-inch slices, arrange flat on a greased baking sheet and brush with the remaining butter. Let rise again for 30 minutes.

4 | Bake the cinnamon rolls in the preheated oven for about 20 minutes. Let cool on a wire rack.

SLICED ALMOND COOKIES

These well-traveled cookies have their origins in Greece and are now enjoyed in several Eastern Mediterranean countries, including Israel.

3/4 cup butter or margarine
2 cups self-rising flour,
plus extra for dusting
1/2 cup sugar
1/2 teaspoon ground cinnamon
1 egg, separated
2 tablespoons cold water
1/2 cup sliced almonds

MAKES ABOUT 30

1 Preheat the oven to 350°F. Rub the butter or margarine into the flour. Reserve 1 tablespoon sugar and mix the rest with the cinnamon. Stir into the flour and then add the egg yolk and cold water and mix into a dough.

2 Roll the dough out on a lightly floured board. When 1/2 inch thick, sprinkle on the almonds. Continue rolling, pressing all the almonds into the dough until it is about 1/4 inch thick.

3 Using a fluted round cutter, cut the dough into rounds. Use a spatula to lift them on to an ungreased baking sheet. Re-form the dough and cut more rounds to use it all up. Whisk the white of the egg lightly, brush it onto the cookies, and sprinkle on the reserved sugar.

4 Bake in the center of the oven for 10–15 minutes or until golden. To remove, slide a spatula under the cookies. They will still seem a bit soft, but will harden as they cool. Let sit on a wire rack until cooled.

SEMOLINA AND NUT HALVA

Semolina is a popular ingredient in many desserts and pastries in the eastern Mediterranean. Here it provides a spongy base for soaking up a deliciously fragrant, spicy syrup.

1 Preheat the oven to 425°F. Grease and line the bottom of a deep 9-inch square cake pan.

2 Lightly cream the butter in a bowl. Add the sugar, orange zest and juice, eggs, semolina, baking powder and hazelnuts and beat the ingredients together until smooth.

3 Put into the prepared pan and level the surface. Bake for 20–25 minutes, until just firm and golden. Let cool in the pan.

4 To make the syrup, put the sugar in a small, heavy saucepan with 2¼ cups water and the half cinnamon sticks. Heat gently, stirring, until the sugar has dissolved completely.

5 Bring to a boil and boil rapidly, without stirring, for 5 minutes. Measure half the boiling syrup and add the lemon juice and orange-flower water to it. Pour over the halva. Reserve the remainder of the syrup in the pan.

6 Leave the halva in the pan until the syrup is absorbed, then turn it out onto a plate and cut diagonally into diamond-shaped portions. Sprinkle with the nuts.

7 Boil the remaining syrup until slightly thickened, then pour it on the halva. Sprinkle the shredded orange zest on the cake and serve with lightly whipped cream.

FOR THE HALVA
8 tablespoons (1 stick) unsalted butter, softened
½ cup sugar
finely grated zest of 1 orange, plus 2 tablespoons juice
3 eggs
1 cup semolina
2 teaspoons baking powder
1 cup ground hazelnuts

TO FINISH
1½ cups sugar
2 cinnamon sticks, halved
juice of 1 lemon
¼ cup orange-flower water
½ cup unblanched hazelnuts, toasted and chopped
½ cup blanched almonds, toasted and chopped
shredded zest of 1 orange
SERVES 10

COOK'S TIP
Be sure to use a deep, solid cake pan rather than one with a removable bottom; otherwise, the syrup might seep out.

GAZELLES' HORNS

Kaab el Ghzal is one of Morocco's favorite and best known pastries—so popular, in fact, that the French have honored it with their own name, Cornes de Gazelles. The horn-shaped, filled pastries are commonly served at wedding celebrations.

1¾ cups all-purpose flour
pinch of salt
2 tablespoons butter, melted
2 tablespoons orange flower water
1 large egg yolk, beaten
confectioners' sugar, to serve

FOR THE ALMOND PASTE
scant 2 cups ground almonds
1 cup confectioners' sugar
2 tablespoons orange flower water
2 tablespoons butter, melted
2 egg yolks, beaten
½ teaspoon ground cinnamon

MAKES ABOUT 16

3. Knead the dough for about 10 minutes, until smooth and elastic, then place on a floured surface and roll out as thinly as possible. Cut the dough into long strips about 3 inches wide.

4. Preheat the oven to 350°F. Pinch off small pieces of the almond paste and roll them between your hands into thin "sausages" about 3 inches long with tapering ends.

5. Place these in a line along one side of the strips of pastry, about 1¼-inch apart. Dampen the pastry edges with water and then fold the other half of the strip over the filling and press the edges together.

6. Using a pastry wheel, cut around each "sausage" to make a crescent. Make sure that the edges are firmly pinched together.

7. Prick the crescents with a fork and place on a buttered baking sheet. Brush with the remaining egg yolk and bake for 12–16 minutes, until lightly colored. Cool and then dust with confectioners' sugar.

1. First, make the almond paste. Combine all the ingredients to make a smooth paste.

2. Make the pastry. Mix the flour with the salt. Stir in the melted butter, orange flower water and about three-quarters of the egg yolk. Stir in enough cold water to make a fairly soft dough.

CHURROS

These Spanish doughnuts are commercially deep-fried in huge coils and broken off into smaller pieces
for selling. Serve this homemade version freshly cooked with hot chocolate or strong coffee.

1¾ cups all-purpose flour
¼ teaspoon salt
2 tablespoons sugar
¼ cup olive or sunflower oil
1 egg, beaten
sugar and ground cinnamon
for dusting
oil for deep-frying

MAKES 12–15

1 Sift the flour, salt and sugar onto a plate or piece of paper. Heat 1 cup of water in a saucepan with the oil until it boils.

2 Pour in the flour mixture and beat with a wooden spoon until the mixture forms a stiff paste. Let cool for 2 minutes.

3 Gradually beat in the egg until smooth. Oil a large baking sheet. Sprinkle plenty of sugar onto a plate and stir in a little cinnamon.

4 Put the dough in a large pastry bag fitted with a ½-inch plain piping nozzle. Pipe little coils or S shapes onto the baking sheet.

5 Heat 2 inches of oil in a large pan to 336°F or until a little dough sizzles on the surface.

6 Using an oiled metal spatula, lower several of the piped shapes into the oil and cook for about 2 minutes, until light golden.

7 Drain on paper towels, then coat with the sugar and cinnamon mixture. Cook the remaining churros in the same way and serve immediately.

ALMOND FINGERS

This is a very simple pastry, which is especially popular in the countries that border the Eastern Mediterranean. In Arab countries, it is known as Zeinab's Fingers.

1¾ cups ground almonds
½ cup ground pistachios
¼ cup sugar
1 tablespoon rose water
½ teaspoon ground cinnamon
12 sheets of phyllo pastry
½ cup butter, melted
confectioners' sugar, to decorate

MAKES UP TO 48

1. Preheat the oven to 325°F. In a bowl, combine the ground almonds, ground pistachios, sugar, rose water and ground cinnamon for the filling.

2. Cut each sheet of phyllo pastry into four rectangles. Work with one rectangle at a time, covering the rest with a damp dish towel to prevent them from drying out.

3. Brush one of the rectangles of phyllo pastry with a little melted butter and place a heaping teaspoon of the nut filling in the center.

4. Fold in the sides and roll into a cigar shape. Continue making "cigars" until all the filling has been used. Place the fingers on a greased baking sheet. Bake for 30 minutes, until lightly golden. Cool, dust with confectioners' sugar and serve.

COCONUT HALVA

This delicious coconut cake can be served either hot as a dessert or cold with tea or strong black coffee.

½ cup unsalted butter
¾ cup sugar
½ cup all-purpose flour
scant 1 cup semolina
1 cup shredded coconut
¾ cup milk
1 teaspoon baking powder
1 teaspoon pure vanilla extract
almonds, to decorate

FOR THE SYRUP
½ cup sugar
⅔ cup water
1 tablespoon lemon juice

SERVES 4–6

1. First, make the syrup. Place the sugar, water and lemon juice in a saucepan, stir to mix, then bring to a boil. Simmer for 6–8 minutes, until the syrup has thickened. Let cool and chill.

2. Preheat the oven to 350°F. Melt the butter in a pan. Add the sugar, flour, semolina, shredded coconut, milk, baking powder and vanilla extract, and mix thoroughly.

3. Pour the cake mixture into a shallow baking pan, flatten the top and bake for 30–45 minutes, until the top is golden.

4. Remove the halva from the oven and cut into diamond-shaped bars. Pour the cold syrup evenly on top and decorate each bar with an almond placed in the center.

DATE MA-AMOUL

From Gibraltar to Baghdad, women used to get together to make hundreds of these labor-intensive, date-filled pastries. Making a small amount is not nearly so laborious. These make a delicious sweet snack that will be particularly appealing to children.

6 tablespoons butter or margarine, softened
1½ cups all-purpose flour, sifted
1 teaspoon rose water
1 teaspoon orange flower water
3 tablespoons water
¼ cup sifted confectioners' sugar, for sprinkling

FOR THE FILLING
⅔ cup pitted dates
½ teaspoon orange flower water

MAKES ABOUT 25

 To make the filling, separate the dates from each other. Chop the dates finely with a very sharp, smooth-edged knife. Add 4 tablespoons boiling water and the orange flower water and beat the mixture vigorously until it almost becomes a purée. Set the mixture aside and let it cool.

 To make the pastries, rub the butter or margarine into the flour. If the butter is hard, it may be helpful to chop it into small pieces first. Add the rose and orange flower waters and the water, and mix to make a firm dough.

 Preheat the oven to 350°F. Press your finger into each ball so that it forms a small container in which to put the date mixture. Press the sides around and around to make the walls quite thin. Put about ¼ teaspoon of the date mixture carefully into each one. Then seal each ball by pressing the edges of the pastry together.

5 Arrange the date pastries, seam sides down, on a lightly greased baking sheet and prick each one with a fork or, if you prefer to use the traditional method, use tweezers. Bake for 15–20 minutes, then remove the pastries from the oven and let cool.

6 When the pastries are cool, put them on a plate and sprinkle generously with sifted confectioners' sugar. Shake the plate lightly and make sure that the date ma-amoul are all well-covered with the confectioners' sugar.

COOK'S TIP
The secret of good Ma-amoul is to get as much date filling into the pastry as possible, but you must be sure to seal the opening well. The traditional way to decorate them was to make a pattern using tweezers, but it is quicker to use a fork. Orange flower water is now readily available at most supermarkets; it is usually found in the baking section.

3 Shape the dough into about 25 small balls by rolling teaspoonfuls of mixture between your hands. Keep your hands cool.

BAKLAVA

———

*This is the queen of all pastries, with its exotic flavors. It is served in Greece, Turkey and further east,
often with a cup of strong black coffee.*

3 cups ground pistachios
1¼ cups confectioners' sugar
1 tablespoon ground cardamom
⅔ cup unsalted butter, melted
18 sheets phyllo pastry

FOR THE SYRUP
2 cups sugar
1¼ cups water
2 tablespoons rose water

SERVES 6–8

1 First, make the syrup. Place the sugar and water in a saucepan, bring to a boil and then simmer for 10 minutes, until syrupy. Stir in the rose water and let cool.

2 Combine the nuts, confectioners' sugar and cardamom. Preheat the oven to 325°F.

3 Brush a large rectangular baking pan with melted butter. Taking one sheet of phyllo pastry at a time, and keeping the remainder covered with a damp dish towel, brush the sheets with melted butter and lay on the bottom of the pan. Continue until you have six buttered layers in the pan. Spread on half of the nut mixture, pressing down with a spoon.

4 Take another six sheets of phyllo pastry, brush with butter and put on the nut mixture. Sprinkle on the remaining nuts and top with a final layer of six phyllo sheets, brushed again with butter. Cut the pastry diagonally into small bars using a sharp knife. Pour the remaining melted butter on top.

5 Bake for 20 minutes and then increase the heat to 400°F. Bake for 15 more minutes, until light golden in color.

6 Remove from the oven and drizzle about three-quarters of the syrup on the pastry, reserving the remainder for serving. Arrange the baklava on a large dish and serve with extra syrup.

CINNAMON BALLS

Ground almonds or hazelnuts form the basis of most Passover cakes and cookies. These balls should be soft inside, with a very strong cinnamon flavor. They harden over time, so it is a good idea to freeze some and only use them when needed.

3   Wet your hands with cold water and roll small spoonfuls of the mixture into balls. Place these at intervals on the baking sheet.

4   Bake for about 15 minutes in the center of the oven. They should be slightly soft inside—too much cooking will make them hard and tough.

5   Slide a spatula under the balls to release them from the baking sheet, and let cool. Sift a few tablespoons of confectioners' sugar onto a plate and when the cinnamon balls are cold, slide them onto the plate. Shake gently to completely cover the cinnamon balls in sugar. Store in an airtight container or in the freezer.

oil, for greasing
1 1/2 cups ground almonds
6 tablespoons sugar
1 tablespoon ground cinnamon
2 egg whites
confectioners' sugar, for dredging

MAKES ABOUT 15

1   Preheat the oven to 350°F. Grease a large baking sheet with oil.

2   In a bowl, mix the ground almonds, sugar and cinnamon. Whisk the egg whites until they begin to stiffen; fold enough into the almonds to make a fairly firm mixture.

INDEX